Pathways

Books by Sam Polson

In His Image

By Faith: Timeless Insights for Staying on Course from Hebrews 11

SonLight: Daily Light from the Pages of God's Word

Corona Victus: Conquering the Virus of Fear

Life Changing Prayer

Pathways: Ancient Paths from the Pages of the Old Testament

PATHWAYS

Ancient Paths from the
Pages of the Old Testament

Pastor Sam Polson

PATHWAYS
Written by Pastor Sam Polson

Text copyright © 2022 Sam Polson

CAUTION: All rights reserved. No part of this publication may be reproduced, stored in a retrieval system, or transmitted in any form or by any means electronic, mechanical, photocopy, recording, or other, except for brief quotations in written reviews, without the prior written permission of the publisher.

Most Scripture quotations are from the ESV® Bible (The Holy Bible, English Standard Version®), copyright © 2001 by Crossway, a publishing ministry of Good News Publishers. Used by permission. All rights reserved.

Published in 2022 by:
Climbing Angel Publishing
PO Box 32381
Knoxville, Tennessee 37930
http://www.ClimbingAngel.com

First Edition: November 2022
Printed in the United States of America

Cover photo: Shutterstock
Graphic Design: Climbing Angel Publishing

ISBN: 978-1-956218-23-7
Library of Congress Control Number: 2022915843

This book is dedicated to the
congregation of West Park Baptist Church.
Serving as your pastor continues to be
the great privilege of my life.

Contents

Foreword   *ix*
Introduction   *xi*
R.E.A.P.   *xiii*

January	1
February	35
March	77
April	123
May	165
June	209
July	241
August	273
September	305
October	341
November	383
December	425

Author's Biography   *468*
Acknowledgments   *469*

Foreword

The first time I heard Sam Polson from West Park Baptist Church preach over the radio, I told my husband, "That's where I want to go. That pastor believes what he's saying, and he cares." We had been searching for a church home for quite some time. That week we visited West Park and have been attending there ever since.

But all this book business didn't start until about five years ago. My husband and I were having lunch with Sam and Sue after church at a local eating establishment. Sam had been preaching a new sermon series entitled, *In His Image*, and I was now fully convinced that the series would make an excellent book. Halfway through the meal, I pitched the idea to him. Ideas are safe with Sam because I knew he would seek God's will.

A couple of weeks later, the Polson family and my husband and I were at yet another restaurant discussing the progress of publishing Sam's first book when Sue and Sam began sharing about their upcoming mission trip to Romania. The next thing I knew, Sam and Sue's son, Stephen Polson, tossed out this thought. "How 'bout publishing a Romanian translation of the book?" A hush came over the table, which rarely happened during our meals. "You could take the book to Romania," he added.

Trivia question for the day: What was Sam Polson's first published book? If you say the English version of *In His Image*, you're wrong.

With only six weeks before the Polsons planned to board that plane to Romania, the book was translated, edited, designed, and published by God's grace. Sam and Sue had 100 copies tightly strapped into their hard-case luggage, and we drove them to the airport. It's all quite difficult to believe now, looking back.

Climbing Angel Publishing released the Romanian edition of *In His Image* on August 17, 2017, the English version on October 17, 2017, and the Mandarin translation on May 25, 2019. Then came *By Faith: Timeless Insights for Staying on Course from Hebrews 11*, published in November 2018, which Sam and Sue took with them to Romania following its August 2019 publication. Then in November of 2019, Sam's first devotional, the prequel to this book, was released—*SonLight: Daily Light from the Pages of God's Word*, which was reverently received.

In March 2020, the pandemic hit, and Sam preached a deeply edifying sermon series on the subject of fear. The church's technical staff quickly adapted to a new way of sharing the gospel, called "live streaming on Facebook and YouTube," and our beloved church members were on a "temporary" lockdown. The sermon series on fear became the book *Corona Victus: Conquering the Virus of Fear*, which was released on July 4, 2020, Independence Day. Then the book *Life Changing Prayer* was published in November 2020, and the Romanian edition of *Corona Victus* in September 2022 (which Sam and Sue once again took with them to Romania). And now, Sam's second devotional—*Pathways: Ancient Paths from the Pages of the Old Testament*, is being released in November of 2022, which you now hold in your hands.

Sam's books have been faithfully utilized for personal examination, family devotion, and group Bible study. The responses he receives, particularly from his first devotional, *SonLight*, are reliably generous, constant, and heart-warming.

I've always said, "If you want to know the writer, read their books," and knowing and understanding Sam is no different. But you will consistently find in Sam's books that they aren't about Sam. Though he uses personal antidotes that provide us with emotional access to the point he's about to make, all his books are about Christ. He doesn't point you to *himself*; he points you to *the One* who can actually save you from this world and equip you with a freedom that can never be taken away. He points you to our living savior Jesus Christ, over and over again.

This new book, *Pathways*, is no different. But as his publisher, I must say Sam is at his best here. All of his 42 years of invaluable experience learning to genuinely love people and minister to them, all of this treasured knowledge is applied to these nearly 500 pages. He forges a path to help us assimilate the Old Testament in a fresh and personal manner, inspiring us to "read on" using insights only Sam could provide.

"Every good thing given and every perfect gift is from above, coming down from the Father of lights, with whom there is no variation or shifting shadow" (Jas. 1:17 NASB). And now these books, created to help us break down and assimilate God's Word, exist when before they did not. What I thought would be fun, God thought necessary. Over a period of five years, those books helped Christ followers study, prepare and usher in a whole new world in which we all now live. Perhaps this new world is not as predictable. Maybe it is not as much fun, but we stand here, on the Rock, more solidly. And if there be more shifting sand ahead, we are better prepared because this preacher from Indiana prayed, sought God's will, and was obedient to Him first and foremost.

We are all grateful for you, Sam. It is no surprise that you dedicated this book to your church family, the ones you helped prepare. We feel dearly loved by both you and Susan, and we thank you for helping us understand just how much we are dearly loved by our Heavenly Father. Thank you both for your love and sacrifice. God be with you.

Lisa Soland
Senior Editor
Climbing Angel Publishing

Introduction

One of the most beautiful images used so often in the Bible to illustrate the life of faith is that of a journey along a road or path. "But the path of the righteous is like the light of dawn, which shines brighter and brighter until full day" (Prov. 4:18). Certainly, the life journey of a disciple is one that is often challenging and, at times, marked by unexpected detours. Still, for the follower of Jesus, it is a path that grows brighter and brighter until that perfect and endless day in heaven.

Our journey through a dark world is made bright by the presence of the One who travels with us, for we do not make the journey alone. Just as Jesus did with those two disciples walking the road to Emmaus, our resurrected Lord joins us on the journey. Also, just as then, Jesus is not a silent companion, but as we walk with the Lord, He conducts a strolling Bible study, revealing from the Scriptures amazing truths concerning Himself.

What enlightenment we receive as we journey with Jesus! He is our Companion, He is our Teacher, and He is our Curriculum. As He did that Sunday afternoon so long ago, our Lord still opens our understanding to see Him in the Words of Scripture. My continual prayer during the months of writing this book, and my prayer today for all who read these pages, is that on the journey along these Old Testament *Pathways*, our gracious Lord will reveal "in all the Scriptures the things concerning Himself." May the encounters be so personal and powerful that all will rejoice, saying, "Did not our hearts burn within us while He talked to us on the road, while He opened to us the Scriptures?" (Luke 24:27, 32)

Sam Polson
Knoxville, Tennessee
October 2022

How to **R.E.A.P.** the Word of God

Read: Read the passage carefully and prayerfully.

Examine: Read the passage again, noting key words or phrases. Be careful to note the context surrounding the passage. Ask questions about the passage. Who is the audience? What situation is the speaker or author addressing? What is the main theme of this passage? Note in particular what you learn about the Lord from the passage.

Apply: Consider carefully the impressions on your heart as you read. How does this passage touch on specific areas or situations in your life? What wisdom are you gaining from this passage? What are you learning about your Lord in relation to your current spiritual experience?

Pray: Use what the Lord has revealed about Himself or about you personally in this time as an opportunity to respond directly to Him. Pray to Him in praise, or repentance, or in petition for others as the Holy Spirit guides you. Treat this time in God's Word not as a devotional exercise, but as a personal encounter with your holy God and your loving Savior.

JANUARY

"His mercies never come to an end;
they are new every morning."
(Lamentations 3:22-23)

JANUARY 1
Genesis 1-3

"LIGHT IN THE DARKNESS"

And God said, "Let there be light," and there was light. And God saw that the light was good. And God separated the light from the darkness.
(Genesis 1:3-4)

The first words of God recorded in the Scriptures are those of His command, "Let there be light." From the center of His own being, the source of endless glory, came rushing into the void of darkness the brilliant radiance of Light. Light defines the very character of our Creator. The Word of God tells us that "God is light and in Him is no darkness at all" (1 John 1:5).

In reality, "Let there be light" is the message of the entire Word of God. They are words of hope, words of *gospel hope* to all mankind who, like Adam and Eve, walk and live in darkness, away from the Light of the Father. In fact, the first ray of gospel light shines into the darkness of sin's rebellion and curse in Genesis, Chapter 3, verse 15, "I will put enmity between you and the woman, and between her offspring; he shall bruise your head and you shall bruise his heel." This is what theologians refer to as the "proto-evangelism," the first gospel message. The promise is that sin will not win, and that darkness will be defeated by the virgin-born Son of God, the Light of the world, Jesus Christ.

The Bible is a book about Jesus and the redemption provided through Him. By His sinless life, sacrificial death, and glorious resurrection, Christ has conquered the darkness. Through His victory, all who believe become children of God, children of Light.

The darkness is powerful, but it cannot overcome the Light of the Lamb. He will return, His Kingdom will come, the darkness will be banished, and there will be "no more night."

JANUARY 2
Genesis 4-6

"THE PLACE OF REST"

The dreadful fruit of Adam and Eve's sin is fully displayed in the chapters of our reading today. Paradise was truly lost, and death, the wages of sin, quickly began to permeate every aspect of life on the earth. Adam and Eve named their first child Cain. They evidently hoped that they had "gotten" the man-child who would be the Lord's promised deliverer, but he turned out to be so corrupted by sin that he murdered his brother, Abel. Within a few generations, the world was filled with violence, so much so that the first recorded song in the Bible is Lamech's anthem of revenge and murder.

The world God created and described as "very good" had become so completely filled with wickedness that the Lord determined, "I will blot out man whom I have created from the face of the earth." However, in the justice of judgment, God also revealed His grace. "But Noah found favor in the eyes of the Lord" (Gen. 6:8). The word for "favor" used here means "grace." The name Noah means "rest."

We are also told that Noah found this grace in the eyes of the Lord. Noah's works did not earn this gracious favor with God. It was an unmerited gift from a Holy God. It was this grace that brought a special rest to Noah and his family when he was 800 years of age. This "gracious rest" was found in an ark of salvation that provided deliverance from God's judgment on sin. The Ark was covered with "pitch," a word later in the Bible used to describe the atoning blood of sacrifice.

This Ark was massive, but it had only one door on its side. Here we see prefigured in the opening chapters of God's Word the Gospel hope provided in Jesus. He is the source of all grace, the One who makes us accepted and favored by God. He covers us with His blood and saves us from the wrath of God. Christ is the door of salvation, and in Him, we are sealed and safe forever. Yes, through the new birth, we are each one "Noah"... we find favor with God and rest for our souls.

JANUARY 3
Genesis 7-9

"Under the Rainbow"

"I have set my bow in the cloud, and it shall be a sign of the covenant between me and the earth."
(Genesis 9:13)

Since it was first so beautifully sung by Judy Garland in the 1939 film *The Wizard of Oz*, the song "Over the Rainbow" has been loved and enjoyed by millions of people around the world. There is something in a rainbow that captures and encourages our hearts whenever we see it.

The amazing spectral colors of light are truly breathtaking. Also, the beauty of the rainbow is usually seen in dramatic contrast to the dark storm clouds and rain that often surround it. The rainbow brings comfort and hope to our souls in an amazing way. God intended it to do this. He told Noah, "I have set my bow in the cloud, and it shall be a sign of the covenant between me and the earth" (Gen. 9:13). The rainbow is a beautiful symbol given by God that He can be trusted to keep His covenant promise.

A rainbow gives us a hope that is not focused "over the rainbow" but ultimately "under the rainbow." The Bible tells us that there is a throne in heaven surrounded by a rainbow, and seated on that throne is the covenant-keeping Lord of glory (Rev. 4:3). He is the source of our hope. In His great love, He has provided another covenant, the covenant of eternal salvation through the sacrifice of His beloved Son, Jesus Christ. Through faith in Jesus, we are given hope that is as secure as the throne of God. So, the next time you see a rainbow, you may recall the beautiful song, "Over the Rainbow," but make sure to offer a prayer of praise to the One sitting on the throne "under the rainbow." He keeps His covenant with you forever and ever.

JANUARY 4
Genesis 10-11

"Humanism Humbled"

There are only two ways in which any human being can live their life, and each of these is a result of focus. Life can be lived either with a focus on God or a focus on self. There are ultimately no other options. We either live to exalt the name of our Lord, or we live to exalt our own name. These two options and their outcomes are set in graphic display and contrast in the earliest chapters of the Bible.

We are told about people like Seth and his descendants, who aligned themselves with the name of God (Gen. 4:26). After the Flood, Noah (one of Seth's descendants) blessed his son Shem and his allegiance to God, declaring, "Blessed be the Lord, the God of Shem" (Gen. 9:26). This Semitic family becomes the servants God uses as the lineage through which will come the Redeemer promised by God (Gen. 3:15). They will be the people who identify themselves by the name of the Lord.

In contrast to the people of His Name, we are told of those who sought to promote their own name. They focused on their own exaltation. This idolatry and its origins are found in defiance of God at a place that came to be known as Babylon. God commanded people to spread over the face of the earth. The rebellious response of most of mankind was a resounding, "No!" "Come, let us build ourselves a city and a tower with its top in the heavens, and let us make a name for ourselves, lest we be dispersed over the face of the whole earth" (Gen. 11:4).

Notice the phrase "a name for ourselves." Men and women wanted their own names exalted rather than God's. The tower would be a testimony to their religion of self. "Humanism" is the term behind which this rebellion and idolatry usually masquerade. God in His power confounds this wicked attempt at unity through the religion of humanism by confusing the languages. The unity that God will bring to the earth will be the united nations, as all their languages join in the exaltation of the Name of the Redeemer of humanity.

There is the spirit and message of Babylon, and there is the Spirit and the message of Pentecost (Acts 2:4). Which spirit will be ours, which name will we exalt, and which message will we share today? The Spirit of Pentecost or the spirit of Babylon? Choose carefully, prayerfully, and definitely.

JANUARY 5
Genesis 12-13

"THE JOURNEY OF FAITH"

People in the United States are often referred to as "constantly on the move." Recent studies reveal that this is not only true regarding transportation, but also about location and habitation. Census data from recent years indicate that an American citizen moves every five years and can expect to move about 11 times throughout their life. That's a lot of moving, not to mention packing!

Genesis 12-13 describes a great deal of moving. There was moving *against* the will of God, as the previous chapters described—the rebellious refusal by multitudes to spread across the earth, replenish, and populate it. That resulted in judgment and confusion and did not work out well.

In Chapter 12 we are introduced to a man who moved *within* the will of God, and on another occasion *without* the will of God, and then finally back *within* the will of God. The man's name is Abram, and his responses in Chapter 12 are filled with "moving lessons" for us. Prompted by God, Abraham obeyed by faith and moved from Chaldea to Canaan. This was a long and challenging journey, but it was a move made according to the will of God. This is always a safe move because God's will is always "good and perfect" (Rom. 12:2).

Abram dwelled in this land living in a tent and built an altar where he "called upon the name of the Lord" (Gen. 12:8). There, near Bethel (the house of God), Abram dwelt with his kinsmen, and in the enjoyment of fellowship with his Master. However, when a severe famine visited Canaan, Abram came up with a reasonable idea. He would move from the drought-stricken hill country of Bethel to the sunny, sandy, but well-irrigated land of Egypt. On the surface, this seemed like a practical and prudent decision, except for one thing—Abram did not discuss his plans with God. He did not "call upon the name of the Lord" and receive permission for the move. Any move *without* God's permission is never a smart one.

Things literally and spiritually "went south" for Abram and his family through "getting ahead of the Lord." Thankfully, by the Lord's Divine intervention, the foolishness of Abram's rash move did not end in moral and spiritual disaster. However, his testimony as God's servant was seriously compromised. Thankfully, in humility and submission, Abram journeyed back to Bethel, "...to the place where his tent had been at the beginning...where he had made an altar at first. And there Abram called upon the name of the Lord" (Gen. 13:3-4). Smart move.

JANUARY 6
Genesis 14-16

"RIGHTEOUSNESS THROUGH FAITH"

Anyone vaguely familiar with the Bible knows that the book has two great divisions, the Old Testament and the New Testament. Someone slightly more knowledgeable might further understand that the Old Testament deals primarily with the nation of Israel. The New Testament contains the record of the life and ministry of Jesus and the sharing of the message of Jesus throughout the whole world by the testimony of His apostles and disciples. People having an even deeper understanding of the Bible would recognize that the Old Testament focuses deeply on the message of the Law given through Moses, while the New Testament emphasizes the Gospel through Jesus Christ.

So far, all of these levels of Bible knowledge are correct. But then, for so many would come a common but mistaken conclusion—that in the Old Testament, people were made right with God by good works, and in the New Testament, people are made right with God by grace. Multitudes of people, even those who attend church faithfully, believe the Old Testament and the New Testament teach two distinctly different plans of salvation. Nothing could be further from the truth.

There is only one God, one who is completely Holy. There is only one kind of person in comparison to this Holy God, and that is a wholly sinful person. There is only one way a sinner is accepted by God, and this is only by grace on the basis of faith. Salvation is by grace alone, through faith alone, in God alone.

Abram, who lived over 600 years before the giving of the Law through Moses, is the timeless witness of the gospel of salvation by grace through faith. That gospel message and example are contained in today's reading. "And he [Abram] believed the Lord, and He [God] counted it to him as righteousness" (Gen. 15:6). Abram was saved by faith; not faith in himself, but faith in God. Certainly, Abram did not have a fraction of the revelation we possess now in the Scriptures. However, he did understand that his God loved him and had promised, since the days of Adam and Eve, that a Redeemer would come. God, in His grace, made this promise. Abram believed God and God credited Abram's faith as righteousness. Salvation by grace through faith is the one and only Gospel.

JANUARY 7
Genesis 17-19

"FATHER ABRAHAM"

Like many reading these pages, I have had many titles associated with my name over the years. But only recently did I finally obtain a cherished title I have longed for so many years—and that title is " Grandpa." I now understand the joy I have often heard people "of a certain age" exclaim, "If I had known that grandchildren were going to be this much fun, I would have had them first!" There is indeed something profoundly moving about holding and looking into the faces of your children's children.

It must have seemed for decade after decade to Abram that his own name was a cruel reminder that he and Sarai were childless. The name "Abram" comes from the root word that means "father." How much more powerful it must have been when the Lord informed Abram that his name would now become "Abraham" because God promised that Abram would become "a father of nations" (Gen. 17:5). This childless man was told this "good news" again when he was nearly 100 years old, and Sarai was almost 90. Hearing that their tent would be transformed from a "geriatric ward" to a "nursery" was just too much for Sarai, who was secretly eavesdropping on the conversation and could not stifle the incredulous chuckle that came out of her mouth (Gen. 18:12). Little did Sarai know that with her response, she had just named the baby! The little boy would be called "Isaac," which means "laughter." Sarai also got a new name, "Sarah," which means "Princess."

What a covenant promise God made to this elderly couple. A childless man would become a father of nations, a woman without a son would become the princess of her people, and a little baby boy would cause his aged parents to dance and laugh.

God is "able to do far more abundantly than all that we ask or think" (Eph. 3:20). What God promises, He can do, and He will do because He is a faithful, covenant-keeping God. Abraham was promised the land, descendants of nations, and an heir through whom all the nations of the earth would be blessed. It's enough to make you laugh, isn't it? Go ahead. Sarah will understand, and she will enjoy it. "God has made laughter for me; everyone who hears will laugh over me" (Gen. 21:6).

JANUARY 8
Genesis 20-23

"JEHOVAH-JIREH"

Many years ago, when our church was constructing a new building, I noticed that many construction projects in our area had signs in front of the site that said, "Financing Provided by...." Then the name of the bank or lending institution would be printed. Since our congregation was providing all the funding for this particular project, I came up with the idea to put up a sign that celebrated God's financial provision. We had a beautiful, large sign that shared the message, "Financing Provided by Jehovah-Jireh."

One day not long after setting up the sign, a person from the community saw me at a local store and commented on our construction. Then the gentleman asked me, "Now, pastor, I'm unfamiliar with the Bank of Jehovah-Jireh. Where is that located?" Well, I knew my brilliant communication strategy may have been slightly flawed! However, the man's question did give me a wonderful opportunity to share the amazing gospel drama orchestrated by God and carried out by Father Abraham and his son Isaac. Truly, it is the story of Calvary in the Old Testament. Notice in Chapter 22 the incredible images of redemption:

> ~ The story begins by focusing on the love between the father and his son. This is the first use of the word "love" in the Bible—the father's love for his son.

> ~ Isaac is his "only son," and Abraham is required to offer his son as a burnt offer of sacrifice to God.

> ~ The terrible event is to take place on one of the tops of the mountain ridge Moriah, the same area Jerusalem is located.

> ~ Isaac carries the wood of his own sacrificial altar on his back up the hill, while Abram holds the knife and the fire to carry out the dreadful mission.

~ Isaac, a strong young man who could resist and refuse, willingly lays himself on the altar.

~ At the last moment, as Abraham is about to take his beloved son's life, the Lord stays his hand and shows him a ram "crowned with thorns" to be offered as a substitute for Isaac.

The moment and the experience are so life-changing that Abraham names the place and also names his God Jehovah-Jireh, "The Lord who provides." For the rest of their lives, Abraham and Isaac would never forget that event and what they learned about God.

Dear friend, may we never forget to trust the love of our Heavenly Father, who spared not His only Son for us. "He who did not spare his own Son but gave him up for us all, how will He not also with Him graciously give us all things?" (Rom. 8:32)

JANUARY 9
Genesis 24-26

"THE COVENANT LIFE"

As we read through the pages of the Bible, it is very insightful to consider the events that God has chosen to record in His word in comparison to the events taking place concurrently on the world stage that would have been perceived as much more significant. The events described in our reading today are a perfect example of this contrast. During these years in the Middle East, all the attention was on Egypt. The nation was spreading its domination over the entire region and was the power center at the convergence of three continents.

Egypt was the focal point of the world but not the focus of God. God's attention was on the desert landscape of the Negev and on a man worried about his family, his safety, his sheep, his wells—survival. The man is Isaac, who had been redeemed from death years before by a God-given substitute. He is the heir of the covenant God had made with his father, Abraham, and the covenant that God reconfirmed with him twice (Gen. 22:2-4, 23-24). In these two sets of verses and Isaac's response to God's declaration, we are given an example of how not to live and also how to live as God's covenant people.

We are not to live by fear. Despite God's covenant promise to protect and bless him, Isaac surrendered to a spirit of fear and then resorted to scheming and lying to safeguard himself and his family. The result of his fear only led to the loss of his testimony before the unbelievers among whom he lived. God graciously protected Isaac and his family from the vengeance of the enemies he had made. In fact, God reaffirmed with Isaac the covenant promises of His love (Gen. 22:23-24). This time, Isaac responded not in fear but in faith—he built an altar, pitched his tent, and dug a well.

That is how covenant people should live. We are worshipers. The rhythm of our lives should revolve around the sacred center of our personal love and devotion to God. We are pilgrims. We should not think of this world as our home. We must be careful to "keep our tent pegs shallow" so that we can always be ready to move at our Lord's direction. We are wells. Within us flows the artesian spring of life in Christ, and our mission is to freely share His grace and love with others. The covenant life we have in our Savior is one of the altar, the tent, and the well. It is not a desert. It is an oasis.

JANUARY 10
Genesis 27-29

"THE TRICKSTER TRICKED"

There is a reason that the most beautiful and costly diamonds are usually displayed against a very dark background. It is the darkness behind the gems that serve to help highlight their brilliance and dazzling qualities. In the Bible, it is certainly true that the precious jewel of God's grace is magnified by the sin-marred lives in which the Lord demonstrates His inexpressible and undeserved kindness.

There is no better example of this contrast between messed-up lives and God's mercy than the family dynamics of the patriarchs. What a dynasty of dysfunction! Whenever we think our families are a wreck and beyond redemption, reading a few chapters from the book of Genesis will cause us to feel more encouraged about ourselves and our relatives.

The family dynamics in Abraham's extended family involve almost every imaginable type of infighting and intrigue, and no one is a better schemer and conniver than Jacob. This trickster does not quite live by the principles of being "his brother's keeper" or "honor your father." First, Jacob leverages Esau's weakness and stress to rob him of his birthright. Then, with the assistance of his plotting mother, Jacob deceives his father, nearly blind, to also rob Esau of the patriarchal blessing Isaac planned to confer upon him. With a brother like Jacob, who needs enemies!

It is on this dark family tapestry that the beautiful story of God's sovereign grace will be displayed. But it is also true that the law of sowing and reaping always holds steady. And what a harvest Jacob reaps from his sowing such deceptive seeds! As hard as it is to believe,

Jacob meets someone trickier than he is—good old "Uncle Laban." Jacob's seven years of devoted and honest toil are rewarded on his wedding night with deception and betrayal just as great as that which he carried out seven years earlier on his brother and father.

Yes, Jacob is God's man; however, that is a testimony to the *God of Jacob*, not *Jacob*. Like so many of us, Jacob must also come face to face with his own reflection before he can truly come face to face with the God of grace. That is the rest of Jacob's story. Let's all look in the mirror of these chapters and keep reading.

JANUARY 11
Genesis 30-32

"The Heel is Healed"

The neighborhood in which I grew up was closely associated with a manufacturing plant where most of the men worked. So, it was definitely what one would call a "working-class" community. This meant that the language regularly spoken was a "working-class" dialect that included a lot of vocabulary that could be generously defined as slang. It would not be appropriate for me in this devotional to give you a sampling of some of those words! However, I can tell you that one thing no one ever wanted to be called was a "heel." The word probably had its origin as a reference to the tough, end piece of bread on a loaf. ("Loaf" was another slang term, but that is for another devotional entry.) Eventually, a "heel" came to mean someone who lacked character and could not be trusted.

Now, imagine actually being named "Heel" by your parents and then growing up to express a character that conformed to your name, "a heel." This is exactly the case with the patriarch Jacob. "Jacob" means "one who grabs the heel," or we could also say, "a deceptive manipulator." That character was ingrained in Jacob literally from the moment of birth through most of his adult life. He deceptively manipulated his father, Isaac; his brother, Esau; and his uncle, Laban.

Jacob has become rich in the land of Paddan-Aram. This is a result of God's blessing on him as Abraham's grandson and Isaac's son, but it is also because Jacob has worked hard and also worked deceptively. Finally, he shares with his wives the plan to sneak out of the area and take all his family and possessions back to the Land of Canaan. Laban learns of Jacob's "night flight" and pursues him in a rage. Only by God's protection is a bloodbath averted.

Shortly after this, Jacob learns that his brother, Esau, is riding out to him with a small army of 400 men! Once again, Jacob springs into full-bore manipulation in an effort to "soften up" his brother, Esau.

That night, Jacob experienced a "close encounter of the divine kind" that forever changed his life, name, walk, and faith. In the strongest wrestling match of the ages, God appears and wrestles Jacob to the dirt, weakening him so that all he can do is cling to the Lord and pray for a blessing. That changed everything for Jacob. Finally, he realized that he could trust God to provide for and protect him, not trust in himself and his manipulation of others. No longer was he Jacob. He was Israel, "He who strives with God." He has become something so much greater than a self-reliant man. He is a God-reliant man, clinging to God and praying for His blessing. Amen.

JANUARY 12
Genesis 33-35

"God is in the House"

As I write these words today, I am nearing the 35th anniversary of serving as pastor of our church. Through those years, I have had the privilege of sharing thousands of experiences with people as they walk through life with the Lord. Many, if not most of those relationships and experiences are, in some way, connected to the place we have worshiped together—the church building on Middlebrook Pike.

That building has become a sacred place for me, as I am sure for many others. It has become, in so many ways, the house of God.

Countless times over the years, I have gone early in the morning or late at night to just sit in the building and read the Scriptures, pray, meditate, sing, or weep. It is a sacred place for me, a personal "Bethel," the house of God. However, through our reading in Genesis today, I have been reminded that it is not "the house of God" that makes the building on Middlebrook Pike sacred. It is the "God of the house of God" who truly makes any location sacred. Jacob came to this realization when he named, or rather, renamed, the spot in the land of Canaan, El Bethel, "God of Bethel" or literally, "God of the house of God." It was the presence of the living God and Jacob's personal encounter with Him that made the spot holy.

Only God Himself makes places, moments, or experiences holy. Jacob testified of this truth when he said to his family, "Then let us arise and go up to Bethel so that I can make there an altar to God who answers me in the day of my distress and has been with me in the day of my distress and has been with me wherever I have gone" (Gen. 35:3). Jacob recognized that his whole life had been "Bethel," and that even in his darkest seasons, each of them was sacred as his God has sustained him.

Jacob's words reveal that he had experienced a radical change in his view of God and, as a result, his *view of life*. For Jacob, God was no longer the "God who is there," now He is the "God who is here." Without taking a single step, Jacob crossed a universe in his soul. He now saw his life not as a journey *occasionally* to a place where God is but as a journey *continually* where God is. My friend, when by God's grace we begin to view our lives as *lived in the presence of God*, then every place is "Bethel," and what a beautiful place that is to live!

JANUARY 13
Genesis 36-38

"Grace in Disgrace"

The Bible is not an easy book to read. First of all, it is quite a long book, as some who are reading all the chapters to this point are already starting to feel. The Bible contains 1,189 chapters and 23,145 verses. It is a long book. The Bible is not easy to read also because of the very different cultured contexts and the historical events focused in the Middle East and Mediterranean region of the world, spanning thousands of years.

The Bible is also difficult to read because it contains descriptions of family and personal behavior that are just really messed up. You might feel like you need a good "brain-washing" after reading Genesis, Chapters 36-38 today. The family of Abraham, "the friend of God," in less than three generations has become dysfunctional, distasteful, and downright despicable. No TV mini-series on a mob family of organized crime could outdo Abraham's family in intrigue and infidelity.

Why in the world would a holy God write a book that is so unholy at times? We need to remember many reasons as we continue our journey through the Old Testament. I want to point out two reasons on which we should focus: *Truth and Testimony*. The Bible is a book of truth— the truth about mankind and the truth about God. The Bible is a testimony to the glory of a holy God and His boundless, redeeming love. It declares the truth of the testimony of the God who came to us in the form of His Son, Jesus Christ, who was "full of Grace and Truth" (John 1:14). The Bible is the testimony of truth about God and mankind so that lives that are as empty clay pots can know once again the water of life, and worship the Father in grace and truth (John 4:24).

The Bible is truth and testimony to our own hearts. Let's face it. We are encouraged when we read about lives and families that are more messed up than our own! Most of all, we personally embrace the grace for the pages of our own darkness and disobedience when we read the stories in the Bible of God's grace for lives of disgrace. So, let's keep reading some real dirt in the Bible and receive the brain-washing we desperately need daily.

JANUARY 14
Genesis 39-41

"From the Pit to the Pinnacle"

The phrase "rags to riches" has existed so long in our culture that it has become an accepted modifier in our American-English vernacular to describe a person who has risen to wealth and influence from a life of poverty, struggles, and obstacles. The phrase was first used to describe the literary genre made famous by the novels of Horatio Alger in the late nineteenth century. Alger's stories nearly always were based on the storyline of a boy or young man who, through the strangest turn of events and due to his character and virtue, journeyed from pain and hardship to a place of prominence and influence for the good of others.

The story of Joseph is undoubtedly the ultimate "rags to riches" story in the Old Testament. And what a story it is! Joseph is the beloved and favored son of his father, Jacob. He is a young man blessed with visions, the visions that were given to him by God. These visions indicated that he would be exalted to a place of prominence in the family, even above that of his older brothers and his elderly father.

It was Joseph's favored position and his visions of exaltation by God that made him despised by his brothers, even to plotting his murder and eventually selling him into slavery. In that strange land, the young slave Joseph was tempted, falsely accused, imprisoned, and forgotten even by the people he had graciously served in their trials. For years, Joseph was the forgotten man by his fellow men, but God never forgot him. Jehovah had never for a moment taken His eyes off Joseph. Though it was impossible for Joseph or anyone else to see, Joseph was "descending into greatness." As Joseph faithfully served his God by serving others in his season of oppression and obscurity, he was being used by God in the lives of others that would ultimately bear fruit for them, others, and Joseph. Joseph was not buried and forgotten. He was planted and prepared for the life-giving ministry to come.

Joseph's "rags to riches" story is the story of Jesus, who "although he was rich, became poor, that we through his poverty might become rich" (2 Cor. 8:9). Our Lord's story is one of "riches to rags" so that we might have a grace story of "rags to riches." Those who desire to follow our Lord and become more like Him must embrace the truth—we have never been buried and forgotten. We have been known, loved, and planted to produce life for others. This is the journey to greatness—true greatness. Like our Master, we do not ascend into greatness. We descend into greatness. Children of the King kneel and serve before they receive the crown from the Ruler of heaven and earth.

JANUARY 15
Genesis 42-44

"JOSEPH REMEMBERED"

Clara Barton is a name not recognized commonly today, but her influence is worldwide over 100 years after her death as the founder of the Red Cross. Clara spent the years of the American Civil War serving as a nurse and had literally been covered with the blood shed by the horrible human destruction of war. Her experiences so deeply impacted her that she was determined to devote her life to training others to care for people whose lives were wrecked by war and disasters that were not of man's making. Her determination and commitment to help the suffering gradually produced a movement of workers and volunteers that has ministered to countless millions of suffering people over the decades.

Clara Barton was a healer and helper because she *could not forget* and also because she *chose not to remember*. On one occasion, Clara was reminded by a co-worker about how terribly a person had lied about her and sought to discredit Clara and her work. Clara quickly responded, "Oh yes, I distinctly remember having forgotten that." What an amazing statement! Even more, what an insight Clara Barton's words give to her character that made her such an instrument of healing. She chose not to let her emotional wounds become weapons to wound others. She could not forget, but she chose not to remember.

Joseph is an ever-living example from God's Word of a person who healed and rescued others because he could not forget that God had a plan for his sufferings. With that knowledge, Joseph chose not to remember the evil that had been done to him by his enemies. In Genesis 42:9, we are told that when Joseph saw his brothers who had sold him into slavery for the first time in years, "And Joseph remembered the dreams that he had dreamed of them." Joseph remembered that before he was so terribly wronged by his brothers, he had already come to know that God had a sovereign plan for his life. Joseph could not forget the certainty of God's plans for him, so he chose not to remember the terrible wrongs his brothers had committed against him.

This is the miraculous opportunity available for God's children in their own lives. Many people will often say, "Well, I can forgive, but I cannot forget." Exactly right! Forgiveness has nothing to do with forgetting; that would be denial and delusion. Forgiveness is *choosing not to remember* the wrongs done and refusing to return the wrong. As believers, we do this because we remember that God has a greater plan and that God has a greater grace. God planned for our lives to reflect His glory, and God, in His grace, forgot and forgave our sins through the sacrifice of His only Son on our behalf. God, in His greater grace, through the greatness of His Son, chooses to forgive His enemies. May we never forget that, so when it comes to wrongs done to us, we will make the greatest choice and choose not to remember.

JANUARY 16
Genesis 45-47

"God Sent Me Here"

"And we know that for those who love God, all things work together for good, for those who are called according to His purpose."
(Romans 8:28)

This is truly a mountain-top truth in Scripture that provides us with a sweeping view of the providence and purpose of God for His people. However, this most beloved verse in the Bible is most needed and comforting when we walk through the deepest and darkest of valleys.

Imagine the faith of Joseph, who, living 1900 years before the Apostle Paul shared the truth of Romans 8:28, believed that the God of his father, Israel, was at work in the terrible events he was experiencing. So much of Joseph's early life was "not good," yet he came to the certainty that his God was using his struggles "for good." By God's grace, Joseph had come to a confidence that he could tell his betrayers, his brothers, that through their evil actions, "God sent me before you to preserve life" (Gen. 45:5). In fact, Joseph is so sure of this that he tells his brothers three times that God had sent him ahead of them to preserve their family. Wow. Joseph's words are so incredible that many therapists or counselors today would probably tell him that he not only lived by the Nile, he lived in denial!

Joseph's words, though, are not those of someone who is mentally ill but of a man spiritually healthy. They are words of faith and grace—faith in a sovereign God of saving grace and a willingness to believe that his life is part of that saving plan and purpose. By believing this, Joseph saved himself from himself. If Joseph only focused on the betrayal, abuse, and injustice he had experienced (all of which were true), it would have poisoned his heart and prevented him from participating in the joyful, incredible, gracious mission of God's salvation.

Forgiveness is the gift we give to others and to ourselves. The person who has the faith to forgive is the person who knows the freedom to truly live. Bitterness is a poison that we pour into the well of our own hearts.

Joseph was able to be a deliverer of those who delivered him to slavery because he was a free man. He was free in the faith that his almighty, all-gracious God had chosen to display His glory through transforming his identity from a victim of wrongs to a deliverer of lives.

That same grace is available to us as believers who have known the pain of being misused. We can know the joy of being used by our God as an instrument of His peace.

JANUARY 17
Genesis 48-50

"The Scepter of Judah"

"The scepter shall not depart from Judah, nor the ruler's staff from between his feet, until tribute comes to him; and to him shall be the obedience of the peoples."
(Genesis 49:10)

The theme of the Bible can be summed up in one word, "Redemption." The theological concept of redemption is one of a payment that is made to set free and restore someone or something that has been lost and is held in bondage. To use the titles of two of John Milton's epic poems, the Bible is the account of "Paradise Lost" and "Paradise Regained."

The Bible begins with the Creation of a world that was paradise. God and His children, who bore His image, shared the perfect love relationship in an environment characterized by perfect peace and total harmony. Sadly, paradise was lost by the treason and rebellion of God's children against their Heavenly Father. Paradise was lost, but not forever. The Bible concludes with paradise restored. God Almighty, and His beloved children once again enjoying perfect, loving communion in a creation renewed and filled with light, peace, and eternal joy.

How was this restoration accomplished? In a word, it was "Redeemed." For that redemption to be accomplished, a redeemer would be required—someone worthy, willing, and able to meet the requirements necessary to set at liberty and restore the relationship between God, His children, and the harmony of creation. The first promise in the Bible is the good news of that Redeemer who would restore all that had been lost by sin (Gen. 3:15).

In our journey through Genesis, we have tracked the lineage of the Redeemer. He would come through the line of Seth and Shem's descendants, Abraham's family, the rescued son Isaac, and the younger son, Jacob. Now, Jacob, his 12 sons, and their families are in Egypt. Knowing his time of dying draws near, Jacob is prompted by the Spirit of God to speak a word of prophecy over his 12 sons, who will become the patriarchs of the Twelve Tribes of Israel. In his message, Jacob speaks a blessing upon his son, Judah. Jacob refers to Judah as a lion (Gen. 49:9) and that his family will be the line of kings among his brothers... "the scepter shall not depart from Judah" (Gen. 49:10). Then Jacob prophesied that from the kings of Judah would arise one to whom "tribute comes," or as it is also rendered in Hebrews, "Shiloh comes." The meaning of the phrase is "until the coming of the one to whom it belongs." This is the promise of the ultimate kind, the King of Kings, to whom the honor and tribute of all peoples will be given.

At the end of Genesis, the promise of the Redeemer is made clear for the coming generations. The Redeemer is the Lion King of the tribe of Judah who will gather the peoples of the earth back to the liberating, loving rule of God. The Lion of the Tribe of Judah will prevail and provide redemption. Paradise will be regained and never lost again. Amen.

JANUARY 18
Exodus 1-3

"Silent Not Absent"

During the spring of 1940, the bombing of London, England, by the Nazis was dreadful and relentless. Night after night, the tracer bullets, exploding anti-aircraft shells, and thousands of floodlights would illuminate the black skies for weeks on end. While in the city below, hundreds of thousands of people would huddle in basements and subway tunnels, awaiting the all-clear siren and the coming of the gray dawn to slowly emerge from their hiding places and survey the destruction. Sometimes, citizens would return to find their entire neighborhoods reduced to unrecognizable rubble. The relentless, horrific bombings took a toll on the citizens physically, emotionally, and even spiritually.

On one occasion, a city resident, completely overwhelmed in his spirit, picked up a piece of mortar from the rubble and scrawled upon a tattering wall the lament of his heart—"God is nowhere!" Several hours later, a volunteer aid worker sat upon a pile of bricks to rest and saw what had been written on the wall. The volunteer sat focusing on the words for several minutes while meditating on the message the letters shared. Finally, a look of illumination and insight appeared on the man's face. Walking slowly to the wall, he picked up the same piece of mortar. Crossing out the previous message, the volunteer rewrote the same letters but created a very different message—"God is now here." Same rubble. Same letters. Very different outlook.

Between the last chapter of Genesis and the first chapter of Exodus is a span of about 350 silent years. A radical change of circumstances has taken place. The Jewish people have been transformed from a small clan of privileged and honored immigrants to a nation of oppressed and abused slaves. They are the people of the covenant, but where is the God of the covenant? He is silent, but he is not absent.

He is present in the courageous hearts of two midwives. He is present in the faith-filled souls of a young mother and father. He is present in the bulrushes along the banks of the Nile, where a baby boy cries from a basket. He is present in the halls of Pharaoh's palace, where a young child of enslaved people is raised as a prince of Egypt. He is present when that same man, at age 40, must flee from Egypt with a death warrant on his head. He is present in the barren, sunburnt desert of the Midian wilderness where, for the next 40 years, this fugitive lives and works in obscurity. He is present in the bush that burns but is not consumed and in the amazing, life-changing revelation of His Name.

The Lord finally spoke, but He was never absent. Throughout 400 years of silence, it was still true. "God heard... God remembered... God saw... and God knew" (Ex. 2:24-25). God's silence is never God's absence. For His people, it is never "God is nowhere." It is always "God is now here."

JANUARY 19
Exodus 4-6

"What is That in Your Hand?"

Moses was a master of excuses, no doubt about it. However, we need to recognize the magnitude of what God required of him compared to the situation he faced and the qualifications he realized he did not possess. First of all, he is 80 years of age. Secondly, he is a fugitive from Egyptian justice with an outstanding warrant for his life. Thirdly, he possessed no military training and no military. Fourthly, he will demand the world's most powerful leader to emancipate over one million slaves who represent a significant portion of the labor force and economic backbone of Egyptian society. Fifthly, he was not known or respected by his own people that he was being called to lead. Sixthly, he was not a persuasive public speaker and seemed to have a speech impediment that caused his communication skills to be significantly impaired. Seventhly, Moses had no understanding of a plan to lead or provide for the needs of such an enormous number of people, and he did not even know where he was being called to guide them.

So, when we consider Moses' situation and his qualifications, it is probably just a little more than fair to say that his excuses for God's call on his life make a lot of sense. As we read the account of Moses' call to the most daunting task asked of any individual until that day, we see that the only personal possession Moses held as he stood before the presence of God was a shepherd's rod.

All Moses had was a large stick, which is exactly what God asked him about. "What is that in your hand?" was the question from God (Ex. 4:2). Moses replied, "A staff." God commanded Moses to lay it on the ground before Him. The staff became a serpent, and then Moses was commanded to pick it up by the tail. Definitely an act of faith! Moses obeyed, and again, it became a staff in his hand. A few moments later, the Lord said to Moses, "And take in your hand this staff, with which you shall do signs" (Ex. 4:17).

In obedience to God, Moses stopped making excuses and began his journey down the mountainside toward Egypt. But then, we are given an amazing statement regarding Moses' staff. No longer is it *Moses' staff*. Rather we are told Moses walked away from Jehovah with "*the staff of God* in his hand." This stick of wood is never referred to as Moses' staff again. It is "the rod of God."

Moses was called to an unimaginable task. All that he had was a stick. But, that piece of wood surrendered to the Lord became an amazing resource for ministry. God's question to fearful excuse-makers today is the same as He asked of Moses, "What is that in your hand?" Whatever we have with our Lord's power *is enough*.

JANUARY 20
Exodus 7-9

"IN HIS NAME'S SAKE"

In the fall of 2010, I had the privilege of meeting and having an extended conversation with the President of the International Mission Board of the Southern Baptist Convention. He had updated the leaders of the mission board on which I served concerning the work of God in global evangelism, especially within countries that were officially closed to the ministry of Christian missionaries. I vividly recall how this mission leader spoke of the growth of house churches in repressive countries where church buildings would never be permitted. I was astounded when he shared that through their contacts in Communist China, they had discovered the existence of five house church associations, each larger in number than the entire Southern Baptist Convention's 50,000 churches!

As staggering as that statistic was in 2010, it was magnified by the reality of what the Communist leader, Mao Zedong, had instituted just 61 years earlier in "The Great Purge." This was the name given to Chairman Mao's sweeping "anti-foreigner" program that included the expulsion of all Christian missionaries from China and the arrest, imprisonment, or execution of all Chinese pastors. In 1949, an estimated one million followers of Jesus lived in China. These believers and those who followed them suffered terrible persecution for decades and continue to do so until the present moment.

What impacted the church's growth in China during such opposition? Today, the number of believers in China is conservatively estimated to be 50 million and perhaps as many as 100 million. Chairman Mao's plan to eradicate Christianity in his country not only failed but also fueled a devotion among believers that inspired fervent evangelism and exponential growth.

Chairman Mao's evil and hard heart against God and His people was not unique. The history of God's redemption plan through the centuries is one of continual, unstoppable victory over the forces of oppression and opposition. Our God, in His wisdom, has ordained that the persecution of His people will only serve to magnify the power of His might and the glory of His name.

Our reading in Exodus today shares how Pharaoh continually hardened his heart against the will of God and refused to obey. Pharaoh considered himself to *be* God and was worshiped as such by his people. Pharaoh was head of an empire that had existed for thousands of years and, in his day, he was the mightiest military force in the world. Mighty, but not *Almighty*. The Almighty One replied to Pharaoh's obstinate resistance, "But for this purpose, I have raised you up, to show you my power so that my name...be proclaimed in all the earth" (Ex. 9:16).

The mega-maniac Pharaoh was just a megaphone for the voice of God to proclaim His power to all the world. My friend, many voices of evil and hatred of God are broadcast in our day, but there is only *one Voice* that controls all things and can calm the storms of fear in our hearts. Listen. That Voice, the Father's Voice, is speaking to you right now. Selah.

JANUARY 21
Exodus 10-12

"The Lamb of Passover"

For nearly 3,500 years, one evening has bound together the Jewish people in their identity, and that is Passover. Just how many millions of times Jewish families have observed Passover would be beyond calculation. For the Jewish people, Passover is the event of their independence, emancipation, and the origin of their spiritual and national identity. It is also for followers of Jesus, the event that symbolizes the hope that is the "scarlet thread," binding together the people of God under the Old Covenant and the New Covenant. The Apostle Paul states, "Christ, our Passover, is sacrificed for us" (1 Cor. 5:7). So, it is clear that Passover is in its essence connected to Messiah and His sacrificial death.

The focus of Exodus, Chapter 12, is on the Passover lamb. The lamb must be carefully observed for four days to reveal that it is free from all illness and defects that would disqualify it from being offered. Likewise, the four Gospel writers carefully examine the life of Jesus, each concluding as did Pilate, "I find no fault in Him." The Passover lamb was sacrificed, and its blood was applied to the lintel and sides of the door. The blood of the lamb was applied, literally, in the markings of a cross on each doorway. The image is of a door of escape from death and entrance into life. The blood of the Lamb on the door was also a covering from the judgment of God, and His promise for all was "and when I see the blood, I will pass over you" (Ex. 12:13).

Notice that God did not say that the tribes of Israel were to kill their lambs but to kill "the Passover Lamb" (Ex. 12:21). There were countless thousands of lambs slaughtered that day in Egypt. Still, the external eyes of Jehovah were only on one Lamb—the Lamb slain in the redemption plan of God before the foundation of the earth (Rev. 13:8).

Messiah in these details is prefigured just as He would be presented and proclaimed by John the Baptist 1500 years later, "Behold the Lamb of God who takes away the sin of the world!" (John 1:29) The Passover Lamb is not just the Lamb for the people of Israel but also for all the peoples of the earth. The Lord's instructions regarding the Passover and the lambs to be slain was a message, not just national and international but also personal. Notice again God's instructions concerning the Passover: "Every man shall take a *lamb*" (v. 3). "You shall make your count for the *lamb*" (v. 4). "*Your lamb* shall be without blemish..." (v. 5)

Note the progression: "a lamb," "the lamb," "your lamb." The designations of this lamb are also the progression to a personal salvation. It is *information* to know that Jesus is "a lamb." It is *illumination* to know that Jesus is "the Lamb." But, it is *salvation* to know that Jesus is "*your Lamb.*" Can you praise God this moment by saying, "Jesus is my lamb?"

JANUARY 22
Exodus 13-15

"THE BATTLE IS THE LORD'S"

When my children were small, one thing we enjoyed doing as a family was watching old movies—film versions of Broadway musicals, the "Road Movies" of Bob Hope and Bing Crosby, or epic Bible stories. My children would often memorize some of the lines from these movies and weave them into conversations around the house—sometimes involving total strangers.

One of these "unfiltered" pronouncements of a line from a movie was loudly declared by our son, Stephen, who was about six years of age at the time. We had gone to a neighborhood swimming pool. During rest time, when everyone was to leave the pool for 15 minutes, my wife and I were stretched out on blankets enjoying the warm sunshine when the sound of our son's voice came ringing out high above the pool, shouting a Biblical declaration, "Behold the salvation of the Lord!" We looked up and saw our small son standing on the edge of the high diving board with floaties around his arms which were outstretched toward heaven.

When Stephen was certain that all eyes were on him, he made a gigantic leap into the air and came down into the water with a huge splash. He popped right back up to the surface thanks to the floaties on his arms and was beaming a smile of appreciation for all the laughter and applause he had generated. My thoughts were a little different as I escorted him to our family area! I was sure I could hear chuckled whispers from every adult we passed, "Preacher's kid." When I asked my son what in the world he was thinking, he explained that he got the idea to pretend he was Moses and part the Red Sea from the movie we had watched. Thank you very much, Charlton Heston!

Over the years, our family has recalled with laughter that "epic moment" when Stephen proclaimed the power of God, "Behold, the salvation of the Lord!" It has also caused me to imagine how many times through the coming years, the eyewitnesses to God's parting of the Red Sea would recount the miraculous deliverance of God for the nation of Israel. Generation after generation would come to know the testimony of God's love and power on behalf of His people.

Each generation would learn that the God of Israel is a deliverer who can defend His people and fight their battles for them. "The Lord will fight for you, and you have only to be silent" (Ex. 14:14.) Yes, we can rest secure and silent when we surrender our battles to the Lord. Then, when we see our God faithfully act on our behalf, we can declare with all the exuberance of the six-year-old boy with floaties on his arms, "Behold the salvation of the Lord!"

JANUARY 23
Exodus 16-18

"The Lord is My Banner"

Recently, I listened to some old recordings made in the early 1900s containing interviews with men and women who were former slaves before and during the American Civil War. It was hard to listen to these recordings because the testimonies recounted what these men and women, 60 or 70 years later, still recalled of the unimaginable toil, abuse, and heartache they had experienced and witnessed. No one could listen and honestly conclude anything else than that slavery is an awful evil and sin.

As I listened, I was struck by the reality of just how traumatic the experience of sudden freedom was for these former slaves. Most of them were simply turned out by their masters. They were free, yes, but they were completely unprepared for life outside the only existence they had ever known. They could not read or write, possessed no understanding of their location or geography, were without money or adequate clothing, and had no guidance about where to go or what to do. Freedom for so many liberated slaves only brought new nightmares of life without the basic support of kindness, care, and provision.

In our Scripture reading today, we see on display the love and care of the Heavenly Father for His people whom He delivered from 400 years of terrible bondage. We learn that the God who liberates His people from bondage is also Provider for everything they need as He leads them to the Promised Land. Just consider what would be required to sustain a nation numbering more than one million people for over 40 years. It is the greatest supply chain project in the history of the world!

God supplied everything—shade from the burning sun, light in the inky darkness of night, water from the rock, a frost of food every morning, clothing that did not wear out, truth to fill their minds and feed their souls, and also His presence and power to defend them and defeat their foes. In a word, these former slaves, now freed by Jehovah, were covered by His love. Truly, they could say, "The Lord is my banner" (Ex. 17:15).

Everything the Father provided for His people on their journey to Canaan is as true for us in Christ as we make our faith journey to heaven. We have been redeemed from our spiritual bondage by our Lord's precious blood as the Lamb of God. He is our shelter and light, living water, daily bread, guide, defender, and the Captain of our salvation. He intercedes for us with arms that are never wearied. When we look up in our struggles, we see that our Master is always there. Truly, we can proclaim, "The Lord is my banner!"

JANUARY 24
Exodus 19-21

"A Treasured Possession"

I learned one of the greatest lessons I ever learned as a teenager through a television commercial. As I look back on it even to this day, it rather amazes me. The commercial was a public service message because it was not really an attempt to sell anything. I don't recall all the details or much of the dialogue, but the theme of the video went straight to my heart and never left.

In the commercial, two teenage boys are riding on a motorcycle, and it is clear they come from two very different lifestyles. The young man driving is the stereotypical "street hood" with the leather jacket, tight faded jeans, and the "coolest" of sunglasses. The other teen is wearing penny loafers, khaki slacks, and a sweater. In the video, they stop to smoke cigarettes under a tree, and the street-wise teen suggests they cruise over to a house he knows is hosting a great party. The other teen says he can't go because his parents have set a curfew for him. The final scene shows the two teens pulling up on the motorcycle in front of a house, and the one on the back hops off and trots up to the door. As the door closes, the young man in the leather jacket is sitting on the motorcycle. He stares at the home for a few moments and then, with a sigh, says, "I wish someone cared what time I got home."

When I heard his statement, my whole perspective on my parents changed in one moment. I got it. For all the griping I did about my parents' rules and restrictions, I understood that I was incredibly blessed to have parents who cared enough to set guidelines for me. Their limitations and rules were expressions of sincere love and concern for me. Their laws were based on love.

These chapters of our daily readings in Exodus introduce an entire section of the Bible known as The Law. God calls Moses to the top of Mount Sinai and shares with him the Ten Commandments. These ten foundational commands of God are only the first of hundreds of commands from Jehovah. Why? Does the Lord intend to be the new slave master to the slaves He has just freed? Is God determined that His people will not waste their time seeking happiness or joy? Hardly. God says they are His "treasured possession" and a "kingdom of priests and a holy nation to Him" (Ex. 19:5-6).

Connect two words in that statement—"treasured" and "holy." God is giving His law to the people of Israel because they are precious and special to Him in a covenant relationship of love. God is love; therefore, His laws are expressions of love.

Take a few moments to let that sink into your heart. You are loved by a Father who cares enough about you to tell you when to come in from the dark.

JANUARY 25
Exodus 22-24

"Lift the Burdens"

"Do not think that I have come to abolish the law or the Prophets;
I have not come to abolish them but fulfill them."
(Matthew 5:17)

When Jesus began His ministry in Galilee, some of His earliest messages were guidelines about how His followers should live their lives. These principles were considered so revolutionary by the religious leaders of the day that he was accused of destroying the Law. Over the centuries, the Law of God had been so encumbered with man-made traditions that God's commands were no longer expressed as the path to freedom but as a ponderous burden to bear on the trail of legalism. In His teaching, Jesus turned that understanding of the Law of God "upside down" so that His disciples could live life from the inside out—Spirit-liberated, not law-dominated.

Our reading today from Exodus, Chapter 23, is a perfect example of how God's true law produces a spirit of burden-lifting, not burden-making. Notice, Jehovah said that His people were to show concern and care for their enemies: "If you see the donkey of one who hates you lying down under its burden, you shall refrain from leaving him with it; you shall rescue it with him" (Ex. 23:5). Jesus: "And as you wish that others would do to you, do so to them" (Luke 6:31).

Likewise, Jehovah instructed His people to never forget the bondage they had experienced. He made it a law in Israel that immigrants and refugees were never to be oppressed but rather to be blessed: "You shall not oppress a sojourner. You know the heart of a sojourner, for you were sojourners in the land of Egypt" (Ex. 23:9). Jesus: "By this all people will know that you are my disciples, if you have love for one another" (John 13:35).

God's people have always been a people of law, but the Law of God is the law of liberty; it is fulfilled in love. In His law of love, we find rest, not stress. God's law is the way to Sabbath: "Six days you shall do your work, but on the seventh day you shall rest; that your ox and your donkey may have rest, and the son of your servant woman, and the alien, may be refreshed" (Ex. 23:12). Jesus: "Come to me, all who labor and are heavy laden, and I will give you rest" (Matt. 11:28).

In His instructions for us, our Lord fills the Law full of His mission of freedom for ourselves and burden-lifting for others. God's laws are meant not only to give us light but also to make light our burden and guide us in lightening the burdens of others. "For the whole law is fulfilled in one word: 'You shall love your neighbor as yourself'" (Gal. 5:14).

JANUARY 26
Exodus 25-27

"The Tent of Meeting"

The Bible is the Word of God. Of the more than 700,000 words it contains, not a single word is without significance. God is incapable of doing anything without a purpose. The words God chooses to include in His book are divinely ordained to communicate the message and theme of His divine plan. If we just read the words of the Bible, we can overlook how they are connected to the Word of the Bible. The Apostle John reminds us of this truth in the opening phrase of his Gospel: "In the beginning was the Word, and the Word was with God, and the Word was God" (John 1:1).

In this simple statement, John shares the most profound truth. In the Godhead, there eternally exists One who is the message and the Messenger of God. If possible, even more astounding is the truth John shares about this Divine Message/Messenger: "And the Word became flesh and dwelt among us, and we have seen his glory, glory as of the only Son from the Father, full of grace and truth" (John 1:14).

John is describing the amazing truth of the incarnation, God, the eternal Word, coming to earth in human flesh. In sharing this incredible reality, John is led by the Spirit to use a very specific and somewhat unusual term. The literal translation would be, "And the Word became flesh and tabernacled among us." The word John uses means to "pitch a tent." The phrase "tabernacled" or "pitch a tent" is significant because it connects the incarnation of God's Son with the tabernacle of the Old Testament.

Over 400 years before Solomon constructed the temple in Jerusalem, Jehovah dwelt with His people in a tabernacle, often referred to as the "tent of meeting." Therefore, to understand and appreciate all the specific details shared in chapter after chapter about the construction of the tent of meeting, we must see that they are all symbolic types of the majesty and ministry of Jesus Christ—the "meeting place" for God and all mankind. As we read through the endless details, we will be blessed if we look for Jesus. The tent of meeting speaks of Christ. This tent was plain and ordinary on the outside, but inside it was stunningly beautiful and glorious. Likewise, Jesus possessed no striking beauty or stature (Is. 53:2), but in Him dwells all the glory of God (Col. 2:9). Jesus is the one door to God (John 10:7), the sacrifice on the altar (Heb. 13:10-12), the lampstand for the world (John 8:12), the manna from heaven (John 6:41), and the continual incense of intercession (Heb. 7:25). His is the Mercy seat of propitiation between a Holy God and sinful people (Rom. 3:25).

As we read these chapters, let's take a fresh look at the descriptions of the tabernacle and pray to see the "glory as of the only Son from the Father, full of grace and truth" (John 1:14).

JANUARY 27
Exodus 28-30

"In His Presence"

The tent of meeting served as a portable temple. It was the sacred center for the people of Israel and the Twelve Tribes of the nation encamped around it. It was portable so that when the glory cloud of the Lord's presence lifted up and stood above the tent, the tabernacle could be carefully disassembled and transported to the next place the Lord chose for the encampment.

The tent of meeting was the visible expression of God's covenant promise: "I will dwell among the people of Israel and will be their God. And they shall know that I am the Lord their God, who brought them out of the land of Egypt that I might dwell among them. I am the Lord their God" (Ex. 29:45-46).

The tent of meeting was a continual reminder to the people of Israel that their God was with them, living among them, and they were precious to Him. Likewise, the tent of meeting was a continual reminder that the Lord was separate from them. He is holy, and they are not. Approaching this completely perfect God in the sinfulness of their condition would bring total, immediate, and well-deserved judgment. To approach this absolutely holy God, the people must have a representative who could take their place and bring their needs before Almighty God. The Lord met this need through the provision of the High Priest. Aaron, the brother of Moses, was designated by Jehovah to be the priestly representative for the people of Israel in His presence. Like the tent of meeting itself, the High Priest, his garments, and his duties all prefigure the coming, ultimate, and final High Priest, Jesus Christ.

For this reason, the Lord gave very specific instructions to Moses concerning Aaron's wardrobe: "And you shall make holy garments for Aaron your brother, for glory and for beauty" (Ex. 28:2). Aaron's garments were testaments to the glory and beauty of the Promised One. The colors of his clothing speaks of our Savior: brilliant white, representing His absolute purity; gold, speaking of His royalty; scarlet, the hue of His sacrifice; blue, the color of His heavenly origin.

Also, two jewelry items worn on the High Priest's garments brought great comfort and peace to the people of Israel and should do the same today for every believer in Jesus Christ. The High Priest had attached two precious stones to the shoulder pieces of his garment. In these jewels were inscribed the names of the tribes of Israel. These two stones represented that everything the High Priest did was on behalf of his people. The High Priest, for all purposes, *was his people*. Likewise, on his chest, the High Priest wore a breastplate that contained 12 precious gems, one for each of the Twelve Tribes. These stones were worn over the High Priest's heart. What an image! Every believer in Jesus is on the shoulders and over the heart of their Master today. He is *walking with us* on earth, and He is *standing for us* in Heaven, and we are safe in both places. Amen.

JANUARY 28
Exodus 31-33

"Rock of Ages"

Many people mistakenly believe that when Moses received the Law from the Lord, he journeyed up to the top of Mount Sinai and shortly returned to the people. However, Moses was on the mountain for 40 days and 40 nights (Ex. 26:18). Tragically, the people of Israel quickly proved just how deeply their hearts were still infected by the idolatry of Egypt. They turned this sacred gathering before God's presence on the mountain into a mass party of drunkenness and debauchery. Worst of all, they soon decided that, like other nations, they needed a physical image to assist them in their worship. They coerced Aaron into blessing and even guiding their blasphemous plan. In his direction, they melted golden jewelry to create the image of a bull that would symbolize the God of Israel.

When the Lord revealed to Moses the wicked treason being carried out by Israel, Moses literally placed himself between the just and holy wrath of God and His idolatrous people. In the following interaction, Moses demonstrates the incredible ministry and privilege of intercessory prayer. As an intercessor, Moses stands or, more probably, kneels between his people and his God. As an intercessor, his heart is drawn in love and identification with his God and his people.

Moses pleads even to the point of requesting that God blot his own name out of God's book if He does not pardon the sin of the Israelites. In merciful response to Moses' intercession, God spares the sinful people the punishment they rightly deserve. No greater intercession will ever occur until, on another hilltop, God hears the prayer of intercession from One filled with devotion to sinners even greater than Moses. "Father, forgive them for they know not what they do."

As a devoted intercessor, Moses not only longs for the needs of others before God, but his heart also longs for his own needs before God, his need of God Himself above all things. Moses, who has boldly requested much from God for the tribes of Israel, now boldly makes his own personal request, "Please show me your glory" (Ex. 33:18).

In God's presence, Moses experienced the completeness that only worshipers of their Creator-Father can ever know. Yet, the experience only made him long for more of the Father's presence. God was pleased with Moses' request and placed him in a location where he could be protected from God's pure holiness and experience God's goodness and glory—the cleft in the rock. There in the side of the rock, Moses would "see God," "know God," and be "transformed by God."

Through the centuries, the people of God who have longed for intimacy with their Creator-Father, have found the secret place of that experience, abiding securely in the "Rock of Ages." Listen as a blind woman, Fanny Crosby speaks of what she has seen:

> *A wonderful Savior is Jesus my Lord,*
> *A wonderful Savior to me;*
> *He hideth my soul in the cleft of the rock,*
> *Where rivers of pleasure I see.*
> *He hideth my soul in the cleft of the rock*
> *That shadows a dry, thirsty land;*
> *He hideth my life in the depths of His love,*
> *And covers me there with His hand.*

("He Hideth My Soul" by Fanny Crosby)

JANUARY 29
Exodus 34-36

"SHINING BRIGHTLY UNAWARE"

> *"Moses did not know that the skin of his face shone because he had been talking with God."*
> (Exodus 34:29)

In many ways, Dwight L. Moody was the Billy Graham of the nineteenth century. He was converted as a teenage shoe clerk in Boston, and in his zeal and gifting, within a few years became renowned in America and Europe for his evangelistic meetings that saw thousands and thousands of conversions to Christ. Moody knew the struggles of childhood and young manhood in poverty. As a result, he established Sunday Schools for boys and girls and summer camping programs for young people.

On one occasion at a camp in Massachusetts, after an evening service in which Moody had preached, a group of young adults decided to host a special outdoor prayer gathering. It was a powerful time of joyful prayer. Walking back from the service, a group of young women passed Mr. Moody on the trail through the camp. One of the young women excitedly ran up to the evangelist, exclaiming, "Oh, Mr. Moody, we have had the most wonderful time with the Lord; look how our faces are shining!" To the young woman's exuberant declaration, Moody gently replied, "Moses did not know his face was shining."

To those who seek Him, the manifested presence of God is a blessed reality. However, the subtle danger of self-focus is always lurking, even among those who seek the Lord in prayerful worship. There is the danger of seeking an emotional experience above the spiritual reality of God Himself.

We must be careful not to seek a "blessing" more than the "Blesser." God, Himself is the gift experienced by those seeking Him. Also, those who regularly spend time with the God of Israel do not speak of it as much as they show it. People "take notice of them that they have been with Jesus" (Acts 4:13).

One of the great gifts the Lord gives to those who spend time with Him is that He *inspires* them without *inflating* them. They leave the glorious presence of God to serve Him by serving others. Something of the Divine presence goes with them, but they are oblivious to it; "they do not know that their faces are shining."

I once saw a t-shirt that someone had specially made that said, "Be the Moon." When I asked her about it, she said she had it made in response to something I had said in a message. I couldn't recall ever making that statement, but she reminded me that I had used an illustration about the moon, that it really has no light of its own but only reflects the light of the sun. "So," the lady said, "I thought I would make this t-shirt to remind me and others to Be the Moon." The preacher needed to hear that! Maybe you do, too.

JANUARY 30
Exodus 37-38

"The Only One"

The instructions the Lord gave regarding the construction of the "tent of meeting" were amazing in their detail. Reading the specifications, in reality, is reading architectural design instructions from the Master Architect. Nothing was left to chance. The Lord made it clear to Moses that everything carried out in the construction of God's dwelling place was to follow the exact "design-build" instructions He had given to Moses on Mount Sinai.

Thousands of items would be needed. For this reason, the Lord gifted two men, Bezalel and Oholiab, with supernatural, Spirit-directed abilities to superintend the project. In your mind, as you approach the tent, it is important to make note of the objects that were unique and one-of-a-kind. These items are significant to us as followers of God's One and only Son.

One Gate: The tent could only be entered by the one gate or screen, which provided access to God's presence. "I am the Way, the Truth, and the Life," said Jesus. "No one comes to the Father except through Me" (John 14:6).

One Altar of Burnt Offering: The writer of Hebrews reminds us, "But when Christ had offered for all time a single sacrifice for sins, he sat down at the right hand of God" (Heb. 10:12).

One Bronze Basin: The basin was a very large and ornate water container that provided for the ritual cleansing of the priests as they prepared to serve. The water in this basin represents the sanctifying power of Christ through His Word for the lives of His servants. Christ sanctifies us "by the washing of water with the Word" (Eph. 5:26).

One Lampstand: Jesus is the "Light of the World," and in His grace, He has called us into the light. Now we can "walk in the light, as He is in the light" and "have fellowship with one another" (1 John 1:7).

One Table: Jesus is the true manna from heaven who alone can provide food for our souls (John 6:51).

One Altar of Incense: This fragrant oil was offered continually before the presence of God within the tent. The priests cared for the flaming incense night and day. The burning of incense symbolized intercession for sinners before God. We rejoice in Christ, who is "able to save to the uttermost those who draw near to God through him, since he always lives to make intercession for them" (Heb. 7:25).

One Ark of the Covenant: Above this ark and the golden lid (called the mercy seat), God dwelt with His people. Upon the mercy seat, the blood of the sacrifice was sprinkled each year to atone for the nation's sins. Through Christ, God has made "a propitiation" (literally, a mercy seat) "by his blood, to be received by faith" (Rom. 3:25). There is only One. Take time as you pray, thanking the Heavenly Father for His Son, Jesus, "The One and Only."

JANUARY 31
Exodus 39-40

"The Long Procession Home"

As we come to the closing verses of the book of Exodus, it is very insightful to compare them with the final statements in the book of Genesis. In both sections, we see expressed the faithfulness of God and blessing upon those who have faith in Him.

The book of Genesis closes with Joseph solemnly instructing his family from his deathbed in the palace. We are told that after Joseph died, he was embalmed according to the tradition of the Egyptians, and his body was placed in a coffin in Egypt. Joseph instructed not to *bury him* but to *carry him* to the Promised Land.

How did Joseph know that his people would return to Canaan? Because of the faithfulness of God to the covenant promises He had made with Abraham, Isaac, and his father, Jacob. God told Joseph's great-grandfather, Abraham, that his people would be slaves for 400 years in Egypt. But when the iniquity of the Amorites (the inhabitants of Canaan) was full, He would bring them back to the land He had given as an everlasting homeland (Gen. 15:13-16).

No doubt, it was the knowledge of this promise Joseph learned from his father, Jacob, that gave Joseph the confidence that his own slavery in Egypt was part of God's sovereign plan. Now 400 years later, the first Israelite slave, Joseph, is carried in his coffin by an immense multitude of over a million former slaves (now a nation named after his father, Israel) to be laid to rest with his fathers in the cave of Machpelah in Hebron. It would not be a short trip.

The long procession home would take over 40 years. How could such a vast multitude, surrounded by enemies, endure, and how would they know the way through an uncharted wilderness? Faith in God. Faith is focusing on God and obeying the directions He gives.

"Throughout all their journeys, whenever the cloud was taken up over the tabernacle, the people of Israel would set out. But, if the cloud was not taken up, then they did not set out till the day that it was taken up" (Ex. 40:36-37).

The God who, through a teenage slave, saved his family in Egypt and turned that small clan into a multitude of slaves; the God who led those slaves to freedom by destroying the superpower of their age; the God who dwells with His people and provides for them in the wilderness; *that God* knows how to show the way and lead His people home! Amen.

February

"The Lord is slow to anger and abounding in steadfast love."
(Numbers 14:18)

FEBRUARY 1
Leviticus 1-3

"Holy is the Lord"

For many believers, Leviticus is one of the most difficult books of the Bible to read or even enjoy; let's be honest. The Book of Leviticus is literally filled and flowing with blood. The various rituals and practices described sound like they belong more in a butcher shop or meat processing plant than in the Word of God. No amount of spiritualizing the messages can sanitize the truth that worship in the Old Testament was often a bloody affair. Why is that? Without a proper understanding of the key theme being communicated through the sacrificial system described, we can easily lose our way in a book we know to be of Divine origin.

So, what is the main theme we must hold to like a compass as we navigate through the chapters of Leviticus? It is helpful to answer that question based on two polar opposite realities. God is completely holy, and human beings are completely sinful. Those two absolute and indisputable realities have to be addressed and understood before it is possible for successful reconciliation between holy God and sinful people. The entire system the Lord establishes through the instructions He shares with Moses is based on His holiness. God is holy. The word "holy" is common to anyone who is even vaguely familiar with the teaching of the Bible. But what does it mean, and why is it fundamental to understanding Leviticus (as well as the other books of the Bible)? The word "holy" has, at its core, the idea of being "separate" or "different." When applied to God, it means He is *really* not like us when it comes to sin. God is perfect love and perfect purity at the same time. Therefore, God loves righteousness and hates sin.

We are *unrighteous* and *sinful*; herein lies the dilemma. How can a holy God who loves righteousness and hates sin be reconciled and fellowship with people who are unrighteous and sinful in their very nature? The *temporary answer*, to use that phrase in relation to time on earth, is in the Levitical system of worship. What did that system teach? Firstly, God could only be approached by representatives of the people who were acceptable to Him. Only one designated person could represent the people in Jehovah's actual presence—the High Priest. Secondly, there must be the offering of a sacrificial substitute to make atonement for the people's sins. Apart from the shedding of the sacrificial animal's blood, there could be no remission of the guilt of sin and its penalty. Thirdly, this Levitical system was an expression of God's love and mercy who, despite His perfect holiness and the total sinfulness of His people, still desired a personal and living relationship with His people. They are His covenant people, and His heart is for them in every way. God did not establish the Levitical system of worship because He *did not* desire to draw near and dwell with His people, but because He *did* desire that relationship with all His heart.

As you read these chapters in Leviticus, remember to look for Jesus in all the details of the ceremonies. He is right there pictured and prefigured in all His glory. Jesus fulfilled it all in His life and concluded it all with His dying cry, "It is finished!"

FEBRUARY 2
Leviticus 4-6

"THE CONSTANT FLAME"

"The fire on the altar shall be kept burning on it; it shall not go out."
(Leviticus 6:12)

One of the noteworthy aspects of the Levitical system of worship was that it operated night and day. The incense from the altar constantly rose and filled the tent of meeting with a beautiful aroma. The "bread of the presence" was always sitting upon the golden table. The light from the golden lampstand shined continuously. The priests constantly watched and tended the fire upon the altar of burnt offering. The solemn command of Jehovah was that they were never to let the flame burn out.

Why was this command given? What is the significance of that flaming sacrifice? First of all, as we have already noted, everything specified in the worship system of the tabernacle speaks of Christ. Jesus is the Lamb slain before the foundation of the world (Rev. 13:8). The sacrifice of His Son is eternal. In the constant flame on the altar, we are reminded that the sacrifice of Christ is from *everlasting to everlasting*.

Secondly, the constant flame on the altar symbolizes the continual offer of God's sacrifice for sin. Jesus is not just a part-time Savior. He is the way of forgiveness and acceptance always available for those who will come by faith. Like Jesus Himself, His sacrifice is the same yesterday, today, and forever (Heb. 13:8).

Thirdly, the priests were to constantly minister and care for the flame for the offerings to God. Likewise, the work of the Gospel in Christ is to be continuously provided by His followers. Because Jesus is the continual sacrifice, the witnesses of the Lamb of God can always affirm that today is truly the Day of the Lord's salvation, the acceptable Day of the Lord (2 Cor. 6:2). The "everyday gospel is the gospel every day" because there is never a day when there does not exist the good news of the faithful saying, worthy of all acceptance, that Christ Jesus came into the world to save sinners (1 Tim. 1:15).

Finally, the never-dying flame on the altar testifies to the type of sacrifice we now offer as members of the New Covenant, presenting our bodies as living sacrifices, holy, and acceptable to the Lord (Rom.12:1). All the sacrifices of the Old Covenant had one common denominator—they were all dead. The only exception was that the "scapegoat," on The Day of Atonement, symbolically bore the sins of Israel away from the presence of God. Of course, Jesus fulfilled this symbol as "the Lamb of God, who takes away the sin of the world" (John 1:29).

Many wonder whether they are devoted enough to *die* for Christ when the devotion the Lord asks of His followers is a heart-burning love to *live* for Him daily. Sometimes, the embers on the altar would burn long at night, and the priest, assuming their duties in the morning, would find it necessary to stir up the flame. I wonder if that might be the situation of your heart's altar today. Yes, the flame kindled there long ago by the Holy Spirit still burns, but does it need to be stirred and fanned for *this* day? The Holy Spirit is a never-ending source of fuel for our loving, living sacrifice. Flame on!

FEBRUARY 3
Leviticus 7-9

"THE FIRE FROM THE LORD"

In the previous reading from Leviticus, we noted that the fire upon the altar of the burnt offering was to be carefully tended by the priest day and night. The fire was never, under any circumstances, allowed to go out. The reason for this was that it was a sacred fire. Calling the fire on the altar *a sacred fire* is not just a symbolic literary expression; the fire originated with God. "And fire came out from before the Lord and consumed the burnt offering and the pieces of fat on the altar, and when all the people saw it, they shouted and fell on their faces" (Lev. 9:24). What an incredible, awe-inspiring moment that must have been!

We cannot begin to calculate how many offerings must have been sacrificed on the altar of burnt offering over the centuries, but the origin of the flames that consumed each one was God Himself. The fire from God is a visible manifestation of His judgment on sin. In relation to evil, our God is a consuming fire (Heb. 12:29). God is absolutely and completely holy, and sin is a terrible and repugnant affront to His holy nature. Sin is also a horrible, wrongful betrayal by God's image bearers against the perfect love and devotion of our Creator and Heavenly Father. Sin is so wicked in the sight of the perfect Holy One that His only verdict is all-consuming wrath. That is why the fire fell from God's presence on the sacrifice that bore upon it the sin of His people.

What I have just expressed may seem fearful and oppressive in its evaluation. It certainly is a fearful thing to consider the wrath of God against sin. However, the gospel message in the fire of God's wrath falling on the sacrifice is the truth that the fire of God's judgment did not fall on *the people*. The good news in this event, and the sacrificial system it inaugurated, is that the offering of a substitute for the place of the guilty was acceptable to God. Sin is a wrong against holy God. That injustice must be punished. Sin is a debt that must be paid. Without the acceptance of the sacrifice, there is no hope for sinners who have violated God's holy Law. The fire from the presence of God on the sacrifice was both awful and wonderful at the same time. It was an awful display of God's justice and a wonderful display of His grace.

What happened that day upon the altar of burnt offering inside the tabernacle could represent, in the faintest of ways, the reality of what would take place on the hill at Calvary and the altar of the cross. It was God's awful cup of judgment that overwhelmed Jesus as He prayed in the Garden of Gethsemane and drank fully on Golgotha. There, the complete wrath of God's justice fell on our substitute, Jesus Christ, as he suffered, "...the righteous for the unrighteous, that he might bring us to God" (I Pet. 3:18). When we try to wrap our minds around what God the Father and God the Son accomplished on the cross, all we can do is say, "Amen" to the exclamation of Martin Luther: "God forsaken by God, who can understand it?" Thank God we are not called to *understand it* but to just *believe it*. Meditate on these beautiful words from the song "Man of Sorrows, What A Name" by Philip P. Bliss:

> *Man of sorrow, what a name,*
> *for the Son of God who came.*
> *Ruined sinner to reclaim,*
> *Hallelujah! What a Savior!*
> *Guilty, vile and helpless we,*
> *Spotless Lamb was He*
> *Full atonement can it be?*
> *Hallelujah! What a Savior!*

FEBRUARY 4
Leviticus 10-12

"Different, Really Different"

"For I am the Lord who brought you up out of the land of Egypt to be your God. You shall therefore be holy, for I am holy."
(Leviticus 11:45)

Over the years of serving as a pastor, I have often had people recommend to me a book or series of messages by Christian authors that claim to have discovered codes that can unlock the hidden messages in the Bible. These works have spanned topics from the Bible, prophecy, astronomy, mathematical codes, sabbath day practices, investment strategies... Well, you get the idea. Someone has well said, "To not accept the plain sense of the Bible is just plain nonsense."

One area of discussion by many authors has to do with a *believer's diet*. According to their varied interpretations, the Bible instructs us to include in our diet the healthiest type of food, and various foods that believers should *exclude* from their diet for optimal health. Some of the Bible's passages about "clean" and "unclean" food sources, like the one in our reading today, are often cited as "proof texts" for the healthiest diet. It is wise to take care of the bodies our Lord has given us to serve Him. But to take the Bible's lists of "clean" and "unclean" foods as *the* way of doing that is to miss the entire point of why God instituted such detailed lists. The reason is not that these animals are inherently unhealthy or dangerous.

God is definitely concerned for the health of His people, but the health He most desires for us is *spiritual health*. This is the fundamental reason for the lists of acceptable and non-acceptable food, and it is plainly stated at the conclusion of the list. God says, "You shall therefore be holy, for I am holy" (Lev. 11:45). Remember, the key concept in the word "holy" is to be "separate" or "different." Because God is completely unique and has set Israel apart as His people, He wants us to remember our special relationship with Him. To constantly remind the people of Israel that they were to be "holy" to the Lord, God determined that the fundamental activity of life—eating—would be a sacred reminder of Jehovah and their relationship with Him. Every day and several times a day, the people of Israel would be reminded that God had graciously saved them and set them apart for Himself. They completely belonged to God, and every morsel they put in their mouths would remind them of this.

As we can imagine, this divinely directed diet plan would impact not only the Israelite's view of food but of life itself. When your food is different, then life is different. "Oh, taste and see that the Lord is good," said the Psalmist (Ps. 34:8). The diet plan of Israel reminded them throughout life that the Lord Himself was the sustainer and nourisher of their lives (Ps. 119:103). Of course, under the New Covenant, all of these dietary laws have been set aside because the fulfillment of all they foreshadowed has come in Christ (Col. 2:17). Now, by the indwelling presence of the Spirit of God, we are continually reminded that we are a holy people because of the grace of salvation from a holy God. We have been bought with a price, and we are no longer our own. "So, whether you eat or drink, or whatever you do, do all to the glory of God" (1 Cor. 10:31). Yes, we definitely need to think about what we *put into* our mouths, but we need to be infinitely more concerned about what *comes out* of our mouths, for out of the mouth, the heart speaks (Luke 6:45).

FEBRUARY 5
Leviticus 13-15

"Unclean"

If you have taken the time to read the appointed chapters for today, I am sure that you will agree they provide a major "cringe factor." Even though you know you are reading sacred Scripture, you may have inwardly muttered, "That's gross!" Don't feel guilty about how you feel; these passages *are gross*. It is hard to read three chapters almost entirely committed to detailed descriptions and provisions for skin diseases and bodily discharges. You may have found yourself asking, "Why in the world is this even in the Bible?!" The answer to that question can only be found in understanding the world in which the people of Israel lived. And, more importantly, gaining an understanding of the spiritual imagery regarding "uncleanness" and, more specifically, leprosy in the Bible.

Leprosy was the horror of the community in Bible times. We are not sure how leprosy described in the Scriptures compares to the variety of skin diseases in modern times. It is clear that leprosy was deadly, a terrible slow death, and that it was also very contagious. For that reason, inspecting in detail every form of infection or mold that even appeared to suggest the presence of leprosy was so vitally important. With the limited medical resources of that time, the first and considered safest response after detection was isolation. Leprosy was the cruelest disease—a slow deadening of nerves that resulted in deformity and destruction of body parts and then the loneliness of suffering apart from family, friends, and community. Lepers were forced to live in a community of "the walking dead," magnified by the cruel humiliation of identifying themselves with croaking voices crying, "Unclean, Unclean!" Truly a tragic existence.

Leprosy is the most powerful image of sin's effect on God's image-bearers. Before a holy God, sinful people are more abhorrent than the most grotesque forms of leprosy could be to the most sensitive-souled human beings. The diagnosis of leprosy was the most terrible form of "bad news." For this reason, it is the perfect expression of the "good news" of the gospel of God's grace! Jesus loved and cared for lepers—physically and spiritually. Some of Jesus' most compassionate actions was the healing of lepers by *touching them*. The people from whom all others fled are the very people to whom Jesus was drawn. The power of

His love and the healing virtue in His touch made the skin of the worst lepers like a child's. Jesus did not just improve the condition of lepers. He transformed the very DNA of their bodies. After Jesus' interaction, they were not "recovering lepers." They were completely healed and liberated lepers. Lepers became His disciples, His greatest witnesses, and the talk of the towns and villages to which they returned.

A question for us to consider today is whether we are *grateful* former lepers. It is easy to travel through life rejoicing in our healing, but we seldom fall on our knees in adoring worship of the One who healed us. Yes, leprosy is terrible, and so is the leprosy of sin. The age-old question, "Can a leper [leopard] change its spots?" has the emphatic answer, "No!" But, praise God, the lover and healer of lepers still touches and cleanses lepers today!

FEBRUARY 6
Leviticus 16-18

"YOM KIPPUR"

Of all the sacred festivals of the Jewish people, none is more solemn and full of national and personal importance than that of Yom Kippur, or as it is translated into English, the "Day of Atonement." This holiest of all days for the people of Israel generally occurs during our month of September and is the day on which one sacrifice is offered on behalf of the entire nation. Of course, sacrifices are no longer offered in the Jewish religion. However, Yom Kippur is still regarded as an annual day of reflection and repentance. Leviticus, Chapter 16, gives the foundational instructions from Jehovah concerning this observance, and it is filled with imagery that foreshadows the perfect sacrifice of Jesus Christ.

To understand this sacred observance, it is important to be clear on the meaning of the word "atonement." The current usage of the word is generally associated with "making things right" with another person or group based on the payment of a penalty. That understanding is the focus of the Lord's message in this passage. Atonement has in its primary meaning the idea of "cleansing," specifically the cleansing of guilt by sacrifice. In the New Testament, the word used to translate the concept of "atonement" literally means "an offering that makes for peace."

In Leviticus, Chapter 16, the Lord gave instructions regarding the designation of two (not one) goats that would express the atonement for the nation's sins. The High Priest would cast lots for two goats that had been presented to God. According to the results of the lots, one of the goats would be designated for the sacrifice, and some of the blood of this goat would be carried behind the curtain in front of the Ark of the Covenant and then sprinkled on the solid gold lid, the Mercy Seat. The blood of the sacrifice was sprinkled between the tablets of the Law (which Israel had not kept) and the holy presence of Jehovah. The High Priest would then approach the other goat and, placing his hands on the head of the animal, confess the sins of the people. The goat was then led into the wilderness by a man designated for this responsibility. This goat was designated as being for "Azazel" (Lev. 16:10, 26).

There has been much debate among scholars about the correct meaning of "Azazel." In 1530, William Tyndale created a new English word to describe this term, "scapegoat," which meant the "goat which bears away." The word has also been understood as a rocky cliff from which the animal was thrown or as a reference to a place in the wilderness where the goat was led. Regardless of which is most accurate in translation, it is clear that this animal represented the good news that the people's sins were carried away from the presence of the Lord.

As believers in the Lord Jesus, we can rejoice that every day is, in reality, "Yom Kippur" for us! Our Redeemer has made the perfect and complete atonement for our sins by His death on the cross. His sacrifice was perfect, once for all, and eternal. Jesus has carried our sins away from God into the wilderness of His "forgetfulness," and they will be remembered by Him no more (Ps. 103:12). Our Redeemer lives and provides for us, as His people, the everlasting Day of Yom Kippur!

> *My sin, oh the bliss of this glorious thought,*
> *My sin, not in part but the whole,*
> *Is nailed to the cross and I bear it no more,*
> *Praise the Lord, Praise the Lord, oh, my soul!*

("It is Well with My Soul," by Horatio G. Spafford)

FEBRUARY 7
Leviticus 19-21

"THE LAW OF LOVE"

If a survey asked who first made the statement, "You shall love your neighbor as yourself," undoubtedly, the most frequent answer would be Jesus. That would be wrong. Jesus is known for teaching His disciples to love their neighbor as they loved themselves; however, Jesus was not the *first* to make that statement. The quote is actually from Jesus' Father, Jehovah, and He issued that command over 1,400 years before the birth of His Son.

Many people would be shocked to know that the command to love their neighbor as themselves originated in the Law given by God to Moses. The conception of God's Law is commonly believed to be one of an "eye for an eye and a tooth for a tooth" rather than the law of love. Sometimes, that belief even extends to the point of trying to separate the God of the Old Testament from the God of the New Testament. The God of the Old and New Testament are one and the same, and Jesus forever linked them by the term "Father."

The God of the Old Testament is the God and Father of our Lord Jesus Christ (Eph. 1:3). Jesus made it clear that His mission was not to destroy the Law but rather to fill it full of the most profound meaning in His mission and His message (Matt. 5:17). Jesus began His ministry by tearing down the misapplication of the Law, and we must continually tear it down day-by-day through the power of His Spirit. Truly, it is only by His Spirit that we can keep the Law of love, but keep it we must if we intend to be Christ's disciples. To love our neighbor selflessly is to express the love of God and to fulfill His will for our lives (Matt. 22:39). Love does not wait until it "feels." Love "does," love "acts." Regardless of what others do to us, Jesus commands, "Do to others as you would have them do to you" (Luke 6:31 NIV). Love does not permit neutrality; love is the most proactive and positive force in the universe. Imagine if God had waited to love us until we loved Him! No, in reality, "We love because he first loved us" (1 John 4:19).

Jesus forever answered the question of what it means to love our neighbor in the story He shared that is often called "The Good Samaritan" (Luke 10:25-37). Our "neighbor" is not limited by ethnic, national, or religious boundaries. The command to love our neighbors is as wide as the world. The command to love others is as personal as taking a walk and seeing the person who is on your path. Loving our neighbors as ourselves is as sacrificial as our safety, as priceless as our time, and as deep as our pocketbooks. There is only one measurement for love—giving. Until we give of ourselves, we have not really loved at all. God loved us as sinners and *gave* His only Son. Jesus loved us and *gave* Himself for us.

It might be good to pause for a moment and examine whether we are actually exhibiting the symptoms of love. Who are you treating today with the kindness they *do not deserve*? For whom are you making personal sacrifices that has never sacrificed for you or perhaps has personally "used you?" Loving our neighbor also means loving our enemy. We must not allow ourselves to say, "I can't do it," because we can by the power of the One who has poured out His love into our lives (Rom. 5:5). His love is "poured into us." Now, we must "pour it upon others" in His Name.

FEBRUARY 8
Leviticus 22-24

"Feasts of Faith"

The calendar of the Jewish people was directly and completely connected to sacred observances that the Lord had established for them to follow. The weekly calendar was determined by the Sabbath. As the Lord had created all things in six days and then "rested" from His work on the seventh day, so also His people were to work six days and rest on the seventh. The Sabbath was a weekly reminder that they were God's people and truly blessed to belong to Him. As they rested and enjoyed a family day each week, they would also be reminded of the restful trust they could have in Jehovah and the blessing of His covenantal love in that divinely established rhythm of life. The Sabbath of the Old Testament is fulfilled for us in Christ, who is our place of rest (Heb. 4:9-10). Our lives are not to be characterized by relentless labor, but instead, we are to experience Jesus as the "easy yoke," the "light burden," and the sabbath "rest" for our souls (Matt. 11:28-30).

For us believers in Jesus, all the festivals of the Jewish nation are testimonies of our faith. We have already seen the beautiful aspects of Jesus expressed in the observance of Passover and the Day of Atonement. In Chapter 23 of Leviticus, we also see beautiful symbols of Christ and His work in the other feasts established by Jehovah to be observed by Israel.

The Feast of First Fruits

This festival was observed the day after the Sabbath following Passover. The observance included the priest taking a few sheaves of wheat just beginning to sprout from the winter planting and waving them before the Lord. This was a celebration of God's provision and an expression of trust in Him for the harvest. How wonderful to know that on the day after the Sabbath following the Passover, the Lord Jesus rose from the dead. He is "the firstfruits" of the promised harvest of the resurrection of His people (1 Cor. 15:23).

The Feast of Weeks

This celebration was to be held 50 days after the Sabbath following Passover. The number 50 eventually led to this festival being called "Pentecost." It was a time of celebrating the full harvest the Lord had provided since the "firstfruits" had appeared out of the ground. The Day of Pentecost, recorded in Acts 2, occurred seven weeks after our Lord's resurrection. How beautifully it testifies to the harvest of souls from around the globe and the praises of Jesus being declared in languages worldwide!

The Feasts of Trumpets

The sounding of the trumpet was used in Israel to call the people to God's presence for worship. Trumpets sounded from the top of Mount Sinai as God called His people to gather for the giving of the Law. The priests sounded trumpets to call the people to appointed worship hours in the Tabernacle and later in the temple. As Christians, we are to wait expectantly for the sound of the "trumpet of God" when the dead in Christ shall rise, and we who are alive shall be caught up to meet the Lord in the air (1 Thess. 4:17).

The Feast of Booths

The Feast of Booths is a week-long celebration following the Day of Atonement, involving the entire nation living under arbors made of the branches and leaves of trees. This joyous week of "national camping" reminded the people of Israel that their ancestors had lived in tents on their journey to the Promise Land. As believers in Jesus reading about this festival, we recall that this world is not our home. We are pilgrims headed for a city, the City of God, eternal in the heavens (2 Cor. 5:1). Jesus sweetly promised, "In my Father's house are many rooms... I go to prepare a place for you" (John 14:2). Yes, there in our Father's house, we pilgrims will finally be at home.

FEBRUARY 9
Leviticus 25-27

"THE MATHEMATICS OF FAITH"

"I will command my blessing on you in the sixth year, so that it will produce a crop sufficient for three years."
(Leviticus 25:21)

There is an expression used in American English to prove or validate something, and that phrase is "Do the math." It is an idiom that is quite clear in any language. If you want to interpret the plausibility of a plan, especially a financial plan, then it is vital to test it by objective analysis —"Do the math." The numbers of the equation remove the plan from the rosy realm of emotion and place it squarely in the bright clear light of mathematics. The statement, "Do the math," assumes that the correct data has been figured into the calculation. Unless the correct data has been inserted into the equation, even the clearest mathematical equation will have flawed results. To use another idiom, "Garbage in, garbage out." Pardon the pun, but at this point in making financial evaluations, many people "trash their lives." The people of Israel certainly did.

In our Scripture reading today, the Lord gave His people a very clear formula on how they were to manage *His* possessions (not "their" possessions). The mathematical formulas (commands) they were given were very clear. A specific command was that the people were to let the land rest every Sabbath year. The people of Israel "did the math," and "ran the numbers," but they *never* followed this formula as their agricultural guide. Why? The numbers didn't add up. They could not possibly survive by setting aside the harvest every seventh year. Why was their evaluation so flawed (and it certainly was), and why would it eventually cost them dearly? *The people did not include God in their equation.* The absence of God in the nation's numbers was due to their absence of faith. Yes, they were willing to trust God with their souls, but not their sowing. They believed that God could rescue them from slavery but not keep them from starvation. The people of Israel failed the test, but the land did get its Sabbath years, for, during the decades that the nation lived in exile, the soil certainly did rest.

Our evaluations will be totally flawed whenever we leave God out of our calculations. However, when we obey the Lord by faith, the impossible becomes the actual. The containers of flour and oil are never emptied (1 Kings 17:16). A little boy's light lunch is more than enough to feed a crowd numbering in the thousands (Matt. 14:13-21). Our faith-giving of the first fruits fills our barns to capacity and our winepresses to overflowing (Prov. 3:10). Our tithe of 10 percent given to God provides 100 percent of our needs (Mal. 3:10). I recall what the farmer told his son as they filled the grain bin, and he testified to God's faithful provision over the years. "Son, it's like this, I keep shoveling it out, and the Lord keeps shoveling it in. And the Lord's got a bigger shovel."

FEBRUARY 10
Numbers 1-3

"Numbered, Known, Appointed"

The Book of Numbers in our English Bibles is actually titled "Bemidhar" in Hebrew, meaning "in the wilderness." The title "Numbers" is a translation of the Septuagint (Greek) title referring to the numbering of the tribes of Israel in Chapters 1-4. It is quite a number—603,550 men over the age of 20 (Num. 1:46). This number does not include the Tribe of Levi, which was to be designated for serving in worship and not warfare. When we consider that only the adult men of 11 tribes were included in this census, it means the total number of people in Israel would have probably totaled at least 1.5 million. To give perspective to that number, it is approximately equal in size to the population of Philadelphia, Pennsylvania, or San Antonio, Texas. That is a phenomenal number of people to imagine on a journey through the wilderness of Sinai. However, we must be careful not to consider these people as a horde wandering aimlessly but as a chosen nation purposefully being led. They are *numbered*, they are *known*, and they are *appointed*. And so are we.

Only the Lord Himself knows the true number of His disciples on earth at this time. Conservative estimates inform us that over 1.5 billion people of the world's population profess to be Christians, a number 1,000 times larger than the people of Israel gathered at Sinai. When we add to that estimate the number of believers from former generations now in heaven, we can see that Jesus' promise, "I will build my church," is an ever-increasing reality. We are part of an *innumerable company* of believers, but each of us is *individually known*.

In the passage for our reading today, scores of names of the tribal leaders are recorded. God knew their names because He knew each of them. Likewise, we "are the Body of Christ and individually members of it" (1 Cor. 12:27). We are not nameless faces in the crowd of the Church; we are known, and we are loved.

Elizabeth Elliot, missionary, author, and noted speaker (now with the Lord), opened her radio broadcasts with the heart-warming reminder, "You are loved with an everlasting love; that's what the Bible says." Elizabeth was absolutely right, and we should never let our thoughts drift to the wrong. We are known, and we are loved. "But God's firm foundation stands, bearing this seal: 'The Lord knows those who are His'" (2 Tim. 2:19). Paul reminds us in this verse that being a Christian in its essence means "being known by God."

God's love is universal, but His redeeming love is always personal. It is never childish to say or sing, "Jesus Loves Me." It is the glorious, unfathomable truth of God's grace. We are *numbered*, we are *known*, so, therefore, we are also *appointed*. Just as the Lord had an appointed place for every tribe and family surrounding His presence in the Tabernacle, He also has an appointed place and plan for each of us in His family. "You did not choose me, but I chose you and appointed you that you should go and bear fruit..." (John 15:16). Jesus has appointed us to participate in His Kingdom work. He has purposed to save us, and He has saved us for the purpose of glorifying God by producing good works (Eph. 2:8-10). Our lives on this earth really matter—they matter for time and eternity. It is never pride to say of yourself what God says. So today, take a few moments to praise God and profess His truth about your life. "Thank you, Father, that because of Your grace in Jesus, I am one of the numbered. I am known, and I am appointed. Amen."

FEBRUARY 11
Numbers 4-6

"The Blessing"

"The Lord bless you and keep you; the Lord make his face to shine upon you and be gracious to you; the Lord lift up his countenance upon you and give you peace."
(Numbers 6:24-26)

"God bless you." These three words are spoken countless times every day, most often in response to someone sneezing. Sometimes they are used as a thoughtful way of ending a conversation just before walking or driving away. It becomes an expression for "Goodbye," which is close to the origin of that word, "God be with you." Regardless of how often or in how many different situations the phrase "God bless you" is used, there lies within it a sacred quality.

A blessing invokes the reality of Divine presence and provision. A blessing involves God Himself. "So shall they put my name upon the people of Israel, and I will bless them" is how the Lord gave instructions about blessing the people (Num. 6:27). Notice that God connects blessing with His name. This means much more than the Lord simply wanting Himself identified in a blessing. He means that He *is* the blessing. He is the origin and source of all that can be conceived as a blessing. A blessing is the loving favor of God upon a person's life that cannot be measured in any value system of this earth. Being blessed is not defined by finances, success, or health. The truly blessed life experiences the treasures that can only be experienced in the Lord Himself. Notice the gifts the Lord shared in the blessing He defined for Moses to express: "keep you," "shine upon you," "be gracious to you," and "give you peace" (vs. 24-26). The blessing is the *Blesser*. God is the blessing.

Read the words of this blessing slowly and prayerfully. I encourage you to read them aloud so you can hear your voice expressing the truth they contain. They are beautiful words, and they are so powerful. They change everything. The words of this blessing lift us from the temporary to the eternal. They realign everything around God. All that matters for us and all that matters for others is found in God alone. His loving favor is life itself now and forever. Ultimately the favor of God, His blessing, is experienced in Jesus our Savior. He is the blessing. Jesus is our safety. Jesus is the face of God shining upon us. Jesus is the light of God in our lives. Jesus is God's grace incarnate. Jesus is our shalom, our peace. God did not just say words of blessing. He came as the Word, who is the blessing. As believers in Christ, we are truly blessed! The blessing of the Lord has made us rich (Prov. 10:22). And the Lord has called us to be a blessing (1 Pet. 3:9). So, perhaps the best way for us to enjoy this special blessing of God upon Israel is to practice this blessing by sharing it with others.

"The Lord bless you and keep you [*through me today*]. The Lord make His face to shine upon you and be gracious to you [*by my presence today*]. The Lord lift up His countenance upon you and give you peace [*by my words today*]." What a prayer to live! What a blessing to give!

FEBRUARY 12
Numbers 7-9

"HE LEADETH ME"

One Sunday in 1865, a young pastor named Joseph Gilmore arrived early for the services at a church where he was to preach as the guest speaker for the day. Sitting in one of the pews, he noticed new-looking hymnals provided for the congregational singing. As Joseph randomly looked at some of the hymns included in the new books, he was startled to see that one of the new hymns was a poem he had written on a Sunday three years earlier. As the new pastor of the First Baptist Church in Philadelphia in the spring of 1862, when the news of the Civil War was so terribly discouraging, Gilmore felt directed by the Spirit to preach from the beloved 23rd Psalm. One day in his preparation for the message, the pastor was struck by the phrase in verse three of the psalm, "He leadeth me."

As Joseph meditated on that truth of God's faithful leading of His people, phrases came powerfully to his mind as a way to express that wonderful hope. Quickly, he picked up a pen and paper and wrote the words as they tumbled from his soul:

> *He leadeth me, O blessed thought!*
> *O words with heav'nly comfort fraught!*
> *What'er I do, where'er I be,*
> *Still 'tis God's hand that leadeth me.*

Later that day, Gilmore's wife discovered the poetry her husband had written, copied the words, and sent them to the well-known writer and publisher of Christian works, William B. Bradbury, in Maine.

Bradbury set the words by Pastor Gilmore to music and promptly published them in one of his periodicals. The hymn "He Leadeth Me" so moved some leaders in the Methodist church that they decided it must be part of their new Methodist hymnal. That is how the young Baptist pastor came to be so amazed to find the notes from one of his sermons included on a page in the Methodist hymnal. Certainly, these amazing events bear witness that even while Pastor Gilmore was writing his own personal thoughts about the phrase "He leadeth me," God was doing just that—leading him.

In our reading from God's Word today, it is clear that the people of Israel were not wandering; they were *being led*. The great cloud of Jehovah's presence hovered over the tabernacle night and day. It was their guide. When the cloud remained, they stayed at that location. When the cloud lifted and moved, they moved. God led them on their journey through the wilderness to the Promised Land.

God still leads His people. He is our Shepherd. He leads us collectively and personally. We may not have the cloud of glory over us, but we have guidance just as clear—God's Word before us, God's Spirit within us, God's people around us, and God's sovereignty upon us. How wonderful to rest and rejoice in the blessed truth that gripped the heart of young Pastor Gilmore so long ago—"the Lord is *my* Shepherd, He leads *me*."

The Lord leads us at all times and in all seasons of our life's journey. As the pastor wrote, sometimes God leads through "scenes of deepest gloom, sometimes where Eden's flowers bloom," but still, it is "God's hand that leadeth me." Regardless of how and where God leads us on our journey, we rest in peaceful confidence that He is leading us to our "Promised Land."

> *And when my task on earth is done,*
> *When by Thy grace the vict'ry's won,*
> *E'en death's cold wave I will not flee,*
> *Since God through Jordan leadeth me.*

Thank you, Pastor Gilmore. Thank you, Blessed Lord and Shepherd!

FEBRUARY 13
Numbers 10-12

"And the Lord Heard It"

I was named after my grandfather, Samuel Polson. I never had the joy of knowing him since he passed away 15 years before I was born.

Samuel is a name that has been in my family for a long time. My great-grandfather was also named Samuel. As a child, I did not like my name because I thought it was old-fashioned. After all, I did not know any other kids named Samuel. Also, some adults referred to me as "Sammy," which irritated me to no end. However, as I grew older and learned that the name "Samuel" was the name of one of the great judges of Israel and that two books of the Bible share the name, I began to feel better about it. It was not until I was in seminary that I learned the meaning of my name. "Samuel" is a Hebrew expression that means, "God has heard," or it also has the possible translation of "name of God." Both translations convey the idea that the Creator, the God of Israel, is not remote and distant, but is the God who is personal, involved, and listening to His people.

In our reading today, we are dramatically reminded of this God who is close and listens to His people. God "heard" the grumbling and complaining of His people as they complained about the lack of variety of food. They were tired of manna from heaven every day and began to long for the free food they enjoyed in Egypt (Num. 11:5). Yes, they longed for the "free food" of "slavery." Rather than remembering the unrelenting toil and bondage they experienced in Egypt, they focused on the "free meal plan." God heard this. He heard the murmuring of the multitudes. God also heard the "secret conspiracy" led by Moses's own sister and brother—Miriam and Aaron. These two used religious speech to cloak their insubordination against God's appointed leader and prophet for the nation. Even worse, their mutinous discussions were rooted in racism, as Moses had recently married a Cushite woman, a black woman (Num. 12:1-2). No doubt, these were very private discussions among the leading family of Israel; but no conversation is ever private because the always-present, all-knowing God, is listening.

Perhaps there is no more powerful truth that can guide us as believers in our discussions than recognizing that every conversation is being heard and recorded by the Lord. Jesus said, "I tell you, on the day of judgment people will give account for every careless word they speak…." (Matt. 12:36). "The Lord hears" is sobering truth indeed. However, there is also a personal and powerful example of responding to the truth that "the Lord hears," and Moses models it for us. We are told that Moses was "very meek, more than all people who were on the face of the earth" (Num. 12:3). When we hear the word "meek," we often translate it in our minds by the word "weak." Meekness is the farthest thing from weakness. It actually contains the idea of strength, the strength of self-control. To be a meek person is "others-focused" because it is a strength expressed in humility of spirit. It is the meek and humble whom "the Lord hears" (2 Chr. 34:27).

Aaron and Miriam had great reason to be thankful for a meek brother who believed in and prayed to a God who hears. His own family had terribly wronged Moses, but did he cry out to God for justice? No, knowing the heart of his Lord and knowing his Lord would hear, Moses interceded and pleaded for mercy on his enemies. "And the Lord heard it." Selah.

FEBRUARY 14
Numbers 13-15

"INTERCESSION"

Many years ago, I experienced a long season of physical struggle with a severe illness. For over seven months, my symptoms were so pronounced and challenging that, for all practical purposes, I was unable to perform my ministry responsibilities. In fact, at times, the symptoms were so severe that I could not function in any meaningful way outside of my own home. It was a challenging and, at times, very fearful season. However, as I look back on those many months, I also see amazing experiences of God's love and care, especially as it was expressed through the kindness and compassion of His people.

One of the most powerful moments occurred when I received a phone call from a dear ministry friend to tell me about a city-wide pastor's prayer gathering that had been held at our church. On the phone, my friend exclaimed, "Brother, if I have ever heard anyone prayed for in my life, it was you today!" He went on to tell me that during the prayer service, a local pastor stood up to pray and then began to pray for me. My friend described the powerful and heartfelt intercession the pastor prayed on my behalf. "Lord, I am standing in the gap today for my brother, Sam Polson. I am standing up to pray to You today for Sam Polson. Lord, before You in prayer today, *I am* Sam Polson." As my friend described my fellow pastor's prayer and the prayers offered to me by so many others that afternoon, tears of gratitude streamed down my face. That was over 20 years ago, and I sincerely believe it is because of intercessory prayer like that, offered by hundreds and hundreds of God's people, that I am writing this page today. I know personally and deeply the power of intercessory prayer.

The word "intercession" comes from two Latin words that could be translated as "to go between." So, intercessory prayer fundamentally means "going between another person and God." It means taking up the personal circumstances or needs of another and bringing them as our cause in petition to the Lord. Apart from the intercessory prayers of Christ in the Garden of Gethsemane and from the cross, there is no greater example of intercessory prayer than that of Moses in our reading today. Consider *who* Moses was interceding for in prayer to God. Not people who had been nice to Moses and needed a "little blessing." Moses is praying for people who have rejected him and ridiculed his leadership. Far worse, these people have declared God to be false and have betrayed the One who has provided for their every need, delivered them from slavery, and brought them to the Promised Land. Moses is interceding for *those* kinds of people. Also, notice *how* Moses intercedes for the people of Israel. He reminds God of His character and His testimony. In his prayer, Moses quotes the Lord's own words to the Lord. His intercessory prayer is focused on the glory of God and not on the worthiness of the people for whom he is praying (Num. 14:16-19). Moses, the intercessor, "goes between" a desperately needy and undeserving people and a holy God, and the Lord heard Moses' plea.

I am writing this page today, and you are reading it because people interceded for me and people interceded for you. The reason we can even approach God at all is because Jesus intercedes for us (Heb. 7:25). We are never more like the Master than when we "go between" God and others. Right now, in prayer, fill in the blank, "Lord, I am standing up today for _____."

FEBRUARY 15
Numbers 16-18

"PRICELESS"

Each year, thousands and thousands of films are made in the United States. The general public will never view the vast majority of these, which is probably a very good thing for most of them! A limited number of the other films will gather some level of attention or popularity among viewers. A very tiny fraction of these films will be considered worthy of being called classics. And then, there exists just a handful of films that have been so loved over decades and even generations that they have become part of the American culture.

One of these timeless films is the Christmas classic, *It's a Wonderful Life*. This film, directed by Frank Capra and starring Jimmy Stewart, has brought families together around television sets for nearly 70 years. Sure, it is nostalgic and over-the-top in its portrayal of basic human goodness. But who has not felt a lump in the throat when war hero Harry Bailey arrives on Christmas Eve, just as friends of his brother, George, have gathered to give their financial gifts for his crisis, and makes the toast, "To my big brother, George Bailey, the richest man I know"? It makes perfect sense in a value system that is not measured in dollar signs.

I will never forget the simple formula for calculating your net worth shared by pastor and teacher Adrian Rogers. "The sum of your net worth is this," he said. "Whatever you possess that money cannot buy and death cannot take away." Brilliant and so very true.

In our reading today, we are informed that the Lord very clearly stated the tribe of Levi would have no allotment in the Promised Land. They would not receive a single acre of property when the land of Canaan was apportioned to the tribes of Israel. And yet, one single statement by Jehovah made the Levites infinitely richer than their brothers in the other tribes, "I am your portion and your inheritance among the people of Israel" (Num. 18:20). To this tribe which served Him in the Tabernacle, the Lord gave Himself as their inheritance. This gift is breathtaking when seriously considered. It is an inheritance that is literally "out of this world," or perhaps better said, it is an inheritance that is "not of this world." It is an inheritance that is not in the future; it is a present reality. The Lord said, "I *am* your portion and your inheritance."

As believers in Jesus Christ, we are not adopted into the tribe of Levi, but we do share in the inheritance. We are "heirs of God and fellow heirs with Christ." We have received the down payment of this incredible inheritance through the gift of the Spirit, which causes us to cry, "Abba! Father!" (Rom. 8:15-17) The truth of our inheritance in the Lord is beyond all calculation because to measure it would be to measure the infinite God Himself. A friend and dear brother in Christ walked over to me during our congregational worship one Sunday morning and said, "Sam, imagine it, all this and heaven too!" Wow. What is the value of our inheritance? We can't measure it and can't begin to understand it, but every believer in Jesus can experience it. We do that by faith. Read, by faith, your financial statement today—"I am your portion and your inheritance." Breathtaking.

FEBRUARY 16
Numbers 19-21

"The Gospel in the Wilderness"

Imagine this scene with me. While hiking a trail, a close relative of yours is bitten by an extremely venomous snake. Thankfully, a friend accompanying your relative on the hike is able to use his cell phone and make a 911 call. Within a matter of minutes, paramedics arrive and carry your relative down from the trail to a waiting life flight helicopter that transports him to the nearest medical center. Wonderfully, doctors can quickly administer antivenom, and your relative's life is saved. Still, he is a very sick person and must stay a few days in the hospital for further treatment and observation. You decide to sit with him for a few hours in the hospital room, and while you are there, your relative's pastor comes to visit. He has thoughtfully brought a wrapped gift, which he presents to your relative, saying, "I thought this might encourage you and lift your spirits." When your relative opens the package, you are incredulous and infuriated to see that the pastor has brought a brass piece of art to hang in front of the hospital bed. It is a replica of the snake that nearly took his life! Let me quickly say that I am *not* the pastor in this story! The thought would never cross my mind, not to mention that I *really* hate snakes!

However, the thought did cross the Lord's mind. In fact, we are told that it was a brass snake lifted up on a pole in the camp of Israel that was the antivenom for the deadly judgment of poisonous vipers on the nation (Num. 21:4-9). The question that begs to be answered is why the Lord would choose such an incredibly strange way to heal the people of Israel from the judgment upon a snake as healing for snake bites. That question would undoubtedly be on the minds of the generations of Israelites until the Lord Jesus answered the question and then became the answer Himself over 1,500 years later. Jesus answered the question one night in response to the question of the religious leader, Nicodemus, "How can a man be born again when he is old?" (John 3:4) Jesus answered that question of the ages by citing the event recorded in today's reading regarding the brass serpent. "And as Moses lifted up the serpent in the wilderness, so must the Son of Man be lifted up, that whoever believes in him may have eternal life" (John 3:14-15). Jesus told Nicodemus that He, the Messiah, would be the ultimate fulfillment of healing from the poison of sin and the certain, eternal death it produces. He would be "lifted up" (a reference to His crucifixion), and all who believe in Him will be saved.

The imagery of the Gospel is so perfect, so profound, and so simple. Jesus, on the cross, became the poison that flows through the veins of every human being. He became the curse of sin. "Christ redeemed us from the curse of the law by becoming a curse for us—for it is written, 'Cursed is everyone who is hanged on a tree'" (Gal. 3:13). The word of promise in that quote from Paul is "redeemed." It means we are set free from the terrible, death-producing, judgment-bringing penalty for our poisonous rebellion against God. And it is a freedom that is free to us because Jesus purchased it. Eternal life is freely given to all, the dying sons and daughters of Adam, if by faith they will "Look to Jesus." Look and live!

FEBRUARY 17
Numbers 22-24

"Blessed of the Lord"

On May 24, 1844, most of the members of the United States Congress assembled beneath the dome of the Capitol in Washington, DC, to observe the testing of a strange apparatus that was alternately considered one of the most important inventions of the ages, or one of the biggest hoaxes ever devised by a deceptive trickster. Samuel F.B. Morse sent over his invention and, using a cable stretched all the way to Baltimore, Maryland, tapped out a language code that was electronically sent to his assistant, Alfred Vail, at the railway station nearly 40 miles away. What should be the message transmitted in this revolutionary manner and historical moment? The daughter of the Commissioner of patents in Washington, Annie Ellsworth, had a recommendation for Morse, "What hath God wrought?" Morse liked Annie's suggestion, and Morse's inaugural message for the telegraph was clicked out and immediately received by Vail in Baltimore. It was truly a historic moment, and so was the message—historic indeed. It was a message that was uttered over 3,300 years earlier. It is an eternal message because God has included it in the Bible. "What has God wrought!" was the exclamation by the mysterious prophet, Balaam, as he pronounced by the Spirit the blessing of God on His people Israel (Num. 23:23).

This amazing exclamation by Balaam, later transmitted by Samuel Morse, is part of one of the Old Testament's most unique and powerful stories. Four chapters of the Book of Numbers are given to share it. And the story has scenes that are downright comical. Balaam was a prophet who experienced and expressed revelations from Jehovah. Because of this, King Balak of the Moabites, in one of the most unwise decisions any king ever made, attempted to bribe and hire the prophet to pronounce a curse on the people of Israel. While riding on his donkey to a viewpoint from which to pronounce the Divine message, Balaam fails to recognize the Lord standing in his path, but the donkey does! The Lord speaks to Balaam through the donkey's voice (this would not be the only time in the centuries to come that the Lord would speak through a similar spokesperson), revealing the terrible danger of opposing the Lord. The story becomes even more comical when King Balak's "prophet for profit" not only does not curse Israel but actually pronounces a blessing. And he does this three times! Despite the truly humorous events in the saga, they contain some of the most beautiful and powerful expressions of God's sovereignty over all things and His devoted, changeless love for His people. God has promised to bless His people and blessed they are and will be. "God is not man, that he should lie, or a son of man, that he should change his mind. Has he said, and will he not do it? Or has he spoken, and will he not fulfill it?" (Num. 23:19)

These are the words of a questionable prophet, but they are a prophecy of unquestionable truth. It is impossible for God to be unfaithful. No one in heaven, earth, or hell can curse those God has blessed. So, regardless of your circumstances today, Christian, you can say and know it is true—"I am blessed!"

FEBRUARY 18
Numbers 25-27

"FORTY YEARS OF FUNERALS"

Over the years of ministry as a pastor, I have conducted or participated in hundreds of funerals. Several of these services have included a procession of vehicles from the church or funeral home to one of the local cemeteries. Sometimes the processions have involved just a few vehicles, while others have included numerous cars and trucks and have required law enforcement officers to provide for traffic safety. Most funeral processions involved a brief trip, while others required traveling many miles and took a significant amount of time. However, not one of those funeral processions or any other funeral procession in the history of the world can compare in the slightest degree to the one recorded in the Book of Numbers!

The 40-year journey of the people of Israel through the wilderness was one continual funeral procession. It might be more accurate to refer to the nation's journey as a 40-year *procession of funerals*. In response to the rebellion and unbelief of His people, Jehovah decreed that all the males 20 years and older would die in the wilderness over a period of 40 years before Israel would enter the Promised Land. Think of that— over 600,000 funerals. If this judgment by God also extended to the women, that would mean a staggering 1,200,000 funerals or an average of 82 funerals each day for 40 years! Truly, the death march of the ages. We are told in Numbers 1:46 that the census of the men of Israel over the age of 20 when they left Mt. Sinai was 603,550. That means 603,548 men died and were buried during that 40-year-long procession of funerals. Only two men over 20 entered the Land of Canaan—Joshua and Caleb. Two out of 603,550.

It is important to remember why these two men were blessed by God to enter the land and consider what that means for us. The reason these men experienced the great promise of Jehovah is both simple and profound—faith. These men trusted God. These two were not necessarily more courageous than the others, but they did have more faith, and faith trumps fear every time. Remember, Joshua and Caleb were two of the 12 spies sent by Moses to investigate the Land of Canaan before Israel entered. The 12 men returned with their report, and Joshua and Caleb definitely delivered the minority opinion. All 12 agreed that the land was indeed "flowing with milk and honey;" it was the most desirable land imaginable. However, the majority report of the 10 men said the situation was hopeless. Why was that? They possessed a vision problem; their vision was faithless. They measured the men of the land in comparison to themselves and saw them as giants. Joshua and Caleb had a faith-filled vision, so they measured these "giants" to their awesome God. Their decision? No contest!

Faith measures all of life by the standard of God. What is little to men is big with God, and what is big to men is little with God. Faith is not living in denial, ignoring problems, obstacles, and challenges. However, faith sees these things and measures them to God. Faith is ultimately determined by where you look. Faith is not found in looking within or looking around but in looking above. "Looking to Jesus, the founder and perfecter of our faith..." (Heb. 12:2)

FEBRUARY 19
Numbers 28-30

"The Sacredness of Words"

"If a man vows a vow to the Lord, or swears an oath to bind himself by a pledge, he shall not break his word. He shall do... all that proceeds out of his mouth."
(Numbers 30:2)

When I was growing up, there was an annual pilgrimage I was required to make by my mom, which annoyed me greatly. Every summer, late in August, when I was trying to enjoy each day to the fullest before school resumed in early September, I had to accompany her to Main Street in our small town to spend time shopping for school clothes for the new year. It was a frustrating and humiliating experience because my mom would make me try on jeans that were so long that they had to be rolled up with cuffs about four inches wide. Her response to my protests was always the same, "They will shrink, and you will grow into them." Yeah, right. That was very small comfort to an elementary-age boy who had to walk into school wearing stiff, new, blue jeans with cuffs reaching halfway up his shins!

I still remember the incredible relief I experienced the year my mom let me shop with my dad for my new school clothes. "Finally," I thought, "I get to shop with someone who understands what it means to be a man!" As it turned out, I learned a lifelong lesson that day about what it means to be a real man. My dad and I shopped in a local men's store, and I was pretty satisfied with our selection—not a single pair of the "giant jeans." We walked to the store's checkout counter, and my dad said to the young clerk, "I would like to purchase these on a credit account, please." The young man looked suspiciously at my dad and said, "Sir, we usually require a cash purchase." Dad said, "I've done this before. It will be all right."

The young clerk responded as he picked up the phone, "Well, I will have to clear this with the owner." My dad said, "That will be fine." I was beginning to feel a little nervous and slightly embarrassed as the young man spoke over the phone to the owner, "Sir, sorry to bother you, but there is a Mr. Luther Polson here at the counter who wants to place a rather large order on store credit." I will never forget the response from the owner. I heard him quite loudly through the receiver, "Luther Polson? Sell him the whole store!" At that moment, my dad looked different to me. *I saw him differently.* I had always loved my dad, but now I also loved and deeply admired him. I knew he had proven himself to be a man of his word. What he said he would do, he did.

Unfortunately, that is a rare quality in people today, but it should be the norm for every follower of the Lord. Jehovah made it clear to the people of Israel that their vows and oaths were to be understood and upheld as sacred. Yes, they were the physical descendants of Jacob, but all forms of trickery and manipulation that were part of Jacob's character as a young man were never to characterize their interpersonal relationships. Jesus, who "filled the Law full of meaning," raised the standard of trustworthiness to an even higher standard. Our Lord utterly rejected the hypocritical and deceptive oath-taking tactics taught by the scribes of His day and declared that, for His followers, every promise they made was sacred before God and required no oath to truly make it binding. "Let your 'yes' be yes and your 'no' be no..." is His command (Jas. 5:12b). Jesus said of His Father, "Your Word is truth" (John 17:17). Our words should possess the same sacred quality—truth.

FEBRUARY 20
Numbers 31-33

"The Battle is the Lord's... and Our's"

"Every armed man of you will pass over before the Lord, until he has driven out his enemies from before him."
(Numbers 32:21)

"But if you do not drive out the inhabitants of the land from before you, then those of them whom you let remain shall be as barbs in your eyes and thorns in your sides, and they shall trouble you in the land where you dwell."
(Numbers 33:55)

I have often seen on bumper stickers for cars and also printed on various forms of items in Christian bookstores the simple phrase, "Let go and let God." It is a beautiful turn of a phrase and also a challenging reminder to stop struggling and simply rest in the Lord. The question that needs to be considered is whether the expression "let go and let God" is accurate or, more importantly, Biblical. The definite answer to that question is, "Sometimes." The phrase "let go and let God" must be evaluated in the context to which it is applied.

To say, "Let go and let God," in reference to experiencing the salvation of our souls, is correct. Salvation is a free gift, purchased totally by Jesus and received completely by faith alone, apart from any work on our part. To try, in any way, to convert ourselves is to remain unconverted. We absolutely must "let go and let God," trusting the finished work of His Son to be accepted for our salvation. We must also remember that an aspect of our salvation is being accomplished daily in our lives *after* our regeneration, and that is our sanctification. It would be wrong to approach our sanctification with a "let go and let God" attitude. As has been well said, "We have not been saved by faith *plus* works, but we have been saved by a faith *that* works."

This is exactly the partnership in salvation that Paul admonished the believers at Philippi to pursue. "Work out your own salvation with fear and trembling, for it is God who works in you, both to will and to work for his good pleasure" (Phil. 2:12-13). We are never to be passive or neutral when it comes to the practice of our salvation. We are not permitted to sit idly and wait for God to do everything. This is not faith —that is, a failure to obey, which is, in its inactivity, active disobedience.

Our guiding principles for life are to be the same that were to guide the people of Israel, "The Lord has given us this land, He will drive out our enemies, now we must go into the land and drive them out." God had *given* them the land, he was *giving* them the land, and now they must *give themselves* to driving out their enemies, the Canaanites. The Israelites were to, as Paul would tell the Jewish and Gentile believers in Philippi 1500 years later, "Work out your salvation." The "Promised Land" is not a symbol of the believer's home in heaven. It is a type of the "abundant life" promised by our Savior here on earth. This is the promise to His disciples who follow Him obediently, an experience of the eternal life here on earth that will ultimately be fully experienced in heaven. It is the promise of a "present tense" salvation whereby through faith and obedience, we experience the living reality of the "fellowship with the Father and the Son" and the "victory that overcomes the world" (1 John 1:3, 5:4). We are not to be *passive*. We are to be *propelled* to action by the greatest of all incentives—Love.

> "For the love of Christ controls us, because we have concluded this: that one has died for all, therefore all have died; and he died for all, that those who live might no longer live for themselves, but for him who for their sake died and was raised."
> (2 Corinthians 5:14-15)

FEBRUARY 21
Numbers 34-36

"The Place of Refuge"

As we have seen in our Scripture readings so far, the Law of God governed practically every area of life for the people of Israel. All matters related to diet, calendar, holy days and festivals, the treatment of animals, clothing, and the practice of medicine were guided by the precepts of God. In reality, the government of the nation and the governing of individual lives was tied directly to Jehovah—it was a theocracy. This "nation under God" principle also extended throughout the legal system. The judges of the nations, the Elders, were not to *make* the Law; they were to *interpret* and *apply* the Law that God, the Law-Giver, had pronounced. As these elder judges interpreted and applied the Law, they were commanded to keep in mind a very important legal principle often referred to as the Lex Talionis, or as it is translated from Latin into English, "The law of retribution." This is most commonly referred to as the principle of "an eye for an eye and a tooth for a tooth." Over generations of use, this expression has become a figure of speech that denotes a harsh and vindictive spirit or response to any personal wrongs, perceived or actual. However, God's purpose in establishing the Lex Talionis as a guiding legal principle for His people had a very different purpose. It was specifically intended to limit the punishment of the crime to the nature and level of the crime.

For example, a man was not executed for stealing a loaf of bread, as was prescribed for centuries in Europe. Nor was a thief sent to prison for years with murderers and rapists but was required, instead, to make restitution and payment of financial penalty to the person from whom he had stolen. Today, in the American justice system, the concept of restitution and financial penalty for non-violent crimes has been replaced with incarceration in prison, which has turned prisons into "crime colleges" for producing more corrupt and trained criminals to be then turned back into society. That is not a system of justice for the victims, safety for the public, or responsibility with restitution and the potential of reformation for the convicted person. God's justice system also provided for cities of refuge, where people accused of causing a person's death could flee for protection from retaliation until the Elders heard their case. Here, a person accused but found not guilty of premeditated murder could live protected from the danger of unjust vengeance by friends or relatives of the deceased person. The cities of refuge were, in a sense, "federal court cities" where justice and mercy were both provided.

As believers in Jesus, we can rejoice today that in the deepest and most spiritual sense, the Lord is our "place of refuge." In Christ, justice and mercy have met together on the cross. Justice has been served because Jesus, our perfect representative, accepted and made full payment for our crimes against a holy God. Mercy is now free to us through the love and grace of our advocate-attorney-substitute, Jesus Christ. Jesus is also our place of safety from the "enemy of our souls"— the Devil. His hatred and schemes are terrible and powerful, but they cannot harm us. Martin Luther wrote in his great hymn, "A mighty fortress is our God, a bulwark never failing." We are safe now and safe forever in the fortress of our God.

> *"The name of the Lord is a strong tower;*
> *The righteous man runs into it and is safe."*
> (Proverbs 18:10)

FEBRUARY 22
Deuteronomy 1-3

"No Fear"

"No Fear." That challenge is often heard in various advertising today, from the armed services to gym memberships. In fact, "No Fear" has been a brand of "lifestyle wear" and "sports equipment" since 1989. You can purchase very attractive "No Fear" outfits for your preschoolers. Just imagine the intimidation factor that clothing will provide for your children or grandchildren as they "go forth to battle" every day! Seriously? The phrase "No Fear" seems to be used today as just an expression of arrogant hubris or, as is more probable, a self-help method of compensating for an internal battle with fear. Now, there is no discounting the very real and powerful truth. However, it is wrong to lump all fear into one category and then avoid it at all costs. All fear is not harmful. Some fear is *helpful*. There is good and healthy fear and wrong and harmful fear. Dutiful parents teach their small children to fear some things—electrical sockets, hot stoves, strangers, etc. Those same good parents teach their children not to fear learning to walk, running in the yard, or leaping off the stairs into their waiting arms.

Likewise, our perfect Heavenly Father guides us into understanding "good fear" and "bad fear." The highest form of fear is the fear of the Lord. "The fear of the Lord is the beginning of wisdom" (Pro. 9:10). I have often defined godly fear as "love-inspired awe." Jehovah meant this when He taught the people of Israel that He should be their fear (Lev. 25:17). The fear of the Lord is the virtue that overcomes all the evils and traps of the wrong and harmful types of fears. The great Scottish reformer, John Knox, said he "feared man so little because he feared God so much." The fear of our God sets us free to the abundant life, but the fear of man only ensnares and entraps us (Prov. 29:25). The fear of the Lord is the basis of faith. The fear of the Lord causes us to *remember* that God is a covenant-keeping God despite how long the delays or how great the obstacles may appear:

> "See, I have set the land before you. Go in and take possession of the land that the Lord swore to your fathers, to Abraham, to Isaac, and to Jacob, to give to them and to their offspring after them."
> (Deuteronomy 1:8)

The fear of the Lord also causes us to *forget* the threats and the empty boastings of those who threaten us in our obedience to the Lord:

"Do not be in dread or afraid of them."
(Deuteronomy 1:29)

"You shall not fear them, for it is the Lord your God who fights for you."
(Deuteronomy 3:22)

When it comes to the issue of fear, our response as believers should be "Know Fear, No Fear." We glory in the fact that we "Know Fear," the fear of the Lord that produces faith in our hearts because our focus is on our Heavenly Father and not on ourselves or our earthly enemies. The fear of God sets us free from fear. Because of that, we as Christians can live in the spirit and the humble boldness of "No Fear," even if we don't own any articles of the "lifestyle wear." The brand is imprinted on our hearts by the greatness and grace of our God.

FEBRUARY 23
Deuteronomy 4-6

"Declaration, Devotion, Dedication"

Usually, the first passage of Scripture committed to memory by every Jewish boy and girl is designated in our Bibles as Deuteronomy 6:4. In the oral tradition of the people of Israel, it is referred to as the "Shema," which is the word for "hear."

"Hear, O Israel: The Lord our God, the Lord is one."

This *declaration* was the cornerstone of all the revelation of God and the substance of their faith. It is a declaration that amid polytheism and the worship of innumerable gods by all the nations and people groups surrounding them, the people of Israel worship one God. This God is one in essence and one in existence. He eternally exists as the one and only God; beside Him, there is no God. He cannot be added to the pantheon of gods because the pantheon only exists in the mind of man. The reality is a "monotheism" of one supreme, unrivaled, eternal God.
The Shema teaches that God is one also in essence. "The Lord is one." God is indivisible in His nature. Theologians refer to this truth as the unity of God. The teaching of the Trinity of God in the New Testament does not contradict the declaration of the Shema about the unity of God. As believers, we declare that there is one God eternally existing in three persons—Father, Son, and Holy Spirit—yet sharing one eternal

substance. The Trinity is three in *One*. The Shema is a declaration that is a preamble to a *devotion*:

> "You shall love the Lord your God with all your heart and with all your soul and with all your might."
> (Deuteronomy 6:5)

This expresses the wonderful reality of a personal love relationship with God. Yes, God is holy, completely "other" than any thing or any person in all His creation. Yet, the God of Israel has shared His "image and likeness" with human beings, and so the purpose of mankind is, as the shorter catechism teaches, "to know God and enjoy Him forever." God is love (1 John 4:8). By God's grace through faith, our hearts have the ability to respond to God, to know Him, which is to love Him. To be known by God and to know God, and to be loved by God and to love Him back, is life itself.

> "And this is eternal life, that they know you the only true God, and Jesus Christ whom you have sent."
> (John 17:3)

The Shema also serves as the preamble to what is the constitution for the Jewish—the Law given by God to Moses. The Law is not just Ten Commandments etched in two tablets of stone, nor is it just a summary of many words on many pages. The Law is life itself. It is not just to be carried in a golden box, written on scrolls, or carried in tiny leather boxes on the arm or forehead. The Law is to be written on the fleshly tablets of the heart. It is to be inscribed into the mind. The Word of God is to be constant communication—when lying down, rising up, walking around, or sitting at a table. The Word of God lives because it is God's Word. Therefore, God's Word should live in us. Shema, O Christian!

FEBRUARY 24
Deuteronomy 7-10

"Affluent Amnesia"

> "Beware lest you say in your heart, 'My power and the might of my hand have gotten me this wealth.' You shall remember the Lord your God, for it is he who gives you power to get wealth, that he may confirm his covenant that he swore to your fathers, as it is this day."
> (Deuteronomy 8:17-18)

I recall reading the story several years ago of a very devoted Christian man who, while on a business trip out of state, suffered an accident that left him with complete amnesia about anything that preceded that event. Added to a number of strange "coincidences" associated with this man's experiences was the tragedy that all forms of his identification were separated from him and lost. Since this was before the day of cell phones and other personal media devices, no technological way existed to identify him. And because he had no police record, there existed no way of identifying him through fingerprints or photos in police records. It was as if, before his accident, he did not exist at all. However, he did exist in the heart of his family, and he very much existed in the heart of his God, and both were working to bring him home.

To shorten a lengthy story, as the man walked a city street one day, he heard the sound of Christian music coming from a service in a local rescue mission. Somehow, the man was drawn by a sense that the music and the message were part of his story. Soon, the kind and concerned leaders of the mission went "on mission" to share the story of this brother's situation with other ministries and churches around the country. Eventually, in answer to the prayers of so many, the Lord amazingly restored the man to his family.

I have never forgotten that story, and I share it with you now about the importance of never forgetting. Amnesia is terrible; scriptural amnesia is disastrous. Moses so strongly warns the people of Israel about this kind of amnesia in his passionate message recorded in our passage today. His constant theme to the Lord *could* have destroyed and *should* have destroyed them. They deserved it. But God is not only a God of justice. He is also a God of grace, showing undeserved and unmerited kindness and favor. The Lord was bringing them to this bountiful and beautiful land, not for them, but for His Name's sake and the covenant He made with their fathers. They must never forget that. And we must never forget it as well. This is one of the greatest dangers of living in affluence. All of our needs are met and more. It is the danger of "affluent amnesia," forgetting who we are by forgetting *whose* we are and forgetting all He has done for us. When we feel like we are not getting what we deserve in life, we should thank God for it! Getting what we deserve is the worst thing we could ever get. Don't forget that!

FEBRUARY 25
Deuteronomy 11-13

"THE WORD TEST"

Not long ago, one of the college students at our church approached me after the morning service with a question, "What is the difference between a test from God and a temptation?" Great question. Admittedly, the difference between a test and a temptation in what it "feels like" to us, is not easy to discern. One of the reasons for this difficulty has to do with identifying the origin and the motive. It is important for us to know that a "test" can be sent to us by God, but as I explained to the college student, God is never the author of temptation. "Let no one say when he is tempted, 'I am being tempted by God,' for God cannot be tempted with evil, and He himself tempts no one" (Jas. 1:13). This helps us to identify temptation as opposed to a test. Temptation can always be recognized by its motivation.

Temptation is always motivated by evil intent—a goal to draw us away from God, who is the source of all that is good. Temptations to do evil always come from an evil source—the world, the flesh, the Devil, or a combination of these three (1 John 2:16). Now, even though we can intellectually understand that the difference between testing and temptation has to do with the source and motivation, how do we discern and address temptation? The answer is in the word "test."

We test all things by the one and only infallible standard of measurement—the Word of God. If something or someone is genuinely of God, that situation, recommendation, or guidance will *always* align with the Word of God. This is why the early Church Fathers referred to the Scriptures as the "canon." The root meaning of the word "canon" is "a reed or a rod for measuring." The meaning, then, behind the "canon of Scripture" is that we are to lay all things next to God's Word for measurement. We are to ask, "Does this measure up or line up with the Bible?" This question helps us discern between temptation and testing and also truth from error. It is a question that should especially be asked when a person is sharing what they purport to be a message from God.

> *"If a prophet or a dreamer of dreams arises among you and gives you a sign or a wonder, and the sign or wonder that he tells you comes to pass, and if he says, 'Let us go after other gods,' which you have not known, 'and let us serve them,' you shall not listen to the words of that prophet or that dreamer of dreams..."*
> (Deuteronomy 13:1-3)

What Jehovah shared through Moses with the people of Israel is crucial for us to hear today. The test for evaluating any messenger is not their miracles but the message being shared. Is it a message that aligns with God's Word, and does it base its authority on the Word of God? If the messenger does not pass the Word test, then do not accept the message regardless of what "signs and wonders" may accompany the person's ministry. God's challenge has never changed. Test the spirits as to whether they are from God (1 John 4:1-3). Test them by the truth and the source of truth. Jesus said, "Your Word is truth" (John 17:17). When it comes to discerning truth, we must always "look with our ears." Don't focus on the manifestations of the miracles. Focus on the message and then measure it by the Word of God.

FEBRUARY 26
Deuteronomy 14-16

"Blind Justice"

"You shall not pervert justice. You shall not show partiality, and you shall not accept a bribe, for a bribe blinds the eyes of the wise and subverts the cause of the righteous. Justice, and only justice, you shall follow, that you may live and inherit the land that the Lord your God is giving you."
(Deuteronomy 16:19-20)

All around the United States, in thousands upon thousands of locations, you can see a sculptured figure immediately recognizable, "Blind Justice." This sculpture is almost always of a robed female holding a balance in her hand and wearing a blindfold around her head. The image is rooted in the concept etched into the constitution of our nation and the laws and ordinances of our states and communities—equal justice before the law. This justice is to be upheld and applied without any influence from the individual's station, background, or race, as represented by the blindfold over the eyes of justice. "With liberty and justice for all" is the final line of the nation's *Pledge of Allegiance*. Those are such moving and noble words that express the highest of aspirations.

Sadly, the reality of the "justice" system in America is all too often "justice for some." The reasons for decisions that are "blind to justice" are as varied as those sitting on the juries or the judges themselves. However, the ultimate cause of injustice is in the blindness of the human heart darkened by sin. Injustice is ultimately insubordination to the Just One—God Himself. As David sang, "Righteousness and justice are the foundation of your throne" (Ps. 89:14).

Therefore, justice is to be an essential expression of the Kingdom of God. That Kingdom does not reside, at times, in the halls of justice of our land, but the Kingdom of God does live within our hearts as believers. Therefore, His justice should dwell there as well. However, justice is not just a quality to be stored in our hearts like a reservoir. Our God says, "But let justice roll down like waters, and righteousness like an ever-flowing stream" (Amos 5:24). The justice of God is to flow from us, His people, into the communities in which we live.

Justice does not mean that we are the judge. Justice means that we are to do all we can to bring equality of God's justice into every arena of life in which we have personal influence. Justice is to flow *from* us into our homes, neighborhoods, churches, schools, workplaces, and relationships. Justice is not just to flow from us, but *to and on behalf* of others. Justice is what we should seek and attempt to provide for those who are victims so often of injustice—the poor, the immigrants and refugees, the widows and the fatherless, and the oppressed and victimized. Justice does not flow to the nations from the polling booth. It flows from the river of life that finds its source at the throne of Jesus. And it flows through His people into the lives of others, people we see, for justice isn't blind at all.

FEBRUARY 27
Deuteronomy 17-19

"THE PROMISED PROPHET"

> "I will raise up for them a prophet like you from among their brothers. And I will put my words in his mouth, and he shall speak to them all that I command him."
> (Deuteronomy 18:18)

The word "Deuteronomy" has as its origin two Greek words that could be translated as "second law." Deuteronomy is a restoration of the Law given by God through Moses 40 years earlier. An entirely new generation of Israelites had been born during those many years in the wilderness. Now, as the nation prepared to finally enter the Promised Land, it was crucial for the people to promise again, by the renewal of the covenant, the pledge to Jehovah and His commands. This would especially be important as they were about to enter a land where the inhabitants worshiped false gods and served them with abominable practices. The renewal of the covenant would be the national rededication to the words of the Law shared with them by God through Moses, their great prophet. However, their prophet would not be accompanying them into the Promised Land. Because Moses disobeyed and dishonored God before the people regarding the provision of water from the rock (Num. 20:9-11), God declared that Moses would see the Promised Land but not enter it.

So, in many ways, the book of Deuteronomy is the record of Moses' farewell address to the people of Israel, providing them with words to guide their lives and those of generations to come. We can only imagine how grieved the people must have been to learn that their leader for over 40 years would not be leading them into the Promised Land. However, as they prepared to cross the Jordan River, Moses shared God's promise of a coming prophet. This prophet, who would come directly from the presence of Jehovah, would bring the living words that God had placed in Him. Of course, this is the promise of the Prophet from Galilee—Jesus of Nazareth.

Jesus is the Prophet of the New Covenant (Heb. 8:6-13). He Himself is the Word, the message of the covenant (Heb. 1:1-2). Jesus is the Word of God, and He is the final Word (John 1:1). In Him alone is contained all the treasures of wisdom and knowledge (Col. 2:3). The words of our Prophet Jesus are light, and they are life. Regardless, many people, most people, in fact, will not follow Jesus and His words. The words of Jesus are not always comfortable and easy. One season in Jesus' ministry, multitudes began to leave Him because His message was not "seeker-sensitive" and pleasing to their self-focused desires. So many people left Jesus that, in sadness, He turned to the 12 disciples and asked, "Do you want to go away as well?" May the answer of Peter be the response from each of our hearts to our Prophet, "Lord, to whom shall we go? You have the words of eternal life" (John 6:67-68). Amen, Peter!

The words of our Prophet Jesus bring eternal life, not just life after death, but life before and after death, life now and forever. Our Prophet's words are our Promised Land, for in keeping His commands, we experience the abundant life. Yes, this world is truly a desert wilderness; but in the midst of it flows streams in the desert (Isa. 43:19), and it abounds with the fruit of the Spirit (Gal. 5:22-23). As a child, we used to sing a song in Sunday School, "My Lord knows the way through the wilderness, all we have to do is follow."

FEBRUARY 28
Deuteronomy 20-22

"No Man is an Island"

> "No man is an island, entire of itself; every man is a piece of the continent, a part of the main. If a clod be washed away by the sea, Europe is the less, as well as if a promontory were, as well as if a manor of thy friend's or of thine own were: any man's death diminishes me, because I am involved in mankind, and therefore never send to know for whom the bells tolls; it tolls for thee."
>
> (Written by John Donne, 1572-1631)

John Donne was a minister of the Anglican Church during the Elizabethan age of England. He is also considered one of the greatest poets of any generation. From his work, which I cited above, have come countless phrases that have become idioms used in the English language for centuries. "No man is an island" and "for whom the bell tolls" are expressions that are still used in daily communication and conversation (not to mention as titles for books and films). Donne's phrase, "No man is an island," came to my mind as I read the chapters in Deuteronomy today. Perhaps you feel as I felt; these are difficult passages to read. Many are brutal in nature and filled with commands for the shedding of blood. It is hard for us, 3,500 years removed from the setting and as people living under the New Covenant, to comprehend God's purposes in giving some of these directions. We can be thankful that these practices are no longer part of the operation of God's Kingdom in His people and the church.

That being said, we cannot think that such passages have no message or application for us today. This is part of the Word of God, "Now these things happened to them as an example, but they were written down for our instruction, on whom the end of the ages has come" (1 Cor. 10:11). Paul said these messages from the Old Testament "were written down for our instruction." What instruction can we receive from passages such as those in today's reading? "No man is an island" is a crucial lesson for us, I believe, to take away from these verses.

All of us are a part of the community of mankind and, more significantly, the community of faith. The answer to the question, "Am I my brother's keeper?" is a resounding, "Yes!" For the positive or for the negative, all of us have influences, and therefore, our lives have significance. "For none of us lives to himself, and none of us dies to himself. For if we live, we live to the Lord, and if we die, we die to the

Lord. So then, whether we live or whether we die, we are the Lord's" (Rom. 14:7-8).

It is a glorious truth in the Gospel that by grace through faith, we can experience a personal relationship with God. However, we must never for a moment believe that a *personal* relationship with God means a *solitary* relationship with God. It doesn't. We are members of the church of Jesus, members of His Body, and fellow citizens in His New Community. So, what we do and who we are is not just our own private existence. We impact and are an influence on others. Our spiritual life increases the lives of others, and our spiritual sickness and death diminish others. This is what John Donne was saying, but God said it first. Not one of us is an island surrounded by ocean. Each of us is a lake surrounded by people. May refreshing, living water flow from us to each life we touch!

FEBRUARY 29
Deuteronomy 23-25

"The Second Harvest"

"When you reap your harvest in your field and forget a sheaf in the field, you shall not go back to get it. It shall be for the sojourner, the fatherless, and the widow, that the Lord your God may bless you in all the work of your hands."
(Deuteronomy 24:19)

Verses like the one above were easily understood by countless generations of God's people, but not so much by millions of believers throughout the past 150 years or so. As a result of the Industrial Age and the population movement to towns and cities, fewer and fewer believers are personally aware of the rhythm and activities associated with agricultural life. We may have some awareness of cultivating, planting, and harvesting, but we are blissfully (and thankfully) unaware of the experience of that arduous work. However, much of the Bible, especially the Old Testament, expresses God's laws, principles, and messages in expressions that are either directly or indirectly related to an agrarian society. So, if we want to understand God's Word, we *must* understand the agricultural references to accurately apply them to our lives. God chose these expressions to be part of His eternal Word, so all of God's people through the ages must understand them. His message *beyond* agriculture, to all of life, is in them.

The verse quoted above is a perfect example of a timeless principles to guide God's people. They are principles of what could be called "The

Second Harvest." The Lord instructed his people not to go back into their fields after the harvest and ensure every single sheaf of grain made it into the barn. Instead, what was left from the first harvest would be the "second harvest" that could be reaped by those in need—the immigrants, refugees, fatherless, and widows. By this generosity, the needs of the poor and the at-risk, who lived on the margins of society, would be met. This was an act of compassion, and it was also an act of faith in God, believing that He would more than provide. He would bless the ones who remembered the needs of others. The blessing and joy of the Lord would be experienced by the ones who gathered the second harvest as well as the ones who provided the second harvest. This practice that was established millennia ago is still the principle that should guide God's people in every season throughout the ages. Our God is the ultimate owner of all things. He is the Lord of every harvest. As the owner of everything, the Lord delights in sharing His possessions with others. God enjoys giving and providing, and He desires His people to experience the joy that comes through generosity —the joy of giving and receiving.

To live in greed is to live a miserable life that robs ourselves of the treasure of joy. The word "miserly" comes from the same root word for "miserable." I once heard a pastor say that an ungenerous person lives by the philosophy, "Get all I can, can all I get, sit on the lid, and spite the rest." That's very plain, and it is also very true. The admonition runs throughout the Laws of God: "Never forget you were slaves in Egypt." God reminded His people that they had been exposed to a brutal existence without generosity. He had delivered them from the heavy yoke of bondage, and now as His people, they were to do the same by lifting the burdens of others. This is the principle of the "second harvest" shared with others. Who have you shared with lately?

MARCH

"Sow for yourselves righteousness; reap steadfast love…"
(Hosea 10:12)

MARCH 1
Deuteronomy 26-28

"Our Profession, God's Profession"

"You have declared today that the Lord is your God, and that you will walk in his ways, and keep his statutes and his commandments and his rules, and will obey his voice. And the Lord has declared today that you are a people for his treasured possession..."
(Deuteronomy 26:17-18a)

As mentioned earlier, the title of the book of Deuteronomy means "second law." Before entering the Promised Land, Moses again shared with the new generation of Israelites the commands from God and their application to them as a nation and as individuals. The words Moses shared, however, were more than just a litany of laws. They were the expressions of a Covenant relationship. As we have read in the above verses, Jehovah and His people pledged themselves to each other. The Law was more than the constitution; it was a covenant, a personal pledge bound in devoted love.

Over the years of my ministry, I have been blessed to stand with several hundred couples as they committed themselves to each other in marriage. These wonderful events have been as different and diverse as the couples themselves. Some services have been grand and impressive, while others have been the epitome of simplicity. Yet, regardless of all the different expressions within these weddings, one thing has united them all—the exchanging of vows. Vows are more than words two people share. They are sacred pledges made in the presence of God while calling on Him as a witness to the covenant. It is a huge moment, intended to be one that will never be forgotten and continually be a living reality guiding and guarding the couple in their marriage.

It is not surprising then that in both the Old and New Testaments, the Lord uses the imagery of marital love and covenant as an emblem of the eternal relationship that binds Him and His people. Israel is called "the wife of the Lord" (Jer. 3:14 NKJV). The church is designated as "The Bride of Christ" (Eph. 5:25). These descriptions are not just words on paper, even as marriage is infinitely more than two names inserted into a document and stored in a courthouse records office. Marriage is the deepest and most devoted of all human relationships, written not on paper but inscribed into the very fabric of a man or woman's being. It is a covenant of love.

What I have just written is not a romantic notion but a wonderful reality understood by anyone reading this page who has been blessed to know the gift of a marriage expressing covenant love. A love covenant changes everything. Duty is devotion, principle is privilege, commitment is consecration, and service is sacred. A covenant changes everything. Perhaps today, a renewal of your covenant with Christ would change everything. What an amazing power there is in reveling in the love of God, praising and thanking the One who has loved you with an everlasting love (Jer. 31:3). What a peace comes in pledging your love to the lover of your soul and confessing the truth that you love Him because He first loved you (1 John 4:19). Yes, love changes everything. May our Lord's covenant love change us again today.

MARCH 2
Deuteronomy 29-31

"Secret Things"

"The secret things belong to the Lord our God, but the things that are revealed belong to us and to our children forever, that we may do all the words of this law."
(Deuteronomy 29:29)

A few years after I began working in the ministry, the pastor of the church where I was serving on the staff informed me that he thought the time had come for me to be officially ordained by the church as a minister of the gospel. This process involved contacting the pastors of other churches in the area and having them serve as an ordination council. The purpose of this council was to interview me about my call to the ministry and ask me questions regarding my knowledge and understanding of the Bible. I had previously attended a few of these ordination councils for other prospective ministers; usually, less than six pastors attended, and the entire interview lasted about one hour. Well, you can imagine my panic when, on the morning of my council, 35 pastors arrived to interview me. Not only that, but the process lasted six hours! My pastor did not offer much encouragement when he approached me before the interview. He chuckled, "Boy, are you going to get grilled today!" And he was right. It was quite a nerve-racking ordeal, but the pastors mercifully recommended me for ordination by our church. Despite his smug humor at my impending ordeal, my pastor did give me a wise piece of advice. He said, "Sam, remember sometimes the best answer you can give is 'I don't know.'" I recall having to give the pastors on the council that answer more than a few times that day!

Now, saying that you don't know is never an excuse for a lack of diligence in seeking the truth or greater knowledge. However, there are times in our growth as disciples of the Lord when it is true wisdom to acknowledge we don't know and sometimes can't know the truth about all situations. There are "secret things" that only the Lord in His infinite wisdom understands (Deut. 29:29). Some of the "secret things" we are incapable of understanding as mere fallen mortals. That level of understanding would require infinite wisdom, which is an attribute belonging only to the infinite One, the all-wise God (Jude 1:25).

So, how should we respond when we come face-to-face with truths in the Scripture or, just as often, inscrutable situations in life? Let me suggest three "very wise" responses to the things of God you don't understand:

Humility: God resists the proud but gives grace to the humble (Jas. 4:6). It is the humble heart that God enlightens (Ps. 25:9).

Trust: It has been well said regarding our Lord, "When you can't trace His hand, trust His heart." We cannot always understand the work of God's hands, but we can always rest in the *wounds of His hands*.

Worship: Not understanding everything should not lead us to fretful worry but fervent worship. Listen to the doxology of the greatest master of theology, "Oh, the depth of the riches and wisdom and knowledge of God! How unsearchable are his judgments and how inscrutable his ways!" (Rom. 11:33).

MARCH 3
Deuteronomy 32-34

"THE EVERLASTING ARMS"

"The eternal God is your refuge, and underneath are the everlasting arms."
(Deuteronomy 33:27)

Benjamin Franklin was an incredibly brilliant man. So many inventions and institutions that are part of the fabric of life in America and, for that matter, around the world trace their origins back to the incredible brain of the printer from Boston, Massachusetts. From the postal service to the fire department to the street lights to the indoor stove, and yes, to critical phrases in the Declaration of Independence, all were conceived in his thinking. However, I think practically every United States citizen is grateful for one idea of Franklin's that never "took flight." He strongly believed the living symbol of the newly formed nation should be the turkey. That's right—the turkey. He was quite certain that this bird, native to North America, represented the best qualities of the new republic. But, it just did not fit. It's hard to imagine our currency (Franklin had a big part of that as well) imprinted with the outstretched plume of a turkey. That's just wrong.

There is something majestic and mighty about the image of an eagle. It seems the Lord created this magnificent, soaring bird to elicit the awe and admiration of all who watch it in flight. The eagle is incredibly powerful and yet also tenderly protective of its young. Clearly, God chose the eagle as the image of His own nature and His care for those who belong to Him. The eagle is used repeatedly in the poetry and songs of Scripture to describe the Lord's constant oversight, protection, and provision for His people. In his final words to the tribes of Israel, Moses shares the beautiful lyrics found in our passage today. He reminds the people of Israel that it is their "eagle-like" God who plucked them out of the bondage of slavery, carried them on His wings through the wilderness, provided for their shelter and food, and protected them from all their enemies.

Moses assures them that for 40 years, Jehovah has guided and guarded them and will continue to lead them safely into the Promised Land. The scene is bittersweet but beautiful as Moses, from Mount Nebo with a death-dimming gaze, looks out upon the vista of his people preparing to cross the Jordan River. He knows they are safe because "the eternal God is your refuge and underneath are the everlasting arms." What is true for the people about to cross the river to the land of their fathers, is true for the prophet who is about to cross the river and "be gathered to his fathers." In life and in death, the Lord surrounds and upholds His people. We are never homeless because the Lord is our refuge, our dwelling place, for all generations (Ps. 90:1).

We grow tired and weak on our journey, but we are never unsupported, for the "everlasting arms" of unlimited might and unconditional love firmly uphold us. We can always confidently rest on our Lord's "everlasting arms!"

> *What have I to dread? What have I to fear?*
> *Leaning on the Everlasting Arms!*
> *I have blessed peace with my Lord so near,*
> *Leaning on the Everlasting Arms!*

(Song written by Elisha A. Hoffman and Anthony J. Showalter, based on the text of Deuteronomy 33:27.)

MARCH 4
Joshua 1-2

"THE SCARLET CORD"

Sometimes when a person is so very ill that their survival is uncertain, it may be said that their life is "hanging by a thread." The origin of that phrase goes back to the ancient Greek tale of King Dionysius. He became so tired of the constant hypocritical pandering by one of his court officials, Damocles, that he invited him to sit upon the king's throne at a royal banquet. Damocles was enjoying himself tremendously until he happened to look up and see dangling over his head a sharp sword suspended from the ceiling by a single hair. This "Sword of Damocles" convinced the conniving, ultra-ambitious official that perhaps he did not desire to be king as much as he previously thought!

In today's Scripture reading, we learn about the account of a woman and her family whose lives were "saved by a thread." Rahab, a prostitute in Jericho, kept two Israelite spies safe in her home while officials from the king sought them. After the soldiers left her home, Rahab begged the Hebrew spies to show mercy to her and her family when they returned with the people of Israel to destroy Jericho. As she pleaded for mercy, Rahab also made an amazing confession of faith, "For the Lord your God, He is the God in heaven above and on earth beneath" (Josh. 2:11). The two spies responded with a solemn vow that if Rahab hung the scarlet cord from her window (the same one used to lower them to safety), she and her family would be completely safe.

This story from the pages of Joshua has fascinated countless generations of children listening to family devotional readings or gathered in Sunday School classes or synagogue Sabbath school. However, this story is not just an amazing tale of rescue. It is also a testimony and illustration of amazing grace. The image of a family huddled in a small home behind a thin cord of scarlet reminds us of the deliverance experienced by hundreds of thousands of Israelite families on the night of the Passover. The Lord promised His people that, as He passed through Egypt, bringing the final plague of judgment, if He saw the red blood of the sacrifice on their doors, He would spare them from His wrath. Now, the judgment of Jehovah is about to descend on the city of Jericho, and not a piece of its massive walls would remain intact except for the small section containing a window from which a thin cord of scarlet red swayed in the breeze. Rahab certainly did not earn the salvation granted to her and her family. Even among the pagan people of Jericho, her lifestyle was far from exemplary. Rahab was granted salvation along with her family for one reason—the grace of a merciful God.

This Canaanite prostitute was saved by the same means as Abraham, the patriarch of Israel—she "believed God and it was counted as righteousness" to her soul. Salvation has always been obtained on the basis of grace received by faith. The Lord sees the blood of His Son and forgives sinners who believe. Today, thank God for the "scarlet cord" of redemption in Jesus. Above all, make sure His blood is your only hope. His blood is enough!

MARCH 5
Joshua 3-5

"Stones for the Ages"

I freely admit that I have a serious compulsion about historical markers. I want to stop, get out of the car, and read all of them. My very patient wife can bear witness to this. I don't know the origin of this interest I have for all things historical. It has been part of my life for as long as I remember. I find it fascinating to stand at a spot where history was made, read about it, and imagine in my mind what took place there.

History is powerful. The Lord knows the power of history. I recall a professor in college reminding us so often that history is, in reality, "*His story*." The acts of God are a living witness and powerful influence throughout the ages. In fact, the very rocks cry out in praise and adoration of God's mighty deeds. Our reading tells us of the living witness of a pile of stones stacked up not far from the Jordan River at the place named Gilgal. The Lord commanded that from the riverbed of the Jordan, 12 large stones, each carried by a representative from the Twelve Tribes, be stacked as a "historical marker" of one of the greatest moments in the life of the nation. Just as He had done at the Red Sea when God parted the waters for His covenant people to bring them into the land He had promised their forefathers centuries before. Now, these 12 stones would stand, declaring a testimony for the generations to come:

> "That this may be a sign among you. When your children ask in time to come, 'What do those stones mean to you?' then you shall tell them that the waters of the Jordan were cut off before the ark of the covenant of the Lord. When it passed over the Jordan, the waters of the Jordan were cut off. So these stones shall be to the people of Israel a memorial forever."
> (Joshua 4:6-7)

The past speaks today and through the ages to proclaim the glorious deeds of God. The power of "His story" is amazing and should be part of our vocabulary. Our words shared with our Lord in prayer should include our praise for the specific and personal ways He has acted on our behalf. Our prayer life should often be "piled high" with stones of praise to our Master for times that He has shown His love, faithfulness, and provision to us.

We should also lead others to these "rocks of remembrance" as we witness and testify. Our children, grandchildren, and the young people we influence need to hear the testimony of God's marvelous deeds in our lives. They will listen, and they will not forget. I vividly recall sitting so many times and listening as my father shared stories of the things he had seen the Lord accomplish! Those stories became "my father's gospel" that impacted my life. His testimonies helped me believe that God was real and personal, and they caused me to long for my father's God to be my God as well. Each one of us is a living epistle that is not only being seen and read but is also being "heard." Take people often to those "piles of rocks" in your life. They are His story. Tell them the stories again and again.

MARCH 6
Joshua 6-8

"Weapons of Our Warfare"

"For the weapons of our warfare are not of the flesh but have divine power to destroy strongholds."
(2 Corinthians 10:4)

What a way to win a war! For decades, the Lord had told the Israelites that they would drive out the pagan idolaters who lived in the land beyond the Jordan. Now they had crossed the river at last, and before them stood one of the most heavily fortified and defended cities in all of the Middle East—Jericho. What incredible strategy and unique tactics would Jehovah share with Joshua as the plan for defeating such a citadel? The long-awaited plan—a silent, daily stroll. That's right. The Israelites were to do nothing, say nothing, and simply walk around the walls of the city.

Not only did such a plan sound ludicrous, but it also appeared counterproductive. For seven long days, the people of Israel would have consecutive opportunities to gaze at the walls of Jericho. No doubt, during that time, the walls seemed to grow higher and more impenetrable every day. You can imagine the curse-filled taunts and laughter that the guards on the walls must have hurled at the silent parade of men, women, boys, and girls. Day after day, the routine never changed, just shuffling feet in the silence, dust, and sweltering heat. For seven days the people circled the city, and seven times on the seventh day—7 7 7, the Divine and complete number of God Himself, for this victory would be accomplished by Him alone. Out of the silence, one long blast from the ram's horn and then a million or more voices united in a great shout of praise to the God of heaven and earth. The walls of Jericho shuttered at the reverberating praise and then fell down flat in submission to Jehovah.

A day never to be forgotten by all who experienced it and a day to be remembered by the people of God throughout the ages who need to experience it for their own Jerichos.

Every believer faces these types of fortress encounters on their journey of faith. Yes, the Lord gives us minds to think and plan, and He also provides us with a will to initiate those plans for addressing challenges in life. Faith is not laziness. However, for all of us, there come obstacles and challenges for which no amount of personal training, talent, or hard work is sufficient. They are Jericho moments, mountain-like before us, that demand seed-like faith in a sovereign God and prayer for His intervention. We face these trials not because we are *out* of the will of God but because we are *in* the will of God. These fortresses looming before us, drive us to a deeper reliance on the Lord, our Master, for whom nothing is impossible.

Sometimes, the strongholds are not *before* us. The entrenched and fortified bastions of evil are *within* us. They are walls of selfishness, fear, and hatred—rock-like castles of corrupt thinking. These Jerichos of the mind must also come down if we are to truly be free. Who can accomplish such a deliverance? Listen to Paul, "Thanks be to God through Jesus Christ our Lord!" (Rom. 7:25) Like the journey around Jericho, the victory does not come immediately, but it will come. Through faith, perseverance, praise, and persistence, the battle for the mind is won by the Spirit.

> "We destroy arguments and every lofty opinion raised against the knowledge of God, and take every thought captive to obey Christ."
> (2 Corinthians 10:5)

MARCH 7
Joshua 9-11

"The Best Made Plans"

"So the men took some of their provisions, but did not ask counsel from the Lord."
(Joshua 9:14)

A great title is often quite helpful to any work of literature. One of the most noted of these in American literature comes from the novel by John Steinbeck, *Of Mice and Men*. That's a great title and, in many ways, a great novel. The title is equally classic; however, it does not come from the pen of Steinbeck but the quill of the eighteenth century poet Robert Burns. Burns created the phrase as part of his poem, "To a Mouse." It tells how he upturned a mouse's nest while plowing a field one day. The poem that emerged was written as an apology from Burns to the mouse and includes the expression of sad resignation.

> *The best laid schemes of mice and men*
> *Go often askew,*
> *And leaves us nothing but grief and pain,*
> *For promised joy!*

There is a tinge of fatalism in Burn's philosophical musings on the unpredictable outcomes of all best-made plans. However, there is also wisdom unmentioned by Burns in recognizing that there is a way of planning far above the "schemes of mice and men," and that is consulting with the Lord.

Chapter 9 of Joshua recounts a terrible, unnecessary deception carried out on the people of Israel by the Gibeonites. The inhabitants of this region in Canaan recognized that their days were numbered, and doom was inevitable. By means of shrewd tactics, they convinced Joshua and the leaders of the tribes that they had traveled from a distant country to make a peace treaty. This seemed like a great financial opportunity for the Israelites, so they made the covenant treaty, only to learn that they had been deceived and had made a terrible mistake in judgment with consequences that could not be altered. To a great extent, their decision was driven by greed, but the root cause was from a deeper source—the tap root of pride. The leaders, with pride-filled confidence in their own decision-making abilities, "did not ask counsel from the Lord" (Josh. 9:14). They talked to each other at great length about their plans, but they did not speak to God. The leaders came up with a very logical, practical, *good* idea, but it was not a

God idea. *Good* is determined by God. Wise plans always align themselves with the wisdom of the all-wise One. Master planning is only masterful if it adheres to the Master's plan. I once heard a pastor say, "Sometimes we follow the advice 'get all you can' only to find out later we don't 'want all we got'!"

Mercifully, there is a way to respond when we recognize we have made unwise decisions. That is to make the wisest decision and take our mess to the Master. He already knows all about it, but we must confess our sin to Him, not "our mistake"—"our sin." To confess means "to say the same thing" about our attitudes or actions that the Lord does. If our unwise decisions were rooted in pride, we need to tell him just that. His gracious promise is that He will freely and completely forgive us. The consequences of our decisions may remain, but the guilt between our Lord and us will be totally removed. With a clear conscience, we can begin again to make wise plans, which always begin with seeking the counsel of our all-wise, all-loving Master.

MARCH 8
Joshua 12-14

"Re-fired, Not Retired"

"So now give me this hill country of which the Lord spoke on that day..."
(Joshua 14:12)

When I was just a child in Sunday School, our gatherings started with all the children assembled for singing. In my memory these many decades later, I can still see us and hear us singing with enthusiastic (and sometimes tone-deaf) voices the praise songs our leaders would teach us. I am amazed that through the years, the words of practically all those songs are still etched in my mind. I am grateful for that because those songs of my childhood have often helped guide me as an adult. Now, as I have reached that special but loosely defined status of "Senior Adult," one of those songs comes back to me again in connection with our Scripture reading today. I remember singing those words with all my might:

> *I want that mountain! I want that mountain!*
> *Where the milk and honey flow,*
> *Where the grapes of Eshcol grow.*
> *I want that mountain! I want that mountain!*
> *The mountain that my Lord has given me!*

I did not know where that mountain was, and I certainly did not know what the grapes of Eshcol were. I don't think some of those leaders knew either! However, I did recognize that the mountain was something worth having, and I certainly wanted to have it. Over 50 years later, after years in college and seminary, after years and years of ministry, that song from my childhood gives me the wisdom to reject the commonly accepted thought about "the golden years." Those lyrics from the children's praise song by Bill Harvey are based on the faith-filled testimony of an 85-year-old Israelite warrior, Caleb. He and Joshua, 45 years earlier, brought back to Moses and the congregation of Israel, the testimony of a land "flowing with milk and honey,"—a garden of Eden for God's people to take in His name. It may very well have been Caleb and Joshua who carried the gigantic cluster of grapes from the Valley of Eshcol (Num. 13:23-24).

Yes, there were giants in the Land of Canaan, especially the fierce and famous Anakim who dwelled in the hill country of Judah. But, who were these giants compared to the God of Israel? Caleb had seen the lush land and the giants who defended it, and, for 45 years by faith, he believed that Jehovah had given it to him and his family. This "Senior Adult" was still fueled by the dream of seeing the Lord conquer and drive out the giants before him, his sons, and his grandsons. Caleb was the farthest thing from "retired." He was "re-fired" by a vision of faith and the glory of God.

Certainly, there is a time when we may retire from the work of our "career," but we never retire from the work of our Creator. We have been created in Christ Jesus for the purpose of good works (Eph. 2:10). Good works are God's works done in love for Him and others. There should never be a mindset in God's people of retirement when "For to me to live is Christ, and to die is gain" (Phil. 1:21). Yes, we should long for our "retirement," for it is truly a retirement that is "out of this world." But until that day, let a childhood song be a lifelong vision: "I want that mountain that the Lord has given me!"

MARCH 9
Joshua 15-17

"FAITH THAT WORKS"

Faith is not laziness. Trusting in the Lord is never in conflict with active obedience to His promises and the opportunities He graciously gives.

Many years ago, I recall a preacher saying in his folksy way, "Some people confidently sing 'Standing on the Promises,' but they are always comfortably sitting on the premises!" We can certainly chuckle at that turn of a phrase, but it is a serious problem and not a laughing matter. The people of Israel are a living testament to the long-lasting results of a lazy faith.

God promised to give the nation all the land promised to their patriarch Abraham. Yes, the land was occupied by fierce and ungodly people groups. However, the Lord had already demonstrated on numerous occasions that the inhabitants of Canaan were no match for His people empowered by His strength. God promised the tribes of Israel the land, but they must also go in by faith and take the land. The tribes did drive out the inhabitants—mostly, but not completely. Throughout the Promised Land, pockets of enemy strongholds were permitted to remain. No doubt, these few areas of partial victory did not seem like a significant issue. But in years to come, what a price the nation would pay for their own complacency, laziness, and incomplete obedience! Permitting these pockets of resistance to exist, they became pockets of infection and cancer that would soon threaten the nation's health and life.

As followers of the Lord living 3,400 years later, we need to consider the lessons from these chapters carefully. We must be careful not to permit the "taking a break" mentality to apply to our spiritual lives. Yes, we are to care for our physical and emotional health with appropriate rest, time with family and friends, and seasons of Sabbath. These are all gifts from God to be regularly experienced and enjoyed. However, we must never forget that our enemies of the world—the flesh and the Devil—are constantly resisting and opposing us. They are terrible relentless foes, and they do not rest. They are defeated through the victory of our King, but they are not yet destroyed. In His Name, we must resist them and root out their corrupting influence. If we do not, we are in danger of becoming like the people of Joseph, the tribes of Ephraim and Manasseh, in providing whining excuses for failing to drive out the enemy (Josh. 17:13-18).

Faith never speaks like that. Faith is not a language of complacency but a compelling vision. Our faith fuels our witness and our work for the Lord. By faith, we *know* that our risen Lord has all authority and His presence is always with us. Therefore, we work to make disciples, teach, and share the gospel everywhere (Matt. 28:18-20). By faith, we *know* that we have been saved. Therefore, we work out our salvation in fear and trembling (Phil. 2:12). By faith, we *know* that all believers who have gone before us have finished their challenging race. Therefore, we look constantly to Jesus and run with endurance the race that is set before us (Heb. 12:1-2). I do not know what time it is in your life, and you do not know what time it is in mine, but one thing is absolutely certain—it's not quitting time! Press on.

MARCH 10
Joshua 18-21

"The Master Plan"

Some of the most frustrating and yet illuminating hours I have experienced in recent years took place a few miles away from the site of the biblical city Ephesus in Western Turkey. My wife and I hosted a tour group that followed the journeys of Paul in the New Testament. Part of the tour included spending most of a day visiting the excavated ruins of this city so significant in the New Testament narrative. A local guide was assigned to lead our group that day, but I became a bit concerned when I realized that I knew more about the history of Ephesus than he did. This was not a good thing for our tour group. Also, I was bothered by how quickly our guide seemed to push the group through the remarkable archaeological remains of the area. It did not take long to discover our guide's "other agenda" as he stopped our bus for refreshments at a place that "just happened" to be connected to a local carpet-making business. We were cordially invited to a "personal tour" conducted by the owner displaying the amazing process involved in crafting the fine rugs. I must admit that I was a little more than frustrated with our local guide, "George," and in my mind could see myself joyfully rolling him up in one of those beautiful rugs. We did not come to look at rugs!

It was a frustrating experience but, as I mentioned earlier, an illuminating one as well. For as much as I was "seeing red," I could also see the incredible artistry and knowledge involved in creating the famous and beautiful Turkish rugs. The process seemed far removed, sometimes even counterproductive, to the results. Clearly, there existed a master plan that connected every step, from capturing the very first threads to the completed work of beauty and functionality. What seemed unplanned, haphazard, and disconnected was actually all a part of a necessary and carefully planned process to produce the finished product.

The chapters of our reading today can honestly be tedious and frustrating to digest. We don't know many of the names and locations associated with apportioning the land to the various tribes. Even more, we have no idea why God chose these various plot lines of survey in assigning the tribes their inheritance. Yes, with patience and a very detailed geographical map of Canaan, we can know the "what" and "where" of these sections of real estate, but we do not know the "why." God simply has not told us. These are some of the "secret things" that belong only to God (Deut. 29:29).

All the same, we can take great personal encouragement from the specific details of the division of the Promised Land. The same God of all creation with a master plan for the real estate He created is also our Heavenly Father who created us and then redeemed us to be His children. The same loving God who planned all the details and paid the full price for our salvation has a plan for each of our lives. At times, the "Master Weaver's" process in our lives seems to make no sense. The threads of His work often seem dark, disconnected, and purposeless. However, we must remember a few things.

First, our God is too good to be unkind, and He is too wise to be mistaken. Second, the process is not yet completed. We are the workmanship of God (Eph. 2:10), and the work is not yet finished. Third, we must never forget that we are standing on the "wrong side" of our Master's work. Only our perspective from the "right side," from heaven, will allow us to see that every thread of our lives was part of a Master plan—the infinite, amazing, and glorious tapestry of redemption. How blessed we are to be threads in that Masterpiece!

MARCH 11
Joshua 22-24

"Blessed Intolerance"

"And if it is evil in your eyes to serve the Lord, choose this day whom you will serve, whether the gods your fathers served in the region beyond the River, or the gods of the Amorites in whose land you dwell. But as for me and my house, we will serve the Lord."
(Joshua 24:15)

Tolerance.

For generations, this word has described a virtue that defines a person of admirable character. "Tolerance" has meant a disposition willing to concede differences of opinion or even belief in a desire to express respect and a peaceable attitude. Tolerance *was* a virtue. Note the past tense, *was*. Today, the idea of tolerance has come to be considered a vice rather than a virtue.

It is said today that the word *tolerance* contains within it the element of prideful judgmentalism. We are told that tolerance is condescending and elitist. Tolerant people, in reality, *it is affirmed*, are unwilling to embrace "the truth" that other people hold. This thinking says, "We have to fully embrace the reality that the truth others hold is *their* truth, and we must also embrace that *their* truth is true for them." Does that last statement sound strange to you? Good. It is strange. The warped logic ultimately flows from a mind that has been darkened by relativism—the belief that there does not exist a source of absolute truth. This was at the heart of the original lie that Satan spoke to Eve in the garden, "Did God actually say...?" Satan's first attack was an attack on absolute truth, which was an attack on the character of God, the source of ultimate truth.

The reality is that truth is either God or something else altogether. Truth is not, by definition, "relative." It is absolute and fixed in God Himself. Therefore, to "tolerate" a source of truth outside of the God of truth is not a virtue; it is an assault on God and an assault on the minds of those who are made in His image. Choosing your truth is, in reality, choosing your God. Joshua knew this. That is why in his final message to the people of Israel, Joshua challenged them to choose whom they would serve. They must either serve the Lord or the gods their ancestors worshiped beyond the Euphrates River. Joshua's charge was intolerant. The call to worship and allegiance always is. Serving and following competing gods is an impossibility. Always.

This intolerant allegiance, however, is never proud and arrogant. It is following the example and the mind of Jesus. Jesus was "full of grace and truth." These qualities were never in conflict within our Lord, nor should they be for us who serve Him. Jesus was the embodiment of love and the most compassionate person who ever walked the earth; yet, His allegiance to His truth was total. "Your word is truth" was the moral center of all our Lord's thinking and decision-making (John 17:17). It was our Master's "intolerance" to any other source of truth except that found in His Father that made Him the merciful, gracious, friend of sinners that He truly was. Truth is not cold, remote, and unfeeling. Truth is the character of God on display. "Love, joy, peace, patience, kindness, goodness, faithfulness, gentleness, self-control..." (Gal. 5:23) A relentless commitment to truth is a devoted pursuit of these virtues. Truth does not tolerate any other kind of character. Living in truth is living with love and grace.

MARCH 12
Judges 1-3

"Drifting Away"

"**W**here did your mother go?" I remember asking two of my children that question one afternoon as we enjoyed a great time riding the waves rolling into a beach on the gulf coast of Florida. Just a few minutes earlier, I had looked to see my wife enjoying the sun as she sat reading a magazine in a beach chair. Susan had now simply vanished. Startled, I began scanning the beach to see where she could have possibly gone. That's when I saw her, still sitting enjoying her book but several hundred yards up the beach. I understood what was happening. Susan had not moved at all, but while the kids and I were riding the waves, we drifted further and further from where we had initially entered the water. We were drifting with the current, utterly oblivious to the reality. But slowly and imperceptibly, we were being pulled by the current further and further down the beach. Thankfully, it was easy to ride the surf to shore and then race the kids back to where their mom was sitting.

Spiritual drifting is just as deceptive but far more dangerous and difficult to reverse. Spiritual drifting is so deceptive because it is not characterized by tsunami-like catastrophe but by the slow, comfortable drifting of compromise. This was exactly the experience of the Tribes of Israel. They did not simply wake up one morning and decide to forsake Jehovah and begin worshiping Canaanite gods. It was a slow drift into idolatry. It started with laziness—taking a break from the relentless battle of taking the land from the idle-worshiping inhabitants. Then, the people of Israel became comfortable sharing their inheritance with the Canaanites and living at peace with them. This led to communion with their enemy, sharing life, and even sharing in marriage. The final surrender to the current compromise was to share in the Canaanite religion—to try to add the worship of Baal with the worship of Jehovah. Comfort, compromise, and communion with ungodliness eventually caused the Israelites to drift into complete *covenant-breaking* with their God. The nation blissfully floated to disaster and judgment.

The danger of drifting is a constant danger for the people of God before we reach the golden shores of our eternal homeland. The only protections we have against this deceptive drifting are the ever-reliable instruments of navigation charts, a compass, and an anchor. These navigation charts are the written testimony of believers who have sailed what are for us as yet, uncharted waters. God's people, by the written and spoken testimonies of voyagers over the ages, give us the wisdom of insight into what we have not yet experienced. Beyond these navigation charts of Godly men and women, we possess the perfect, unfailing compass—the Word of God. In the worst storms of life, when for seasons we are driven into darkness, completely at a loss for our location on the seas, we can always find "true north" by the source of truth—the Bible. Our compass of the Word will never steer us in the wrong direction. Of course, the greatest protection against drifting is a secure anchor—the anchor of our soul, faith in the Rock of Ages—Jesus Christ. The waves may surge and roll, and the storms may batter us (and they surely will), but we don't have to drift!

MARCH 13
Judges 4-6

"JEHOVAH-SHALOM"

*"Then Gideon built an altar there to the Lord and called it,
The Lord Is Peace."*
(Judges 6:24)

One of the fiercest forces on our planet is the incalculable power and incredible size of a tropical storm—a hurricane. These awful and awe-inspiring occurrences are capable of spreading hundreds of miles in diameter, dropping untold billions of gallons of water, all the while clocking wind speeds capable of reaching in excess of 200 miles per hour! Only those who have endured one of these (and I am grateful to say I have not) can begin to describe their impact. However, as all of us are aware and perhaps a few of you have experienced, something amazing exists in the center, in the eye of the storm—calm and peace. It is hard to imagine that with one of the most cataclysmic phenomena in nature raging all around, in the very heart of it all there is peace. The Hebrew word that translates, or is transliterated into numerous languages is "shalom."

If ever a man needed shalom it was Gideon. He lived in a country completely dominated and oppressed by the most violent and wicked people—the Midianites. To describe some of their rituals and practices would be entirely inappropriate for these pages or public or even private discussion. So awful were the Midianites and their outrages on the Jewish people that vast numbers of the population had to hide in forests, mountains, or underground caves. The most basic of activities, like threshing wheat, had to be carried out in hidden places such as a winepress. That is where Gideon was when greeted by a stranger who called him "a mighty man of valor" (Jud. 6:12). It was the Angel of the Lord, a preincarnate appearance of the Christ, the Messenger of Jehovah, who spoke to Gideon.

And so, like our Lord, He called Gideon not according to how he saw himself, but as the Lord saw him—for who he *could be* and *would be* because "the Lord is with you," He said. Within a few minutes, Gideon was gripped by a fear greater than that produced by the Midianites, a fear brought by the recognition that as a sinful human being he had gazed upon the face of God. It was to this godly fear that the Lord spoke, "Peace be to you. Do not fear; you shall not die" (Jud. 6:23). Peace had come to Gideon, peace from the Prince of Peace.

My friends, peace is powerful. It is a completely safe dwelling place for those who fear the Lord. "Therefore, since we have been justified by faith, we have peace with God through our Lord Jesus Christ" (Rom. 5:1). There is no greater power than the peace in knowing you are fully accepted by God through faith in His Son. This shalom is not passive. This peace compels us to action for the cause of the Lord. Peace with God makes us enemies against idolatry, even if it costs us the approval of our family and closest friends.

Gideon's peace with his God caused him to reject the pagan practices of his father and his family. Gideon's peace with God gave him a witness with a new identity—"Jerubbaal," which means "Baal contends" or "Baal needs to show he can contend with this man of God." You've got to love that! In the shalom of the Lord, Gideon was a new man, clothed with the Spirit of God (Jud. 6:34). Think about it. People with the peace of God on the inside are people with the power of God on the outside. May the shalom of God be within us and upon us this day!

MARCH 14
Judges 7-9

"The Seventieth Son's Sermon"

From the top of Mount Carmel in Israel, on a clear day, you can experience a breathtaking view. Turning to the north, you can see the top of Mount Hermon rising over 8,000 feet in the distance. The springs flowing from this majestic mountain unite to form the Jordan River that flows through Israel. Looking to the south from Mount Carmel's summit, you can see the coastal plain that slowly rises to the hills of Judah. Gazing to the west, you look out upon the emerald and blue waters of the Mediterranean Sea. Then, as you turn to the east, you can see off in the distance Mount Tabor and below the famous Valley of Jezreel. This valley has been the scene of thousands of battles over the centuries—"the greatest battlefield in the world," as Emperor Napoleon once described it. The soil of the Valley of Jezreel is literally soaked with blood, but the most horrendous bloodshed of the ages is yet to come in this valley—the epicenter of the coming Battle of Armageddon.

It was in this valley that Gideon and a small band of 300 men armed with swords, pitchers, torches, and trumpets, by the power of God, routed the amassed armies of the Amalekites numbering over 120,000. For this exploit, Gideon was rewarded with the allegiance of Israel as their judge for nearly 40 years. After his death, he was rewarded by treachery and the slaughter of 69 of his 70 sons by the fratricide of his son (by one of his concubines), the wicked and cruel Abimelech. I said 69 of his 70 sons because Gideon's youngest son, Jotham, escaped the butchery of his brothers by his half-brother. We cannot imagine the shock and grief that filled Jotham's heart, but we do hear his pain. Jotham climbed to the top of the rugged pulpit, Mount Tabor, and from that height to the natural amphitheater below, shouted a parable of curse upon the brother who had carried out such an awful crime and on the citizens of Shechem who had conspired with him. Years later, that curse fell down upon these people and Abimelech as they turned upon each other in hatred.

What lessons can we take from such a dark passage of the Word of God? Of course, there are many, but we can see and learn the lesson of sowing and reaping. It has been said that the wheels of God's justice may grind slowly, but they grind exceedingly small. That is a substantial part, the final part at times, of the law of sowing and reaping. Ultimately, the seeds sown produce fruit that is ground beneath a grist mill, which is precisely what a lady threw down upon the head of Abimelech, crushing his skull!

The Lord seems completely absent in the events of this sordid story, but He is very much there, as also is His justice. What we sow, we reap, and it literally comes down upon our own heads. What do we want raining down upon our heads—showers of blessings or arrows (millstones) of justice? We reap what we sow, and what is the field? The field is the world. What is the world? The world is the individuals who form it. The law of the harvest is absolute and fixed. What we sow, we will reap. So, let us look at the fields and the people around us and ask, "What are we sowing into their lives?"

If it is the seed of selfishness, then the harvest will be the shouts and millstones of cursing. If we sow love, that is what we will reap—the shouts of praise and the showers of blessing.

MARCH 15
Judges 10-12

"WORDS HAVE CONSEQUENCES"

One of the most priceless gifts we can ever be given is the treasure of a loving reproof from a true friend (Prov. 27:5-6). It is valuable because it is an investment into our character development that produces profit in our lives and the lives of others we influence. I will always be thankful for the painful but profitable deposit a friend made into my life many years ago. I don't recall all the specifics, but I definitely remember sensing that I had said something to her in a moment of frustration that may have wounded her emotionally. When I saw my friend again, I mentioned what I had said to her and apologized if my words or tone had hurt her. I so vividly recall her response; I never want to forget it.

She looked at me with tears in her eyes but kindness on the expression of her face and said, "Pastor Sam, just remember we love you, and your words have power." God bless her! She kindly, gently gave me a loving rebuke. "We love you, and your words have power." Yes, our words do have power. We are told in the Scripture that our words have the power of life and death (Prov. 18:21). We need to learn that lesson from the many examples our Lord provides us.

Today's reading offers us two *negative* examples of the power of words that bring destruction to others and ourselves. The chapters today include the record of what has been known for centuries as "Jephthah's rash vow." Without thoughtful consideration, Jephthah bound himself by an oath to the Lord to offer as a burnt offering the first thing coming from his homestead as he returned victorious over the Ammonites. No doubt, he probably expected it to be some animal from among his livestock; but imagine his horror when it was his only daughter, as of yet unmarried, who came joyfully running to him! There is debate among Bible scholars as to whether Jephthah offered his daughter as a burnt offering or whether the text meant she was to live devoted to God and without a husband or children for the rest of her life. Regardless, this young woman's life and her dreams for the future were ruined by the words of her father—a "father wound." I cannot begin to tell you how many women and men who, for years and years, have borne the never-healing scars from the words, and the influence of a father not under the control of his spirit. Often, that father is passing on the wounds inflicted by his father. Words have power. Let every father, mother, or role model to children reading this page heed this lesson.

We also have the tragic, negative example shared with us by the men of Ephraim. Our reading tells us of the second time they came to threaten a leader because they were not informed ahead of time about a course of military action. In reality, their attitudes and not their accents brought their ruin. They were unable to form the word "Shibboleth." The lack of diction destroyed over 42,000 members of the tribe. Our words identify us. The words of our mouths reveal the condition of our hearts (Luke 6:45). Not only is it prudent, but also *safe* to make sure that our words are gracious and "seasoned with salt" (Col. 4:6). That certainly doesn't mean using no "salty speech," but it does call us to make sure our words are for the benefit and help of others. Our words have power. May our words this day be a power for good.

MARCH 16
Judges 13-16

"Tragically Unaware"

"But he did not know that the Lord had left him."
(Judges 16:20)

It is often said, "Ignorance is bliss." To this, a quick-witted person once added, "Only for the ignorant!" There are ways in which it is a blessing not to know everything that is taking place. What we *can see* is enough to deal with, at times. However, the verse quoted above is not describing a blessing but a personal tragedy.

The Lord has devoted four chapters in the book of Judges, almost twenty-five percent of the entire book, to inform us about the life of one man—Samson. Clearly, God wants us to consider the life of this judge of Israel carefully. And what a life it was, from the announcement by the Lord himself to the epic ending of Samson's life among the ruins of the Temple of Dagon and the thousands of bodies of Philistines. Bookended between these two incredible events is the triumphant and tragic story of Samson's life. He is a study in contradictions—a devoted servant of God and a self-focused, self-consumed bully. He is incredibly strong and amazingly weak at the same time. He glorifies God, and he promotes himself. He is stronger than a lion and more fragile than a kitten. He is a lot like us in many ways, and we can learn from his victories and defeats.

In most movies or books that share the story of Samson, he is generally portrayed as looking something akin to the bodybuilders of our day. However, if we carefully read his life story, it seems to be just the opposite. His enemies were determined to find the source of his great strength. This indicates that nothing in his physical appearance would cause people to believe that standing before them was the strongest person on earth. I remember as a teenager listening to the strongest man on earth, Paul Anderson, give his testimony at a camp I attended. Judging from his huge arms and torso, you could believe it. We were not completely surprised when, in a demonstration of strength, he lifted a table off the floor on which sat the 12 biggest guys in the auditorium!

No one would ever think that about Samson, though. His strength was supernatural because it was spiritual. Samson was strong because of the Spirit of God. His power was not because of the long hair that rested upon him but because of the Spirit of God resting upon him. Apart from God's Spirit, he was just a very weak man with a terrible attitude. Without God, he could do nothing. His prideful presumption caused him to believe he could do anytime he wanted, just as he had always done before. He was blind to the fact that the Spirit had departed from him. Only when his enemies physically blinded him could Sampson truly see that his pride and arrogance had blinded him to his utter dependence on the Lord.

Recognizing and embracing our weaknesses is necessary for us to be strong. Our Master has told us, "...apart from me you can do nothing" (John 15:5). There is hopelessness in our Lord's words, "...you can do nothing," but there is hope as well because He said, "without me." This is an encouragement to a strength we can know "with me." There is strength in weakness—*His strength, our weakness.* Weakness is a prerequisite for strength. Always.

But he said to me, "My grace is sufficient for you, for my power is made perfect in weakness." Therefore I will boast all the more gladly of my weaknesses, so that the power of Christ may rest upon me."
(2 Corinthians 12:9)

MARCH 17
Judges 17-18

"A LITTLE LEAVEN"

No one who has ever lived on this earth has been able to capture the deepest of spiritual truths in the simplest of terms, as did our Lord Jesus. He took the most easily understood examples from daily life and transformed them into timeless expressions of eternal truth. One of Jesus' most remembered and easily understood expressions was simply this, "A little leaven leavens the whole lump." In a time when bread was the "stuff of life," everyone who heard Jesus utter this expression immediately understood.

It was not the dough that impacted and changed the leaven, but just the opposite. A tiny amount of leaven, or yeast as we would term it now, invades and spreads throughout the dough. Also, Jesus' Jewish audience understood the spiritual application symbolized by leaven. Each year the faithful of Israel observed the seven-day festival of Unleavened Bread that was associated with Passover. It was a continual reminder that the people of Jehovah were to be a holy people, set apart for Himself, and separated from the leaven of sinful worship and practices of the heathen. Over the years, leaven became a synonym for sin and the danger it brings to every person.

Like leaven, what is considered "a little sin" has an incalculable impact. In the two chapters of our reading today in Judges, we have a terrible living example of how far and deep and how long the influence of sin can spread and permeate.

A woman, in gratitude to the Lord for stolen silver returned by her son Micah, decided to observe the event by having a small shrine crafted from the silver and return the coins to her son in the form of a household shrine. Although this gift was "in the name of the Lord," it was far from being a sacred gift, for it was a direct violation of the commands of God against all forms of idolatry. Also, it was a "little leaven" that would only expand and deepen the idolatry in her son's heart. He decided to turn the gift from his mother into a shrine and then ordained one of his sons to act as a priest in this "home-grown" cult.

When a man from the priestly tribe of Levi happened to pass through the neighborhood, Micah saw a way to "legitimize" his cultic shrine by ordaining the Levite as priest. The "little leaven" of religion in "the Name of the Lord" no doubt proved to be a lucrative business for Micah as people came to visit. But soon, this self-established religion and self-ordained priest became missional in its impact as 600 rogues from the region of Dan seized the silver shrine and the Levite and carried them both to their homeland. Chapter 18 ends with the terrible, enduring legacy of this "little leaven" from a silversmith shop for generations to come:

> *"And the people of Dan set up the carved image for themselves, and Jonathan the son of Gershom, son of Moses, and his sons were priests to the tribe of the Danites until the day of the captivity of the land. So they set up Micah's carved image that he made, as long as the house of God was at Shiloh."*
> (Judges 18:30-31)

Think of that! This Levite is Jonathan, the grandson of Moses himself! He and his descendants became priests to a shrine in one tribe, a shrine that operated in a contemporary and competitive fashion with the very "house of God" constructed under the direction of Moses for the worship of Jehovah! Could that mother in Bethlehem ever have imagined how immense the consequences of her "little leaven" of compromise would be? Absolutely not, and neither can we. Selah.

MARCH 18
Judges 19-21

"A Nation's Epitaph"

"In those days there was no king in Israel. Everyone did what was right in his own eyes."
(Judges 21:25)

Some passages in the Bible are just hard to read. In the blazing light of Divine revelation, sin's hideous and sordid depths are placed on bright display. To me, the final chapters of the book of Judges are some of the most distressing and depressing in all of the Word of God. Civil corruption and civil war are the final scenes of a book that begins with the descriptions of triumph as the Lord leads his people Israel into the Promised Land. Now, just a few generations later, the values and morals of God's chosen people are as bad, if not worse, than the heathen nations they dispossessed.

Spiritual death and decay corrupt every aspect of society. How is this possible? The answer is found in the sacred commentary etched upon the tombstone of the nation of Israel. "In those days there was no king in Israel. Everyone did what was right in his own eyes." A legacy summary so accurate and all-encompassing that it is written twice. (Judg. 17:6, 21:25). This is the reality of what "human freedom" will produce because it is inseparably connected to "human depravity." Every man in Israel could fully express his "free will."

But as Martin Luther so clearly communicated in his treatise, *The Bondage of the Will*, mankind's free will isn't free. The will of all men, apart from God's redeeming grace, is captive and enslaved to sin. The will, apart from submission to God, is not freedom; it is anarchy and societal suicide. A people left to themselves is not in the process of evolution but rather in a bottomless spiral of devolution. Following its own "mental advance," mankind will soon reveal that "every thought and intention of the heart is only evil continually" (Gen. 6:5).

This wretched condition was so tragic in Israel during the time of the Judges because "there *was* a King in Israel." Israel was not intended to be a monarchy but rather a theocracy. Israel was the people of Jehovah, and He was their true Master. The King of Heaven was the rightful King of Israel. The manifestation of the Kingdom of God on earth was represented in the Twelve Tribes descended from Abraham, the friend of God (2 Chr. 20:7). God had given them the land He promised to their fathers. Israel was the covenant people of God in the covenant land He alone had provided the nation. There truly was a King in Israel. The issue was that He was not enthroned in the *hearts* of

Israel. *Self* was ruling in the people's hearts, and "King Self" produced a kingdom of darkness, or more accurately—a kingdom of blindness. When everyone does what is right in his own eyes, it will soon be evident that his eyes are blind. Darkness is the domain of people who throw off the restraint of God's loving reign. "God is light, and in him is no darkness at all" (1 John 1:5). "But if we walk in the light, as he is in the light, we have fellowship with one another, and the blood of Jesus his Son cleanses us from all sin" (1 John 1:7).

True freedom is ultimately found in this "declaration of dependence," as penned by John, the "beloved disciple." He had been a freedom-loving "Son of Thunder," but he had come to learn the "blessed freedom of submission" to the One who said, "follow me." Jesus offers us "abundant life" (John 10:10). That life is experienced each day as He lovingly saves us from ourselves. Take a moment and pray for the King of Israel to reign with freedom-producing dominion in your life today.

MARCH 19
Ruth 1-4

"The Love Story of Redemption"

"Blessed be the Lord who has not left you this day without a redeemer, and may his name be renowned in Israel!"
(Ruth 4:14)

The book of Ruth is wonderfully and providentially placed in the Bible. The story it shares is a ray of hope and love amid a terribly corrupt age. Through this beautiful narrative, we are reminded once again that the Lord's grace is always at work even in the darkest of days, and that the promises He made to provide salvation for all the people groups of the world will never fail.

The book of Ruth is a love story, a story of *redeeming* love. However, this love story begins with scenes of grief, bitterness, and hopelessness. Naomi, whose name means "pleasant," felt such desolation she even asked the people to refer to her as Mara, meaning "bitterness." Humanly, she had every reason to be filled with bitterness, because over a span of a few years, her husband and two sons died in Moab, where they had immigrated as a family. Naomi pleaded with her two Moabite daughters-in-law to remain in their own country as she returned grief-stricken to her family in Judah. One of her daughters-in-law finally relented and stayed in Moab, but the other, Ruth, devotedly refused to leave her. "For where you go I will go, and where you lodge I will lodge. Your people shall be my people and your God my God" (Ruth

1:16). Ruth's words of devotion revealed a work of God's grace in her heart as she renounced her homeland and pledged herself to the God of Israel.

Sometime later, Ruth is gleaning the leftovers from the fields of the man Boaz, who "just happens to be" the person in Israel able and willing to redeem the family inheritance belonging to Naomi's husband and sons by marrying the young Moabite widow, Ruth. The story begins as a tragedy of hopelessness and grief and concludes as a triumph of love and a legacy of grace. To understand just what a legacy of grace is contained in the story of Ruth, we need to carefully examine the ancestry involved.

The book of Ruth concludes by telling us, "Salmon fathered Boaz, Boaz fathered Obed, Obed fathered Jesse, and Jesse fathered David" (Ruth 4:21-22). Boaz and Ruth are the great grandparents of King David. Wow! But wait, there's more! Who was the mother of Boaz? Rahab. That's right, Rahab the Canaanite prostitute of Jericho who hid the two Israelite spies, one of them being Salmon, the father of Boaz. (Matt. 1:5) Double wow! But wait for it—notice the Bible reference I just cited; it is part of the genealogy of Jesus, the Son of David, and the Son of God! The Savior of the world is the direct descendant of people who would be considered the ultimate outsiders—a Canaanite prostitute and a Moabite woman.

This love story of the book of Ruth is the love story of not just the redemption of a piece of property in Judah but the love story of God's redemption of the whole world. And the story takes place in Bethlehem! How great is our God, and His sovereign control of all things, causing the darkest of seasons and the most unlikely of people to be the trophies and messengers of His redeeming love! Take some time to stop and praise him for this story of redemption—your redemption. Also, encourage yourself through this living reminder of the book of Ruth that you, too, are a "living epistle" of God's redemption story. God wants your story to be known, for it is His story. Live and share the story today.

MARCH 20
1 Samuel 1-3

"The Prayer of a Child"

"Speak, Lord, for your servant hears."
(1 Samuel 3:9)

Like the Book of Ruth, the book of 1 Samuel opens with beautiful and touching scenes of God's faithfulness and grace, set against the background of the spiritual darkness that enveloped the land. The nation lived under the leadership of the judge/priest, Eli. He is a tragic figure of a man who seems to possess a sincere love for the Lord. However, he has separated the service to his God from his life's priorities as a spiritual leader and father. Eli had become fat and lazy in his position as priest and judge, and he had also abdicated his leadership over to his sons, who were priests, allowing them to defile the house of the Lord by practicing larceny and licentiousness at the very entrance. Eli was so dull of spiritual understanding that he failed to recognize the fervent, desperate, silent prayer of a young woman named Hannah as she poured out to the Lord, her plea for a son. Here we see the light of God's love shining in the darkness of a wicked generation. Simple and devout couples like Elkanah and Hannah still served the God of their fathers in faith and hope.

Hannah prayed silently, but the Lord of Heaven heard her prayer of faith. What a beautiful and touching scene, a few short years later, as Hannah returns to Eli at the temple, bringing her little boy Samuel with her. She named him Samuel, meaning "heard of God," because the Lord had graciously heard and answered her prayers for a son. She has brought her son to the priest in fulfillment of her sweet pledge, "I have lent him to the Lord. As long as he lives, he is lent to the Lord" (1 Sam. 1:28). What a mother. What a worshiper. Standing in the court of God's house, Hannah breaks out in her "Magnificat," praising Jehovah for his strength, kindness, and faithfulness. Eleven hundred years later, another young mother will quote from Hannah's song as she praises the God of Israel for the gift of a son, His Son (Luke 1:46-55).

Samuel grew up serving in the Tabernacle of God. Again, what a touching scene as the small child sleeps on his bed near the Holy Place and hears his name called by the Lord. Not recognizing it was the Lord, three times Samuel runs to ask the sleeping priest Eli what he requires of him. Finally, Eli understands it is the Lord calling the little boy and wisely counsels the child on how to respond. It is not long until Samuel once again hears the Lord call for him, and we can only imagine his trembling heart and voice as he responds, "Speak, Lord, for your servant hears" (1 Sam. 3:10). It is then that God in his mysterious, sovereign wisdom shares with the little boy a revelation of the judgment on the house of Eli of which He had long ago warned the priest. The next morning, the old priest resigned himself to what he knew to be the righteous decision of God, "It is the Lord. Let him do what seems good to him" (1 Sam. 3:18). How different would have been the ministry and legacy of Eli had that been the sincere testimony and diligence of his service for God over all the years!

One day, our Lord Jesus exulted in His Spirit that the Heavenly Father had revealed to childlike followers the Kingdom truth hidden from the religious leaders (Luke 10:21). That joy-filled exclamation of Jesus is still the reality today. The wise of the world only babble on in foolishness, but the people of childlike faith and willingness to respond can clearly hear the voice of the Lord and gain the mind of Christ. The prayer of little Samuel is still the greatest expression of wisdom, "Speak, Lord, for your servant hears."

MARCH 21
1 Samuel 4-7

"GOD IN A BOX"

The renowned eighteenth century French author and publisher Voltaire once blasphemously quipped, "God created man in his own image, and then man returned the favor." As terrible as that quote is, it sadly communicates much that is true. Everyone worships. In reality, no person or people group exists that does not worship. We are hard-wired in our very being to worship. Tragically, Voltaire was right; much of the history of mankind is just an outworking of worshiping a God made in our own image.

God is made in the image of man. Sadly, tragically, that transference of the qualities of human beings upon God creates a false god that is pathetically weak or pathologically evil. This idolatry can take the form of paganism, as manifested in the myths of the polytheistic religions of ancient Egypt, Greece, Rome, or the infinite varieties of deities in the Far East. Just as tragic, or more so, is when the *true* God is worshiped in a *false* manner—the God of the Bible, the One and only true God, "used" in a form or expression that suits His worshipers' selfish desires.

In our reading today of 1 Samuel, we have recorded just such a vain attempt to manipulate the God of Heaven. When the Philistines marched against the tribes of Israel and defeated them, the leaders wondered how this was possible since they were God's chosen people. In a flash of logical human wisdom, they comprehended the problem—the Ark of the Covenant had to be carried by the priests before the army as it marched into battle. Of course! That was the issue, and it had a simple solution—fetch the Ark and follow it into battle.

We read in the passage how well that brilliant plan worked for them. You see, the leaders of Israel foolishly believed that if they had the Ark, they had God. The basis of their decision was they believed they had "God in a box." He was *their* God, and they could march Him out and use Him whenever it suited them. *But God will not be used.* The Philistines, interestingly, possessed the same philosophy. They believed that they had captured the God of Israel in capturing the

Ark. *But God cannot be captured.* Very soon, the Philistines recognized that, while they got what they wanted, they did not want what they got. Putting it politely and mildly, they were "in a world of hurt." Believe it or not, the milk cows had more sense than the people toward the glory of God. Leaving their calves behind, the milk cows, joyfully lowing in praise, pulled the cart carrying the Ark back to Israel. Sadly, even then, some men of Beth-shemesh peered into the Ark, and seventy of them were struck dead. *God will not be objectified.*

As followers of the Lord, we must beware of the deceptive paganism of "using" or "leveraging" God. The Lord is not a God to be given lip service at football games, Nascar races, patriotic rallies, or political conventions. He is not the God to be used in "Christian marketing," making Him the power source for selfish, unbridled capitalism. Likewise, God is not contained in a building on a Sunday morning where we meet and leave Him once a week. He is not the God of meaningless words sung heartily in worship services. He is God alone, God everywhere, God at all times, God when we desire Him, and God when we don't. He delights to be worshiped and seeks worshipers (John 4:23). But worship is not special places with special activities. True worship is not *where* we worship but *how* we worship. "God is Spirit, and those who worship Him must worship in Spirit and truth" (John 4:24). All we are, responding to all He is—that's worship.

MARCH 22
1 Samuel 8-10

"THE PEOPLE'S KING"

*"No! But there shall be a king over us, that we also may be like
all the nations, and that our king may judge us and go out
before us and fight our battles."*
(1 Samuel 8:19-20)

From generation to generation, children have used the leverage of three little words—"all my friends." And parents have felt the leverage of those words. "But all my friends have one," or "but all my friends are going." There is an almost irresistible force to be like others. I am still amused by many young people who assert that they want to be individualistic and non-conformist. But when you see them at the mall or school, they seem to be with a group of similar, individualistic, non-conformists! It is not easy being different. That is one of the reasons it is not easy to live as a God-follower because the call to follow the Lord is a call to "be different."

That is the root idea of the word "holy," "to be set apart," and "to be unique and different." Now we must quickly recognize that the call to be different is not a call to be weird. The work of the Kingdom is not advanced by "the odd for God squad." However, disaster lies ahead when God's people want to fit in and align with the values, morals, or even priorities of the majority of the population. The adjustment may seem logical and appropriate, but if it is a decision not aligned with the Word and will of God, it will be a logical, appropriate, *disastrous* decision. The people's choice is rarely God's choice and practically never a wise decision.

Our reading today contains "Exhibit A" of the fallacy of popular opinion. The people were tired of being governed by very unimpressive leaders like their judges and like old Samuel, for instance. We cannot imagine how the desire for a king must have wounded the heart of the man who had faithfully led and served Israel for decades. However, the Lord made sure Samuel knew what was being expressed in the "people's choice." They were, in reality, rejecting their great, faithful, and invisible King, Jehovah (1 Sam. 8:7). The Lord made sure the people knew specifically, clearly, and in advance the price they would pay for establishing a king to rule the nation. So, the Lord judged His people's sinful desires by giving them what they wanted. Sometimes the worst experiences of bondage are the Lord permitting us to exercise our free will.

With the greatest respect for Abraham Lincoln, "government of the people, by the people, and for the people" is often not the expression of the freest life. As Lincoln himself said in quoting the Scripture, "Blessed is the nation whose God is the Lord" (Ps. 33:12).

Saul was a natural for the "people's choice award." He was humble, handsome, and head and shoulders taller than anyone else. A man to be admired, looked up to, and respected, and a choice to be regretted before long. The people's choice to conform to the practices of the nations around them was so logical and appropriate, but as they soon came to see, it was so disastrous. The "Jiminy Cricket" philosophy of "always let your conscience be your guide" is a sure path to a dead end experience unless your conscience is informed and conformed to the Word of God.

MARCH 23
1 Samuel 11-13

"A Man After His Own Heart"

"The Lord has sought out a man after his own heart, and the Lord has commanded him to be prince over his people, because you have not kept what the Lord commanded you."
(1 Samuel 13:14)

"Looks can be deceiving." That is a truism—a statement that is self-evident to people across continents, cultures, and centuries. The deceptiveness of how things appear is not just a force mentally acknowledged but also a physical, optical reality that builders, artists, and architects have, through the ages, implemented into the creation and construction of notable works of art.

A fantastic example of this "deceptiveness" from the days of classic Greek architecture still exists in the awe-inspiring beauty of the Parthenon in Athens, Greece. This incredible structure, which has captured the gaze and the hearts of admirers for over 2500 years, is actually full of intentional deceptiveness. The master architects and designers of that temple understood that for the building to be admired at a distance, it had to be designed and constructed concerning the tendencies of the human eye. The Parthenon had to be created with practically no straight lines, either vertically or horizontally, so that the building would *appear* perfect, aligned to the tendencies of the brain to interpret what it is viewing from a distance. In effect, part of the beauty of the temple lies in its understanding and embracing of optical illusion. It is a masterpiece of architecture built on the reality that "looks can be deceiving."

King Saul appeared to be a masterpiece of a ruler, but eventually, it was revealed that he was a "disaster piece." Even in the latter years, Saul looked the part of a king. Any modern film studio would have considered his tall, rugged, handsome form to be "a natural" for playing the role of a king. They would be right. If you wanted someone to "play the part" of the king, then Saul is your man. However, if you wanted someone to be the king, especially the King of Israel, Saul would be completely miscast. The problem was not outward. It was inward.

Saul did not have the heart of a king for Israel because his heart was not aligned with *The King* of Israel, the Lord. The disqualifying issue for Saul was pride; it always is. Pride is the origin of all sin, tracing its crooked path back to the angel, Lucifer, whose heart was lifted up in pride, placing his desires above those of the Most High. We see this in Saul as he "lifted himself up" in assuming the role of a priest and not only as king. Of course, he was under pressure, but the external pressure only revealed what was internal in Saul. His heart was concerned with what *appeared* to be right rather than being focused on what was *inherently* right, desiring the will of God. So, when it came to Saul, "Looks *were* deceiving." He appeared bold and brave, but in reality, he was self-focused and cowardly. He was more concerned with what people thought of him than what God knew of him.

Fear of people more than the fear of God is always rooted in pride, and the roots of pride always produce the same fruit. The fear of man will prove to be a snare (Prov. 29:25). "Looks can be deceiving," and the greatest deception is self-deception. Self-deception has only one prevention—allowing the Lord to lovingly, honestly look into our hearts and show us what is there. When we do this, we expose our deceptive darkness to the blazing light of God's redeeming love. The light of the gospel, the light of Christ our Lord, transforms our hearts and conforms our hearts "after His own heart."

MARCH 24
1 Samuel 14-16

"The Shepherd King"

"Do not look on his appearance or on the height of his stature, because I have rejected him. For the Lord sees not as man sees: man looks on the outward appearance, but the Lord looks on the heart."
(1 Samuel 16:7)

Only someone who has known the lonely isolation of the "wall of shame" can truly understand the feeling.

When I was a boy, every kid in the neighborhood dreaded experiencing the final moments of the "pick-out-teams" process to organize a baseball game on our elementary school ballfield. Two of the older boys would call "captain!" That meant the rest of us had to line up against the towering brick wall of our school and wait while the self-designated leaders, one selection at a time, called out the names of individual draftees for their respective teams. It was a humiliating and painful experience to be the last guy standing with your back to the wall and all the other boys looking at you. Trust me. I know.

No one wants to be the least wanted, the overlooked, but that is precisely who God chooses. God not only chooses the overlooked, the last one against the wall, but He also appoints them team captain. God's team has never been the "dream team." On the contrary, His teams are more often "the bad news bears." God does not choose champions; He chooses ones considered by man to be "losers" and then makes them champions.

Perhaps in our reading today, as nowhere else in the Bible, does God choose the most unlikely of candidates as His leader. So absent of kingly qualities was David that his own father overlooked him. He was overlooked because He didn't look like a king, especially when the concept of a king was King Saul. Now there was a man who looked like a king! David's older brother, Eliab, looked like a king; even Samuel was impressed and convinced (1 Sam. 16:6). But, as the Lord instructed Samuel, He does not look at a person's height or countenance but at his heart and character. And the Lord liked what He saw in David, a heart fashioned like His own, the heart of a shepherd that would carefully and courageously lead and guard the sheep of Israel.

Have you ever asked the Lord to help you value what He values? To see in others and themselves what most cannot see? Do you praise and affirm abilities or skills of temporary, earthbound importance or the qualities of the heart that are eternal and heavenly? Do you see people only for what or who they are now, rather than what or who they can be in time, by the grace of God? I freely admit my failures in this regard. Still, over the years of ministry, I have learned to look for the overlooked and watch for the qualities that are expressions of the character that our Lord embraces and encourages—humility, integrity, meekness, and faithfulness. I have learned the amazing, sacred power of encouragement—the hand on the shoulder, the sincere word of affirmation, the assurance of the Lord's love. It is a powerful moment to feel someone believes in you when you don't believe in yourself.

As always, our Lord has expressed this ministry better than anyone ever could. "So whatever you wish that others would do to you, do also to them..." (Matt. 7:12) Let's choose to invest in ones who are often left standing at the wall. After all, didn't our Lord choose us?

MARCH 25
1 Samuel 17-19

"THE GIANT SLAYER"

"You come to me with a sword and with a spear and with a javelin, but I come to you in the name of the Lord of hosts, the God of the armies of Israel, whom you have defied."
(1 Samuel 17:45)

Israel rocks! No, literally, Israel is a land full of rocks.

Never in all the places I have visited is there a country with soil as rocky as that in Israel. I recall once a member of our tour group from our church asking our Israeli guide if it was okay to pick up a few rocks to take back as souvenirs. Our guide's response was classic, "Please do! Please take some of these rocks; it is our country's chief export product. We have more than we need!" I'm not sure the Department of National Antiquities would have affirmed our guide's response. The number of tourists doing that in a few years would once again "scatter Israel among the nations!"

I readily admit to having picked up a few rocks over the years as mementos of my visits to the Holy Land. In particular, I recall picking up five small, smooth stones in the Valley of Elah. As I did, I imagined the moment 3000 years earlier when a handsome, young Israeli carefully selected five similar stones and placed them in his pouch. The young Israeli, of course, is the son of Jesse—David of Bethlehem. Standing there in that valley, I felt the same excitement as I had when first hearing the story and gazing at my teacher's flannel graph as a Sunday school child. Only the Lord knows how many billions of times the events of 1 Samuel, Chapter 17, have been recounted, and how often they have inspired His children of all ages to be "strong in the Lord."

The event is truly a turning point in the history of Israel and in the history of the world. It is almost an encounter symbolic of an even greater and more influential conflict. It is not representative of the battle between good and evil. Nor is it primarily an example of our spiritual warfare (though my own messages from this passage have pressed that image too strongly). When it comes to the Champion of the Lord of Hosts, there is only One who has fulfilled the victory of the conflict between David and Goliath. Only the Son of David, the Child of Bethlehem, the Lion of the Tribe of Judah, has accomplished the ultimate victory over all that is evil and of the evil one.

Goliath stood six cubits high, wore six pieces of armor, and carried a spear whose head weighed 600 shekels of iron. He stands there defined by 666, shouting his blasphemies against the people of Israel, and in many ways, they deserved them. But this cursing giant is about to learn he is no match for 777—the Holy, Holy, Holy God of Israel. The victory of Israel that day was won by the anointed One of God. His victory was the victory for his people.

And so it is for us, the weak, cowering, and unworthy sons and daughters of Adam. We have consistently failed the test, as did the soldiers of Israel during those 40 days of testing before the cursing, slandering giant of Satan. However, praise God, there is One who has undertaken for our cause, who has faced the enemy after 40 days of testing and overcame him with the Word of God. He is our Champion who overcame the evil one every day of His life on earth and defeated the enemy by His death. We have our Champion, our David, who met the enemy on our behalf and triumphed over him in His glorious resurrection. His victory is *our* victory. All praise today to the Son of David!

MARCH 26
1 Samuel 20-22

"A Friend and Brother"

*"The Lord shall be between me and you, and between
my offspring and your offspring, forever."*
(1 Samuel 20:42)

Abraham Lincoln once wrote, "The better part of one's life consists of his friendships." How very true is that insight! It is friendships that truly make a person rich. Sadly, in our culture, most people do not make any significant investment in that most valuable commodity. Friendship is so little understood today that "friend" has been redefined as any person who shares information with us on social media. We have become a society of "click-on" friendships. People we do not even know and will never meet become our "friends."

Now, to be clear, this is not to say that, as believers, we are to refrain from "being friendly" to all. The Bible is clear that Christians are to do good to all people, especially our faith family (Gal. 6:10), but deep friendship is based on more than good manners and general politeness. Friendship is sacred in nature and is an expression of a covenant relationship. Nowhere in the Bible do we find a more powerful model of friendship than that between David and Jonathan.

We are told that their friendship was so deep that it was as if their souls were bonded together, a fusion of friendship (1 Sam. 18:1). What are some of the fundamental qualities of deep friendship modeled for us by David and Jonathan? First, in its essence, deep friendships are spiritual. David and Jonathan believed their relationship was a gift from God. They talked to each other about the Lord. They regularly had "covenant conversations." Second, David and Jonathan trusted each other. They assumed the other's good intentions. These were two amazingly gifted and competent individuals! However, they refused to view each other as competitors. Third, these two men valued their friendship and defended one another, even at the risk of "offending" other people and their selfish agendas. We can only imagine how many of David's companions who were enemies of Saul might have looked with a jaundiced gaze at his friendship with Saul's son. And it is apparent that Saul was a little more than "slightly disapproving" of his son's friendship with David! Fourth, true friends pledge themselves to seek the best interest of each other. Paul tells us that love does not seek its own interest but rather seeks what is best for others (1 Cor. 13:5). As has been said, a friend is "the one who comes running in when everyone else is running out." It was truly dangerous to be David's friend, but Jonathan was gladly willing to endure that risk.

One of my dad's favorite stories to tell about me as a child was the "lisping response" he heard me give to my brother, Lonnie, when I was trying to "borrow" some money from him. My dad would tell how he overheard my brother, in great frustration, respond to my request for a quarter, "Sam, you always blow your allowance; you never have any money!" My dad was amused and delighted by my response, "Yeah, but I gotta lot of fwends." Through the years, my dad would remind me of that story and say, "Son, never forget that you are never poor if you have a lot of 'fwends.'"

Friends are priceless, and it is never too late to invest in that precious commodity.

MARCH 27
1 Samuel 23-26

"Victorious Over Vengeance"

"May the Lord judge between me and you, may the Lord avenge me against you, but my hand shall not be against you."
(1 Samuel 24:12)

"**P**ower tends to corrupt, and absolute power corrupts absolutely. Great men are almost always bad men...." So wrote Lord Acton, the famous nineteenth century British historian, politician, and writer. Lord Acton was famous in his day, but now he is not as well-known as this one statement, which he made in a letter to leaders in the Anglican Church. Lord Acton's quote has been confirmed so many times in the lives of powerful people that it has almost reached the status of indisputable truth. Indeed, in this day of instant information and awareness of the abuse of power, Lord Acton's evaluation has never been more fully endorsed.

Blissfully, there can be, and have been, notable exceptions to Acton's rule. These are the testimonies of true greatness—men and women for whom the corrupting influence of power was overcome in their lives by the power of a greater influence. The expression of the rule contained in Lord Acton's quote and the *exception* to that rule are both personified in our Scripture reading today.

King Saul was corrupted by power to the point of the betrayal of his friends, the murder of godly men, the annihilation of peaceful communities, and the deadly pursuit of his greatest supporter, David. Saul pursued David relentlessly until he cornered him in the Valley of Engedi. There, David and his men were forced to hide in the caves the mountain goats called home. Having seen this rugged canyon, the caves, and the descendants of those mountain goats, I can attest that it is a perfect place for hiding and carrying out an ambush. David certainly could have prepared that attack for Saul, but he did not have to because Saul walked right into it. He walked right into the cave where David was hiding and placed himself in (how to politely say this?) a "very vulnerable position." The Lord delivered Saul into his hands. David had the opportunity to take vengeance, the supporting counsel from friends, the means to do it, and a boatload of reasons to do it. David only lacked two things keeping him from executing Saul—freedom in his spirit and permission from the Lord. And David did not have freedom in his spirit because he did not have permission from the Lord.

David was a godly man—a man after God's own heart (1 Sam. 13:14). Nothing was a greater power in his life than the power of God's Word and will. To take Saul's life would be taking the place and the prerogative that belonged only to the Lord. When it came to vengeance, David believed and embraced the truth that only Jehovah was Judge, Jury, and Executioner. David already had written in his heart the words the Lord would later have written in His Word, "Vengeance is mine, I will repay says the Lord" (Deut. 32:35).

As believers, we also live under this standard. In fact, grace has raised the standard even higher than the Law. It isn't enough to *not* take vengeance; our Master Jesus says we must be on the offensive, "Do not be overcome with evil, but overcome evil with good" (Rom. 12:21). We are not just to *endure* our enemies, but we must *embrace* them with kindness. "Impossible," some say! Not with the power of God, which is the power of love. Our God, in His great love, embraced His great enemies—us. With His love in our hearts, we can do the same.

MARCH 28
1 Samuel 27-30

"BEWARE OF STINKING THINKING!"

"Then David said in his heart, 'Now I shall perish one day by the hand of Saul. There is nothing better for me than that I should escape to the land of the Philistines.'"
(1 Samuel 27:1)

"Welcome to Gath." That was never a road sign David expected to see in front of him! And not in a million years did his family or friends imagine that David would bring them here!

"Gath," perhaps you recall the name. That's right, *that* Gath—the hometown of Goliath and his family of giants, the same Goliath David killed in battle and then beheaded. What in the world was David doing here with his family and friends? Had he lost his mind? Yes, in some ways, he had, for when our thinking processes are controlled by anything other than the truth of God, that is insanity.

We can understand that the relentless stress of fleeing from Saul and the fear for his family with him and his family back in Bethlehem had taken a toll on David. However, fear was no longer just a battle in David's mind; fear had *won* the battle for David's mind. Fear had caused David to forget *who* he was because, through fear, he had forgotten *Whose* he is.

No one could have had more assurances that he was the anointed one, the man destined to be king. Samuel had told him; Jonathan had told him; Abigail had told him; even Saul himself had told him! However, rather than remembering these faith promises, David took counsel with his fears, which is never wise counsel.

So, David "said in his heart," which means he talked to himself. When we start talking to ourselves, it is probably a foolish conversation! It certainly was for David at this moment, for he actually fooled himself. Foolishly, he left the land of Judah and moved himself and his family and friends to a place where no one would ever think to look for him. David was undoubtedly right about that! But he was wrong in every other dimension and certainly had not counted the cost of his "bright idea." As we read the passage today, we see "the high cost of low thinking" in David's life. Notice the price tag.

David compromised his *integrity*. He left the land of his inheritance and lived among the pagans. This lover of God lived among the haters of God. David compromised his *influence*. Rather than being a force for good, he was leading his family and his followers into an evil place. David compromised his *testimony*. The enemies of the Lord received him, but they did not trust him. He was not seen as a witness for the Lord but as a traitor. Then, David compromised his *joy*. If you carefully read the chronology, you will see that while David was 18 months a citizen of Gath, he wrote no psalms of praise. How could he sing songs of Zion in the city of the enemies of God? Only God's sovereign providence, using the doubts of the enemy, kept David from potentially involving himself in an attack on Judah. David's thinking was *wrong, wrong, wrong, wrong*.

But finally, he was rescued from this terrible detour by doing something *right*—something he should have done 18 months earlier. David finally did two things that ended this downward spiral and disastrous detour. First, amidst disaster, David went to his source of light and truth. "David strengthened himself in the Lord his God" (1 Sam. 30:6). David got a grip on himself by gripping, or rather, being gripped by the truth that God was for him and with him. Secondly, "David inquired of the Lord" (1 Sam. 30:8). Finally! After 18 months of working his own plan, David asked God for guidance. David went to God, and God was there.

Regardless of where you are today or how long you have been there, reject the "stinking thinking" that took you there. Do the wise thing—encourage yourself in the Lord and ask for His guidance right now. He has been there all the time.

MARCH 29
1 Samuel 31 - 2 Samuel 1

"How the Mighty Have Fallen"

Most people familiar with the Bible recognize that the book, chapter, and verse divisions, part of all translations over the past several hundred years, are not found in the original text. They were placed there to make the reading of Scripture and the location of passages much simpler. This is true of our Scripture passage today since the separation of the two books of Samuel did not occur until the late Middle Ages. These "two books" were actually a unified and continuous recording of the ministry of the last of the *Judges, Samuel,* and the account of the *Kings* of Israel beginning with Saul.

The text of what we know as 1 Samuel concludes with the death of King Saul and his son, Jonathan, and what we know as 2 Samuel begins with David being informed of the deaths of these two men he so dearly loved. The passing of Saul and Jonathan devastates David and leads him to compose his famous "Song of the Bow," which praises their lives and laments their deaths. His requiem's repeated phrase and theme is "How the Mighty Have Fallen!" In his lyrics, David also writes, "In life and death they were not divided" (2 Sam. 1:23). When we connect those two themes, we can see how wandering away from the Lord is never a solitary journey. Saul's journey was, in reality, Jonathan's journey. "No man is an island," famously wrote John Donne, and we see that tragically displayed in Saul's life. His spiritual downward spiral pulled his son and his nation down as well. Choices bring consequences, and morally wrong choices bring terrible collateral damage for others to experience.

First Samuel concludes with the gruesome image of King Saul's body fastened to the wall of Beth-shan, but the body of his son, Jonathan, is fastened there as well, and the bodies of thousands of his soldiers lie exposed to the elements in the Valley of Jezreel and on the slopes of Mount Gilboa. "How the Mighty Have Fallen!" and how many the mighty one, Saul, brought with him!

This passage is scary, and we need to be scared by it—scared straight. Saul could never have imagined the day he was anointed by Samuel or the day he was acclaimed as the king by the people that his last 24 hours on earth would see him involved in witchcraft, pierced by arrows of the Philistines, or fastened to the wall of Beth-shan. Never would Saul have wanted to be instrumental in the death of his son, the death of thousands of his fellow Israelites, or the defeat and near destruction of his nation. How did he get here? How did he lead people here? *One step at a time.*

Another king tells us that the path of the just is as the shining of the dawn that grows steadily brighter until the fullness of day (Prov. 4:18). Likewise, the path of a sinful person descends further and further into the abyss of darkness. Sadly, tragically, that person takes others with him. King Saul's life is a warning for all generations of the awful consequences of sinful choices:

> *Sin will take you farther than you want to go,*
> *Sin will keep you longer than you want to stay,*
> *Sin will cost you more than you want to pay.*

(Author unknown)

MARCH 30
2 Samuel 2-4

"GOD'S TIME AND GOD'S WAY"

A recurring theme constantly appears in the Psalms of David, which is about the importance of "waiting on the Lord." Many times, as David crafts his songs, he directs them to his own heart, challenging himself to "wait patiently on the Lord." For many of us, two words that don't easily unite in our minds are "wait" and "patently." Honestly, "waiting patiently" in our hyperactive culture can seem like an oxymoron. The problem is that we often fail to recognize the spiritual nature and opportunities for spiritual growth in waiting. Now, I'm not trying to spiritualize the frustration of sitting in a doctor's office or sitting in traffic. However, even those "tribulations" can help us see that "the need for speed" permeating our modern existence can be toxic to our spiritual health and our need for peace of mind. Peace and stress are mutually exclusive. Peace and waiting are not.

"Waiting" involves faith. "Waiting on the Lord" means we believe God is at work even when we don't currently see his active involvement in our lives. This is especially an expression of faith when we wait for God to do what we know he has promised. "Waiting in faith" means we don't "take things into our own hands" even when we know what we want to see accomplished is a good or right thing.

Consider David's faith-filled waiting in our Scripture reading today. David knows he is to be king of all Israel. He has known that since he was a teenager, and God's plan to make him king has been reaffirmed to him by many people in many situations through the ensuing years. Now, he has people surrounding him who are very willing to take matters into their own hands and make him king. David even has associates of the son of Saul, who are willing and plotting to make David king. However, David waits on the Lord. He knows by faith that he will be king of all Israel one day, but he is committed to seeing that happen in "God's timing and in God's ways." Accomplishing the plan of God by personally taking the life of Saul's son is something David will not do. A God-honoring outcome must only be achieved by a God-honoring process. Accomplishing the right thing the wrong way is still wrong. The ends do not automatically justify the means.

At the risk of dating myself, Larry Weiss' lyrics to the song "Rhinestone Cowboy" unmask what drives many driven people, "There'll be a load of compromisin' on the road to my horizon, but I'm gonna be where the lights are shinin' on me." The sense of achievement in reaching a good goal is not worth the price of a guilty conscience when you arrive. When we take matters into our own hands to accomplish our objectives, we ultimately rob ourselves. We may end up where the "lights are shinin' on us," but we look back on a dark path of "compromisin'" that got us there.

"Heavy sits the crown" on the head of the person who placed it there themselves. If he puts the crown on his head, someone else can remove it, so inside the crowned head is a mind without peace. Jesus is "the Prince of Peace" who brings peace. However, His gift of peace is only for those who have surrendered their agenda, objective, and timetable to Him. "Be still before the Lord and wait patiently for him" (Ps. 37:7).

MARCH 31
2 Samuel 5-7

"God's Worship, God's Way"

In the previous reading, we saw in David the virtue of waiting on the Lord and seeing His promises accomplished in His time and in His way.

In our Scripture passage today, we read how the Lord finally fulfilled the promise He had made to David years before establishing him as the king of Israel. In God's timing and God's ways, David had seen the Lord bring him from shepherding the few sheep of his father, Jesse, to being the shepherd of the millions of people in God's flock of Israel. His conscience is clear from the blood guilt of personal vengeance as he finally ascends to the throne of all Israel. Now, his plan is to unite the nation with a new national capital.

Since childhood, David often lifted his eyes from his father's flocks outside of Bethlehem and looked upon the Jebusite fortress of Jerusalem. Secure and defiant, it had stood since the days of the tribes' entrance into the Promised Land. In one of his first acts as king, David conquered that fortress as a place for his palace and the site for the house of the Lord, which He desired to build there. All of these plans were plans of faith that he sincerely desired, in God's timing, to see accomplished. Quickly, the mocking enemy was routed from Jerusalem, and David established his home on a large rock out-cropping that became known as "the city of David."

Next, David excitedly made plans for the sacred Ark of the Covenant to be brought from the home of Abinadab to Israel's new capital city. Not a more joy-filled and united day of praise to God had ever taken place than the one dedicated to bringing the Ark, the most sacred treasure of all Israel, to its new resting place and permanent home in Jerusalem. So, we can imagine the stunned shock that spread through the joyous parade of worshipers when Uzzah tried to stabilize the rocking Ark by touching it and fell dead. David and the throng were filled with fear, and David was also filled with anger that his worship festival had been ruined. The key phrase is "his worship festival."

Remember, the right thing done the wrong way is still wrong. The worship processional was inherently wrong because it did not align with God's will and God's Word. The Ark was not to be pulled on a cart, which is how the Philistines transported it decades before. It was to be carried by the priests, the sons of Aaron, and it was to be transported by the poles the Lord had prescribed. No one else was to carry it, and no one else was to touch it. God would not be lightly esteemed or trifled with as an object to be carted about, and He would not tolerate "Philistine methods" replacing His divinely ordered practices for worshiping Him.

When David and the leaders realized and repented of their wrong, self-focused, and flippant approach to worship, they could worship the Lord "in spirit and in truth" (John 4:23). Then, with a clear and informed conscience, they could worship with joy before the Lord. Sadly, people with no appreciation for the mercy and majesty of God, like David's wife Michal, will condemn expressions of exuberance in worship. To see someone "dance before the Lord" (yes, "dance") will seem for them undignified and unbecoming. Indeed, not every devout and devoted believer dances in worship, and quite frankly, some should never try. However, if in the presence of your Savior-King and Redeemer, you are not at all times dancing on the inside, it might be time to check to see if the dial of your soul is really in tune with the music of His majesty.

APRIL

"For it is time to seek the Lord, that he may come
and rain righteousness upon you."
(Hosea 10:12)

APRIL 1
2 Samuel 8-10

"Covenant Kindness"

When the soldiers arrived from King David, no doubt Mephibosheth believed it was a death escort. He had been summoned from his hideout home in Lo-Debar. Mephibosheth was the only surviving member of King Saul's family. His grandfather, Saul, had been a maniacal and relentless foe for his descendants.

Mephibosheth's uncle, Ishbosheth, had refused to recognize David as the Lord's chosen king. He had ruled over the northern tribes, and his generals had plotted to destroy David. That is until they were persuaded to switch their allegiance to David. Then, two leaders of the raiding parties of Ishbosheth came into his royal chamber while he napped and murdered their master. Everyone connected with the family of Saul was dead except Mephibosheth. Year after year, he lived in Lo-Debar, which means "a place of no pasture," praying and hoping that his existence in this desolate place would not become known to King David. Mephibosheth could not even run away because he had been crippled at the age of five. His nurse was carrying him as she fled from the Philistines who had killed his father, Jonathan. She fell and landed on his legs, crushing them.

For years, Mephibosheth lived in the wilderness, believing King David wanted him dead, unable to flee, existing in continual fear and hatred of the king. Mephibosheth had no way of knowing that he was believing a lie. King David was not his worst enemy—just the opposite; David was his greatest friend. How was that possible? It was possible because of a blood covenant of undying love and devotion. Years before, Jonathan, Mephibosheth's father, and David pledged themselves to each other and each other's family as long as they lived. As a sign and seal of the covenant, they cut their wrists, shared their blood, exchanged clothes, and took a vow before God Almighty. Can you imagine the dumb-founded amazement of Mephibosheth as David pledged to him his safety in the palace, invited him to be part of his household, and take an honored place at the king's table?

I once heard a pastor describe the response of Mephibosheth as he sat for breakfast the first morning at the table of King David in this folksy fashion: "Well, I sure don't understand this, but I sure can't deny it. Would you pass the biscuits, please?" Perfect.

So amazing as the story is, it is only an example of the far greater transformation that has taken place in the life of every believer. We were born into a family, the human race, that is an enemy to the King, rejecting His rightful rule. We, too, were crippled by a fall. We lived in a wilderness, hiding from and hating the King for years. Then, one day, we received the summons that brought us into the King's family. We wear His garments of righteousness and sit in fellowship with Him at His table. What a wonder! We cannot understand it, but we cannot deny it, so we might as well enjoy it. Let's share the biscuits!

APRIL 2
2 Samuel 11-13

"A Vacation from God"

"But David remained at Jerusalem."
(2 Samuel 11:1)

As I write these words, I have just finished reading a chapter of a book dedicated to renewing the call and importance of sabbath in our lives. And yes, I am feeling very convicted. Sabbath is more than just a day the Lord designated in the Creation week. Sabbath is a principle that guides us toward having a sacred rhythm in our lives rather than a secular agenda. In reality, sabbath is a gift from the Lord in making space for enjoying physical, emotional, and spiritual seasons of rest in the goodness of God. It is a preface to the eternal sabbath that we will enjoy with Him and in Him forever.

Sabbath is much more than a vacation. While the root word for sabbath has the idea of "rest," the origin of the term "vacation" involves the concept of being free or exempt, a time for leisure. It is inaccurate to think of sabbath as good while vacation is evil. A vacation that provides a rhythm for sabbath is undoubtedly a wonderful thing for an individual or a family. However, when we think of vacation as a season of "exemption from responsibility," that can be extremely treacherous.

It is especially dangerous when taking a vacation involves getting free for a season from "God-ordained responsibilities."

Our reading today indicates that kind of "vacation" in David's life. It is instructive that the Bible begins this whole tragic season in his life by saying, "In the spring of the year, the time when kings go out to battle.... But David remained at Jerusalem" (2 Sam. 11:1). The inference is clear that David was not where he should be as king. He was "taking a vacation" from his responsibilities to the Lord, and tragically what occurred on his "spring break" would change the whole course of his life, his reign, and his family terribly.

A lazy attitude toward the serious things of life is when Satan works overtime. He made sure that David saw what he should not see at the very weakest moment for David to see it. The "it" was Bathsheba, and that is how David saw her—not as a woman with an identity, as one of the Lord's people, not as the daughter of Eliam, and not as the wife of his faithful soldier, Uriah. David viewed Bathsheba as an object to satisfy his lazy, lustful desires. While on his spiritual and moral vacation, David forgot his identity. He experienced temporary amnesia about who he was and whose he was. That type of "vacation" is, in reality, a "journey into a far country"—a place to which it is very easy to travel but very difficult to return. Worse yet, David did not just take this vacation as "personal days." David took his family, his companions, his nation, and his testimony with him. To be blunt, it was a "vacation from hell" from which David and his people would never fully recover. A vacation *from* God follows the road signs marked "Lust," "Sin," "Death," —L.S.D.—and that is always a bad trip!

APRIL 3
2 Samuel 14-16

"TRUST DURING THE TRIAL"

Through the advances in technology over the past several years, we have the ability to be present in real time at some of the most momentous nationwide and even worldwide events. This technology has brought us directly into courtrooms, where cases that capture the highest levels of public interest are presented to the judges and juries involved. We can now witness live that "hold-your-breath" moment as the spokesperson for the jury announces the verdict that determines the defendant's future and also has a significant impact on society. There is not quite another moment like it, as the decision of a few men and women will often be a matter of life and death for one person and the joy or sadness of millions of others. It all hangs on the decision of the judge and jury.

Our reading today takes us to a season in David's life, and that of the entire nation of Israel as the grip of ever-growing tension tightens toward a verdict of unparalleled significance. Rebellion, treason, and impending civil war have taken hold of the country as Absalom, supported by some of David's most "loyal" associates, invades Judah and converges on Judah. "How will King David respond?" is the question on everyone's mind. "What will he do?" The answer to that question, and I believe even more instructive for us to consider, is what David determined *not to do*. He would not presume to take the actions which rightly belonged only to God. We see this character quality of David displayed in a couple of scenes during the early moments of the rebellion.

First, David refused to bring the Ark of the Covenant with him as if it were his personal possession or the guarantor of his safety and success. The human king was leaving Jerusalem but not the Divine King. Though Israel was in a crisis, the God of Israel was very much in control, and David believed the Lord would decide *if* and *when* he would return to Jerusalem. David knew he did not have to carry the Ark before him for the God of the Ark of the Covenant to go before him. The God of Israel was the Lord in every direction and every location.

Secondly, we see David's refusal to act in the place of the Lord concerning his personal enemies. As David crested the top of the Mount of Olives, dirt, stones, and curses showered down upon him, compliments of Shimei, a relative of King Saul. With the movement of a finger, David could have had the head of this road-rage attacker removed from his shoulders. However, as David would not presume to take God's vengeance on Saul, he would not do so on his rampaging relative. David had the authority, the opportunity, and the affirmation of his friends to take vengeance, but he did not have the Judge's verdict and decision. David knew he was not the judge, so he did not carry out or call down judgment.

Whatever place or position we may occupy in this life, the seat of the Judge is always filled. Let's trust the Judge and His judgment "Do not judge, or you too will be judged" (Matt. 7:1).

APRIL 4
2 Samuel 17-19

"The Counsel of the Lord"

"No wisdom, no understanding, no counsel can avail against the Lord."
(Proverbs 21:30)

I recall chuckling out loud once in a worship service when I heard the pastor make the following statement: "Sin is not just wrong. Sin makes you stupid." Several people looked at me disapprovingly (and I do not blame them), but they failed to realize that my chuckling outburst was not to mock the pastor's words but rather to affirm the truth and brilliance of his short statement, "Sin makes you stupid." Our actions and attitudes have consequences, not just in the lives of others but also in our own. Virtue brings its own reward, and so also does vice. The "children of light" are those who walk in the light of God's truth and will. The "children of darkness" are those who walk in disobedience to God's truth and will, and therein lies darkness, death, and destruction.

In the Book of Romans, Paul declares that those who reject the light of the knowledge of God will soon experience a darkened conscience that can no longer recognize and receive the most simple and fundamental truths. They tragically become spiritually stupid (Rom. 1:18-21).

This spiritual stupidity is a sovereign judgment of God on sinners and also a self-inflicted judgment by the sinners on themselves. To judge sin, the Lord allows, at times, the sinful attitudes and actions of people rebelling against Him to produce their own consequences. Theologians refer to this as the passive judgment of God, and it is on full display in the thinking of Absalom through our Scripture reading today.

This beautiful, brilliant man who carried out one of the most conniving coups of history suddenly goes stupid. He has David on the run from Jerusalem with his army dispersed and disorganized, the perfect opportunity for a military coup de grace. And Absalom decides to wait because he rejects the wise counsel of the gifted Ahithophel and follows the recommendation of Hushai, who is secretly an agent in King David's service. How could Absalom possibly accept such terrible advice? "For the Lord had ordained to defeat the good counsel of Ahithophel, so that the Lord might bring harm upon Absalom" (2 Sam. 17:14). God was beginning the process of judgment upon Absalom by causing him to experience the darkness and the stupidity of his own rebellious thinking. Absalom had sinfully followed his dark thinking, and now the darkness flowed back into his thoughts.

Our God is sovereign over sin and sinners. Our sovereign God can even cause men's wrath to praise Him (Ps. 76:10). The most hideous crime ever committed, the murder of His beloved Son, has been used by God to bring the ultimate glory to Himself and the eternal blessing to Adam's fallen race. Wicked men, in their determined hatred of Jesus, only accomplished the predetermined plan of Almighty God (Acts 2:23, 4:28).

The only time we are told in the Bible that God laughs is His scoffing laughter at wicked people who believe they will "break the chains" of submissive bondage to His Anointed One. "He who sits in the heavens laughs; the Lord holds them in derision" (Ps. 2:4). So, go ahead, read the newspapers, watch the broadcasts, listen to the podcasts of people who declare their freedom and demand their rights to do whatever they choose to do. And then, join in a good laugh with your Heavenly Father.

APRIL 5
2 Samuel 20-22

"The Song of Deliverance"

"In my distress I called upon the Lord; to my God I called. From his temple he heard my voice, and my cry came to his ears."
(2 Samuel 22:7)

The very first images from the Hubble space telescope started arriving at NASA on May 20, 1990. If you want a jaw-dropping experience, I encourage you to log on from a computer that has a large screen and view the images that Hubble is relaying to the earth of the universe that surrounds our tiny planet. There are no words. Even the most skeptical astronomers were unprepared for the beauty and vastness of creation that Hubble captured through its lens.

Though the telescope has captured images of only the tiniest portion of space, it has revealed a galactic choreography of swirling galaxies that span distances beyond human comprehension. The speed of light is calculated at 182,282 miles per second, and even at that mind-boggling speed, the nearest star to our sun is 4.3 light-years away! The distances spanning the galaxies already viewed and the number of stars revealed in those galaxies are innumerable by any meaningful calculations we possess. And yet, the Word tells us our God numbers them all and calls each one by name (Ps. 147:4). Who can comprehend such a God who created the heavens by the Word of His command? (Ps. 33:6)

Yet, greater than the infinite might of our God is the depth of His intimate care. Our Heavenly Father, who by His Word, created a universe so immense our finite minds cannot conceive it. Yet He is so close and so personal that He hears the prayers of our hearts never articulated by our lips. When we call Him, He hears because He is not the God watching us *at a distance*. He is the God who is *here* caring for us. He is an ever-present help in trouble (Ps. 46:1).

Our weakness and our trouble are not obstacles to our Master. Our times of struggle are the very things that attract Him and call Him into action. In these trials, we most deeply and profoundly experience our Father's pity and provision. They testify to our God's greatness. We need to see our times of challenge as another opportunity to *know* God's love so we can *show* and then *share* his love. God's great love expressed in our lives becomes our life's story, or perhaps to follow David's example—our life's song. Moses had a song, Deborah had a song, Hannah had a song, Samuel had a song, David had a song, and you and I have a song. We may not have an attractive voice, but we do have a beautiful song—"The Song of Deliverance."

APRIL 6
2 Samuel 23-24

"Mercy on Mount Moriah"

It is a moment that lasts for a lifetime, and how I wish every believer could experience it! I'm referring to the sensation of cresting the ridge of the Mount of Olives and seeing, for the first time, the breathtaking vista of the City of Jerusalem spreading out before you. In many ways, Jerusalem is not an attractive city and pales in comparison to the timeless beauty of cities such as Athens or Rome. However, for a believer in the God of Abraham and His Son Jesus Christ, no place on earth and moment in time can compare to the view before you.
Immediately, your eyes are drawn to the city's southeast corner and the ancient cream-colored walls adorned by a sizable blue-tiled structure with a glittering gold dome. It is the Al-Aqsa Mosque, or as it is more commonly referred to, the Dome of the Rock.

The mosque sits within a vast enclosure on the Temple Mount, the site of the temple constructed by King Herod and the same location as the temple built by King Solomon one thousand years earlier. The Al-Aqsa Mosque is beautiful, but it celebrates the myth from the eighth century AD of the prophet Muhammed's nighttime ride on a winged creature from Mecca in Saudi Arabia to Jerusalem. However, for believers in the God of Abraham, Isaac, and Jacob, the site of the Temple is connected to two events that took place on that ancient ridge of Mount Moriah and that prefigured the salvation provided by the Lord for all mankind.

It was on the ridge of Mount Moriah that Abraham, in obedience to Jehovah, prepared to offer his son Isaac as a burnt offering. In the impending death of Isaac, the Lord intervened by providing a ram as a substitute. One thousand years later, judgment was once again about to take place on that site as, in punishment for David's sin, an angel from God was poised to strike the city of Jerusalem with a plague. The angel hovered over the threshing floor of Araunah, located on Mount Moriah. Upon seeing him in broken-hearted repentance, King David cried out to God for mercy. In response, the Lord stayed the angel's hand and spared the city (2 Sam. 24:15-25). It was this site of the threshing floor that David purchased from Araunah, on which he built an altar to offer burnt offerings and peace offerings to God (2 Sam. 24:25). And it was on this same spot so identified with the Lord's mercy for sinners, that several years later, David's son Solomon built the beautiful temple, the dwelling place of God with His people.

Then, another thousand years later, further down the ridge of Moriah, God, in His infinite mercy, carried out the work of eternal redemption. On a craggy knoll, our Savior offered Himself to God as a sacrifice for sin and a substitute for sinners. The Lamb of God was offered on the altar of the cross, and the judgment for sin (our sin and our judgment) was paid in full. My friend, whether you ever gaze upon the City of Jerusalem on earth, you can be absolutely certain to look one day upon the heavenly Jerusalem and the resurrected King who lives there. You are lovingly, personally invited to live there with Him forever!

> *"If you confess with your mouth that Jesus is Lord and believe in your heart that God raised him from the dead, you will be saved."*
> (Romans 10:9)

APRIL 7
1 Kings 1-3

"The Gift that Keeps on Giving"

> *"Give your servant therefore an understanding mind to govern your people, that I may discern between good and evil, for who is able to govern this your great people?"*
> (1 Kings 3:9)

"The gift that keeps on giving" is a phrase that has been employed for many years to inspire generosity and stimulate spending. It certainly is an excellent turn of phrase that has been used in the past and present, and no doubt will continue to be used in the future as a motivation for charitable purposes. Generosity truly is a "gift that keeps on giving." However, that phrase has also been employed for a little less than altruistic purposes. "The gift that keeps on giving" seems to have no expiration date as a marketing motto, convincing consumers that an endless variety of things are those they cannot deny themselves—radios, appliances, electronics, cameras, chocolates, etc. In fact, a Google search brings up thousands of results in response to the query "the gift that keeps on giving."

The fact that this phrase has become so pervasive in our culture begs some questions to be asked and answered. For example, what is "the gift" and exactly "who is this gift for?" It's not surprising that King Solomon is the one who knew those answers and possessed the wisdom to ask for that gift to be given to him. His wisdom was to ask for the *gift of wisdom*. Think about this gift of wisdom that Solomon treasured and desired above all gifts. *Wisdom is a heavenly gift.* Wisdom comes from

God, who is the all-wise God. Wisdom is not something we can "work up"—it must be called down from the Source of wisdom in prayer.

Wisdom is an invaluable gift. But what exactly is wisdom? Perhaps the simplest definition would be this: "Wisdom is the application of divine truth to earthly life." Wisdom is more than education alone. Wisdom involves using truth to discern what is right, wrong, or best. Priceless. Wisdom is a beneficial gift. News flash—life is confusing at times! With all the conflicting voices giving an unending flow of advice and guidance, having a companion who shares with you the direction of "true north" is invaluable. The Bible says the person who walks with the wise will be wise, but a companion of fools will be brought to ruin (Prov. 13:20). Foolishness, in the Biblical sense, does not simply mean childish or silly. Foolishness describes life decisions and direction that are in opposition to the will and ways of God. One translation of foolishness renders it as "moral perverseness." A friend who will guide us away from the path of deception and destruction by sharing wisdom with us is truly a gift from the Lord we should treasure.

Finally, and perhaps most wonderful—*wisdom is an available gift.* Our God is generous, and He graciously shares His gifts with all who will humbly receive them. This is true of the gift of wisdom. "If any of you lacks wisdom, let him ask God, who gives generously to all without reproach, and it will be given him" (Jas 1:5).

God was pleased when Solomon prayed for wisdom, and He answered that genuine request with a wisdom unmatched in human history. God's promise to us is unchanged. He offers wisdom to those who ask. So, pray a wise prayer right now. Pray for wisdom.

APRIL 8
1 Kings 4-6

"The Measure of God's Blessing"

"The blessing of the Lord makes rich, and he adds no sorrow with it."
(Proverbs 10:22)

"**H**ave a blessed day!" I regularly hear people working in various businesses in our community make that parting statement as other customers, or I am finishing a transaction. For me, when someone makes that statement, "Have a blessed day!"—they have already fulfilled their wish because their words of blessing have just blessed me!

There are many places in our country and around the world where you would never hear those words shared with any customer. It is a real encouragement to receive and share a statement of blessing. Perhaps though, it would be good for us to be clear about what we mean or should mean when we bless people. What does it really mean to be "blessed"? If we are not careful, it can become just a pleasant expression but void of any more thought than a three-word response when someone sneezes, "God bless you!"

Most people would undoubtedly define the life of Solomon described in our Scripture reading today as a blessed life. When it came to wealth, wisdom, power, or prestige, Solomon was certainly "blessed" according to almost any definition. However, what really made Solomon and his people blessed was the *gracious favor of God*. Ultimately, that is the essence of being blessed, and without it, there is no blessing. To be blessed is to know by experiencing the gracious favor of God.

I think there is a statement generally overlooked in our reading that measures the blessing of God far beyond the dimensions of Solomon's reign and riches. "In the four hundred and eightieth year after the people of Israel came out of the land of Egypt..." (1 Kings 6:1). Four hundred eighty years earlier from the date Solomon began construction of the temple, the Israelites had been enslaved. Stretching before that were over 400 years of the harshest existence living in bondage in Egypt. One hundred or so years before that, the entire "nation" existed of 75 people, the family of Jacob, who came to live with Joseph, now a prince in Egypt. Almost 1000 years have passed, and that band of refugees, then a nation of slaves, then emancipated immigrants, are now in 964 BC, the most powerful and prosperous nation in the entire Middle East. They were blessed indeed! The nation was blessed because of the favor of God. It was not deserved or earned; it was all of grace. True blessing always is.

So, an incredibly important question for us to consider today is this, "How do we measure blessing, and do we see ourselves as blessed?" An old gospel song says, "Count your blessings, name them one by one." That is a great and helpful thought, but ultimately no amount of blessings will make us *feel* blessed if we don't *know* in our souls that we *are* blessed. The knowledge of blessing is eventually calculated by the wonder of knowing "the Blesser." Truly, the blessing of God Himself and not His gifts should be the focus of our lives as a "blessed people."

Let me encourage you to read these words of 1 Peter 1:3 aloud and make them your invocation of worship today:

> *"Blessed be the God and Father of our Lord Jesus Christ! According to his great mercy, he has caused us to be born again to a living hope through the resurrection of Jesus Christ from the dead."*
> (1 Peter 1:3)

APRIL 9
1 Kings 7-9

"Consecrating the Temple"

In all the long history of the people of Israel, there had never been a day as full of meaning as that described in 1 Kings, Chapter 8. Over 1,200 years had passed since Abram, the father of the nation, had arrived childless with his wife, Sarai, into the land of the Canaanites. Now his descendants, numbering like the stars in the heavens or the sand on the seashore, gathered to consecrate a dwelling place, a temple for the God who had called Abram out of the pagan region of Babylon and promised him and his descendants the land stretching from the River of Egypt to the great Euphrates. On the ridge where Abraham had shown himself willing to offer up his beloved son and heir, Isaac, Solomon had constructed an altar and temple to Jehovah-Jireh. The sacred Ark of the Covenant, the mercy seat and throne of God, was brought up from the City of David to Mount Zion as sacrifices beyond number were offered. The songs of the priests and Levites filled the air, and the responding praise of untold thousands of Israelites echoed off the slopes of the surrounding hills.

As indescribable as this scene was, we cannot begin to conceive of what was unseen, as angelic beings beyond number in the heavenlies offered their praise and worship to the God of the Ages. God Himself was dwelling in the cloud of glory among His people. Since the Garden of Eden, there had never been anything to compare to it. God in His temple, dwelling with His people, and His people with Him.

Has there ever been anything on earth to even approach this? Oh yes, indeed. Not just equaling the miracle and majesty of the scene described, but in reality, far surpassing it. What could exceed the wonder of God in His temple with His people and His people with Him? The truth and reality of the gospel. God's people *are* His temple, and He does not just dwell *with* them but *in* them. That's right. God dwells on earth in His people. His people *are* the temple. This is amazingly true, *collectively* and *individually*. This miracle did not occur upon Mount Zion but in an upper room because of what was accomplished on Mount Calvary. In answer to Jesus' dying prayer, the God of the temple tore the curtain in two (Matt. 27:51). Then, 50 days later, in answer to another prayer from His Son, the God of the temple in heaven sent the Holy Spirit to fill and indwell his people individually and collectively (Acts 2:1-4, 1 Cor. 3:16, 6:19).

As God's people through faith, we are His temple; each of us is a living stone brought by redeeming grace to create a house for God's Spirit (1 Pet. 2:5). What a mystery! What a privilege! What a responsibility! I ask myself, and I ask you to consider with me today, what it would mean if we thought of "church" in this way or our "bodies" in this way. I offer a prayer of repentance from my heart as I ponder that thought even as I write these words today. But let us not only be humbled by this truth but also motivated by this truth. We are the temple of God, collectively and individually. May we, by God's grace, determine then to be a holy temple.

APRIL 10
1 Kings 10-12

"THE WISEST FOOL"

"For when Solomon was old, his wives turned away his heart after other gods, and his heart was not wholly true to the Lord his God, as was the heart of David his father."
(1 Kings 11:4)

"There is no fool like an old fool," says an ancient epigram. The reason for this biting evaluation is that the words "old" and "fool" should not normally be conceived as belonging together. "The foolishness of youth" is certainly foolish, but how much more foolish is the abandoning of common sense, common decency, and common grace by people advanced in years? Even more foolish is that of the wisest of men who warned his young son and the youth of the ages with these words, "Keep your heart with all vigilance, for from it flow the springs of life" (Prov. 4:23). What deceptive power had overwhelmed the guard of Solomon's heart and poisoned the springs of his life—a greater passion, a greater love than the love for God. The sad commentary is written by the Holy Spirit in 1 Kings 11:1-2, "Now King Solomon loved many foreign women...from the nations concerning which the Lord had said to the people of Israel, 'You shall not enter into marriage with them...'"

Solomon loved the Lord; no doubt about it. His extraordinary prayer of praise and adoration recorded earlier in 1 Kings was completely sincere and the expression of his heart. Never in a million years could he who labored in love for years to build a temple to his God have ever imagined he would build places of worship to false gods and personally offer sacrifices to those idols. But having untethered himself from the anchor of obedience to God's Word and listening to the seductive siren voices of pagan princesses, the wisest of Kings drifted in blissful, blended lust toward cataclysmic disaster. Sadly, Solomon did not just ruin his own life. The poisoned springs from his heart flowed into the minds and morals of his family and nation. In many ways,

Israel and Judah's awful legacy of disobedience and destruction over the next 400 years finds its source in the poisoned springs of King Solomon's heart.

What is the timeless warning for us to receive from the example of "the wisest fool"? It is a warning regarding idolatry. Most of us have not constructed secret shrines to idols in our homes. However, idolatry does not begin in a place but in a replaced preeminence within our affections. We permit a rival to exist in our hearts and compete against our first love, the Lord our God. What is an idol? Any person, place, or thing that distracts from our devotion to the Lord our God. Sometimes the reflection of the idol can be seen in the mirror. If we do not see self-denial as an essential part of our worship, then the poison of idolatry is already polluting the springs of our hearts. Beware of the greatest form of deception—self-deception.

Listen to the loving admonition of a wise, old man: "Little children, keep yourselves from idols" (1 John 5:21).

APRIL 11
1 Kings 13-15

"Rags to Riches"

Not long ago, I read an article that described how a famous NBA basketball player recently filed for bankruptcy. At first, I thought I must have misread or misunderstood the article because I could not comprehend how a man whose annual contract reached millions of dollars only a few years ago could be financially bankrupt. However, as the article shared in detail some examples of this player's extravagant lifestyle, it all began to make sense. Well, his decisions made no sense at all. Still, it was possible to do the math and recognize that any amount of money is a finite sum, and it can be wasted by the infinite capacity of selfishness and greed.

Our Scripture reading today tells us the story of the most incredible waste of inheritance the world has ever known. No child in history has received the inheritance bequeathed from Solomon to his son and successor, Rehoboam. There are no human calculations of wealth that can measure the riches of Solomon. According to 1 Kings 10:14, the amount of gold that came to him each year was 666 talents. How much is that? Wait for it.... 50,000 pounds of gold each year! If you multiply that amount by the current value of gold per ounce, you may break your calculator. Unimaginable riches! Yet, in the space of 41 years, Rehoboam had bankrupted the nation's treasuries. A good portion of that wealth was carried off to Egypt by King Shishak after he invaded and defeated the kingdom of Judah (1 Kings 14:25-26). Think of that. The wealth of the nation set free from slavery flows back to the country that once enslaved them!

The warning of a wasted inheritance is the lesson for us from Rehoboam. As incredible as the inheritance that Rehoboam received as the heir of Solomon truly was, it pales in comparison to the riches possessed by each of us as children of the King of Heaven. We are heirs of God and joint-heirs with Jesus Christ (Rom. 8:17). What we will inherit one day as we share in the everlasting Kingdom, no mind can comprehend, and no tongue can tell. That inheritance will never be wasted because the desire or temptation to do so will not exist. Thank God for that! However, what can be wasted is the present portion of our inheritance that is *already ours*— this life we have in Christ. If all the world and its treasures are not to be compared to the value of one soul, then what is the value of a life and lifetime redeemed by Jesus? Likewise, what could be a greater wasted inheritance than wasting our days and years focusing on things that won't matter ten seconds after our final breath?

No doubt many of us at this moment recognize that we have wasted far too much of our priceless treasure of time on things void of eternal value. However, we must not succumb to despair, for we can "redeem the time" that remains to us and make it count for eternity (Eph. 5:16).

I once heard a minister say, "Never forget, God can do more in a moment than you can do in a lifetime." What a wonderful truth! Likewise, God can do more in the moments that remain to us than we could have ever imagined seeing accomplished in our entire lifetime. The treasure of our life is in the days of our life. Let's not waste this one.

APRIL 12
1 Kings 16-18

"The God of Elijah"

It was such a fantastic experience that sometimes I wonder if I imagined it. However, my wife and a few other people were present and they can attest that it really did happen.

Several years ago, I hosted a tour group to the Holy Land, and the first day of our itinerary brought us to Mount Carmel. I recall it being a rather rainy day in the early spring, and I was feeling a little disappointed that our group could not have a better view of the Mediterranean Sea to the west and the beautiful Valley of Jezreel to the east. As a few of us lingered on the top of the ridge, I expressed what it must have been like to be present at this exact spot the day Elijah called upon Jehovah to bring fire down upon the altar he had built and the sacrifice he had prepared.

No sooner had those words left my mouth than a bolt of lightning descended from the clouds above, striking a location a few miles away. Our small group just stood there for a moment, looking at each other as if to say, "Did that really just happen?" I can assure you we did not stand there long. We immediately scurried down that hill and away from the gathering clouds! Trust me. I will *never* forget that experience!

It would also be impossible for anyone to gather that fateful day as the prophet Elijah challenged and mocked the priests of Baal and then called for God to send fire from heaven. I'm certain no one ever forgot the lightning that consumed the sacrifice and dried up all the water in the trench. What did this event cause the pagans to declare? "Elijah!" They declared the exact meaning of Elijah's name—"The Lord, He is God."

The question we should consider today, and look about us to see answered is this, "Where is the God of Elijah?" Where do we see that the Lord is God? We see the answer in the amazing displays of the presence as those people (or well as our small group did) on the top of Mount Carmel. But we should also see them in other, not so graphic, but just as genuine, revelations in our lives—in the provision of a home for shelter, enough food for another day, the healing from sickness, and answers to our prayers. (Read again 17:8-24.) We see that the Lord is God, "Elijah," in the clear direction from God, in the protection from enemies, and in people who join us in sharing God's message. (Read again 18:1-19.)

Several years ago, in our church services, we enjoyed singing the praise song, "Days of Elijah." You can search the web for the music, and you will find lyrics reminding us that in times of spiritual apathy and opposition, God is yet doing works of revival, life-giving testimony, renewal of praise, strengthening of His people, and declaring His Word. We live in God's sovereign providence on a dark, cloudy day of spiritual apostasy, but the Lord always has His remnant people who, in the power of His Spirit, reveal, "The Lord, He is God!"

Behold, He Comes! Riding on the clouds,
Shining like the sun, at the trumpet call.
Lift your voice, it's the year of Jubilee,
And out of Zion's hill salvation comes.

(From the song, "The Days of Elijah" by Robin Mark.)

APRIL 13
1 Kings 19-20

"What Are You Doing Here, Elijah?"

"There he came to a cave and lodged in it. And behold, the word of the Lord came to him, and he said to him, 'What are you doing here, Elijah?'"
(1 Kings 19:9)

"It's my party and I'll cry if I want to" are the words to a party song of the 1960s, but they also describe the party spirit that has existed for thousands of years—a pity party. That is precisely the kind of party that Elijah was holding by himself on Mount Horeb, that is, until God crashed it. This was a different kind of party, and a different kind of "whine" was flowing. When the Lord asked, "What are you doing here, Elijah?" a torrent of repressed emotions came rushing out from the deep crevices of his soul.

"I have been very jealous for the Lord, the God of hosts. For the people of Israel have forsaken your covenant, thrown down your altars, and killed your prophets with the sword, and I, even I only, am left, and they seek my life, to take it away" (1 Kings 19:10).

Wow, is Elijah ever in a bad place mentally and emotionally! Today, a diagnosis would probably be rendered that Elijah is clinically depressed. There is nothing wrong in using that type of terminology, as long as we think that the answer to clinical depression is not to be ultimately found in any physician apart from the Great Physician. His treatment of Elijah's depression had begun before he checked himself into the Mount Horeb hospital. How does Elijah's depression present itself?

First, he had just come through one of the most emotionally taxing moments of his life—the confrontation with the priests of Baal on Mount Carmel. Valleys of depression often come when a person is emotionally drained, often after a "spiritual high." Someone once asked a pastor, "Do you take Mondays as your day off?" The minister quickly responded, "Absolutely not! I will not take as my day off a day when I am that depressed!" (Any pastor reading this understands.) Elijah was emotionally and physically drained. The prophet had just annihilated hundreds of priests of Baal and then ran in abject fear from the threats of one woman, Jezebel.

What was the first prescription the Great Physician gave to his panicking preacher? First, he gave him a nap, a meal, a nap, and then another meal. Sometimes, the most spiritual things we can do are sleep and eat. Some say, "Well, the Devil doesn't take any time off!" In answer to that, we need to remember the Devil is not our example! And also, the Devil does not have a physical body that needs sufficient rest and fuel. Caring for our bodies is directly connected with caring for our souls. Secondly, the Great Physician made an appointment with his patient at a holy place. God met with Moses, the law-giver on Mount Horeb, and He also made an office appointment there with his great prophet. Our first need is not to "go for God" but to first "be with God." In fresh personal encounters with God, we are refreshed for public ministry.

Thirdly, God reminded Elijah that it was not the incredible displays of nature that brought His living presence but His spoken Word (1 Kings 19:11-13). Fourthly, the Lord gave Elijah an advocate, Hazael, and an associate, Elisha. Aloneness is always, as God said at the first, "not good." We are not to be isolated, solo saints. We need relationships. Fifthly, the Lord let Elijah know he was not "the only one." Seven thousand others were on the Lord's team. The Great Physician is an excellent Psychologist who specializes in depression. Make an appointment today. His calendar is never too full.

APRIL 14
1 Kings 21-22

"God's Ambassador"

"But Micaiah said, 'As the Lord lives, what the Lord says to me, that I will speak.'"
(1 Kings 22:14)

Elijah said he was the only prophet of the Lord left in the land. God corrected Elijah's self-focused and depressed math by letting him know that there were yet seven thousand faithful God-followers who had not bowed their knee to Baal. If Micaiah is characteristic of the Lord's team, what a courageous group it was!

We know practically nothing about Micaiah beyond what we learn about him in this brief account. However, these few verses speak volumes about his character and are a living epistle for the ages of what it means to be an "ambassador for God."

First of all, representing the Lord faithfully is not usually politically correct. Like untold thousands of God's faithful witnesses today, Micaiah was incarcerated because of his faith. All he had to do was "go along with the party line," align with the majority (the immoral majority), and he could go free. After all, had not even the good and wise King Jehoshaphat of Judah joined in a political and faith coalition with King Ahab of Israel? Did Micaiah think he was better than a great man like Jehoshaphat? Didn't Micaiah understand this was a time to "put away religious principles" for the sake of the nation? After all, were they not ultimately "one nation under God?" How could Micaiah possibly do God's will by dividing his own people? It was treasonous to bring a message against the plans made by the government's leaders. After all, had not the Lord, in His sovereign wisdom, appointed Ahab and Jehoshaphat for this season? Micaiah needed to realize that his contentious spirit was contrary to the Spirit of God.

Though not expressly said, everything I have just written was undoubtedly the message contained in the instructions from the "Royal Media Ministry." Their literal words were, "Behold, the words of the prophets with one accord are favorable to the king. Let your word be like the word of one of them, and speak favorably" (1 Kings 22:13). Talk about pressure! All the pressure the "Samarian Ministerial Association" could bring to bear was pressed down on Micaiah. However, this prophet was under a more tremendous pressure—a pressure from within—the force of the Spirit of God. Only one voice mattered to Micaiah, and that was the voice of his Master. Micaiah was not the message's source; he was solely the messenger.

He walked into the presence of those two kings as an ambassador of the King of Kings. "As the Lord lives, what the Lord says to me, that I will speak" (1 Kings 22:14). The response to Micaiah's faithful message was a slap on the face from another "prophet," in reality, a "prophet for profit," Zedekiah, the son of Chenaanah. Also, Micaiah was sent to death row to await execution when King Ahab returned. Micaiah was led in chains back to prison, but he was the freest man in Ramoth-Gilead. His was the inner, peace-filled freedom of a servant-ambassador of the King of Glory. Freedom of speech is the freedom of those who say "what the Lord says." May we live and speak in the freedom of our Lord this day.

APRIL 15
2 Kings 1-3

"Where is the Lord, the God of Elijah?"

Many of you reading these pages may recall the wonderful and amazing fundraising phenomenon that swept across the United States and many other countries for several months in 2015. It was called the "ice bucket challenge," and it became an incredible social media event in which people were challenged to have a bucket of ice water emptied over their heads and to donate to a fund dedicated to finding a cure for the awful disease ALS. ALS is often called Lou Gehrig's disease in connection to the famous New York Yankees baseball player who succumbed to the illness in 1941. I clearly remember accepting that icy challenge and the experience of having my daughters dumping not one but two large buckets of ice water on top of me. I also recall the joy of publicly challenging a pastor friend to accept the same frigid challenge!

Thinking of that event reminds me of another "water bucket" challenge that a nationally known pastor gave me, and many other pastors gathered at a conference. As I recall, the pastor said something to this effect, "Men, here is a good way to remind yourselves how much the Lord really needs you. Go home and fill a bucket with water. Next, stick one of your arms into the water as far as the elbow. Then, very quickly, pull your arm out of the water. After that, look down into the bucket and notice how much of a hole your arm has left. The size of the hole in the water is exactly how much you are essential to the Lord's work being accomplished." Of course, knowing chuckles swept across that audience of pastors. Then, the speaker made the application I have never forgotten and hope I never will. "Brothers, always remember this truth—the Lord *will* use you, but He does not *need* you." Wow. That was a very plain and bold statement. It was also a priceless gift. Every servant of the Lord is valuable, but no one is indispensable or irreplaceable.

Elijah is a timeless reminder of this truth. He was the greatest of the prophets. In fact, in the Mount of Transfiguration, Elijah stood beside the glorified Jesus as the representative of the prophets (Matt. 17:1-3). He was "the man of God," as he was called in his lifetime. His ministry and influence in Israel leading the battle for God's truth and the battle against idolatry and apostasy was incalculable, but he was not irreplaceable because Elisha replaced Elijah. In a moment, Elijah was gone from the earth, transported to heaven in a fiery chariot. All he left behind was his mantle, the outward symbol of the inward anointing and power of God's Spirit upon him. The power of God and the Spirit of God does not leave with Elijah. The worker was gone, but the work continued. Elijah left behind the legacy of his life, residing in the lives of those he had influenced for God and those he had discipled as prophets. By his teaching in words and deeds, Elijah left on earth a school of prophets led by a man who had been his foremost disciple—Elisha. Elijah's successor would go on to do even more miracles than his mentor. "Where is the Lord, the God of Elijah?" He is still here. His work continues. He delights in showing Himself mighty still in and through the lives of his servants. He does not need us, but He will use us. Soon, we will be gone, heaven bound. What mantle of legacy will you leave behind?

APRIL 16
2 Kings 4-6

"Chariots of Fire"

"So the Lord opened the eyes of the young man, and he saw, and behold, the mountain was full of horses and chariots of fire all around Elisha."
(2 Kings 6:17)

On one occasion, a pastor was speaking to his congregation from the passage in Revelation that describes the dragon, Lucifer, pulling down one-third of the stars from the heavens (Rev. 12:3-4). The pastor continued to say that the text indicated that one-third of the angels of heaven, now demons, joined Satan in his awful rebellion against God. At that point in the sermon, a very simple but devout church member responded heartily, "Praise God!" The man's outburst caught the minister somewhat off guard, so he responded, "Brother, I'm not sure I quite understand your joy over what I just shared." The man quickly replied, "Well, don't you see it, pastor? That means we've got two angels for every one of the Devil's demons!"

We may smile at his folksy evaluation, but we sure can't argue with his math! As vast as they are in number, the energized, demonized, mobilized hordes of hell are yet outnumbered by the heavenly host of angels forever loyal to their Lord. However, if one single angel did not exist, the infinite Almighty God is not in the least hindered or challenged by that army of evil adversaries.

With eyes of faith, we can see what Gehazi, the servant of Elisha, needed to see by sight. On our journey to faith in Messiah, we must embrace the reality of the gathering we have joined. "But you have come to Mount Zion and to the city of the living God, the heavenly Jerusalem, and to innumerable angels in festal gathering, and to the assembly of the firstborn who are enrolled in heaven, and to God, the judge of all, and to the spirits of the righteous made perfect" (Heb. 12:22-23). What a family we have joined! Or, more accurately, what a family into which we have been adopted (Gal. 4:4-5).

The story in our Scripture passage today helps to focus our minds on faith, which is the ultimate reality. Our faith is not based on what might be. Faith is based on the unseen reality. The most certain and unmovable things are those which are not visible but invisible. "Now faith is the assurance of things hoped for, the conviction of things not seen" (Heb. 11:1). Living by faith is not living in a "make-believe world." Faith is the ultimate expression of living in the "real world." What Elisha said to his servant was *really true*. "Do not be afraid, for those who are with us are more than those who are with them" (2 Kings 6:16).

As followers of Christ, we are in the minority numerically. (Though we praise God, our number is growing by thousands every day!) However, as Christians, we are not in the minority when it comes to our resources. "What then shall we say to these things? If God is for us, who can be against us?" (Rom. 8:31)

It has been said that, "You and God make a majority." The great truth is that God alone is the majority! Our concern is never whether God is on our side. Instead, we should ask ourselves, are we on the Lord's side? Standing with the Lord is seeing things from the right perspective. It is crystal clear—"God wins!"

APRIL 17
2 Kings 7-9

"This Day of Good News"

I have said many times that if it were possible for every Christian in America to spend just one day in a third-world country, the level of generosity in giving would be completely transformed. We have lived in a nation so blessed financially that we completely forgot that the vast majority of people around the earth could not begin to imagine the standard of living we simply take for granted.

My understanding of how truly wealthy I am in relation to billions of people on this planet was changed forever by an experience that took place over 30 years ago in the Philippines.

I had never been outside of the United States until I traveled to Davao City, Philippines, to speak at a pastors' conference organized by a friend and missionary serving there. One dear lady served as the cook for the entire conference, and for several days, from dawn until after dark, she prepared delicious meals for all of us who participated in the event. On the conference's final day, I asked my missionary friend if it would be all right to give her a small gift of appreciation. He assured me it would and translated for me as I thanked the tiny, elderly woman for everything she had done for us during the conference. She smiled brightly and bowed several times as I spoke, but when I handed her a twenty-dollar bill, she stared at it for several moments. Then her shoulders began to shake, and tears flowed down her face. As I recall, she gripped both of my hands, and bowing again, she pressed them to her forehead.

As we walked away, I asked the missionary what had just happened. "Sam," he said, "you just gave that lady an amount equal to about one month's wages." I was stunned and humbled, and then it was my turn to have tears in my eyes. That experience has never left my mind, and I trust it never will. How rich we are as Americans! Any person in our country who earns minimum wage makes more than 90% of the people in the rest of the world. We need to be generous with the wealth the Lord has provided us. Even more so, as believers, we must not hoard for ourselves the greatest treasure on earth—the gospel of our Lord and Savior, Jesus Christ.

In a true, spiritual sense, we are like the starving lepers huddled outside the gate of Samaria. After they found the camp of the Syrians deserted, feasted on the food, and enriched themselves with the abandoned treasures, their consciences began to condemn them. They thought of the multitudes starving in the city a short distance away. "Then they said to one another, 'We are not doing right. This day is a day of good news... Now therefore come; let us go and tell the King's household'" (2 Kings 7:9). Each one of us, before salvation, was a starving leper. And then, by grace, we discovered the living bread and became members of the King's household. We know where there is food for starving souls and riches for all who are clothed in rags. How can we be silent on this day of good news? After all, what is sharing the gospel but just one beggar telling another beggar where there is free bread to be found?

APRIL 18
2 Kings 10-12

"Operation Rescue"

It is hard to imagine the kind of early childhood Joash experienced. He was born as a son of King Ahaziah of Judah, but while still an infant, his father was killed in battle by the fierce and unpredictable general, Jehu. In fact, on the same day that he killed King Ahaziah, Jehu also executed the king of Israel, Joram. However, as dreadful an enemy the baby may have had in Jehu, the most dangerous person in his life was his own grandmother, Athaliah.

When the queen's mother heard that her son, King Ahaziah, had been killed, she ordered every member of her son's family be put to death and declared herself Queen of Judah. If his Aunt Jehosheba had not grabbed him from his crib and hidden Joash and his nurse in a bedroom, the little boy would have been included in the slaughter carried out by his grandmother. For the next six years, this little boy was kept hidden in the temple under the constant protection of Jehoiada, the high priest. Imagine living as a child unable to go outside and play, meet other children, or make friends lest your monster-grandmother learn of your existence and immediately put you to death! We cannot imagine it. But the love of this child's Heavenly Father was stronger than the demonic hatred of his grandmother and infinitely greater. Joash was brought up in the House of the Lord, guarded and guided by his physical and spiritual guardian, Jehoiada, the priest.

Intrigue and idolatry surrounded the little boy, but he was watched over by angels and loved by his Aunt Jehosheba and "Uncle Jehoiada." Finally, when he was six years old, Joash, surrounded by sworn priest-protectors and supported by his beloved "uncle," was brought to stand beside the sacred pillar in the temple. There, as the guards proclaimed, "Long live the king!" the little boy was anointed King of Judah. Imagine the rage-filled amazement of "Queen" Athaliah as, entering the temple, she saw her little grandson with the Book of the Law in his tiny hands and the crown of David resting upon his curly-haired head! It was a scene that haunted her mind for the next few remaining minutes of her disgusting life.

The epitaph of this child-king's reign that extended for the next 40 years is this, "And Jehoash did what was right in the eyes of the Lord... because Jehoiada the priest instructed him" (12:2). "Just a child" is a phrase that we should never use when it comes to the potential of any "little one" we may know. This rescued baby became the child-king who became the ruler who restored the temple of the Lord and, also to a great extent, restored the worship of Jehovah in Judah.

When we invest in the lives of children, we are entering the expansion of God's Kingdom that is "already, not yet." These little ones are precious to the Lord and recipients of His hand's blessing, just as He did on this earth. They are beloved by Him today and are leaders in His Kingdom advance on earth and His Kingdom to come in the New Heaven and the New Earth. Take a moment to pray for the young ones around you. Ask the Heavenly Father to place on your heart the faces of a few, or even one, whom you can influence with kindness, grace, and truth. Maybe there is a little boy or girl you need to bring to the House of the Lord. He or she may be a king or a queen in the making! You never know.

APRIL 19
2 Kings 13-15

"INTOLERABLE TOLERANCE"

Elisha is one of the most amazing individuals recorded in all the biographies of the Bible. In many ways, he is unique among all the characters introduced to us in the Old Testament. The record of the miracles God performed through him during his lifetime far surpasses those of any other prophet. Elisha, in a fantastic way, even performed miracles *after* his lifetime.

In our Scripture reading today, we are told the amazing account of how a dead man was revived when his body touched the bones of Elisha! (2 Kings 13:21) Elisha finished his long ministry and died in peace with the Lord, but he died an angry man at the end. He was angry with the King of Israel, Joash, who had come to visit him in his final illness. Elisha prophesied from his deathbed that Joash would be an arrow the Lord would shoot in victory over Syria. However, when Elisha commanded Joash to strike several symbolic arrows on the ground, the king responded by only striking the arrows to the ground three times. This angered the dying prophet because it represented that Joash would not repeatedly attack Israel's enemy until Syria was destroyed (2 Kings 13:18-19). The prophet knew that this partial defeat of a terrible foe would, in time, be the source of a total defeat for Israel. Within a few generations, the terrible price would be paid by the nation that would soon be celebrating an incomplete victory over the enemy. To the south, in the kingdom of Judah, that disaster would be delayed by nearly 150 years, but already the seeds of "religious tolerance" were being sown to produce a harvest of judgment on the nation.

Through the long record of the Kings of Judah, a phrase is repeated over and over again, "But the high places were not removed; the people still sacrificed and made offerings on the high places" (2 Kings 14:4). Through generations of "good kings" who did love and serve the Lord, there existed a toleration of unholy sites and practices, first permitted by Solomon to appease his many wives from pagan countries. Sometimes the people worshiped Jehovah in these "high places," however, God forbade such practices since He required He only be worshiped in sacrifices offered where He had chosen to place His Name —Jerusalem. Worshiping the true God in the wrong way was still wrong. Partial obedience is, in reality, total disobedience.

Billy Sunday, the famous and flamboyant evangelist of the early twentieth century, used to say, "The reason sin is so dangerous is we treat it like a cream puff rather than a rattlesnake." Billy was right. Toleration is a virtue except when it is toleration of that which is ungodly. "Righteousness exalts a nation, but sin is a reproach to any people" (Prov. 14:34). How true is that statement, and yet how sad that its author Solomon did not heed his own wisdom in dealing with the sinful toleration of idolatry in his own home and kingdom. His reign of peace was infested with these "high places," cells of contagion that would ultimately poison the entire nation. May the Lord give us the grace to be devoted to justice and mercy in all our dealings with others, but may He grant us the wisdom to ruthlessly root out the seeds we must not permit to germinate in our souls.

APRIL 20
2 Kings 16-18

"A Generation of Grace"

> *"He trusted in the Lord, the God of Israel, so that there was none like him among all the kings of Judah after him, nor among those who were before him."*
> (2 Kings 18:5)

King Hezekiah is truly remarkable. His qualities of mind and character stand out in contrast to his surroundings and culture like a diamond in a pig sty. His father, King Ahaz, was famous in a wicked world for his wickedness. Ahaz was so debased he offered one of his sons, Hezekiah's brother, as a burnt offering to the pagan gods of the Canaanites. He also built an altar in the temple of God that was an exact replica of the high altar to the gods of Syria, whose temple he had visited in Damascus (2 Kings 16:10-11). Ahaz so promoted the practices of idol worship that the land of Judah was filled with pagan shrines. Every high hill was dedicated to false gods and became sites of unspeakable wickedness. It is hard to conceive of a king who had more thoroughly corrupted his nation and people.

This is the influence and legacy that Hezekiah had to follow daily like a sewer into his life. What possible hope could there be for a boy, and then young man, who was constantly exposed to such corruption? A great hope—the hope of God's powerful grace. As awful and pervasive as Ahaz's evil influence, it could not begin to compare to the transforming power of God's grace.

What Paul would write 800 years later was already true for Hezekiah, who was raised in a sinful world and debauched family. "But where sin increased, grace abounded all the more" (Rom. 5:20). So mighty was the power of God in Hezekiah's life that, although his father was the most notoriously wicked King of Judah, Hezekiah became famous in his time and for all time as a king who wholeheartedly followed the Lord as none before him or none who would follow. Hezekiah was a trophy of grace and is the perfect example of what I often call "a generation of grace."

"A generation of grace" is a person who has received much pain and abuse in their past, often from members of their dysfunctional family, and yet determines with the power of the Lord to pass on an influence and legacy of love. It is a life of intervention that receives the pain of sin yet passes on the blessing of righteousness. I know of no other life goal that is more difficult yet more impactful and fruitful. The generation of grace is a scarred generation. There are wounds to the heart and mind that never completely heal. The people of the generation of grace live with that pain. However, these people do not pass that pain and abuse on to others. Instead, they determine that "the abuse stops here; I do not have to treat others the way I was treated." They know by experience that "a greater grace" of the river of life has flowed into their hearts by God's salvation. Their daily determination is to let God's grace flow through them to others. The generation of grace does not live in denial of the abuse they have received but rather lives with a personal determination and declaration, "I will not be overcome with evil, but I will overcome evil with good" (Rom. 12:21).

In reality, each of us as believers is part of the generation of grace, for we have been recipients of God's grace in Jesus Christ. May grace be the legacy we give to our generation and leave to the generations to come.

APRIL 21
2 Kings 19-21

"Take it to the Lord"

"Hezekiah received the letter from the hand of the messengers and read it; and Hezekiah went up to the house of the Lord and spread it before the Lord."
(2 Kings 19:14)

Recently, I heard a statistic that astounded me. During a global mission summit, one of the leaders of a social media outreach initiative shared that 95% of the world's population has access to some type of device that provides satellite-based communication, such as a computer, laptop, pad, or phone. Let that sink in for just a moment, 95%. That means over 6 billion people on this planet have access to devices that allow the transfer of global communication. Astounding. Within the span of a few years, the ability to share information has expanded exponentially to include the vast majority of the people on earth. This ability has provided a level of inter-connectedness that boggles the mind.

Sometimes, this ability to connect socially with people everywhere is used in ways that are not helpful and can be harmful. For millions of people, social media has become a global platform for sharing their personal challenges, including their struggles with other individuals, to masses of people who have no connection to the situation whatsoever. Perhaps like me, you have been aghast to see how some people take their personal relationship struggles and proclaim them in the global town square of social media. This only spreads the conflict by needlessly involving others in the problem, and also deepens the pain and bitterness for the ones who are involved. Most sad is this practice when it involves professing believers refusing to follow the principles and examples God has shared in His Word.

Hezekiah is an excellent role model for believers in many things, but certainly in how he dealt with assault, threats, and accusations from the Assyrian leader, "the Rabshakeh." When Hezekiah received a letter that Rabshakeh had already publicly proclaimed and posted, he immediately responded in a manner that is an example for us all. Hezekiah did not take the accusation and assault and post it for public discussion on all available "boards." Hezekiah took the lies and threats straight to the Lord. He presented God with this "open letter" of the enemy and opened it in His presence. Hezekiah first made the matter one of private prayer rather than public posting. Hezekiah talked to God about his enemy's threats and lies before he talked to anyone else. In opening the terrible letter before the Lord, Hezekiah also opened his ears and heart to hear whatever His Master had to say about the matter.

As we read in the passage today, the Lord personally responded to Hezekiah, but He also sent a message to the Assyrians they would never forget! In one night, 185,000 members of their army were struck down by God. It was a complete and total victory—God's victory. When we are threatened or attacked, we need to take time to ask an essential question—who do we want to win? Do we want a victory that vindicates us or glorifies God? When we take the attacks of others against us to the Lord in prayer, we have already won the biggest victory of all—the victory over self.

APRIL 22
2 Kings 22-23

"THE LOST BOOK"

"And Hilkiah the high priest said to Shaphan the secretary, 'I have found the Book of the Law in the house of the Lord.'"
(2 Kings 22:8)

Missiologists tell us that 40 percent of the world's population does not have access to a complete copy of the Bible in their own language. In light of the vast majority of people on our planet having access to some form of web-based or satellite communication, that is truly a staggering reality. It is also a tragedy because we know that the Word of God, shared in some manner, is essential for faith that leads to salvation (Rom. 10:17).

As Christians, we should faithfully and generously support the efforts made by so many Bible translation ministries bringing the light of God's Word to millions and millions of more people each year. There is no treasure on earth as priceless as the Bible. Shared within its covers is the will of God and the way to know our Creator, who, to know personally, is life eternal (John 17:3). It is the Word of God that guides us in the worshiping of God so that our worship is expressed in spirit and in truth (John 4:24).

This understanding of the importance of the Word, and knowing how vital it was to the people of Israel, makes the scene described in our passage so awful and so wonderful. The Book of the Law had been lost. In the space of about 850 years, since Moses completed the writing and presented the Book to the nation, not a single copy of it was known to exist! Neither the high priest nor the king had ever even seen a copy of the Law. During a repair project of the temple initiated by King Josiah, the Book of the Law was discovered in the House of the Lord. Of course, immediately, the king desired to have the Book read to him. The result was *repentance, renewal,* and *restoration.*

When King Josiah heard the Law, he immediately *repented* in sackcloth and ashes. The recognition of his failure and that of the nation to faithfully follow the Lord and keep His Word overwhelmed him. Having called the nation to repentance, the king led them to a *renewal* of their covenant pledge to wholly observe the statutes of Jehovah. This sincere repentance and devoted renewal led to a *restoration* of the worship of God alone. Josiah committed himself to destroying every idol and every high place of pagan worship in the land. In his zeal, the king went so far as to grind all the altars to powder and burn the bones of the leaders who had been buried near the pagan shrines. Josiah destroyed all the mediums and those who had led people in the practices of the occult. So great was Josiah's zeal in restoration to the Lord that at this death it was recorded that no king had ever turned back to God as he had (2 Kings 23:25). What a transformation occurred when the Book of the Law was found! "The Law of the Lord is perfect, reviving the soul" (Ps. 19:7).

The power of God's Word has been undiminished through the ages, yet sadly it is still lost in many houses of the Lord today. Rituals and traditions have hidden the Word so that it is lost to the people in many places of worship. Let's not lose the Bible *in our homes*. But more important than the *reverence* of the Word by our families, is the *reading* of the Word. Find the Book of the Law and read it carefully. Then, let it read you personally.

APRIL 23
2 Kings 24-25

"Far From Home"

It is fascinating how often the approximate span of 400 years appears in the chronology of the people of Israel. For 400 years, they labored as slaves in Egypt. Then, following their liberation by the Passover and parting of the Red Sea, through the wilderness years and until the coronation of King Saul, is another period of about 400 years. Then, from the uniting of the nation under David until the destruction of Jerusalem and the temple and the captivity in Babylon, another period of about 400 years. It is hard to conceive the radical change that has occurred from the scenes recorded in 1 Kings, Chapter 1 until the events recorded in 2 Kings, Chapter 25. The journey begins with the establishment of David's kingdom and then the zenith of power, riches, and glory during the reign of Solomon.

Today's reading recounts the terrible and disastrous results of the nation's downward spiritual spiral in departing from the Lord. In 722 BC, the northern tribes were carried into exile by King Sennacherib of Assyria. Then, in 586 BC, 136 years later, the remaining two tribes, referred to as the kingdom of Judah, were finally and completely overthrown by Nebuchadnezzar, King of Babylon. The millions that had once resided in the "land flowing with milk and honey" were now dead or lost as slaves among the nations, except for a small band of refugees in Egypt and a remnant of survivors living in the provinces of Babylon.

Through the centuries, Jehovah had warned His people of the terrible price their rebellion and treason toward Him would bring. How awful were their "wages of sin," and what a price they were paying for their "freedom." They now were exiles in a far country but were not forgotten. The Lord, their God, knew exactly where they were. And, even in their brokenness and bondage, they were not forgotten. God can never forget His people whose names are engraved on His hands (Isa. 49:16).

The experience of the last legitimate king of Judah, Jehoiachin, is an allegory of the nation. At the age of 26, Jehoiachin surrendered to King Nebuchadnczzar and, along with his family, was taken in chains to Babylon. For the next 37 years, Jehoiachin lived in prison, forsaken, he no doubt thought, but not forgotten. For in the first year of the reign of evil Merodach, king of Babylon, he "graciously freed Jehoiachin king of Judah from prison. And he spoke kindly to him and gave him a seat above the seats of the kings who were with him in Babylon" (2 Kings 25:27-28). Jehoiachin was honored and richly provided for as long as he lived. Likewise, the remnant of Judah was not forgotten. They prospered and multiplied in Babylon as they waited for the Lord to bring them back to the land of their fathers. God had not forsaken them, and, in due season, He would bring them home.

Wherever you are, my friend, as you read these pages, God sees you and loves you. He has not forgotten you. You are not alone even if this hour finds you in "a far country" spiritually, emotionally, or relationally. You are reading these pages today as a reminder that God is with you. Whatever has led you to read from a devotional like this is from God. The power is certainly not in my words, but the message of God's relentless love calls you closer to Him today. The sound may only be like a whisper, but it is the still, small voice of the infinite, glorious God of heaven and earth. Do not be afraid. Listen.

APRIL 24
1 Chronicles 1-3

"JUST NAMES"

Now, let's get honest. The three chapters you read today (*if* you read them!) are not the most exciting passages you have ever considered in the Bible. That does not mean these verses are not as inspired or in any way less the Word of God than any other in Scripture. It does not mean, however, that what is conveyed in these words is as important as the words of John 3:16. Equally *inspired* words do not mean they are equally *important*. Yet, these words are *essential*. Anything God chooses to communicate to mankind is important. So, let's take a few moments to review these chapters and consider what lessons they may possess for us today.

Like 1 & 2 Kings, the Books of 1 & 2 Chronicles are actually one book in the Hebrew text. Internal information shared in the Books of Chronicles indicates that they were written shortly after the first refugees in Babylon returned to Judah, generally thought to have taken place about 538 BC. So, the Books of Chronicles record the history of Israel as a way of encouraging the first Israelites to return to their homeland. They also remind the Jewish people, living in Babylon, of God's covenant faithfulness to them. The Chronicler (we are not sure of their identity, perhaps Ezra) connects the people of Israel, not just back to their father Abraham, but to the father of all mankind, Adam. Through this history, the Jewish people are reminded that there is only one true God of all human beings and also that, in His grace, He made an everlasting covenant with Abraham and all his descendants. God is a covenant-making and covenant-keeping God, and they are bound to Him by covenant. God had not broken faith with them, but they and their fathers had violated their covenant responsibilities to Him time and time again. The history of Chronicles would remind the Jewish people of their identity and their need to keep absolute loyalty to Jehovah. The Books of Chronicles would be a constant reminder never again to practice idolatry. This lesson was learned, for the Jewish people never returned to pagan worship after their years of captivity in Babylon.

So, what are the applications from the Books of Chronicles for us who read these lists of names and events 2600 years later? First of all, we are reminded of the amazing accuracy and detail of the Bible. No other book of antiquity holds a candle to the Bible in the specific individual and national information it shares. The Bible is not a book of misty myths. It is a detailed and careful record of people and events that make up the meta-narrative of redemption shared through its pages.

Secondly, Chronicles, like no other section in the Bible, reminds us of the meticulous and miraculous recording of the contents of Scripture. Untold thousands of people copied and transmitted millions and millions of letters over the centuries as God preserved His Word. They are unknown to us, but their finger-numbing and mind-numbing copying of the text of the Bible is a ministry that must be greatly rewarded in heaven. One day, perhaps, we will have the knowledge and the time to thank each of them personally!

Finally, the Books of Chronicles remind us that God *knows our names*. Our lives matter, and how we live our days on earth has eternal significance. Our lives are living epistles being read and recorded by men and angels. Don't think your life doesn't matter. Segub's did, and so does yours (1 Chr. 2:22).

APRIL 25
1 Chronicles 4-6

"THE PRAYER OF PAIN"

Tucked away in the lengthy and repetitive genealogies of 1 Chronicles are some golden nuggets of spiritual instruction and encouragement for those who have the devoted determination to read them. Let me say, "Thank you and bless you" for being one of those individuals as we take this *Pathways* journey. One of the most valuable of these overlooked treasures is discovered in our reading today as we learn about and listen to the prayer of Jabez. Jabez was virtually unnoticed for 2500 years until Bruce Wilkerson wrote a small devotional book titled *The Prayer of Jabez* in 2000. To date, approximately 10 million copies of the book have been sold.

I recall the fantastic phenomenon of that small volume that swept through the United States and many other countries within a matter of months. According to Wilkerson's challenge, praying Jabez's prayer daily for 30 days would be transformative in a person's character and life circumstances. Very soon, a multi-layered marketing campaign that highlighted various applications and expressions of the prayer caused the prayer of Jabez and Wilkerson's book to be affirmed as a gift from God for spiritual development. The book was condemned by many as the latest prosperity theology, "name it and claim it" heresy. To be sure, Bruce Wilkerson is not a heretic. Throughout his ministry, he has not supported the abuses of the prosperity gospel, which is most definitely not the gospel of our Lord! However, many people, in a sincere desire to experience the Lord in fresh encounters, have taken the prayer of Jabez out of context and sought in it a simple-to-apply "formula for faith."

Let's take a closer look at Jabez and his prayer and consider the personal application of information and insight the Lord wanted to share by providing this brief biography of a man and his prayer. The key to what is shared is the meaning of Jabez's name. Jabez means "pain." His mother called him this because she delivered him in great physical pain. It is easy to understand how difficult it must have been for him, a boy and then a young man, to be known as "pain." Clearly, Jabez's mother caused him years of pain by giving him this name. Being greeted by other children with the words, "Here comes Pain!" could not have been easy! Jabez's name took on a deeper identity that was indeed a source of pain to him. Then, just how and when we do not know, Jabez recognized that his name and all the experiences regarding his name were precisely the key to addressing all they represented.

Jabez realized he needed to take what was causing him the most pain, his name, and bring it to God for His Divine intervention and transformation. Jabez understood that the God of Israel was not a God who delights in causing pain but is gracious, kind, merciful, and generous to all who call upon Him in faith. In his pain (his name), Jabez called on *the Name* (the nature) of the God of Israel. Notice that Jabez's prayer was one of *faith, fervor,* and *focus,* "Oh that you would bless me and enlarge my border, and that your hand might be with me, and that you would keep me from harm" (1 Chr. 4:10). The word for "harm" used here is "pain." Jabez, in bold faith, prayed for a breakthrough in his life. He had ambition and desired influence, but he realized that blessings could only come from God. It was not an ungodly, selfish prayer. He asked to be blessed, and he asked to be a blessing... "that you would keep me from harm [pain] so that it might not bring me pain" (1 Chr. 4: 10). Jabez's prayer from his pain, to be blessed and not to be involved with pain, pleased the Lord, "And God granted what he asked." God's blessing is greater than all our pain, and you can ask Him for that blessing.

APRIL 26
1 Chronicles 7-9

"Salvation Out of Disaster"

Etymology is the study of the origin of words. To say it is a popular hobby or subject of interest would be to do a little more than just stretch the truth! Most people find that mastering the current vocabulary of their own ever-changing language is more than enough of a challenge without adding the effort of discovering word origins to the task. Though I am certainly not an etymologist, I have found that uncovering the root meaning of some words, especially keywords in the Bible, has repaid the efforts in spiritual understanding and application in great measure.

In our reading today, we have a couple of significant examples of spiritual insight in taking the time to trace the source and message of a few words. In Chapters 7-9, we have carefully recorded genealogies of the families of Israel. This was vitally important to the Jewish refugees living in Babylon because when they finally returned to their homeland, according to God's promises, providing evidence of their lineage would help reapportion the land. So, the chronological records of the nation were not just a matter of its knowledge of the past but also its hope for the future. The people of Israel had experienced a terrible disaster brought about by their sin. Still, the covenant promise and constant hope for the nation was of a gracious deliverance and salvation provided by the God of Israel.

In the origin of terms and names used in the chronology of Israel through these verses resides a message of hope for Israel and, as God's covenant people, us as well. An example of one of their hidden etymological gems is found in the tragic account of Ephraim (Chr. 7:20-29). We are told how two of Ephraim's sons (or grandsons, for the text is not clear), Ezer and Elead, were killed by murderous Philistine raiders from the region of Gath. So great was Ephraim's grief that when his next son was born, he named him "Beriah, because disaster had befallen his house" (2 Chr. 7:23). Beriah is the Hebrew word for "disaster," which is also a very interesting word.

Of course, we know that our word "disaster" means an event of terrible extent and proportion. The word "disaster" comes from a combination of two Greek words that mean "bad star." Inherent with the superstitious ancients was the idea that the stars and planets controlled the events in an individual's life and destiny. As a Jewish person of faith, Ephraim would not have held that pagan view, but it is clear that the tragic loss of his sons had produced a crisis of faith in him. In grief, he named his baby Beriah, meaning "disaster." However, what Ephraim had forgotten is that there is a God who controls all things, and because of His sovereign grace and power, He can bring deliverance out of what seems like a disaster. A direct descendant of Ephraim and his disaster-named son Beriah was Nun, who gave birth to a little boy named Joshua (2 Chr. 7: 27). Yes, *that* Joshua—disciple and assistant to Moses, who would lead the tribes of Israel out of the disaster of 40 years of wilderness wandering into the Promised Land.

The name Joshua, as you may be aware, means "Jehovah is salvation," and "Joshua" is the Hebrew name for the Greek word "Jesus." So, rejoice today in the timeless faith lesson from ancient etymology. Life is sometimes characterized by disaster, but our lives are not defined by the stars of the sky. Look up! Our lives are delivered from disaster by the "Bright and Morning Star," Jesus, the God of our salvation.

APRIL 27
1 Chronicles 10-12

"INVALUABLE ISSACHAR"

"Of Issachar, men who had understanding of the times, to know what Israel ought to do, 200 chiefs, and all their kinsmen under their command."
(1 Chronicles 12:32)

The Book of 1 Chronicles picks up the narrative of Israel's history, focusing primarily on David's unification of the nation after the death of Saul. The key reason for this is that the people to whom this history was primarily directed were the exiles of the kingdom of Judah. David was the first king of Judah. And then, after the other tribes united under him, he became the king of the entire nation. In many ways, David was looked to as the father of the nation, while Abraham was honored as the father of the people.

When David first came to rule in Judah, the nation's situation could not have been more dire. King Saul and his son Jonathan were dead, and the Philistines had practically annihilated the army of Israel in the Valley of Jezreel. The conditions within and surrounding Israel were desperate, and the spirit of the people was one of depression and defeatism. But, that was not the mood within the heart of David and the very small band of men who followed him. David had faith in God, and his men had faith in David. David's faith was contagious, and so was his example. As a worshiping warrior, he was a man following God with all his heart. His courageous faith reproduced itself in a band of "mighty men." These exploits of David's warriors described in our reading today are so incredible that, were they not contained in Holy Scripture, we might consider them mythical tales like those of the ancient Greeks.

Courage is contagious, and slowly, from around the scattered tribes, men who saw hope and a future personified in David began to join his ranks. Eventually, after his coronation, King David led an army of hundreds of thousands, representing all the tribes of Israel. The number of soldiers provided by each tribe is noted specifically, except for the one notable exception—the tribe of Issachar. This tribe had always been one of the smallest in Israel, and it would stand to reason that their contribution to David's army might be among the least. Still, in a unique statement, it appears that the little tribe of Issachar may have made the most significant contribution of all. We are told that the tribe provided 200 chiefs and their kinsmen, but they were an invaluable group! "Of Issachar, men who had understanding of the times, to know what Israel ought to do" (1 Chr. 12:32). What a gift they were to King David! Their incredible value was that of wisdom and discernment for their nation and their king.

Today, we would describe these men of Issachar as having "a Biblical worldview." They "had understanding of the times." That is, they understood and interpreted the information they obtained within the framework of God's truth, which is the only source of truth. Jesus said to His Father, "Your word *is* truth" (John 17:17). He did not say, "Your word is true" (though that is correct). He said, "Your word *is* truth." When information is framed and filtered by the truth, it provides the ability for discernment, applying God's truth to life's situations. The men of Issachar were a rare breed, and sadly men and women with their wisdom and discernment are even rarer today. However, if we will prayerfully apply ourselves to hearing and heeding God's Word, we too can be men and women of Issachar. Our Lord desires us to know His truth and apply it to ourselves so we can share it with others.

APRIL 28
1 Chronicles 13-15

"ACCEPTABLE WORSHIP"

"Because you did not carry it the first time, the Lord our God broke out against us, because we did not seek him according to the rule."
(1 Chronicles 15:13)

Sincerity is an admirable quality of character. Few things are more repellant than recognizing a person is insincere—what they portray in word or deed does not align with the motives of their heart. This is the nature of hypocrisy. The word "hypocrite" actually comes to us from the ancient theaters of Greece in which a person wore a mask to portray the character assigned to him in a play. These masks were constructed in a way that included a type of internal megaphone so that the actor's voice would be audible to the audience. The word coined for an actor adopting of a character to portray was "*hupokrités*." Hupokrités literally means "to judge beneath," from which came the idea of pretending to be someone and was eventually used as the word for an actor.

Insincerity is terrible, but to be sincere and yet sincerely mistaken or wrong can be tragic. We are often told that sincerity is all that matters when it comes to the issue of religion. Perhaps you have heard this exact use of expression or something very close to it, "It really doesn't matter *what* you believe as long as you are sincere." Strange, isn't it that people make that comment about religion when they would never say it about traffic lights or speed limits? I don't think the police officer would accept the response, "But officer, I was completely sincere in driving 40 miles per hour over the speed limit." Sincerity can never be an excuse for violating human laws; how much less, then, can sincerity be an acceptable reason for violating God's law?

Early in his reign, David learned that worshiping God *fervently* must also include worshiping God *obediently*. Or, as he says in the verse above, "...according to the rule." We do not tell God how we will approach Him; He tells us how we can approach Him. Coming into God's presence is at the heart of what it means to worship. Worship, in reality, is the ultimate expression of true life, for to "glorify God and enjoy Him forever" is the purpose of mankind, according to the text of the Westminster Shorter Catechism. With all due respect to the divines of Westminster, the Lord Jesus expressed it better this way, "And this is eternal life, that they know you, the only true God, and Jesus Christ whom you have sent" (John 17:3). True life, Jesus said, is to know God the Father through the One who alone can make Him known—Jesus the Messiah, whom God has sent.

Approaching and seeking God "according to the rule," as David said, is to approach Him through David's descendant and Lord, Jesus of Nazareth. "For there is one God, and there is one mediator between God and men, the man Christ Jesus" (1 Tim. 2:5). There is only one God, not many, and there is only one Person who can bring people to God, and that is Jesus. He is the one and only way, but He is the one way that is open *for all*. That is the gospel truth, and it is truly good news. We are welcome to approach God how He Himself has provided—through the perfect life, sacrificial death, and glorious resurrection of His blessed Son.

When we come to God from our heart by faith, through the merit of His Son, *that* is true worship; and it is acceptable worship to God because it is worship "in spirit and in truth" (John 4:23). Now, that is something to sing and dance about just as David did! Maybe you can only sing and dance in your heart, not with your voice or your feet. That's fine. Go ahead. The Lord will enjoy it!

APRIL 29
1 Chronicles 16-18

"REJOICE"

"Let the heavens be glad, and let the earth rejoice, and let them say among the nations, 'The Lord reigns!'"
(1 Chronicles 16:31)

It has been an incredible privilege for me on several occasions to stand on top of Mount Zion in Jerusalem. It was this craggy, rocky hilltop that the Lord directed David to purchase and prepare as the site for the temple that would honor the God of Israel and serve as a house of prayer for all nations. It was to Mount Zion that David brought the Ark of the Covenant and led the people to celebrate and praise the God of Israel.

That is definitely not the atmosphere that generally exists on Mount Zion today. On the contrary, Israeli defense personnel continually patrol the entire area. A discernible sense of tension surrounds the site of the former temple, and today it is the location of the Muslim holy shrine—the Dome of the Rock and Al-Aqsa Mosque. All that remains of the original temple is a portion of the western retaining wall, which is often called the "Wailing Wall" because, in front of it, Jewish people daily lament the temple's destruction and fervently pray for its restoration by Messiah.

Mount Zion is not generally a joyful place. That made the experience so unique several years ago when, above the prayers of lament at the Wailing Wall, I heard the sounds of singing, laughter, clapping, and shouting. Turning around, I saw dozens of orthodox Jewish men carrying a young man in a wooden chair on their shoulders. It was the celebration of his Bar Mitzvah and his installation as an adult member of the faith community. Not only did his family and friends celebrate, but even we, as non-Jewish spectators, were invited to join the celebration. For a few minutes, people from many different nations and ethnic backgrounds united in celebration and praise on Mount Zion. That felt so good, and it felt so right.

Joy in the presence of the Lord is meaningful; in fact, it is *missional*. The mission of God is a mission of joy for the peoples of the earth to rejoice in His reign and His salvation (1 Chr. 16:31). "Let the nations be glad!" is the message of God's mission (Ps. 67:4). Joy in salvation is the mission of God, the heart-message of David, and the heartbeat of the Son of David—Jesus Christ. It was for joy that Jesus died. Yes, you read that correctly. *It was for joy* that Jesus died. *His* joy. "Looking to Jesus, the founder and perfecter of our faith, who for the joy that was set before him endured the cross, despising the shame, and is seated at the right hand of the throne of God" (Heb. 12:2). Jesus died for the purpose of joy—His joy, our joy. "Though you have not seen him, you love him. Though you do not now see Him, you believe in Him and rejoice with joy that is inexpressible and filled with glory" (1 Pet. 1:8).

There *is* joy in Jesus. We who know Him know that joy. But I have a question for us. Is joy our mission? Are we missionaries of the joy of Jesus? Let's pray about that. "Lord Jesus, make us contagious to all people with your joy. Amen."

APRIL 30
1 Chronicles 19-21

"GOD IS FOR US!"

When someone asks me for a good book by which to study the Bible, I answer in a way that surprises them and hopefully helps them. My answer to the question is, first of all, "Study the Bible," and then to follow up with the encouragement to purchase and use a study Bible. The Bible was written to be read with a specific goal. It was not primarily written so that we might know the Bible. It was written so that we might know the God of the Bible. The Bible is a book for the purpose of knowing the Author. The wonderful promise from the Author is that as we read His Book to search for Him, we will find Him (Jer. 29:13). The purpose of true Bible study is to bring us to a personal knowledge of God. Thankfully, the Spirit of God, the Author of Scriptures, is with us and in us to help interpret the Word of God.

Having given that sincere challenge, I then encourage them to purchase a study Bible that includes cross-references, an explanation of terms, a concordance of commonly used words, and general introductions to all the books of the Bible. There is no reason the average person with some discipline and determination cannot, by a few years of carefully reading a study Bible, possess the equivalent of a Bible college-level knowledge of the Word of God.

I have shared this to express what I firmly believe is the most neglected part of a study Bible by most people—the section of maps found at the back. Who would start a journey to a desired destination without some sort of map or guidance on the route and the locations along the journey? Yet, we often do that with the Bible when it is a journey that will take us through 2000 years of history, countless locations, cultures, and civilizations. These maps in the back of our Bibles are priceless when it comes to understanding the people, places, and moments described in God's Word. Thankfully, most study Bibles have already provided maps that guide us through the various times and civilizations from Genesis to Revelation. You will find the maps helpful in understanding and celebrating the God of the nations as He faithfully carries out His great plan. You will see fingerprints of the faithful Almighty inscribed on the very boundaries of the nations.

Our reading today is a perfect example and opportunity. It is filled with the names of strange-sounding places and people but take the opportunity to read it with a map from your Bible or some other source. It is the story of King David's expanding kingdom with the help of God. Look for tiny Bethlehem, David's hometown. Observe how small Jerusalem is in comparison to Israel. Notice how Israel is surrounded—the Philistines to the west, the Syrians to the north, the Moabites and Ammonites to the east, and then mighty Egypt to the south. Now, read these chapters and the chapters ahead with this visual in mind. God has exalted an overlooked shepherd boy to be king of a tiny country surrounded on all sides by hate-filled enemies and also many literal giants. Follow the victories God gives David on the map before you. The map has a message from history, and for us today—our God reigns! "If God is for us, who can be against us?" (Rom. 8:31)

MAY

"The Lord, the God of hosts, the Lord is his memorial name."
(Hosea 12:5)

MAY 1
1 Chronicles 22-24

"HEART AND HANDS"

"Now set your mind and heart to seek the Lord your God. Arise and build the sanctuary of the Lord God, so that the ark of the covenant of the Lord and the holy vessels of God may be brought into a house built for the name of the Lord."
(1 Chronicles 22:19)

During the ministry of Jesus, there is recorded for us the day Jesus and His disciples visited the home of His friends Martha, Mary, and Lazarus. You may recall how upset Martha became when she felt that her sister, sitting at Jesus' feet while he taught, was leaving her to do all the food preparation work. Martha eventually became so frustrated that she rebuked the Lord and told Him to make Mary help her. Jesus gently responded that Martha had become too distracted with all the preparation but that Mary had chosen what was most important at that moment. She was therefore receiving benefits that would never be taken from her.

It has become popular in recent years for people to describe themselves or others as "Marys" or "Marthas." With that categorization, some people are considered more contemplative in nature, while others are identified as more proactive. Still, others have used that passage to define people as either "worshipers" or "workers." While we understand that individuals have basic personality qualities that certainly impact how they express their faith, I think we have to be careful to draw distinctions between those who are "worshipers" and others who are "workers." In reality, worshiping and working are not in competition or conflict. They complement each other and are both essential to healthy discipleship.

In our passage today, David challenged the leaders of Israel to express both qualities in their lives, setting their minds and hearts to seek the Lord and actively construct the sanctuary of the Lord (1 Chr. 22:19). By sharing this challenge, King David called these men to both the worship *of* God and the work *for* God.

As followers of the Lord, we must make a conscientious effort to reject the "secular/sacred" divide that is part of the fabric of our culture. We are instructed and influenced to view work as a necessary evil to be endured to make money, do the things we enjoy, and ultimately not have to work in retirement and be free to do whatever we like. I don't think we see that understanding of tension between work and joy, or secular and sacred, supported anywhere in God's Word. The reality is that the redemption that is in Christ redeems all of life. We, therefore, can do all things to the glory of Christ (1 Cor. 10:31). Even if we work in conditions that are far less than perfect or for people that are exceedingly less than perfect, we are serving Christ (Eph. 6:5-8). This revolutionary concept of the impact of the Gospel caused Paul to plead with us that our entire lives be presented to Christ as "living sacrifices," which is our reasonable act of worship (Rom. 12:1). When we truly begin to see that, because of Jesus, all of life has become sacred, then we are free to enjoy life as a gift to be received from our Heavenly Father and to be offered back to Him.

MAY 2
1 Chronicles 25-27

"Organized Obedience"

Evolution is against the law. That is more than just a wish; it is a reality. Let me explain. Evolution is a *theory* taught by so-called science, which is opposed to the actual *laws* of science. Evolution contradicts science. The theory of evolution presumes to prove that all living organisms are slowly going through mutations of change that are leading to greater levels of diversity and complexity. However, the actual law of science, specifically the second law of thermodynamics, teaches by observation and measurement that living organisms and all matter tend toward greater disorder, disorganization, and energy loss. To put it simply (and scientifically), creation is not slowly charging up. It is, in fact, running down.

This is the *natural* state of things—decay and disorder, but it is not the *supernatural* state of things where the Spirit of God is working. The living reality of God entering a person's life begins a process of spiritual regeneration and renewal. The Lord brings life, and with His life comes a growth in character and conduct that reflects more and more the qualities of the One in whose image we are being remade (Rom. 12:1-2). In theology, we refer to this process of our salvation as sanctification, which means becoming more and more like Jesus. It is a "well-ordered life" in the highest sense of the term.

For this reason, as believers, we need to reject the notion that what is "spiritual" is never to be planned or organized. This philosophy is rampant in many Christian circles and often accepted without question that what is a work of God's Spirit is never planned or structured. Disorganization is spiritual, it purports, but structure and organization are worldly and legalistic. I guess someone forgot to tell King David that great revelation! It would certainly be ridiculous to call the author of most of the Psalms "unspiritual" and "legalistic," yet in our reading today, we see that David spent an enormous amount of time and energy organizing and structuring the worship, government, and armed forces of Israel. David would disagree that planning, organization, and scheduling were somehow "unspiritual." He was a person passionate for God and believed God was honored by service well-planned and well-performed.

In this regard, every believer should be a practicing "Methodist." The term "Methodist" was not chosen as a name for a Christian denomination. Rather, it was the way John and Charles Wesley and other evangelists in eighteenth century England believed the life of a disciple of Jesus should be lived—with determination, planning, and structure. A well-organized life reflects the belief that all of life is sacred and important. Since that is clearly the case, "sacred organization" should never be just a theory for us but a law by which to live.

MAY 3
1 Chronicles 28-29

"A LIVING LEGACY"

It would be almost impossible to imagine a more dramatic and eventful life than King David's. From his youth as a shepherd boy caring for his father Jesse's flocks to reigning as the greatest of the kings of his day, David's life is a saga of proportions that no Hollywood script nor even a multi-volume set of historical fiction could begin to communicate.

The account of his life recorded in Scripture is more moving and eventful than perhaps any other person in all the annals of history. To aspire to live a life that is as powerful and influential as David's would be to set personal goals for ourselves that are far beyond any person's abilities. However, as I read these final chapters in 1 Chronicles and listen to David's valedictory address to his son Solomon and the gathered leaders of Israel, I realize that David's legacy is based on the fundamental qualities that are attainable and transferable by any devoted follower of the Lord. I see in David's character, three crucial qualities that produce a "living legacy."

The Legacy of Faith

At the core of David's life, steadfast confidence and trust in God reigned. This faith *compelled* him to step out and face the blaspheming giant, Goliath of Gath. It was faith in God that *composed* David when

Saul relentlessly pursued him. It was faith that *controlled* David when he had the opportunity to take vengeance against Saul and many other personal enemies throughout his lifetime. David's legacy of faith culminates in his final address to his son, "And you, Solomon my son, know the God of your father and serve Him with a whole heart and with a willing mind" (1 Chr. 28:9). God was real to David.

The Legacy of Worship

David is described forever as a man after God's own heart (1 Sam. 13:14). David loved the Lord and was passionately devoted to Him. The Psalms David left as part of his legacy, overflow with the desire to know the Lord and His ways. They are reflective of a person desperate and hungry for a real relationship with his Savior, not the musings of a framed and matted silicon saint. David's worship was authentic and, at times, ragged with questions. David's worship is a living legacy for our own today.

The Legacy of Generosity

There is no greater test of faith and love than the test of generosity. The greater "Son of David" expressed it this way, "For where your treasure is, there your heart will be also" (Matt. 6:21). Follow the money trail, and it leads to the heart of any person. In David's generosity for the House of God that he was not allowed to build, we see his legacy of love. David was generous because he loved God and believed all he possessed was the Lord's (1 Chr. 29:14). God had David's heart, so He also had his resources.

The qualities of *faith*, *worship*, and *generosity* are David's living, eternal legacy. None of us can live David's life, but by God's grace, each of us can leave his legacy. We leave it by living it, one day at a time.

MAY 4
2 Chronicles 1-3

"Worthy Goals"

I once heard success defined this way: "Success is the accomplishment of goals." I certainly appreciate the value and effectiveness of being goal-oriented. However, a person can accomplish all the goals they have established and yet waste their life. I have seen it done many, many times. A case in point: I received a call from a lady asking me if I would be willing to come and visit her very sick husband. He had listened to some of my messages on the radio and wanted to share some things with me. Of course, I gladly said I would be willing to visit this man and made an appointment to go by his house.

When I drove up the driveway, I checked to ensure I had the correct address, for there, sprawling before me, was one of the most beautiful estates I had ever seen—manicured lawn and gardens, basketball court, tennis court, equestrian stable, and riding trails. However, it was the scene *inside* the house that was so surreal. Propped up in a hospital bed next to an indoor/outdoor swimming pool was an elderly man with one of the saddest countenances I had ever seen. After a few moments of introduction, the man told me about the millions of dollars he had made over his lifetime and the number of people who had become wealthy through him. But, I can still hear his choking voice as he said to me, "Pastor, none of my friends come to see me. My children and grandchildren have nothing to do with me. I have wasted my life and have nothing of value to show for it." I will never forget what that man said to me, and I never want to forget. He accomplished all his goals yet wasted his life. In reality, he was a failure at the only thing which really matters—life itself.

Success is not the accomplishment of goals. Success is the *pursuit* of worthy goals. King Solomon was a success by any *human* measurement. He was the richest man who ever lived and succeeded beyond what could have been predicted or considered possible. We read in our chapters today how Solomon constructed one of the marvels of the ancient world—the temple of God in Jerusalem. However, it was not the *beauty* of the building that made the project and "project manager," Solomon, successful. The purpose and desire for the building made it a worthy goal. "The house that I am to build will be great, for our God is greater than all gods" (2 Chr. 2:5). A worthy goal is not about *us*. It is about *Him*. Success is a pursuit of God Himself. In pursuing our Master above all, we lose our life and find it in Him. Listen to the testimony of one of the most "successful losers" of all time:

> "Indeed, I count everything as loss because of the surpassing worth of knowing Christ Jesus my Lord. For his sake I have suffered the loss of all things and count them as rubbish, in order that I may gain Christ."
> (Philippians 3:8)

Pursuing God. That is a worthy goal. That is success.

MAY 5
2 Chronicles 4-7

"THE MANIFESTED PRESENCE"

I have never learned a foreign language. Well, let me rephrase that statement. I have never learned a *modern* foreign language. I have spent many years attempting (and never succeeding, I might say) to master three ancient languages—Latin, Greek, and Hebrew. As I struggled over the years to gain some ability in those languages, I have often considered what a difficult thing it must be to learn American English. Our language is such a melting pot of idioms from so many cultures that it must be incredibly challenging to understand, let alone begin to use.

There is also the challenge of homonyms—words that sound the same but have different meanings. For example, consider the homonyms "eminence," imminence," and "immanence." "Eminence" conveys superiority, "imminence" means immediacy or about to happen, and "immanence" is a theological term that means God encompasses or is present in all of His creation.

Immanence means all of God is in all places. From this reality of God's immanence flows the corresponding reality of God to His creation, "omnipresence." God is "now here" is the expression communicated in Scripture of God's immanent omnipresence. That is, by His nature, God is present in every part of His creation. There is no place where God is not. King David expressed it this way, "Where shall I go from your Spirit? Or where shall I flee from your presence? If I ascend to heaven, you are there! If I make my bed in Sheol, you are there!" (Ps. 139:7-9) Yes, our God is in all places at all times.

That being affirmed, there is yet all the difference in the world between the omnipresence of God and the manifested presence of God. This occurs when the Lord chooses to display His presence in ways that can be experienced by our physical senses and our spiritual capacities to recognize the presence of our Creator and Savior. Chapter 7 in our reading today contains one of the most amazing and powerful expressions of the manifested presence of God in all of Scripture. In answer to King Solomon's intercession of national confession, praise, and petition, the Lord sent fire from heaven to consume the burnt offering. The glory of His manifested presence filled the temple to the degree that the priests could not enter because of the glory of the Lord (2 Chr. 7:1-2). Wow, talk about a dedication service!

Now, to be clear, the Lord does not usually reveal His presence in such a dramatic physical display. However, that does not mean that, as believers in the Lord, we should settle for dry, dusty, textbook-accurate theology that knows nothing of the warm, living, spiritually-sensed reality of God's presence in our lives. I once heard a preacher warn a congregation in his folksy way, "It is possible to be as theologically straight as a gun barrel and just as empty." Our God is a Divine Person, and He has provided for us, through the indwelling of His Holy Spirit, a personal relationship that can be known and experienced in our spirits. This relationship can be just as warm and genuine as our relationships with loved ones and friends. Jesus said that He no longer calls His followers "servants," but, rather, he considers us in our relationship with Him, to be "friends" (John 15:15).

As we believe and obey our Lord, he promises that both He and His Father will come and make our lives their home (John 14:21). His presence is manifested to us, and others *experience* His presence through us. The noted evangelist D. L. Moody once entered a barbershop to get a haircut. Several of the patrons recognized him but said nothing. Later, one of the men in the barber shop wrote, "It was not anything particular that he said; but when Mr. Moody left that shop, somehow it felt as if he had transformed it into a chapel by his presence." We do not take God anywhere, but His manifested presence in our lives should always go with us every day—*this day*.

MAY 6
2 Chronicles 8-9

"Wisdom Leads to Worship"

The Queen of Sheba traveled a very long way to visit King Solomon. Scholars have identified the land of Sheba with various locations, but the majority now connects it with the people group of Saba in the southern section of Arabia. This means the queen traveled several thousand miles, no doubt many months, to meet with Solomon. It also indicates just how far the fame of Solomon's riches and wisdom had traveled in that ancient day. Solomon was world-famous three thousand years before the availability of worldwide communication. What the Queen of Sheba experienced during her extended visit to Jerusalem astounded her.

> "The report was true that I heard in my own land of your words and of your wisdom, but I did not believe the reports until I came and my own eyes had seen it. And behold, half the greatness of your wisdom was not told me; you surpass the report that I heard."
> (2 Chronicles 9:5-6)

To express the Queen of Sheba's reaction in the vernacular of today—she was utterly blown away!

That would be a sad thing indeed if that were all that happened. But, thankfully, she experienced much, much more. She was dumbfounded by Solomon's wisdom, and she was bedazzled by the magnitude and glory of his architectural feats and the stately beauty of his royal presence. But the wisdom and wonder ultimately led her to the experience and expression of worship. Listen to the worshipful response of this foreigner to the kingdom of Israel.

> "Blessed be the Lord your God, who has delighted in you and set you on his throne as king for the Lord your God! Because your God loved Israel and would establish them forever, he has made you king over them, that you may execute justice and righteousness."
> (2 Chronicles 9:8)

What a priceless gift that the Queen of Sheba did not lose the glory of *God* in the glory of *Solomon* but that she was granted wisdom to see the glory of God in all she beheld!

True wisdom always leads to worshiping God, whose glory is displayed in all things "bright and beautiful." A new dimension of life is provided for the seeker who is enabled to see the glory of God in all things. Then, life itself becomes worship as we experience God's glory in the laughter of a child, the smile of a friend, a delicious meal, a beautiful flower, the singing of a bird, the gatherings of the church, the breeze on our face, and the sunlight filling our eyes. To live life without this type of worshipful wisdom is not to live at all but only to exist. It is so easy to lose God in the wonders of His world when in reality, all creation sings His praise. It is easy also to lose God in the cult of *personality* worship that honors and extols men above God. The Queen of Sheba did not do this even in the courts of Solomon. She was not blinded by his riches, wisdom, and abilities. Instead, she saw the display of God's love and power in them. Hers was the wisdom of a worshiper, which is the greatest wisdom of all.

MAY 7
2 Chronicles 10-12

"THE GREAT DIVIDE"

It was amazing, historic, and incredibly powerful, but it only lasted 80 years. The glory days of Israel, the days of a united people under God's anointed kings, David and Solomon, lasted for only two generations. In that short time span, a defeated, scattered, and disheartened people were transformed to become the dominant nation of the age, controlling the region from Egypt to Syria and the Mediterranean Sea to Mesopotamia.

But it was all lost in a matter of months because of the pride-filled heart of a 41-year-old man, Rehoboam. His arrogant and condescending spirit divided the nation in two, leaving only the tribes of Judah and Benjamin under his rule. The ten northern tribes, henceforth known as Israel, refused to be governed by a man who was concerned only with using power to oppress and not to bless.

The nation would never be united again. Apostasy soon sweep through the ten northern tribes, and the division invited the invasion of King Shishak of Egypt and the plundering of Judah's riches. "Pride goes before destruction and a haughty spirit before a fall," wrote Rehoboam's father (Pro. 16:18), but sadly this son of wise Solomon did not believe this axiom applied to him. He recognized the error of his ways too late and, in some measure, humbled himself for the consequences of his pride.

Unity is precious to God. In Psalm 133, David compares unity to the beautiful fragrance of the high priest's anointing and the life-giving dew that descends to the earth around Mount Hermon. Unity attracts the favor and blessing of God wherever and whenever His people express it. Division is the dreadful result and curse of a proud spirit. In his usual blunt and truth-speaking fashion, the apostle James is clear about the origin of a prideful and divisive spirit. "But if you have bitter jealousy and selfish ambition in your hearts, do not boast and be false to the truth. This is not the wisdom that comes down from above, but is earthly, unspiritual, demonic" (Jas 3:14-15).

Pride is the original sin, for it was pride that prompted Lucifer to be dissatisfied with his exalted position among the heavenly host and wickedly attempt to become like the Most High. Pride divided the angels of God, and devilish pride divided Adam and Eve from their blessed relationship with the Heavenly Father. Pride is the Devil's work and his most powerful and deceptive weapon. For pride, he camouflages and promotes as a virtue in the guise of self-esteem, self-worth, self-confidence, and self-awareness. If only as the people of God, we could recognize that anything, any word, and any thought that begins with "self" begins in the wrong place. The self-life never produces the best life. The best life is a life focused on God and others, just as we are instructed in the Ten Commandments. Pride robs us of real life—a life centered on loving God, loving people, and impacting the world. Now, that is living!

MAY 8
2 Chronicles 13-15

"APPEAL TO HEAVEN"

Many of us are familiar with famous inspirational quotes from the American Revolution. "Give me liberty or give me death," "Don't tread on me," "All men are created equal," and several others are stamped in the collective conscience of many freedom-loving people in our nation. Not as well known in our day are the words, "An Appeal to Heaven," which were sewn into many battle flags carried by regimental units of the Continental Army.

This phrase does not come from an enthusiastic exclamation of a patriot's speech. It originated in the pen of the British jurist and philosopher of the seventeenth century, John Locke. Locke and his essays were fundamental to the thinking of many of the founding fathers of America. Locke wrote that whenever a people suffering under a tyrant king or government have no place or means of appeal on earth, "then they have a liberty to appeal to heaven, whenever they judge the cause of sufficient moment." Locke's phrase "appeal to heaven" fired the faith and will of thousands of Americans over a century later as they determined to resist unlawful subjugation with an "appeal to heaven."

Today's reading shares the overview of two of the greatest and good kings of Judah—Abijah and Asa—who stood against idolatry and intrigue by *appealing to heaven*. "And when Judah looked, behold, the battle was in front of and behind them. And they cried to the Lord, and the priests blew the trumpets. Then the men of Judah raised the battle shout. And when the men of Judah shouted, God defeated Jeroboam and all Israel before Abijah and Judah" (2 Chr. 13:14-15). It was not the shout that brought the victory but *the faith* that prompted the appeal to God. "And the men of Judah prevailed, because they relied on the Lord, the God of their fathers" (2 Chr. 13:18). Years later, King Asa faced an Ethiopian army of over 1 million men, the largest enemy force ever described in Scripture. But at the words of faith and admonition from the prophet Azariah and others,

> *"Asa cried to the Lord his God, 'O Lord, there is none like you to help, between the mighty and the weak. Help us, O Lord our God, for we rely on you, and in your name, we have come against this multitude. O Lord, you are our God; let not man prevail against you.' So, the Lord defeated the Ethiopians before Asa and before Judah, and the Ethiopians fled."*
> (2 Chronicles 14:11-12)

An appeal to heaven is an appeal in faith to God. It is a cry of desperation and powerful because it calls upon God for victory.

Thousands of years have passed since these battle scenes described in our reading today took place, but the principles of faith and the power for an appeal to heaven remain unchanged. God moves when we are moved to desperation for His help and power. When were you last desperate for God to move in power in any situation in your life? What might you be facing today that needs a desperate appeal to heaven from you? Like Paul, we find God's strength in our weakness (2 Cor. 12:9). Appeal to heaven today, my friend. "The eyes of the Lord are toward the righteous and His ears toward their cry" (Ps. 34:15).

MAY 9
2 Chronicles 16-18

"Finishing Well"

There is a quaint saying that shares this encouragement, "Well begun is half done." There is much truth in those five words because no task is ever finished that is not first started. However, it has been my experience over the years that many people, through the excitement of an opportunity, have little difficulty in beginning a project with hard work and enthusiasm. Still, when it comes to seeing a project to completion... Well, that is another matter. Many people are self-starters, but that is all they do—start. "Well, begun is half done," but that's all it is, *half done."*

It takes more than vision and enthusiasm to bring a project to completion. It requires character, determination, and commitment to finish well. If that is true of any task or project, how much more is it true of the greatest endeavor of all—a faithful life of service to God?

King Asa is a living example of a good and godly man who began well but did not finish well. The contrast between the early years of his reign and his later years is quite startling. By faithful devotion and dependence on God, Asa defeated the greatest armed force ever to invade the land of Israel. Beyond that, in his zeal for the Lord, Asa destroyed the places of idol worship throughout Judah and even removed his mother from her royal position because she had commissioned "a detestable image" to be fashioned for worship (2 Chr. 15:16).

Contrast that devotion to Asa's actions in his later years. Rather than calling upon the Lord for deliverance from the wicked King Baasha, Asa confiscated the temple's treasures to hire a mercenary army from the King of Syria to come to his aid. When the Lord in His love sent the seer Hanani to reprove him, an enraged Asa had the man of God put in stocks in prison (2 Chr. 16:10). Finally, during his final two years of life when a disease afflicted him in his feet, even then Asa refused to seek the Lord and only relied on human therapies to cure his disease. What a sad ending to a life and reign that had begun so well. We are not told in the Scriptures the path that led to Asa's spiritual decline and apathy, but somehow over the long years of his life and reign, Asa lost his passion for God. He did not finish well.

The great Bible teacher and preacher of the late 19th and early twentieth centuries, F. B. Meyer, said that he often prayed, "Dear Lord, please let my life flow all the way to the end. I do not want to wind up in a swamp." Amen. A light of promise from the Lord is framed against the twilight of Asa's fading fervor. It is the promise of God's strength to cause us to begin well and continue with faithful zeal to the end of our life's journey. It is the promise of a God who continually looks for people to whom He can reveal His strength and grace. "For the eyes of the Lord run to and fro throughout the whole earth, to give strong support to those whose heart is blameless toward him" (2 Chr. 16:9).

God is looking for people He can help. Are we a people looking for *His* help?

MAY 10
2 Chronicles 19-21

"OUR EYES ARE ON YOU"

One of the most precise tests of a person's character is how they respond to a loving rebuke. As we saw in yesterday's reading, King Asa was lovingly rebuked by a servant of God, and he responded by placing him in stocks in prison. Today, we read of a completely different response from Asa's son, King Jehoshaphat, when Jehu, the prophet of God, rebuked him for allying with Ahab, the desperately evil king of Israel. Jehoshaphat's humble response set the direction for the rest of his life and the challenges to come.

With a shepherd-like heart, Jehoshaphat sought to bring the people of Judah back to the Lord. He established a program of Bible instruction throughout the land. He restored the justice system by appointing judges who would make decisions based on the fear of the Lord and faithfulness to Him (2 Chr. 19:4-10). Nothing was more important to Jehoshaphat than leading the nation to know, serve, and worship the God of Israel faithfully. Because Jehoshaphat made these things his priority, he was ready and the people were prepared when the great trial of their age arrived.

The trial came in the form of an invasion by the ancient enemies of Israel—the Moabites and the Ammonites. How did Jehoshaphat mobilize the nation to meet these foes? He called for a prayer meeting. "Then Jehoshaphat was afraid and set his face to seek the Lord and proclaimed a fast throughout all Judah" (2 Chr. 20:3). Jehoshaphat's first move was to move toward God, and his first plan was not to have a plan but rather to look to the Lord for His plan. "We do not know what to do, but our eyes are on you" (2 Chr. 20:12).

What a scene it must have been! Hundreds of thousands of people, young and old, standing before the Lord their God with upturned faces, worshiping and waiting for their God to give His answer. And they did not have to wait long as the Spirit of God came upon Jahaziel, who, with God-inspired passion, promised them that the battle to come was the Lord's and they would not have to fight for them. This did not mean the people of Judah were inactive or uninvolved in the battle. They were to be worshiping warriors whose weapon against the enemy was the power of praise! "Hear me, Judah and inhabitants of Jerusalem! Believe in the Lord your God, and you will be established; believe his prophets, and you will succeed" (2 Chr. 20:20). It was when the people of Judah began to sing and praise that "the Lord set an ambush against the men of Ammon, Moab, and Mount Seir, who had come against Judah, so that they were routed" (2 Chr. 20:22).

Every believer in Jesus is involved in spiritual warfare. We do not fight against flesh and blood enemies. Our battle is against the demonized, energized, organized, mobilized hordes of Hell. We are no match for them in our own strength or tactics. However, we do have weapons of spiritual warfare that are mighty through God to pull down strongholds (2 Cor. 10:4). Our weapons are the weapons of worship and the Word. We fight like Jesus, who, when He was attacked by the Tempter, overcame him with the Sword of the Spirit, the Word of God, and by a relentless devotion to only worship the Lord, His God, and Father. Brothers and sisters, we are at war. Our foe is mighty, but Jesus has defeated him. We must not lose heart but battle the enemy every day with the Word of God and the worship of God. The battle is the Lord's!

MAY 11
2 Chronicles 22-24

"GRIPPED BY GRATITUDE"

During my years of college and graduate school, there were two common denominators for every one of the thousands of classes I attended. First, every class session began with prayer led by either the professor or one of the students. Secondly, every classroom on the campus had written above the blackboard an inspirational quote from the founder of the university, a fiery Methodist evangelist. Now, I admit that I did not really appreciate this custom at that time in my life and sometimes considered it a little odd or at least old-fashioned. However, looking back today, more than 40 years later, I understand how effective this custom truly was. Seeing those written challenges and words of wisdom hundreds of times etched them forever into my mind and, as a result, has continually brought them into my thoughts over the years. For example, as I read the passage today concerning the life and reign of King Joash, one of those classroom quotations from my college days quickly came to my mind, "When gratitude dies on the altar of a man's heart, that man is well-nigh hopeless." The statement may seem a little "old school" and "preachy" in style, but the wisdom it communicates is Biblical and timeless. When a person develops an ungrateful spirit, his life is usually unsalvageable.

Our reading today in God's Word shares a case study about the danger and disaster of an ungrateful person. If ever anyone should have been grateful all his days, it was King Joash of Judah. As an infant, he was rescued from the murderous plot of his grandmother by his Aunt Jehoshabeath. Then, for seven years, he was hidden and protected by the godly high priest, Jehoiada. At seven, Joash, guarded by Jehoiada and teams of bodyguard priests, was brought to the temple court and proclaimed king. Through the remaining years of Jehoiada's long and devoted life, Joash was counseled and guided by him to be a king that would honor God and bless his people. Finally, Jehoiada died at the age of 130. After his death, how did Joash repay all the kindness and mentoring Jehoiada had provided for him? He yielded to the demands of the leaders to restore idol worship in Judah, and when he was confronted by Jehoiada's godly, Spirit-filled son Zechariah, Joash commanded that he be stoned to death.

Granted, this is a unique and awful demonstration of ingratitude, but it does warn us of how terribly destructive a lack of gratitude can be to our souls. Ingratitude is not only a sin against others; it is a sin against ourselves. Ingratitude desensitizes our mind's ability to receive truth from God. Paul wrote these words of diagnosis over the character of a God-rejecting people, "For although they knew God, they did not honor him as God or *give thanks to him*, but they became futile in their thinking, and their foolish hearts were darkened" (Rom. 1:21).

How do we avoid the terrible consequences of ingratitude? The answer is quite simple and very effective—by practicing gratitude daily. Gratitude should be included in our conversations with God and others, sharing how grateful we are for who God is and what He has done. Tell others regularly of your sincere gratitude for their kindness, and you will experience the power of gratitude. Gratitude, expressed to God and others, produces a grateful spirit and poisons a selfish mindset. Gratitude is an offering to God and a blessing to others and ourselves. "Through him then let us continually offer up a sacrifice of praise to God, that is, the fruit of lips that acknowledge his name" (Heb. 13:15).

MAY 12
2 Chronicles 25-27

"DELIGHTFUL DISCIPLINE"

"So Jotham became mighty, because he ordered his ways before the Lord his God."
(2 Chronicles 27:6)

The title of this devotional may seem like an oxymoron, a contradiction in terms. Many people would regard the words "delightful discipline" the same way they would an expression like "a joyful root canal!" Granted, discipline is not a pleasant experience in itself. Ask any child whose parents believe in it! By its very definition, discipline requires an exercise of the will brought to bear on emotions or desires that sometimes cry out for "freedom." However, it is clear from human experience and the Scriptures that discipline is one of the most helpful qualities we can provide for ourselves or others. Discipline resists immediate self-gratification for the delayed experience of a more delightful benefit and joy.

In our reading today, King Jotham is a timeless example of the benefit of discipline, especially the most significant discipline—a God-honoring discipline. Jotham came to reign in the most jarring of circumstances. At the young age of 25, the responsibilities of the kingdom were thrust upon him when his powerful and popular father, Uzziah, was struck with leprosy because of a *lack* of discipline. Uzziah, proud in his attitude because of all his success, crossed the line of God's limitations by offering incense on the altar, a ministry limited to the priests, the descendants of Aaron. To his credit, Jotham learned from his father's tragic error and was determined to "order his ways before the Lord." As a result of this sacred self-discipline, "Jotham became mighty" (2 Chr. 27:6). Discipline is a divinely ordained character trait that honors God and brings His blessing.

Self-discipline was a character trait of Jesus, who ordered His life to do the things pleasing to His Father. It was self-discipline that brought Jesus His personal victory over fear and dread as He prayed submissively in the garden, "Nevertheless, not my will, but yours, be done" (Luke 22:42). Because self-discipline is a characteristic of Jesus, it is also one of the qualities of the fruit of the Holy Spirit, "self-control" (Gal. 5:23). Discipline does require determination, hard work, and sacrifice. But it also provides the greatest of all gifts we can ever give to ourselves, by God's grace—"godliness." Paul told Timothy, the young pastor in Ephesus, to exercise discipline to attain the precious goal of godliness. "Have nothing to do with irreverent, silly myths. Rather train yourself for godliness" (1 Tim. 4:7). The verb Paul uses for "train" is the root word from which comes our English term "gymnasium." So, Paul is challenging Timothy (and us), "Get into the gym for godliness!" Godliness is not the result of being a "pew potato" in church. No, godliness comes to those who do more than just attend church services. They leave the sanctuary to "work out" their salvation daily (Phil. 2:12). Of course, Paul is not teaching that we are saved by faith plus works, but he does make it crystal clear that we are saved by *a faith that works* (Eph. 2:8-10).

God is serious about our faith; we need to be as well, all the while knowing that God's loving desire is that we experience the joy-filled abundant life provided for those who order their lives according to His precepts. The Father desires us to know His joy. He is serious about our joy, and we should be as well.

MAY 13
2 Chronicles 28-30

"AFTER THE DARKNESS, LIGHT"

A few years ago, my wife and I were blessed to take a group of people from our church on a "Rome and Reformation Tour." On this trip, we visited the sites in the city of Rome associated with the capital of the Roman empire, and then those sites connected with the rise of the Roman Church that succeeded it. Then our group traveled to Germany and followed a study tour of the places associated with the life and ministry of the great reformer, Martin Luther. Finally, we traveled to Switzerland to learn more about the ministry of the Reformation leaders Huldrych Zwingli and John Calvin.

Our final tour day was spent in the lovely city of Geneva. A small park in that city commemorates the influence of the great spiritual reformation that swept through Europe in the sixteenth century. Within that beautiful park stands an imposing wall containing statues of leaders of the Protestant Reformation associated with the city of Geneva and beyond. There, engraved in large letters upon that wall, is this phrase—"Post Tenebras Lux," which translates into English as "After the Darkness, Light." Those words were the motto and the reality of the Reformation. Out of the terrible centuries of spiritual darkness covering Europe, God, by His grace and through His Word taught by brave men and women, brought the dawning of a new day of gospel light.

Our reading today could be described as the age of Reformation in the kingdom of Judah and some sections of Israel. It is hard to imagine a darker time spiritually in Judah as King Ahaz offered his own little children to the Canaanite gods in a valley outside Jerusalem, destroyed the objects for the worship of Jehovah on Mount Zion, and then locked the doors to prevent people from worshiping the Lord in His temple. What a desperately dark and evil season! But then, Post Tenebras Lux—"After the Darkness, Light."

Where did this light of the Lord and His truth first dawn? In the heart of one young man, Hezekiah, the son of the most wicked king Judah would ever know, Ahaz. The first gleams of the Lord's light are described this way in Hezekiah's testimony. "Now it is in my heart to make a covenant with the Lord, the God of Israel, in order that His fierce anger may turn away from us" (2 Chr. 29:10). Hezekiah then called on the citizens of his kingdom and invited the people of the tribes of Israel to join him saying, "For the Lord your God is gracious and merciful and will not turn away his face from you, if you return to him" (2 Chr. 30:9). What was the result of this light in Hezekiah's heart that he determined to share with others? "So there was great joy in Jerusalem, for since the time of Solomon the son of David king of Israel there had been nothing like this in Jerusalem" (2 Chr. 30:26).

Post Tenebras Lux—"After the Darkness, Light." God's light is greater than the deepest darkness. We live in a terribly dark world, that is true. But that darkness cannot extinguish the light of Jesus who shines in our hearts. We are light in Christ (Eph. 5:8), and we are the light of the world (Matt. 5:14). Today, as the gospel song challenges us, "Carry your candle, run to the darkness…and go light your world."

MAY 14
2 Chronicles 31-33

"Mercy Beyond Measure"

For many years, I have believed that the most profound word in all of Scripture is the word "so." Now, of course, many words in the Bible are much longer than this little word, but there is none that is deeper because it is the word that measures the love of God. "For God *so* loved the world, that he gave his only Son, that whoever believes in Him should not perish but have everlasting life" (John 3:16). Jesus said, "For God so loved the world…." Those two little letters that create the word "so" define a depth of love that can never be measured or comprehended. It is a tiny, two-letter modifier that communicates what is infinite and incomprehensible to our finite minds, the love of God.

Of course, we are not surprised in the least that God would love. It is His very nature to love because God is love (1 John 4:8). What is dumbfounding is *whom* God loves and *how much* He loves them. Again, we are told by Jesus that God so loved *"the world."* This means the world of mankind, all mankind. Jesus said that His Father loves *all* human beings, and we certainly take great comfort in celebrating that width of the Father's love and resting in that amazing truth. However, what Jesus said about His Father's love also means that God not only loves *all* human beings, but He also loves *every* human being. This is where it becomes challenging because God loves each individual, and *we know* some of them! Honestly, we can think of individuals so wicked and cruel that we could never imagine loving them, but God does. His love and His grace are greater than their sin. At times, that is hard to accept, especially when we see God's love and grace include people like King Manasseh, whom we read about in our passage today.

If the Apostle Paul is the example of amazing grace in the New Testament, I would offer Manasseh as that trophy in the Old Testament. Manasseh was a monster, "And he burned his sons as an offering in the Valley of the Son of Hinnom, used fortune-telling and omens and sorcery, and dealt with mediums and necromancers. He did much evil in the sight of the Lord, provoking him to anger" (2 Chr. 33:6). What a despicable human being. He was a man beyond any help or hope. But...he wasn't! God's grace and love were enough, even for the likes of him. Under the punishment of God, Manasseh did the most unpredictable and unexpected thing—he repented. "And when he was in distress, he entreated the favor of the Lord his God and humbled himself greatly before the God of his fathers. He prayed to him, and God was moved by his entreaty and heard his plea and brought him again to Jerusalem into His kingdom. Then Manasseh knew that the Lord was God." (33:12-13)

Honestly, I have a hard time with those words, don't you? A wretched person like Manasseh doesn't deserve to be forgiven and restored. And I am absolutely right. He doesn't deserve it. In truth, no one does. I don't. You don't. Forgiveness is never deserved because it is a free gift, offered only by the merit of the perfect life and atoning death of Jesus. God *so loved* a wretch like Manasseh that He saved him— amazing! Yes, amazing. God's grace always is.

"Amazing grace how sweet the sound that saved a wretch *like me!*"

MAY 15
2 Chronicles 34-36

"WITHOUT REMEDY"

"But they kept mocking the messengers of God, despising his words and scoffing at his prophets, until the wrath of the Lord rose against his people, until there was no remedy."
(2 Chronicles 36:16)

During the presidency of Andrew Jackson, a man by the name of George Wilson was convicted of robbery and murder in Pennsylvania. At the persistent efforts of some of his friends who were able to present further evidence calling into question the guilty verdict, President Jackson issued Wilson a full pardon. Then, one of the strangest events in the history of American jurisprudence took place. Some of Wilson's friends traveled to the prison where he was awaiting execution and personally presented the pardon to him. They were stunned when their friend refused to accept the President's pardon! Without a clear explanation, Wilson just adamantly refused to accept it. Well, this resulted in a complicated legal issue. Could the death sentence be carried out on Wilson or not? A jury found him guilty but pardoned by the President, so what was Wilson's legal status? The case quickly came before the United States Supreme Court, and renowned Chief Justice John Marshall wrote a decision: A pardon is a piece of paper that offers forgiveness of the punishment assigned for the guilt of a crime committed. However, if a pardon is rejected, it is not a pardon at all. George Wilson must hang. And that is exactly what happened—George Wilson was hanged for crimes for which he had been offered a full and complete pardon. The legal decision was clear; a pardon rejected is no pardon at all.

As tragic as the case of George Wilson is, it pales in comparison to that of the kingdom of Judah. Through the messages of His prophets, Jehovah continually offered the people a pardon for their crimes against Him and the punishment they so rightly deserved. However, the people of Judah mocked these messengers of mercy because they despised the words of God's peace and pardon offered to them. As a result, the sins and crimes of the nation were *without remedy*. They would not receive their pardon, so the only recourse was to receive their penalty.

It is truly insane to reject the mercy of an offended God when He freely offers it. However, this is exactly the state of the unrepentant sinner before a holy God. Sadly, it could be the condition of someone reading this page. God forbid that it might be you, my friend.

God offers guilty sinners so much more than mercy. You see, "justice" means receiving what we deserve. "Mercy" means *not* receiving what we deserve. "Grace" means receiving what we *do not* deserve. God, in His mercy, offers us grace because of the merit of Jesus. However, if a person spurns and despises His mercy and grace, that person is requesting justice from God, and that is exactly what they will receive—justice from God. What an awful fate—receiving what is fully deserved from a holy, offended God!

Yes, it is "Jesus or justice." Which will you receive from God?

MAY 16
Ezra 1-3

"The Remnant Returns"

The book of Ezra continues the history of the Jewish people where the book of 2 Chronicles ends. It might be helpful to remind ourselves of the approximate timeline for the Jewish nation. Most Evangelical scholars date the Exodus from Egypt, led by Moses, about the year 1444 BC and the entry of the Israelites into the Land of Canaan after 40 years of wandering at about 1404 BC. After a period of governance by judges and then by Saul as the first king, the Twelve Tribes of Israel were united as one nation about 1000 BC. Following only 80 years of reign under David and his son Solomon, the united nation of Israel broke apart under the pride and oppression of King Rehoboam about 920 BC. For the next 200 years, the people of Israel were divided into two nations, known as "Israel," comprised of the 10 tribes in the north, and "Judah," composed of the two tribes of Judah and Benjamin in the south.

In 722 BC, the 10 northern tribes of Israel were defeated and taken into captivity by the empire of Assyria. Beginning about 606 BC and finalizing in 586 BC with the destruction of Jerusalem and the Temple, the two southern tribes of Judah and Benjamin were carried into captivity by King Nebuchadnezzar of Babylon. A few decades passed, and then Cyrus, king of the Medo-Persian empire, defeated Babylon. About the year 538 BC, he published a decree stating, "The Lord, the God of heaven, has given me all the kingdoms of the earth, and he has charged me to build Him a house at Jerusalem which is in Judah." Further, King Cyrus declared to the Jews, "Whoever is among you of all his people, may his God be with him, and let him go up to Jerusalem, which is in Judah, and rebuild the house of the Lord, the God of Israel— He is the God who is in Jerusalem" (Ezra 1:2-3). Just remarkable. Not only did King Cyrus permit the Jewish citizens of his kingdom to return to this sacred project, but he also returned to the leaders of the people 5,400 gold and silver vessels that Nebuchadnezzar had carried away from the temple decades earlier!

It was only a tiny remnant of people, just 42,360, compared to the millions that had once populated Israel's united kingdom that responded to this invitation. Yet, they were God's remnant, not just numerically but spiritually. By far, the vast majority of the Jewish people chose not to return to their homeland. Yet, a remnant did make that choice and responded to the Lord's calling. "Then rose up the heads of the fathers' houses of Judah and Benjamin, and the priests and the Levites, everyone whose spirit God had stirred to go up to rebuild the house of the Lord that is in Jerusalem" (Ezra 1:5). We cannot imagine the faith, courage, and endurance required among these believers to travel hundreds of miles, experience unimaginable hardships, and endure the opposition of violent enemies to follow the Lord and do His will. We can only imagine the joy that filled their hearts when, after two years, the cornerstone for the new temple was laid on Mount Zion. They wept, they shouted, and they sang. "For he is good, for his steadfast love endures forever" (Ezra 3:11). Only those who *hear* and *obey* God's voice can truly sing Isaac Watts' song "We're Marching to Zion." I wonder, can we honestly join the remnant's song today?

> *Come, we that love the Lord,*
> *and let our joys be known;*
> *join in a song with sweet accord,*
> *join in a song with sweet accord*
> *and thus surround the throne,*
> *and thus surround the throne.*
> *We're marching to Zion,*
> *beautiful, beautiful Zion;*
> *we're marching upward to Zion,*
> *the beautiful City of God.*

MAY 17
Ezra 4-6

"Prince of the Persecuted"

> *"Surely the wrath of man shall praise you;*
> *the remnant of wrath you will put on like a belt."*
> (Psalm 76:10)

Jesus said a very strange thing in His famous "Sermon on the Mount" when He declared, "Blessed are those who are persecuted for righteousness' sake, for theirs is the kingdom of heaven... for so they persecuted the prophets who were before you" (Matt. 5:10-12). Now, according to human wisdom, that statement makes no sense at all. However, from the perspective of the Lord (and that is the only perspective that ultimately matters), Jesus spoke *actual* truth, not *theoretical* truth. Our Lord said to be opposed by the power of the earth is to know and experience the privileges of the citizens of the King and His Kingdom. According to the Apostle Paul, persecution is both the proof and the privilege of those who believe and follow Jesus (Phil. 1:29, 2 Tim. 3:12). To be treated wrongly for doing good is to be identified with our Master who experienced the same.

It is also counter-intuitive but absolutely true that experiencing opposition for our faith is an opportunity to experience our God in fresh and powerful ways. It is this "wrath of men" that David said our sovereign God causes to praise Him and that actually adorns His majesty, like wearing of a beautiful belt (Ps. 76:10). It is often incredibly humorous to see how the Lord overcomes His enemies with "Divine Judo," using their forceful assault and aggression against them. Today's chapters are a historical record of our Master using martial arts against His enemies. It is a story celebrated by the Jewish people for over 2500 years, and it should also thrill our hearts and steel our resolve.

You remember that King Cyrus of Persia granted permission for the Jewish people who desired to participate in journeying to their homeland and rebuild the Temple of the Lord. A remnant of around 43,000 returned and committed themselves to the sacred task. This project was massive, and years passed in the endeavor. In time, King Cyrus died, and the Persian King Artaxerxes eventually came to power. This change of administration was just the opportunity the enemies of the Jews had sought to work against them and their building project. They lied to King Artaxerxes about the Jews' motives. They appealed to his selfishness, saying they were a rebellious people and would use the project as fortification and a platform for rebellion and refusal to pay taxes. The king responded by withdrawing his predecessor's "building permit" and, in an edict, forbade the people from continuing the project. In the face of opposition and force, the work on the temple and the city ceased for years.

Then, the King of all kings, who sets up kings and removes them by His power, brought to an end the reign of Artaxerxes and raised up a new king, Darius of Persia. This new administration brought new hope for the Jewish people who, spurred to action by the prophets Haggai and Zechariah and led by Zerubbabel, began in earnest to rebuild the house of God. Then, God worked a miracle on their behalf. He used government bureaucracy to assist them! Buried deeply in the archives of Babylon and Persia a document was found of King Cyrus from years before, authorizing the project. Not only did King Darius decide to permit the rebuilding of the temple, but he was also determined to have his government *pay for it!*

The earth is the Lord's and all it contains (Ps. 24:1). The heart of the king is in His hands, and like a river, the Lord turns it as He pleases (Prov. 21:1). Yes, persecution is a privilege, and opposition is an opportunity. Let's keep the faith and keep being faithful.

MAY 18
Ezra 7-10

"Ezra's Example"

"For Ezra had set his heart to study the Law of the Lord, and to do it and to teach his statutes and rules in Israel."
(Ezra 7:10)

As a father of small children, I remember how much I looked forward to providing Christmas presents for my kids and how much I dreaded it at the same time. Let me quickly explain before you throw this book away in disgust! I loved buying Christmas presents for my children. In fact, my wife will tell you that I was a little fanatical about it. However, I often experienced considerable dread when I purchased gifts for them, a dread associated with three small words—"some assembly required."

Without a doubt, I am the least capable dad on the face of the earth when it comes to using tools and following instructions for assembling toys! I cannot begin to say how many years I left the blissful experience of a Christmas Eve service at our church to spend long hours in the purgatory of assembling toys for the next morning. Yet, there was an exception to the rule of my ineptness if a detailed picture of the process and the end product was included. Then, and only then, could I accomplish the toy assembly mission without weeping, wailing, and gnashing of teeth. Having a pattern or a model, makes all the difference in the world.

The same is true regarding our development as disciples. We need a pattern, a model. The Lord knows this, which is why He has shared instructions and examples of mentoring in His Word. In our reading today, we have some of the clearest directions and one of the best examples of faithful behavior in all of the Bible.

Ezra is a timeless pattern of a God-follower whose life was an inspiration and model for people of his day and on through the centuries. Ezra was a man of devotion, zeal, purpose, and influence. Indeed, these qualities can only be produced through God's grace, but what are the practices in Ezra's life that provided the conduit for God's grace to flow? Well, they are brilliant, and much of their brilliance is in their simplicity. He determined to *study* God's Word, he determined to *do* God's Word, and he determined to *teach* God's Word. *Study it, do it, and teach it.* Simple. Brilliant. Not easy, of course, but these three determinations encompass the totality of life and mission for us as disciples.

We Study God's Word: By studying God's Word we come to know our God and understand His ways. We also come to understand the plan He has for mankind in general and for us individually.

We Do God's Word: This is the way of true life, for it is not the hearer of the Word but the doer who is truly blessed (Jas 1:22). This is the way of wisdom, for wisdom is the application of the Word to life. In *doing* the Word of God, our faith moves from the intellectual to the experiential, and the living reality of God transforms us.

We Teach God's Word: We become missional in this final means and method of God's grace. We become models and mentors for others. We are certainly not perfect and will never be in this lifetime, but we can be genuine and real. We can say to others, "Follow me as I follow Christ" (1 Cor. 11:1). We then fulfill the purpose of our Lord's call on our lives, "Follow me and I will make you become fishers of men" (Mark 1:17).

Study the Word, do the Word, and teach the Word. This is God's Word for us today and every day.

MAY 19
Nehemiah 1-3

"A CAUSE, A CALL, A COMMISSION"

Over the years, one question that I have been asked as much as any other is this: "How can I know the will of God?" Of course, this is a huge question, and its answer could not have greater significance. Many people complicate the issue much more than necessary. I have often found it helpful to think of the will of God in two aspects: the *revealed* will of God and the *discerned* will of God. The latter flows out of the former.

The way we discern the will of God for ourselves, in personal and specific situations, is by aligning our lives in obedience to God's will that has already been revealed. In other words, we should not be concerned about the will of God we *don't know* until we are actively obedient to the will of God we *do know*. We *discover* God's will by *doing* God's will.

Our reading today provides us with a wonderful, personal example. Nehemiah was a contemporary of Ezra the scribe. Both of them were refugees living in Babylon during the reign of the Persian king, Artaxerxes. Ezra was a scribe of the tribe of Levi, while it appears Nehemiah was of Judah and served as a palace official in the king's administration. It seems that Nehemiah was one of the king's most trusted advisors. He served as cupbearer, a position that included close personal contact with the king and also involved guarding his safety.

Now, how did Nehemiah go from being a king's cupbearer to a wall builder in the city of Jerusalem? The answer is, of course, by the will of God, but our attention is on *how* that will of God was understood and undertaken. It began with *a cause*.

Nehemiah's heart was gripped, as he went about his life of daily obedience, with an awareness of something that needed to be done. After nearly 100 years following the first return of Jewish refugees to Jerusalem, the city's wall had still not been rebuilt. The citizens were in danger, and suffered constant harassment. This terrible reality weighed upon Nehemiah's heart, but he did not respond first in plans and action. No, he made it a matter of prayer. Before Nehemiah talked to anyone else, he spoke to God. Brilliant, spiritual, powerful.

Secondly, doing the will of God became a sense of *calling* to Nehemiah. He prayed about the need in Jerusalem, which intensified in his mind so much that it was constantly a part of his thinking process. We could say, "it was heavy on his heart" every day. Nehemiah so identified with the situation in Jerusalem that people around him, including a pagan king, recognized it. In this way, Nehemiah could put words to what was on his heart and clearly express it as a "calling on his life." Then, the final aspect of knowing and doing God's will was reached as Nehemiah received a *commission*. He was empowered and sent by someone in authority to accomplish the *cause* and fulfill his *calling*.

Granted, the one in authority was a ruthless king, but that king was under the control of the King of kings. The King of the universe moved on and through an earthly king to commission a faithful servant to do God's bidding. This process resulted in Nehemiah not just "going for a personal project" but being "sent on a Divine mission." As Nehemiah faithfully worshiped and served God in Babylon, he became aware of a *cause*, sensed a *calling*, and was given a *commission*. In all this, I hear the wisdom of knowing and doing the will of God.

> "Trust in the Lord with all your heart, and do not lean on your own understanding. In all your ways acknowledge him, and he will make straight your paths."
> (Proverbs 3:5-6)

MAY 20
Nehemiah 4-6

"Oh No, to Ono!"

> "I am doing a great work and I cannot come down. Why should the work stop while I leave it and come down to you?"
> (Nehemiah 6:3)

I will never forget the information and insight I received many years ago while attending the annual pastors' conference of one of the largest denominations of churches in America. This fellowship included nearly 50,000 churches and about 15 million church members. It is a powerful association and one of significant present and historical impact. And yet, the executive leaders of this denomination were greatly troubled by the findings of a study revealing that over 200 pastors each month were resigning or leaving their churches under duress due to significant opposition by members of the congregation. The leaders of the denomination decided to investigate further.

Their deliberations led them to conduct a survey of pastors who, in recent years, had resigned due to opposition by members of the church. In the survey, the pastors were asked to list how many church members *actively opposed* them and their leadership. Several hundred pastors responded to this survey, and the results were astounding. When asked to list the people who opposed them, the average number of names on the list of those pastors who resigned due to opposition was seven. Yes, you read that correctly—*seven*. Two hundred pastors left Evangelical churches across America a month because of the resistance from *seven* people each!

Certainly, some of those 200 pastors each month should have resigned because they were not carrying out their ministries faithfully, and good, godly believers could not support them. However, the data revealed the power of criticism, rumor, and slander to undermine the strength and emotional health of faithful servants of God. It also made it clear that if pastors or Christian leaders focus on the vocal minority of the constant complainers, they will neglect the needs of the people who believe in them and their vision, or worse, leave the ministry assignment to which God has called them.

As followers of Jesus, we are commanded *to love everyone* but not *to listen to everyone*. Nehemiah is an example of this commitment of refusing to indulge in conversations that only distract from the work of the Lord and the welfare of His people. Sanballat and Tobiah are in the "hall of fame" of religious complainers. They claimed they wanted to have a ministry "dialogue" with Nehemiah on the plains of Ono. But, in reality they were deceptive discouragers, plants of the ultimate Deceiver, and set only on discouraging and defaming God's servant. Nehemiah's response was to say, "Oh no, to Ono." He knew their motives and that the "great work" to which he had been called required his full attention and complete devotion to duty (Neh. 6:3). If Tobiah and Sanballat were genuinely interested in God's work, they would have proven that by *laying bricks*, not *laying traps*. It is humility from God that makes us seek wisdom and safety from many counselors (Prov. 11:14), but that does not mean taking counsel from *any counselors*.

We need to make sure that we love all people, but we take our counsel from those who demonstrate they are "worshiping workers."

MAY 21
Nehemiah 7-9

"THE WATER GATE REVIVAL"

"And all the people gathered as one man into the square before the Water Gate. And they told Ezra the scribe to bring the Book of the Law of Moses that the Lord had commanded Israel."
(Nehemiah 8:1)

For many, the term "Watergate" has become a synonym for political maneuvering and intrigue at its worst. If you are a person of "a certain age," you no doubt remember the challenging days in America during the Watergate investigation that eventually led to the resignation from office by then President Richard Nixon. If you are not old enough to recall those days personally, yet you possess a basic knowledge of United States history, you are aware that it was one of the most challenging and divisive seasons our country has experienced.

However, that is certainly not the case in the history of the Jewish people. In fact, just the opposite. The term Water Gate is forever associated with a moment of national renewal and rededication for the nation of Israel. Imagine a congregation of over 40,000 people gathered in one of the largest public squares in Jerusalem for one purpose—to hear, read, and interpret the Word of God. It is probably not without Divine intent that this time of national renewal and revival for the "Living Water of the Word" took place where the people regularly came to draw water from the primary water source in Jerusalem.

The wall for the city had been completed in less than 60 days, one of the most amazing construction accomplishments in recorded history. The safety of the city and its people was not in a wall that separated them from their enemies but in a covenant that united them with their God. Theirs was a covenant relationship with the Lord. That covenant was founded on the words of the covenant that the Lord had given through Moses almost exactly 1000 years earlier. The ancient words of the Lord were the living and life-giving words for them as a people. The words were literally the living water for their health. As a result, hearing these words brought incredible joy as they recognized again all the Lord had given and done for them. However, these words of the Law produced sorrow, remorse, and repentance as they realized how false they and their fathers had been to the covenant responsibilities they owed to God. Rejoicing and repenting were the constant and conflicting emotional realities as they interacted with the Word of God.

Rejoicing and repenting is the rhythm of life for any follower of the Lord who is serious about their faith. The Word, like a mirror, shows us the moral dirt that continually clings to us in our daily life. But, the

Word of God is also the water that reflects our Lord's beauty, cleanses us from all unrighteousness, and conforms us more and more to the image of our Master. So, life for a Christian is lived daily at the "Water Gate," the source of cleansing and life-giving water that flows from the Rock of our Salvation, Jesus Christ. We must come to the Water Gate daily to cleanse our lives and renew our souls with the beautiful words of life.

> *Sing them over again to me,*
> *Wonderful words of life;*
> *Let me more of their beauty see,*
> *Wonderful words of life.*
> *Words of life and beauty*
> *Teach me faith and duty;*
>
> *Refrain:*
> *Beautiful words, wonderful words,*
> *Wonderful words of life;*
> *Beautiful words, wonderful words,*
> *Wonderful words of life.*

("Wonderful Words of Life" by Philip P. Bliss)

MAY 22
Nehemiah 10-13

"ZEALOUS FOR GOD"

"Who gave himself for us to redeem us from all lawlessness
and to purify for himself a people for his own possession
who are zealous for good works."
(Titus 2:14)

Several years ago, I heard the rock and roll legend Roy Orbison interviewed a few months before his death. At the interview's close, he was asked, "Roy, how would you like to be remembered?" After a few moments of reflection, the legendary musician replied, "Oh, I think just to be remembered will be good enough." I must say that I did appreciate the humility of his answer, which is not a common virtue among many rock and pop music performers.

Have you ever considered that question for yourself—how would you like to be remembered? It is a compelling and probing question. Perhaps even more important than the issue of being remembered is *who* we want to remember us.

Nehemiah was very clear on this question. Three times in the final chapter of the book that bears his name, he expresses a prayer, "Remember me, O my God" (Neh. 13:14, 22, 31). Nehemiah is not concerned about God forgetting him. Being perfect, God cannot forget anything, nor can He learn anything. Nehemiah is expressing that the Lord will affirm his personal devotion to the worship and work of God. Our reading today makes it very clear that to lead in the physical rebuilding of Jerusalem, Nehemiah also had to be fully committed to the spiritual rebuilding and reformation of the nation. Pursuing God is never an easy endeavor personally, and it is much more challenging to motivate and lead others on that cause. Right beliefs must be expressed in the right behaviors or the public profession, and testimony for truth is as lifeless as a tomb.

God has not provided for us in Christ only orthodoxy of faith but also the orthopraxy of faith. Faith produces and motivates toward good works and God's name. Paul's challenge to the pastor of the church on the Island of Crete, Titus, cited at the beginning of today's devotional, makes it clear that God saves us by grace and then, by that same grace, motivates us to be zealous for good works. The challenge we must embrace is that to be genuinely zealous for God, we must also be jealous for God—jealous in the sense that we believe our lives are a reflection of our God, and therefore we want our actions and attitudes to reflect Him rightly.

Some people think it is a godly road to remain completely unnoticed. The Lord Jesus certainly did not agree with or endorse that aspiration, "Let your light shine before others, so that they may see your good works and give glory to your Father who is in heaven" (Matt. 5:16). Jesus wants us to live in such a way that we *are noticed*. By noticing the uniquely different character and quality of our lives, a credible and powerful witness is shared for our Heavenly Father. Being zealous for good works is never about us; it is *about them*, and it is *for Him*. Pride would make this impossible, but sincere zealousness for God is not a human but a divine characteristic and is a natural expression of God's love that has been poured into our hearts (Rom. 5:5). Zealousness for God is a living, powerful witness. I once read a witty quote I thought found its answer in a Sunday School chorus I used to teach boys and girls. The quote: "I would rather see a sermon than hear one any day."

The children's chorus: "Do you know, Oh Christian, you're a sermon in shoes?" Amen!

MAY 23
Esther 1-3

"Never Mentioned, Ever Present"

The book of Esther is unique in so many ways. Yet, in one characteristic, it is utterly unique among all the 69 books that comprise our English Bibles. The book of Esther never mentions the word "God." Think about that for a moment. In the volume that we know as the Word of God, there is an entire book that does not reference the word "God" or, for that matter, any other term for the Divine Creator!

For this reason, some of the scribes of the intertestamental times (the centuries between the Old and New Testament) were very suspicious of the book of Esther, especially the ultra-orthodox groups like the Essenes, the copyists who created the Dead Sea Scrolls. God is not mentioned in the book of Esther, but His presence and providence are everywhere. This is one of the reasons the book of Esther is so compelling and comforting. The story of a beautiful young woman living in the palace of the king of Persia is the "never-mentioned, ever-present" Master of all things.

The backdrop for this testimony of God is dark indeed: opulence, decadence, sensuality, objectification of women, polygamy, slavery, pride, mercilessness, political intrigue, antisemitism, and genocide—to name a few characteristics of court life in the palace of the king of Persia. It is hard to imagine living under the rule of a king like Ahasuerus, but to live in his palace as a beautiful woman and a slave is unimaginable. It is difficult to conceive of a situation or surroundings where a woman like Esther would be more vulnerable. She is a young woman devoted to God and faithful to His ways and the heritage of her people. Yet, despite those qualities, it *appears* she has lost her parents and her uncle Mordecai's loving care and protection.

However, the key word is "appears." The reality is that Esther is not alone. The walls and guards that separate her from her people do not separate her from her God. He is with her in the palace, in her trial, just as He was with Daniel in Babylon 100 years earlier. There is no place where the God of Israel is not. He has not forgotten this daughter of Israel. Through her story, He will powerfully demonstrate that He has not forgotten His people living in exile. The message for this woman of faith is the same as a young woman who testified centuries before, "You are a God of seeing" (Gen. 16:13). The Lord, "El Roi" who saw Hagar and provided for her and her son, 1500 years later saw Esther and would provide and care for her and her people.

My friend, wherever you are today, God is still "El Roi," He sees you. Those eyes of God that see you are kind and loving eyes. God's eyes are on the righteous, and His ear is attentive to their cry (Ps. 34:15). The

Lord is good, and He does good (Ps. 119:68). Sometimes our circumstances do not seem to demonstrate God's care. Paul told us we must enter the Kingdom through much tribulation (Acts 14:22). However, it is true that we are never alone in our trials. He has said, "I will never leave you nor forsake you" (Heb. 13:5). The certainty of our Master's love is not written in our circumstances but etched into the glorified, nail-scarred hands and feet of Jesus. God's silence is not God's absence. He *is* with us. Immanuel, "God is with us." May we not look around for evidence of that reality. Regardless of our circumstances, may we look up by faith and speak His Names this moment, "'El Roi,' You are 'Immanuel.'"

MAY 24
Esther 4-6

"For Such a Time as This"

"And who knows whether you have not come to the kingdom for such a time as this?"
(Esther 4:14)

One of the great literary works of the Middle Ages, or any age, is *The Divine Comedy*, the epic narrative poem, and allegory written between 1308-1320 by author and poet Dante Alighieri. *The Divine Comedy* is the tale of a vision of the afterlife in which Dante visits the realms of hell, purgatory, and paradise. Through this literary device, Dante advances his understanding of Roman Catholic theology regarding the soul's spiritual journey. Part of *The Divine Comedy* is shared using the allegorical vision that those considered powerful and influential in this life are spectacles of emptiness, vanity, and remorse in the next. In that regard, the section of the book of Esther we have read today could aptly be termed *"The Divine Comedy."* It is funny for everyone, except Haman!

The righteous Jewish man, Mordecai, whom Haman despises with all his heart and plans to exterminate, along with all his people, is the very man the king commands Haman to honor. To add humiliation beyond measure, Haman is commanded to honor Mordecai according to his own pompous plans, leading Mordecai, who is riding the king's horse and dressed in the king's royal clothes, through the streets of Susa, all the while proclaiming, "Thus shall it be done to the man whom the king delights to honor" (Esth. 6:9). Now, that is funny—seriously, divinely funny!

Intermingled with the comedy, however, is a story of incredible bravery. The hero is the young Jewish woman, Esther, now queen of

Persia. When she is informed by her uncle Mordecai of the wicked plot from Haman to destroy all the Jews, Esther risks her life by going unrequested before the presence of the king, which is a capital offense. Esther's only requirement is that people pray to the King of Heaven for three days on her behalf. With total dependence on the Lord, she commits her life to act on behalf of her people, saying, "and if I perish, I perish" (Esth. 4:16). Of course, Esther was afraid. She was young, beautiful, and favored in the realm. She did not want to die. However, Esther knew that there are things more valuable than life. Esther's love for her God and her people she treasured more than life itself.

Also, her loving and faith-filled uncle, Mordecai, helped Esther to see that Divine destiny and sovereignty had placed her in such a unique place for the good of her people. "And who knows whether you have not come to the kingdom for such a time as this?" (Esth. 4:14) Mordecai's statement was not in the form of an assertion but more in the form of an appeal for personal consideration. Of course, the answer was unmistakable and undeniable; it was obvious Esther had come to the kingdom for just this moment.

I wonder, is the same just as obvious to you about your life—the timing of your days in this season of the kingdom? If the Bible teaches us anything about our lives, it affirms that our days are not accidents or without meaning. The Lord who formed us before our first days on earth also created and ordained the days of our lifetime. (Carefully read Psalm 139:13-16.) You and I have come to the kingdom for such a time as this. That truth should humble us so profoundly and inspire us so greatly. *Our lives matter.* They matter to God, and they matter in the lives of others. When you truly believe that God has brought you to His kingdom for such a time as this, you can never live another "ordinary day."

MAY 25
Esther 7-10

"The Proverb of Purim"

"The lot is cast into the lap, but its every decision is from the Lord."
(Proverbs 16:33)

When King Solomon wrote Proverbs 16:33, he was sharing a statement of wisdom about God's providence in all things. But he did not know that he was also making a prophetic statement that would be fulfilled in an amazingly precise fashion 500 years later for the Jewish people.

Many times in ancient Israel and other cultures, when a decision needed to be reached or a settlement made, the determination was achieved by casting dice. Of course, the pagan people did this to express their superstitious beliefs regarding luck or fate. On the other hand, Jewish believers saw the casting of dice or *lots* as a way of looking to the Lord for His affirmation. They believed that the Creator and Sustainer of all things was also present in the smallest details, even to determine how dice would finish their tumbling motion into a piece of cloth. Although we are certainly not instructed as Christians to discern the will of God in this manner, there is Biblical precedence for the practice, and the underlying theology is taught throughout Scripture that God's providence is in all things.

The rolling of the dice, the providence of God, the words of King Solomon, and the story of Esther all blend together in our reading today. Haman had determined the date for the annihilation of the Jewish people by the casting of lots (Esth. 9:24). The Persian word for these stones of lot or dice was "Pur." From Haman's casting of the "Pur," a date was set in early spring, in the Jewish month of Adar, the last month of the religious year. Wicked Haman cast the Pur, but never could he have imagined that not only was God using Haman's hatred to set the date for the deliverance of the Jews and defeat of their enemies. He was also naming and establishing the date for an annual Jewish holiday observed until this day—the festival of Purim!

As mentioned earlier, the book of Esther is unique in that God is not mentioned in the entire story. However, every aspect of it, even down to dice rolling, is His story. Taken with the previous books of Ezra and Nehemiah, the entire age of the Jewish exile exalts the glory of God in His absolute providence and unfailing love. To live in exile from home is not to live in exile from God. The Lord was as present with His people in Babylon and Susa as in Jerusalem. Wherever God's people collectively or one of His people individually finds themselves, God is there.

These pages show that our lives are not pawns on a cosmic chessboard of chance. Jesus said the very hairs of our heads are numbered (Luke 12:7), so we know that wherever we lay our heads, God is there! Think of it, if the festival of Purim celebrates God's presence and control of dice thrown in a lap, then all children of God can certainly and peacefully lay their heads in the lap of the Heavenly Father. Shalom Aleichem. "Peace be upon you."

MAY 26
Job 1-3

"A Chained Devil"

The book of Job can be a challenging and difficult section of the Bible to read. There is much in the book that is depressing, and the dialogue (which encompasses most of the work) is from an ancient culture and mindset radically different from ours. Yet, for people who devote themselves to reading it carefully and prayerfully, it yields some of the finest gold in all the mine of Scripture. I hope you will be one of those devoted and blessed miners.

Job, named after the main character, is considered by most Evangelical scholars to be the oldest book in the Bible. The events take place during a season in the life of Job, "the greatest of all the people of the east" (Job 1:3). The "east" here means east of the land of Israel. It is probably identified with the area of the fertile crescent, the region of Ur, the homeland of Abraham and Sarah. These events, then, describe a period perhaps a thousand years before the time of Moses. Job, though not specifically mentioned, is undoubtedly part of the long genealogy of the descendants of Seth, the people of the east who identified themselves as worshipers of the God and Father of Adam (Gen. 4:26).

The book of Job opens in a wonderful and strange way. We are introduced to the greatest man of his age who, while rich in possessions, is richer in his faithfulness and devotion to God. However, the narrative quickly turns strange in that a day arrived when "the sons of God came to present themselves before the Lord, and Satan also came among them" (Job 1:6).

The "sons of God" here refers to the angels of heaven. Satan, who was once numbered among them but rebelled against God, decides to present himself as well. Admittedly, we don't know how this was accomplished or why it was permitted, but two things are apparent. First, "Lucifer," for that was his original designation, has come before the Almighty as Satan. Lucifer means "shining one," and Satan means "adversary." He is well-named, for he is the arch-enemy of God and man.

Second, it is clear that the Lord has a plan regarding Job because He specifically calls the man to Satan's attention as one of His faithful servants, a man blameless and upright. To this recognition, Satan mockingly replies in his twisted logic, "Does Job fear God for no reason?" (Job 1:9) Satan's slanderous attack against God (and this is, in reality, the theme of the whole book) is that the only reason Job or anyone else serves God is because of what they personally get from it. Job serves God because he benefits from it, not because God deserves it. This is Satan's hate-filled assault on God, "No one really loves you for who you are. They only love you for what you do. You aren't worthy of love or loved for who you are."

Ultimately, this is the thinking behind Satan's plot. In response, the Lord permits Satan to attack His servant Job. However, one divine limitation is placed on Satan—he cannot take Job's life. He may take his wealth, family, and even his health, but Job's life belongs to God alone. This is a troubling narrative in so many ways. We see God's total sovereignty in all things, yet in His will, He chooses to permit evil to exist and even evil to be done against His devoted servants.

I struggle with that, as I am sure you do. Yet one thing is clear: Satan is so powerful but *not* all-powerful. Satan is the Devil, but he is a chained Devil. He *cannot* go beyond God's boundaries, and, in his hatred, he *will* accomplish God's purposes, as we shall soon see.

MAY 27
Job 4-6

"WITH FRIENDS LIKE THESE..."

"As I have seen, those who plow iniquity and sow trouble reap the same."
(Job 4:8)

Job was a beloved man by God and many people. In the last part of Chapter 2, we are introduced to some of Job's "friends"—Eliphaz, Bildad, and Zophar. Undoubtedly, these men were sincere in their friendship with Job because they came a long way to be with him. They identified with him and they spent a great deal of time with him in his sufferings. However, in their desire to help, they were not very helpful at all. They were not helpful because their help was not offered in humility. They presumed they were in a position to "interpret" Job's situation and to "instruct" him regarding how he should respond. By this, they did not help alleviate Job's suffering; they only added to his pain. One of the first things said by Eliphaz, the most esteemed of his friends (since he spoke first), is a theme that will be repeated many times in the coming days, "Can a man be pure before his Maker?" (Job 4:17) The insinuation is obvious, "Job, you have done something wrong to bring these terrible calamities upon you."

Eliphaz's statement is a process of merciless (and graceless) logic—right is rewarded, and wrong is punished. God is punishing Job, so Job is guilty of some evil. Wow, how helpful! As the saying goes, "With friends like these, who needs enemies?" Eliphaz is guilty of judging, and judging is always rooted in pride. He takes the elevated position of presuming that he has such a clear grasp of the laws of sowing and reaping that he can interpret what is happening and what needs to be done.

I recently read the account by an author concerning the time he shared a railway car with a father and his two boys, who were undoubtedly the most misbehaved children he had ever encountered. The father seemed oblivious to their raucous behavior. Finally, when he could stand it no longer, the writer sharply informed the man how impolite and inconsiderate he was being to allow his sons to behave so. The writer was certainly unprepared for what followed. Like one snapped back to consciousness, the father apologized, saying, "I'm sorry, we just left the hospital, and before we boarded the train, I had to inform the boys that their mother had died unexpectedly." The writer was aghast at what he heard and even more by the insensitivity of his judging words. It was a lesson he said that he would take to his grave.

Almost all of us can give thanks that we have never experienced the trauma that were expressed in that train car. However, all of us can take wisdom from that author's presumptuous judgment. Likewise, we can also learn from the negative example of Eliphaz. Before we speak, we need to listen. Before we judge, we need to be sure we have all the facts. Before we give advice, we need to make sure it is requested, or, at least, we need to first ask permission to share it.

Have you ever been judged unfairly? Have you ever had your motives questioned or maligned? Have you ever been slandered? How did it feel? Never forget that, and never pass it on.

MAY 28
Job 7-9

"JOB'S MEDIATOR AND OURS"

"There is no arbiter between us, who might lay his hand upon us both."
(Job 9:33)

"**B**lind Justice." That is a figure famous on the outside and inside of the walls of courthouses and courtrooms throughout America. The figure comes to us from ancient times, where the goddess Justice is portrayed as a woman holding a balance in one hand and a sword in the other. Sometimes associated with this figure are items such as a palm leaf denoting mercy or a broken shackle or chain representing freedom. Central to the idea is that every person, without respect for who they are, will be treated equally and fairly before the law. Justice will be blind. Of course, our judicial system often fails to achieve that goal, as any decision-making process involving deeply flawed men and women would. Notwithstanding, the goal of equal justice for all is worth the efforts of all men and women of goodwill and certainly the support of followers of Christ.

Human justice is flawed. God's justice is not. This reality haunts Job and is the source of his lament in Chapter 9. Job has been challenged to recognize that only a guilty person would suffer as he has. Although he knows that his conscience is clear of any evil deed that brought his afflictions as just punishment, Job is also clear that when it comes to the purity of the Holy One of heaven and earth, he cannot proclaim his *absolute* innocence. The reality of his spiritual sinfulness in comparison to God's holiness causes Job to cry out, "How can a man be in the right before God?" (Job 9:2) Consider His omnipotence (9:3-19), consider His omniscience (9:20-29), and consider Job's complete inability to cleanse himself from sin against an offended God (9:30-32).

At this moment, Job offers up in hopelessness the great need of his soul and, as a result, unknowingly expresses the hope of every sinner in the provision of their deepest need. "For he is not a man, as I am, that I might answer Him, that we should come to trial together. There is no arbiter between us, who might lay his hand on us both" (9:32-33).

Job was absolutely right, and he was gloriously wrong. God was not a man like Job so that they might meet each other in court. Regardless, that would be the last thing Job would want because he knew he was guilty. He could never atone for his sins, and justice would demand that he be thrown into a pit, condemned by God and abhorring himself (9:30-31). Job was right. God was not a man, but God *could* and *would* become a man. The answer for the infinite chasm between a holy God and sinful man was a person who could fully represent both—a God-Man.

Unbeknownst to Job, the plea of his heart was God's plan. God, Himself would come in the form of a man, that being both God and man, He could be the perfect arbiter. Jesus did that; He is that arbiter, the mediator. "For there is one God, and there is one mediator between God and men, the man Christ Jesus" (1 Tim. 2:5). Praise God for Jesus who "can lay His hand on us both" (Job 9:33).

This is the Gospel of reconciliation—in Jesus, justice has been perfectly met by His perfect life and vicarious death. The outstretched arms of Jesus on the cross encircle the whole world, and in His grace, He lays His hand on repentant sinners like the dying thief on the cross —like us— and He brings us to God and paradise. Praise His name forever!

MAY 29
Job 10-12

"God of Wisdom and Power"

"With God are wisdom and might; he has counsel and understanding."
(Job 12:13)

When the Apostle Paul was sharing his personal testimony and message of the gospel before King Agrippa in Caesarea, the king finally interrupted him exclaiming, "Paul...your great learning is driving you out of your mind!" (Acts 26:24) King Agrippa was partially correct. Paul was indeed a man of great learning, one of the great minds of his age, or any age, for that matter. Yet, he certainly was not mad. He was simply a man who had experienced "a close encounter of the Divine kind." Paul had met Jesus.

Later, Paul would write to the believers in the city of Colossae, declaring that in Christ "are hidden all the treasures of wisdom and knowledge" (Col. 2:3). All true wisdom and knowledge flow from their original source, the fountain of the Godhead. Things are true to the extent that they align themselves with the metric of absolute truth, the God of truth. Things are wise to the extent that they adhere to the principles of the "only wise God" (Jude 1:25). Ultimately, all knowledge and wisdom, or science (so-called), is, in reality, foolishness.

That is *definitely* not the evaluation of the world system in which we live. Much that is considered and called "education" in our culture is a learning process (perhaps "indoctrination" is a more fitting term) that actually leads people further and further from wisdom and knowledge. Many sincere men and women have been educated beyond their understanding, and, as a result, they have "died by degrees."

God, in His Word, laments, "My people are destroyed for lack of knowledge" (Hos. 4:6). Think about that—a lack of knowledge will destroy your life. That lesson sadly is proven day after day by people who profess to know God in Christ. Ultimately, the question comes to one of deciding who you want to consider you a fool. Of course, in all sincerity, the reply might be, "Well, I don't want to be considered a fool by anyone." Sadly, that is not an option. We will be considered "fools for Christ's sake" (1 Cor. 4:10), or we will consider that the "foolishness of God is wiser than men" (1 Cor. 1:25) and determine that the "fear of the Lord is the beginning of knowledge" (Prov. 1:7). Job was under the constant barrage of very educated men. Yet, his mind was fixed on the One who "leads counselors away stripped, and judges he makes fools" (Job 12:17).

A man walked down a busy city street wearing a sign that invited people to gospel services at a local rescue mission. The front of the sign on his chest proclaimed, "I am a fool for Christ." On the sign across his back was written a question, "Whose fool are you?"

The truth is foolishness and wisdom will never be clearly and unmistakably affirmed in this world. However, we can make the wise decision now, the same one made by missionary and martyr Jim Elliot so many years ago: *"He is no fool who gives what he cannot keep to gain that which he cannot lose."*

MAY 30
Job 13-15

"LIFE IS SHORT, ETERNITY IS LONG"

"Man who is born of a woman is few of days and full of trouble."
Job 14:1

"If a man dies, shall he live again?"
Job 14:14a

One of the most unique, sobering, and encouraging places I have visited in my entire life is the Catacombs of Saint Callixtus in Rome. The miles and miles of connected caves have served as the burial place of hundreds of thousands, perhaps millions, of people dating back to the earliest days of the Roman republic and empire. However, during the terrible persecutions of Christians that swept through the second and third centuries, these caves and burial chambers not only became the abode of the dead but also of the living. Followers of Jesus were forced to live underground during most of the daytime hours. They would leave for work or to acquire food only during the night. As a result, these catacombs also became centers of worship, education, and community life. As imaginably difficult as this existence must have been, scholars and archaeologists of recent years have discovered that something very identifiable was left by these early Christians inscribed in this city of the dead. And that was, in a word—hope.

The tombs of the Romans were often ornate and beautiful, but missing in the messages carved by the mourners in the stones were expressions of confidence in meeting again and joyful fellowship in the afterlife. The religions and philosophies of Romans varied to the extreme, but they all united in providing no clear answer to the question posed by Job, "If a man dies, shall he live again?" (Job 14:14a)

Later in his trial, Job will make a personal and definite answer to his own question. The early Christians knew the answer, which brought them hope even in the utter darkness of the catacombs. Living in tombs, those believers could hear the promise of Jesus made before the tomb of His friend Lazarus, "I am the resurrection and the life. Whoever believes in me, though he die, yet shall he live, and everyone who lives and believes in me shall never die" (John 11:25-26).

For this reason, the tombs of the Christians in the catacombs were characteristically inscribed with words of hope. The hope they expressed did not take the form of a wish; *a wish is not hope.* Hope in the dictionary of the faith means "confidence," "steadfast assurance." Hope has been described as the "not yet experienced reality" of a believer. As the Reformers were wont to say, it is the "already, not yet" reality of believers in Jesus.

Hope is more certain than death because hope lives and journeys on beyond the grave. We have hope in Christ that addresses and answers the two great realities of human existence—life is very short, and eternity is very long. A human being "born of a woman is few of days and full of trouble (Job 14:1), but any person born of the Spirit of God will never perish but have everlasting life (John 3:15-16).

The empty tomb of Jesus is the eternal answer of our Lord to the question of Job, "If a man dies, shall he live again?" (Job 14:14a) Listen to your Lord's voice speaking hope into your soul. "Because I live, you also will live" (John 14:19b).

MAY 31
Job 16-18

"OUR HEAVENLY ADVOCATE"

"Even now, behold, my witness is in heaven, and he who testifies for me is on high."
(Job 16:19)

A theme runs through Job's long and terrible ordeal as he suffers physically and endures the interrogation of a team of self-ordained prosecutors—his so-called "friends." Job longs to have a personal interview and dialogue with God about his experience. Again and again, he pleads for an opportunity to personally make his case before the Lord. Yet, he knows in his soul that such an experience would be awful beyond the telling. He longs to make his case to his Maker, but *who is he* to speak to the Holy One?

His conscience is clear in the matter he is enduring, but a clear conscience and a sinless life are not the same thing. Job knows this. And yet, what hope is there for Job if abandoned of support on earth? He has no advocate in heaven!

Then, in a glimmer of hope, despite the torture he is enduring, Job knows that God is *not* against him; God is *for* him. God is his advocate.

"Even now, behold, my witness is in heaven, and he who testifies for me is on high" (Job 16:19). Surely, the God who has been his guide and support all the long days of his earthly sojourn has not forsaken or forgotten him. He has hope; the Lord is his witness in heaven and the One who speaks on his behalf on high!

Job sensed in his darkness like a gleam of early dawn, the full light of New Testament grace flooding into our souls. It is the living reality of Christ, our Lord, that God is for us (Rom. 8:31). God was for us in eternity past when He foreknew us in love and predestined us to be adopted as His children. God proved He was for us when, in His mercy, He called us by His Spirit and justified us by faith in Jesus. This God will always be for us because He plans to fully restore and glorify us in His presence (Rom. 8:29-30).

This God is for us because Jesus stands for us in the Holy place. We are not unrepresented on high. Through Jesus, it is wonderfully true that our "witness is in heaven, and he who testifies for me is on high" (Job 16:19). We cannot be unrepresented in the court of heaven because our Master ever lives to make intercession for us (Heb. 7:25).

With that hope, we are permitted—no, *we are invited*—to come to the throne of the God of heaven and earth. Because of Jesus, God's throne is not a throne of judgment but a throne of grace. A blessed thought—grace upon grace.

JUNE

"Have we not all one Father? Has not one God created us?"
(Malachi 2:10)

JUNE 1
Job 19-21

"Strength from the Future"

"For I know that my Redeemer lives, and at the last he will stand upon the earth. And after my skin has been thus destroyed, yet in my flesh I shall see God, whom I shall see for myself, and my eyes shall behold, and not another."

(Job 19:25-27)

Several years ago, while attending a pastors conference, I remember being particularly struck by a statement from one of the speakers. "Pastor, never forget that regardless of how long you serve a congregation, ultimately, you are an interim pastor." "Interim" means "temporary" or "transitional." Before that moment, I had never seen my ministry in that light, but I have never forgotten it, and I pray I never will.

The concept of "interim" and "temporary" should be very prominent in our thinking as disciples regardless of the role or vocation in which we serve. Knowing that we are "interim" humbles us and helps us. It humbles us to remember that regardless of how long we serve, our life is but a vapor that appears for a brief moment and then vanishes away (James 4:14). Also, recognizing that all of our life is "interim" helps us persevere when confronted with terrible problems and sometimes, like Job, to endure what is unendurable.

While enduring unimaginable trials, by God's grace Job was still comforted in knowing they were only "interim," and his deliverance through the Lord would be absolute and eternal. "For I know that my Redeemer lives, and at the last He will stand upon the earth" (Job 19:25).

It is helpful and instructive to note several characteristics of Job's confession. First of all, it was a confession of faith. Job's words were the expression "of things hoped for, the conviction of things not seen" (Heb. 11:1). Job's sufferings were terribly real, but the *ultimate reality* for him were the things yet to come. Secondly, Job's confession was one of complete deliverance. His sufferings might continue unabated, and his days certainly lead to the grave, but the grave would not be the end. Job believed that he would live again, and death was not the final word. Thirdly, Job's incredible hope rested upon a personal Redeemer. Job said, "I know that *my Redeemer* lives." He confessed with confidence that his soul had already been redeemed. And his body (now ravaged by illness) would also be redeemed and restored. Job proclaimed, "Yet in my flesh I shall see God, whom I shall see for myself" (Job 19:26-27). In

Job's terrible, horrible trials, his faith is triumphant. Job is struggling, and his faith is not perfect, but his Redeemer is!

All of us today need to meditate upon this confession of Job. It would be powerful for us to personalize and pronounce it today. Job has been dead for thousands of years, but he still speaks today. As followers of Jesus, Job's confession is our confession. Our Redeemer lives, and he promises that we will also live, "Because I live, you also will live" (John 14:19). Like Job, we complain in our pain and groan in our suffering. Yet, we can also join our voice with his to proclaim the absolute truth of our living hope in our living Redeemer, whom we shall see for ourselves and our eyes shall behold (Job 19:27).

> *Face to face with Christ, my Savior, Face to face—what will it be,*
> *When with rapture I behold Him, Jesus Christ who died for me?*
> *Face to face I shall behold Him, Far beyond the starry sky;*
> *Face to face in all His glory, I shall see Him by and by.*

("Face to Face With Christ My Savior," by Carrie E. Breck)

JUNE 2
Job 22-24

"Rejoice in the Lord"

"But he knows the way that I take; when he has tried me,
I shall come out as gold."
(Job 23:10)

My *life is in boxes!* I had this thought more than a few times last year. After 26 years of living on the same cul-de-sac near the church where I serve as pastor in Knoxville, Tennessee, my wife and I purchased a home in another neighborhood. I knew our move would call for several boxes, but never could I have imagined just how many! The library of books I had acquired over the years filled more than 50 moving boxes alone! Along with these were dozens more needed to contain all the ministry files and mementos from 42 years in the pastorate. Then came the boxes and boxes and boxes of photographs (mostly taken by my dear wife) spanning the decades of our life and ministry together. Of course, many of these boxes contained untold numbers of photos of our three children.

I admit to a few teary-eyed moments as I opened some of those boxes and was immediately transported back to innumerable scenes saved in my memory and captured on film, recording the joys of raising our kids. One of those photos was taken when our daughter Ruth was about four years of age. However, the image carried me back to an event many years before. In the picture, Ruth is flashing a big smile with her eyes wide in excitement as a man wearing a pirate outfit kneels beside her. But this is not just any pirate. This is Ruth's hero, "Patch the Pirate."

Patch and his family were incredibly popular in Evangelical Christian circles for their ministry to children by teaching life lessons from the Word of God through songs and stories. It was a tremendous ministry, but one which had been born, years earlier, out of what seemed a terrible tragedy—one my wife and I observed firsthand. "Patch," a.k.a. Ron Hamilton, and his wife, Shelly, were members of the church that Susan and I joined shortly after we were married and which we attended during my years in seminary. When we joined the church, Ron was diagnosed with a tumor in his left eye. The tumor was cancerous, and Ron's eye had to be removed. Everyone in our church was devastated that this devoted, young couple was experiencing such a terrible ordeal.

I will never forget the Sunday evening service when Ron, with his bandaged eye, stood behind the microphone and, accompanied by Shelly on the piano, publicly sang for the first time the song the Lord had given him following his surgery. In his testimony that night, Ron said the song was based on the words of Job 23:10, "But he knows the way that I take; when he has tried me, I shall come out as gold."

> Ron sang:
> God never moves without purpose or plan,
>   When trying His servant or molding a man.
>   Give thanks to the Lord though your testing seems long,
>   In darkness He giveth a song.
>
> Chorus:
> O rejoice in the Lord! He makes no mistake.
> He knoweth the end of each path that I take.
> For when I am tried and purified, I shall come forth as gold.

Tears flowed freely that Sunday night as Ron sang. I admit that 44 years later, my eyes at this moment are brimming with tears. However, my heart is full of joy for the grace the Lord gave Ron and Shelly Hamilton in their hour of trial and the priceless impact their ministry has had on countless thousands of children. I have an old photo of a delighted little girl with her favorite pirate to prove it!

Rejoice today in the Lord. He makes no mistakes!

JUNE 3
Job 25-27

"BILDAD OR BARNABAS"

"How you have helped him who has no power!
How you have saved the arm that has no strength!"
(Job 26:1-2)

If sarcasm were a weapon, then Job could quite possibly be considered one of the most dangerous men who ever lived! This great man suffered both physically and emotionally from the relentless verbal assaults of his "friends" who questioned his integrity claims. It becomes evident in reading the chapters of the book that bears his name that Job gave as good as he got! In Job's response to Bildad cited above, Job makes it very clear, with biting sarcasm, that he finds Bildad's words just a little less than helpful and empowering.

The thoughtful guidance not to "kick a man when he is down" never connected with Bildad. His friend Job is not just down; he is in mourning, destitute in finances, ridiculed by his wife, and suffering in body and spirit—a perfect time to lecture a friend on the finer points of theology. Not to mention using the thinly veiled metaphor that compares Job to a maggot and a worm! (Job 25:2-6) Bildad is just the kind of guy you want visiting you in the hospital! (Pardon the sarcasm.)

Bildad is certainly not a role model for encouragement. But Joseph is. So much so that the apostles gave him the nickname "Barnabas," which means "son of encouragement" (Acts 4:36). Barnabas is presented to us in the book of Acts as the ultimate encourager. He repeatedly comes alongside people to selflessly provide assistance. Barnabas, in faith and bravery, "takes a chance" on the notorious Saul of Tarsus, the persecutor of Christians now turned professor of Christ. He encourages this incredibly discouraged new disciple and brings him into the faith community in Jerusalem (Acts 9:27). It is Barnabas who selflessly recognizes that the work of the Lord in Antioch is beyond his abilities. So he travels for days across the great distance to find Saul and bring him to lead the ministry of this great church (Acts 11:25-26). Sometime later, Barnabas accompanies and supports this phenomenally gifted Saul of Tarsus on the first great mission to the Jews and Gentiles living in Asia Minor (Acts 13:2).

Many months later, it is Barnabas who, at the cost of fellowship with his beloved colleague, determines that the young and previously fearful and fleeing teammate, John Mark, deserves another opportunity to prove himself (Acts 15:37-39). The investment of Barnabas in this young man paid dividends; for years later, Paul, from his prison cell in

Rome, directs Timothy to bring Mark with him, "for he is very useful to me for ministry" (2 Tim. 4:11).

Discouragement and encouragement are both incredibly powerful. Which of the two is the ministry of the Lord? The answer is revealed by the fact that the word for encouragement is the same used by Jesus as a title for the Holy Spirit (John 15:26). Are we like Bildad or Barnabas? The choice is ours.

JUNE 4
Job 28-30

"THE WAY TO WISDOM"

"And he said to man, 'Behold, the fear of the Lord, that is wisdom, and to turn away from evil is understanding.'"
(Job 28:28)

My father used to delight in telling the story of a simple-minded but mischievous man who would sit for hours upon a bench on the courthouse lawn of Albany, Kentucky. One day, a man from "up north" pulled over to the curb in his big fancy car and asked the man seated on his bench, "Hey buddy, can you tell me the way to Jamestown?" To this question, the man replied, "Well, some folks go this way, and some folks go that way." The man in the fancy car responded with a strained smile, "That's funny. Now seriously, how do I get to Jamestown?" To this, the seated man replied again, "Some folks go this way, and some folks go that way." Thinking an insolent "redneck" was mocking him, the driver of the big car cursed at the man, stomped on the accelerator pedal, and with squealing tires sped away. Some bystanders who happened to overhear the conversation immediately doubled over in convulsions of laughter. As my father loved to explain, "Albany, Kentucky, is located exactly 25 miles north of Jamestown, Tennessee, and 25 miles south of Jamestown, Kentucky. So some folks go this way, and some folks go that way!" Well, it certainly helps in asking for directions to ensure the source of those directions is a straightforward and trustworthy guide to the desired destination!

In our reading today, we are given directions to a destination that no one on earth can serve as a reliable source, for the destination is not found on earth. It is found in heaven, in God Himself. Job asks, "But where shall wisdom be found? And where is the place of understanding?" (Job 28:12) While it is true there are innumerable directions available today and very freely given to arrive at the destination of wisdom, in reality, the answers can be summarized by the words of the man sitting on the bench in Albany, Kentucky, "Well, some folks go this way, and some folks go that way." The truth is this: "the folks" don't know the way to wisdom; only God does. Thankfully, God has shared those directions, which are wonderfully clear and simple. Finding wisdom requires making a U-turn and traveling straight. Job said it much more poetically and beautifully, "Behold, the fear of the Lord, that is wisdom, and to turn away from evil is understanding" (Job 28:28).

If we desire to find wisdom, we must start with a "you turn" of repentance. All of us left to ourselves are headed the wrong way, away from God. God in His goodness calls us to repentance which is "a change of mind that produces a change of direction." The new direction to wisdom requires "driving straight ahead"—"the fear of the Lord, that is wisdom" (Job 28:28). The guardrails to wisdom are, in reality, the "God rails." It is in obedience to God's Word that we stay on the right road. The road to wisdom is not always easy. Jesus said that at times it would be narrow and difficult (Matt. 7:13). It would be a "crossroad" of picking up our cross and following Him (Matt. 16:24). However, this road to wisdom is the "way everlasting" (Ps. 139:24) and the "good way" (Jer. 6:16), for it is the path to knowing God, and He is the ultimate wise destination!

JUNE 5
Job 31-33

"LIGHT IN OUR DARKNESS"

"He has redeemed my soul from going down into the pit, and my life shall look upon the light."
(Job 33:28)

It was an incredible sight and an experience to be remembered for all the days of my life. My wife and I and a group of people from our church were enjoying a wonderful trip to Israel. It was springtime, and the weather was terrific—sunny days, cool nights, and the beautiful inspiring scenes of the Holy Land surrounding us. In particular, the area surrounding the Sea of Galilee was busting with the colors of new life, and the sites associated with the life and ministry of Jesus seemed to come alive with fresh meaning. Very early one morning, while it was yet dark, I walked the short distance from the kibbutz where we were lodging to enjoy some quiet time of devotion by the lake's shoreline. Over thirty minutes, I was blessed to watch the eastern horizon slowly change in color from inky black to purple, to orange, and then to the gold of a new morning.

Watching the yielding of the night to the sun's power reminded me of what the prophet Isaiah, 2,800 years ago, had foreseen taking place spiritually, beginning from Galilee and spreading to the ends of the earth. "In the former time he brought into contempt the land of Zebulun and the land of Naphtali, but in the latter time he has made glorious the way of the sea, the land beyond the Jordan, Galilee of the nations. The people who walked in darkness have seen a great light; those who dwelt in a land of deep darkness, on them has light shone" (Isa. 9:1-2). From where I was seated by the lake, in the dark of the early morning, my soul worshiped in praise to God for the Light of Heaven shining His light into the darkness of this world and graciously onto the darkness of my own heart as well. I was sitting in the dark, but at the same time, focusing on the light I knew would soon come.

Emotionally and spiritually, that is where Job was sitting for a long season. And it is where we sometimes find ourselves—sitting in the dark but looking for the light. For those "dark seasons of the soul," we need to be reminded to look for the light by *looking in the right direction*. I did see the light of the new day that morning by the shore of Galilee, but I would have seen it much later if I had not been looking to the east, the direction of the sunrise! Where should we look for the light in those seasons when we are suffering? Where do we look for a spiritual sunrise?

Look to the Light in Worship...

"God is light, and in him is no darkness at all" (1 John 1:5). "If we walk in the light, as he is in the light, we have fellowship with one another" (1 John 1:7). "The Lord my God lightens my darkness" (Ps. 18:28).

Look to the Light in the Word...

"The unfolding of your words gives light" (Ps. 119:130). "Your word is a lamp to my feet and a light to my path" (Ps. 119:105).

Look to the Light in the Lives of Godly People...

"The path of the righteous is like the light of dawn, which shines brighter and brighter until full day" (Prov. 4:18). "A friend loves at all times, and a brother is born for adversity" (Prov. 17:17).

Look to the Light of your Ultimate Identity and Destination...

"For at one time you were darkness, but now you are light in the Lord" (Eph. 5:8). "And night will be no more. They will need no light of lamp or sun, for the Lord God will be their light" (Rev. 22:5).

JUNE 6
Job 34-36

"The Gift Not the Giver"

"He delivers the afflicted by their affliction and opens their ear by adversity."
(Job 36:15)

I'm not sure how you feel about Elihu after reading his extremely long message directed at Job, but I confess that I have struggled as I have listened once again to his six-chapter sermon. Perhaps I do that because I hear him with the ears of an old man listening to a young man rebuke and admonish an old man! However, even if Elihu's spirit may not be humble, he delivers much truth that Job, Eliphaz, Bildad, Zophar, Sam, and *(insert your name here)* need to receive! There is always a great danger in rejecting a true and helpful message because it is delivered by an insincere and ill-motivated messenger.

I have never forgotten one sentence of wisdom I received years ago after enduring two days of the most boring conference imaginable. I recall nothing significant the speaker shared as he droned through several sessions. But I would gladly endure that conference again for the long-lasting value of one statement he shared near the end. He said it almost in passing, but this challenge he gave gripped me, "If someone hits and hurts you with a rock of criticism, before you throw it back in anger, read the message written on the rock. It just may be a message from the Lord for your good."

That has been priceless guidance for me. I wish I could say I have followed it without fail. However, on countless occasions, painful, unjust criticism has been the delivery system for gifts to help me grow in the Lord. If someone gifted us with a handful of diamonds he had just found in a sewer, would we reject them because of their unsanitized condition? I don't think so. How much less, then, should we reject the insights or truth that may be gold nuggets of character development that come to us from less than sincere or noble people?

If we desire to truly be like Jesus, we must learn as He learned. "Although he was a son, he learned obedience through what he suffered. And being made perfect, He became the source of eternal salvation to all who obey Him" (Heb. 5:8-9). Reread those verses carefully. Jesus learned obedience. That is, He learned by *experience* the lesson of obedience through His suffering. From whom did our Lord receive suffering? It was through the cruel and hateful attack of His enemies and the suffering of enduring the sin debt of others. God the Father used the hate, rejection, and murder of His Son by sinners to make Jesus the source of eternal salvation. What a sovereign, gracious, and infinite God we serve! What Jesus endured *made Him* the perfect and complete Savior and compassionate Great High Priest for all who believe.

And so it is for each of us as followers of Jesus, who are suffering rejection and ridicule, as unjust and undeserved as we may believe it to be. Our Heavenly Father ordained this suffering to conform us more and more to the image of His Son and our Savior. We may not like the "Elihus" the Lord sends into our lives, but if we listen and endure them, they may gift us with a handful of dirty diamonds!

"He delivers the afflicted by their affliction and opens their ear by adversity" (Job 36:15).

JUNE 7
Job 37-39

"WORDS WITHOUT KNOWLEDGE"

"Who is this that darkens counsel by words without knowledge?"
(Job 38:2)

Two simple but essential truths are the foundation of understanding and essential for living a meaningful life. Truth #1: *There is a God.* Truth #2: *I am not Him.* The essence and source of all that is wrong on this planet is ultimately founded on thoughts and actions that proceed from created beings believing and behaving as if they are the Creator. This is as ancient as the Garden of Eden and as current as the untold millions of decisions made worldwide in the time it has taken you to read this page.

Creating a god in the likeness of human beings is the source of paganism from ancient times and the source of so many of our problems. We want to be in charge; we desire to be the masters of our own fate and the captains of our own souls. This is the dark center of our sin nature. Yes, praise God, for, by His grace, He shines the light of the knowledge of the glory of God in the face of Jesus Christ (2 Cor. 4:6) into our dark hearts, yet we must resist the darkness that remains by constantly affirming in our minds "the Lord is God and I am not."

As good and godly a man as Job was, yet he struggled with surrendering to this basis of all truth. We hear it in what he says. Job is a timeless example of the truth—"out of the abundance of the heart his mouth speaks"(Luke 6:45). In his terrible ordeal, his words complain to his friends regarding his own righteousness and the injustice of their challenges and the injustice of his situation. The message behind Job's words is this—if I were God, I would not treat such a devout and dedicated servant as I am this way. In short, *"Job knows best"* rather than *"Father* knows best."

How do we personally grapple with the faulty conclusions and counsel that reigned in the heart and flowed from the mouth of such a fine man as Job? Two relentless practices help us—to constantly focus on the nature of God and to filter our words through the Word of God. When we reflect on God often and rightly, our minds are secured by the realities of God's nature. We *know* that God is just; therefore, it is impossible for Him to be unjust in the world or in our lives. All of the ways of God are like Himself, just and true. God is not the ultimate source of evil and wrong. All that is darkness in this world finds its source in the consequences and curse of sin. Therefore, we must be cautious, as redeemed sinners, that we make sure the advice and guidance we give does not "darken counsel without knowledge" (Job 38:2). God's Word is the source of light in which we can joyfully walk and which we can confidently share with others. There is a God, and not one of us is Him. Let's walk in that light ourselves and talk that light with others today.

JUNE 8
Job 40-42

"Victory in the Ashes"

I am writing these lines during days when our television and computer screens are filled with images of the horrors of the war in Ukraine. Houses, hospitals, schools, apartment complexes, community centers, etc., have all been indiscriminately reduced to rubble and ash by the assaults of Russian military forces. Multitudes of people have lost their dear loved ones and most treasured earthly possessions. Lifetimes and legacies have been obliterated in moments to satisfy the unbridled lust for power and dominance by hate-fueled, maniacal men. If it is better never to have been born than to offend and harm just one of God's little ones (Matt. 18:6), then what an unimaginable punishment must await those who have planned and executed such unspeakable evil! Unless they repent.

I freely admit there is a dark place in me that does not want to admit that forgiveness is even desirable, let alone possible, for people who are guilty of such hate crimes. However, I know my God and the power of His grace is greater than all sin. Only the love of Christ can turn murderers into missionaries and evil people into evangelists. The examples of grace from the Bible and the experiences of my own life and ministry testify that it is true. "This is a faithful saying, and worthy of all acceptation, that Christ Jesus came into the world to save sinners; of whom I am chief" (1 Tim. 1:15, KJV). God is not only able to give beauty in the place of ashes, but through Christ, He is also able to make the ashes a testament of His love and grace.

In Job's life, we see victory in the ashes over error as the truth of God's character overwhelms the error of "learned counselors." They spoke of God but did not speak "what is right" (Job 42:7-8). Job spoke the truth of God to his generation and to those who jeered at him, and in the end, God vindicated his testimony.

There is also victory in the ashes for Job. The attack by his spiritual enemy, Satan, has been terrible beyond the telling, but God ordained the flames of the Old Dragon's hate to purify Job of pride and self-righteousness. In reality, we have the Devil to thank for causing one of the most beautiful confessions of faith ever uttered. "I had heard of you by the hearing of the ear, but now my eye sees you; therefore, I despise myself, and repent in dust and ashes" (Job 42:5-6). "Dust and ashes." What strange yet fertile soil for the fruit of repentance—a profession of faith and worship of a holy, living God.

In the ashes of Job's life, the one who is destroyed is the arsonist himself, Satan. The greatest beauty displayed in these ashes is a gem. God is so wonderful that men and women will serve Him, not for what He *does for them*, but for *who He is to them*. People will serve God regardless of their circumstances because of love. Satan will never understand that, but he can see it, and so can the people in this world he tries to blind. God's love always shines, and nowhere does it beam more beautifully or brightly than from the ashes of life.

JUNE 9
Psalms 1-2

"Rejoice with Trembling"

We associate fear with many things: heights, crowds, dogs, needles, public speaking, etc. But how often, if ever, do we associate fear with joy? I can hear the answer. Never! That makes perfect sense. Fear is not generally a pleasant emotion. However, in Psalm 2, David challenges us to "Serve the Lord with fear, and rejoice with trembling" (Ps. 2:11). That makes absolutely no sense unless you really know God. The fear of the Lord is the beginning of wisdom (Prov. 1:7). Jesus called on His disciples to fear God (Matt. 10:28).

The fear of God is a radically different kind of fear because it is a fear that is rooted in *awe-struck love*—"Awe-struck" in the understanding of God's glory and majesty. And a "love" that is based on God's amazing love for us—a love demonstrated in sacrificing His beloved Son to rescue us from His wrath. We rejoice, tremble, and serve when we behold our glorious and gracious God in worship. Sinful fear is dispelled, and Godly fear delights.

> *"There is no fear in love, but perfect love casts out fear."*
> (1 John 4:18a)

JUNE 10
Psalms 3-4

"A Song in the Night"

I do not remember who said it or even where I was when I first heard it. But it is a simple reminder that has guided and encouraged me so often over the years, and I have been able to share this simple truth with so many others. "Don't forget in the darkness what you learned in the light." Times of darkness not only can make us fearful, but they can also make us forgetful. We must choose to remember the light of truth in the night of fear.

David was a man walking in the darkness. His own son betrayed him, and many of his closest friends deserted him. It seemed there was only a step between him and death. He was afraid; anyone would be. But, David made a decision in his darkness of heartache and fear. He encouraged himself by what he had learned in the light, "But you, O Lord, are a shield about me, my glory, and the lifter of my head" (Job 3:3).

David was not in denial. He realized he was surrounded by his enemies, but he chose to remember a greater truth. Yes, he was surrounded; he was surrounded by God Himself as his shield. That was the truth that brightened his darkness. He cried out to God, and David's darkness blazed with the light of renewed confidence and peace. His position was not changed, but his disposition was transformed. In the midst of terrible conflict, David experienced supernatural peace. That peace is available for you today from the greatest warrior of all—the Prince of Peace. "Peace I leave with you; my peace I give to you. Not as the world gives do I give to you. Let not your hearts be troubled, neither let them be afraid" (John 14:27). *Don't forget in the darkness what you learned in the light!*

JUNE 11
Psalms 5-6

"JEHOVAH-SHAMA"

"The Lord has heard my plea; the Lord accepts my prayer."
(Psalm 6:9)

It does not require a deep and careful reading of the Bible to be struck by the fact that within its pages, a number of different names and titles are used to refer to the One and only God. What makes this even more significant is that it was His people who assigned almost all these names and titles. On one very notable occasion, however, God deliberately assigned a name to Himself. This occurred the day He revealed Himself to Moses from the burning bush on Mount Sinai and commissioned Moses to be the human deliverer of His people. Moses asked God how he should answer the Israelite slaves when they wanted to know who had sent him to lead them to freedom. God responded by saying that Moses should tell them "I AM" had sent him (Ex. 3:14).

God called Himself, "I AM." The English letters for "I AM" in Hebrew are "YHWH," and when the vowel markings are included, it is pronounced, "Yahweh." Most often, "Yahweh" is transliterated into the name "Jehovah" in English. As you may know, when we see the word "Lord" in our English Bibles, it is to inform us that the name "Yahweh" is being used in the Hebrew text. God instructed Moses to tell the Israelites, "I AM" had sent him to them, and in doing this, He communicated so very much about Himself to His people. "Yahweh" or "Jehovah" means that God is the ever-existing, ever-present maker and sustainer of life itself. He is the One *Who I* always present and always present tense. Throughout history, God's people have found comfort in this incredible reality of God's changeless presence.

Our reading today in Psalms is a song of David that celebrates what God's presence meant to him personally in a time of crisis. The song recorded a time in David's life when he was bedridden by illness. It was also a season of deep emotional distress because David sensed that the Lord had brought this ordeal on him. In his physical weakness and emotional depression, David despaired life itself. Yet, in his darkness, David cried out to Yahweh, Jehovah, the One who is present and always present tense. In his darkness, "The Lord" gave David light, and David knew that his prayers had been heard and accepted (Ps. 6:9). David did not give God this name, but he experienced Him that day as "Jehovah-Shama," "the Lord who hears." "Jehovah-Shama" is the greatest prayer promise that could ever be given, for how futile is prayer if there is not a "God who listens," but how powerful is prayer when the ever-present One is listening closely!

As you begin your prayer time today, why not start with the name of the One who is always listening? Go ahead. "Jehovah-Shama..."

JUNE 12
Psalms 7-8

"Praise in the Persecution"

Jesus told us it would happen. He said, "If they persecuted me, they will also persecute you" (John 15:20). The Apostle Paul said that persecution was inevitable for every serious Christian. "Indeed, all who desire to live a godly life in Christ Jesus will be persecuted" (2 Tim. 3:12). It's not easy to be treated badly when trying to live a good life! We know so little about persecution in our culture compared to what our brothers and sisters are experiencing in other parts of the world. But we will experience it. However, more important than experiencing persecution is how we respond to it.

Persecution for our truth and values can make us better or make us bitter. Guess which one our Lord desires? Our sovereign God ordains times of persecution in our lives, not that we might be pressured into depression but be *pressed deeper* into Him. It is when we feel like God is all we have when we discover, in fresh ways, that He is all we need. The Lord plans for our persecution to lead us to praise for who we find Him to be. Listen to the song of David, a man in the pressure cooker of persecution.

> *"I will give to the Lord the thanks due to His righteousness, and I will sing praise to the name of the Lord, the Most High."*
> (Psalm 7:17)

Right now, take a moment to consider those words again. Now, offer them as your own in praise to God. Keep doing that during any experience of persecution and you will always be protected. You won't get bitter; you will get better because praise wins.

JUNE 13
Psalms 9-10

"The Power of His Name"

> *"And those who know your name put their trust in you, for you, O Lord, have not forsaken those who seek you."*
> (Psalm 9:10)

We cannot trust someone we do not know, certainly not in the deepest meaning of the word "trust." We may have quite a bit of confidence that the other driver will stop at the red traffic light, but that is not the same as *trust*. Trust is based on knowledge of another person's character. That requires time and experience.

We often refer to a person who is worthy of trust as having "a good name." We mean that over a period of time and experience, they have proven to be a person who can be trusted. Trust requires *personal* knowledge.

The Lord has a good name. His character has been proven and tested innumerable times throughout the ages. As people have come to experience God's character over the centuries, they have given Him names that communicate His nature. They know Him, name Him, and trust Him. They know His name, His faithfulness, justice, righteousness, salvation, peace, comfort, holiness, helpfulness, strength, joy, provision, goodness, kindness, etc. They know His name, so they trust Him. They become people who know their God.

Take a few moments to reflect on who you know God to be through your personal experience. Express your trust in Him today by praising Him in prayer for some of the ways you have experienced Him in your life. Now, claim one of His names for today.

"Lord, I praise you because you are _____."

JUNE 14
Psalms 11-12

"It Will Be Worth It All"

I have heard him sing the same song several times. Each time, my eyes fill with tears. I am overcome with the profound, guiding truth being shared with such a stammering, halting voice. His name is Stephen, and he suffers significant mental and physical impairment from a brain injury at birth. Life is not easy for Stephen. Every step is a challenge. Each conversation requires incredible concentration to frame the thoughts and form the words. Stephen cannot provide for his own basic needs. He cannot drive, live independently, work a typical job, or balance a checkbook. The world is a difficult place, and life is tough for Stephen, but Stephen knows Jesus. In an incredibly simple yet brilliant way, he views life in the light of the reality of glory to come.

He learned a song years ago that he claimed as his personal testimony. He has sung it hundreds of times to thousands and thousands of people. Stephen has changed the lives of countless people by reorienting their view of *problems* in light of the *promises* to come. Mine included. Listen to Stephen sing this transforming truth:

It will be worth it all when we see Jesus!
Life's trials will seem so small when we see Christ.
One glimpse of His dear face all sorrow will erase.
So, bravely run the race, till we see Christ.

("When We See Christ," lyrics by Esther Kerr Rusthoi)

JUNE 15
Psalms 13-14

"Singing in the Dark"

One reason the Psalms are so dearly beloved is because David often says things we know to be true and feel in our soul, but would never say them in church. Psalm 13 is a perfect example of one of those brutally honest moments. David is in a dark season, not only because of treachery from some of his closest companions and dearest loved ones but also because he feels abandoned by God and utterly alone. So much so that he cries out in despair, "How long, O Lord? Will you forget me forever? How long will you hide your face from me?" (Psalm 13:1)

You know the feeling, don't you? Maybe that is where you are and what you are feeling right now. So, what should we do when we feel the darkness around us and within us, but we don't feel *Him*? Take heart, for that, is precisely the reason this Psalm is included in God's Word. How gracious our dear Lord is to record this song so we can sing it with David!

First of all, confess your feelings. This means to confess to God how you feel. Denial is not a spiritual virtue. Get honest with God, just like David. God will not be surprised, and He will not be offended. Tell God what you are feeling and ask Him the questions that are grieving your soul, but don't stop there. After you have confessed your feelings, just like David, *confess your faith*. Give voice to what you know is true, even if you are not feeling it right now. Make the choice to rejoice. Sing out the truth of your faith in the midst of your darkness and doubt. Sing with David in the dark:

> *"But I have trusted in your steadfast love;*
> *my heart shall rejoice in your salvation.*
> *I will sing to the Lord,*
> *because he has dealt bountifully with me."*
> (Psalm 13:5-6)

JUNE 16
Psalm 15

"God's Neighbors"

Psalm 15 opens with David gazing upon Mount Zion in Jerusalem and on the *Tent of Meeting* where God dwelt with His people. David's home was on the same ridge in Jerusalem; he was God's neighbor. This amazing truth led David to meditate on who could truly be "God's neighbor," not just in physical residence but in spiritual reality. David lists five "zoning requirements" for people who desire to be "God's neighbors." Let's take some time to note those requirements today:

1. (v. 2) "He who walks blamelessly and does what is right." They are guided by truth, refusing to do what is wrong and focused on doing what is right.

2. (v. 2) The person who "speaks truth in his heart" means a person who first applies God's truth to their own soul. They meditate on God's Word for their own benefit.

3. (v. 3) "Who does not slander with his tongue and does no evil to his neighbor, nor takes up a reproach against his friend." This person considers a neighbor's reputation and character sacred and protects it.

4. (v. 4) "In whose eyes a vile person is despised, but who honors those who fear the Lord." They value the character of others on how they value the character of God.

5. (vs. 4, 5) "Who swears to his own hurt and does not change; who does not put out his money at interest and does not take a bribe against the innocent." These people don't live for money. They live for God and others.

Living according to God's zoning laws gives us an eternal title deed to the best neighborhood!

"He who does these things shall never be moved."
(Psalm 15:5)

JUNE 17
Psalms 16-17

"Fullness of Joy"

God is joyful. Please read those words again. *God is joyful.* Honestly, there are many qualities and attributes we associate with God, but how often do we think of His *joyfulness*? But it is true—God is the most joyful being that exists because the joy of perfection permeates all He is! God is *completely joyful*. The only true and lasting joy any person can experience is through knowing and sharing in *God's joy*. In fact, it is God's joy to share His joy with His people.

King David knew God's joy by experience, and he sang about it in Psalm 16:11, "You make known to me the path of life; in your presence, there is fullness of joy; at your right hand are pleasures forevermore." David looks back over his life and recognizes that God, in His grace, revealed the path David should take. It is the "path of life." God has been David's companion on this journey, and David has found God's friendship to be the "fullness of joy." Then, David's heart exults to think that this joy will never end; he will experience "pleasures forevermore" with his God. Wow! What an eternal companion—the God who is contagious with joy!

Dear friend, this song was written by David, but it was recorded for *us* to sing. Life is not always easy. It might be filled with challenges for you right now, but the song is ever true. God's path is life. His presence is joy. His promise is pleasures forevermore. Now that is something to sing about today!

JUNE 18
Psalms 18-19

"The Treasure of God's Word"

In Psalm 19, David sings a song celebrating God's revelation. David exalts the grace the Lord has demonstrated in making Himself known. David especially praises, (in verses 7-11), the infinite value of God's Word to His people. Today, let's focus on the nine qualities of God's Word that are priceless to each of our lives.

1. The Word of God provides *spiritual renewal*. "The law of the Lord is perfect, reviving the soul." (v. 7)

2. The Word of God provides *wisdom*. "The testimony of the Lord is sure, making wise the simple." (v. 7)

3. The Word of God provides *deep joy*. "The precepts of the Lord are right, rejoicing the heart." (v. 8)

4. The Word of God provides *insight*. "The commandment of the Lord is pure, enlightening the eyes." (v. 8)

5. The Word of God produces *holy awe*. "The fear of the LORD is clean, enduring forever." (v. 9)

6. The Word of God is *true and righteous*. "The rules of the Lord are true, and righteous altogether." (v. 9)

7. The Word of God is *invaluable*. "More to be desired are they than gold, even much fine gold." (v. 10)

8. The Word of God is *delicious*. "Sweeter also than honey and drippings of the honeycomb." (v. 10)

9. The Word of God provides great *reward*. "Moreover, by them is your servant warned; in keeping them there is great reward." (v. 11)

What a priceless treasure!

JUNE 19
Psalms 20-22

"THE PSALM OF THE CROSS"

All of the psalms of David rise out of his own experience. Each of his songs are his expression of his life's journey. However, sometimes David writes as a prophet. His words have a fulfillment in the years to come. Psalm 22 is undoubtedly a word of prophecy, for it was not fulfilled in David's experience but in the life of his greater Son, Jesus Christ. Psalm 22 takes us to Calvary, to the sufferings of the Savior.

Jesus quotes from this psalm during His agony on the cross. Verse 1 expresses the ultimate horror Jesus experienced, "My God, my God, why have you forsaken Me?" The only time Jesus referred to Him by any other title than "Father" was as He suffered. Why did Jesus refer to His Heavenly Father as "God" on the cross? You and I are the reason.

On the cross of Calvary, the Lord Jesus bore our sin as He offered Himself to God as the atoning sacrifice for our forgiveness.

There is a mystery in this psalm that the most brilliant of theologians cannot fully comprehend. As he meditated on this verse, Martin Luther declared, "God forsaken by God, who can understand it?" Thank God we do not have to understand it, but we can trust in the gospel message. "For our sake he made him to be sin who knew no sin, so that in him we might become the righteousness of God" (2 Cor. 5:21). Psalm 22 is a terrible song, but it is the wonderful theme of our salvation in the redeeming love of our Messiah and our God, Jesus of Nazareth. Hallelujah, what a Savior!

JUNE 20
Psalms 23-24

"The Gates Will Open"

Standing on the crest of the Mount of Olives and gazing upon the city of Jerusalem is one of the most spectacular sights a believer can ever witness. Just beneath your location is the Garden of Gethsemane and the ancient olive trees beneath whose limbs the Lord prayed in the moonlight. Further beyond is the Kidron Valley, across which He was led in chains by His captors. Then your eyes reach the hillside across the valley, and you look at the walls of Jerusalem atop Mount Zion.

As your eyes follow this wall, you notice the outline of a large set of gates. The gates open directly onto the temple mount, but you can see that these gates were bricked shut long ago to limit access to the area of the Al-Aqsa Mosque that now sits on the temple mount as one of Islam's most holy sites. A few years ago, an archaeologist discovered that directly under the currently closed gates lie the remains of ancient gates that existed in the time of Jesus.

The modern eastern gates are bricked shut and covered with mounds of dirt, but one day those gates will be opened again. Jesus will return to the Mount of Olives and once more ride down the slopes of the hill, not as the humble servant but as the victorious Lord. On that day, the shout from Psalm 24 will resound across the Kidron Valley:

> "Lift up your heads, O gates!
> And be lifted up, O ancient doors,
> that the King of glory may come in.
> Who is this King of glory?
> The Lord, strong and mighty,
> the Lord, mighty in battle!"
> (Psalm 24:7-8)

Even so, come, Lord Jesus.

JUNE 21
Psalms 25-26

"The Secrets of the Lord"

*"The friendship of the Lord is for those who fear him,
and he makes known to them his covenant."*
(Psalm 25:14)

We all have different levels of relationship and personal intimacy in our interactions with others. There are things we are willing to share with acquaintances, and then there are matters we share only with friends. Then there are those things about our lives that we only share with those with whom we have the deepest relationships.

These levels of intimacy are also true of our God. There are things about Himself that He makes known through the general revelation of creation. "The heavens declare the glory of God, and the sky above proclaims His handiwork" (Ps. 19:1). There are those truths the Lord reveals to people who seek Him through His special revelation of Scripture. "And beginning with Moses and all the Prophets, He interpreted to them in all the Scriptures the things concerning Himself" (Luke 24:27). And then, there are, as our text above tells us, personal and intimate insights into God's heart and ways that He shares with those who worship Him in fear or awe-inspired love. David called this "the friendship of the Lord," or as it can also be translated, "the secret counsel of the Lord."

This is a fantastic truth and an incredible invitation! The fantastic truth? *God is not hiding.* The incredible invitation? *He desires to make Himself known.* Our Creator-God desires a relationship with us that is conscious, personal, and intimate! The question for us is how much do *we* desire that kind of relationship. Why not have a "confidential talk" with Him about that today?

JUNE 22
Psalms 27-28

"A Song in My Heart"

*"The Lord is my strength and my shield;
in him my heart trusts, and I am helped; my heart exults,
and with my song I give thanks to him."*
(Psalm 28:7)

There has never been discovered a people group in all the world that does not do two things—laugh and sing. Laughter and singing are somehow imprinted into all the people groups of the world. This is part of the image of God and His nature that we human beings bear, even in our sinful state.

When people come by the grace of God to know Him and trust Him, these qualities of joy and song are sanctified. The response of a human being redeemed and reconciled to their Creator is to exult with joyful singing. Of course, this does not mean that believers in the Lord are automatically given the ability to sing. However, as one country pastor once said, "The Lord, when He saved me, did not put a song in my mouth, but He sure put one in my heart!" This is the same song of joyful praise that David described, "...my heart exults, and with my song I give thanks to him." Praise should overflow our hearts as we reflect on who our God is and what He has done for us. There is also spiritual power in the expression of praise to God, so praise should be a regular part of our prayer time to Him.

We must be careful that our prayer time with God does not become a reciting of only our problems and our needs. This could result in depressing ourselves! The Devil delights when people only talk to God about their problems, but how he hates to hear praises to the Almighty rise from the voices of troubled saints. May we make sure to take time to praise God today. It will bless Him, help us, and irritate the Devil, and that's a good thing!

JUNE 23
Psalms 29-30

"Dancing in the Tomb"

"You have turned for me my mourning into dancing;
you have loosed my sackcloth and clothed me with gladness,
that my glory may sing your praise and not be silent.
O Lord my God, I will give thanks to you forever!"
(Psalm 30:11-12)

It was certainly not what I expected. For so many years, I had wanted to visit a site in Jerusalem that had eluded me on previous visits—the tomb of David. When I stepped into the entry room of the structure, the first thing that surprised me was the music; not the sad and mournful chants I would have expected in a mausoleum, but bright, joyful singing and clapping. Even more amazing was the scene that awaited me in the burial chamber itself, which was the source of the celebration. In the room's far wall was a stone sarcophagus draped by a beautiful blue tapestry with a gold emblazoned star of David. Around the final resting place of David, a group of Jewish rabbis dressed in their black garments were joyfully dancing and singing, their curled ringlets of hair bouncing as they danced. Even we who were non-Jewish visitors were invited to join the celebration of praise. Afterward, our guide explained that since David wrote many psalms of joy and often danced before the Lord, it was the tradition of orthodox rabbis to honor David's life by dancing before his tomb every day.

As we left that praise-filled tomb that afternoon, I thought of another tomb just a short distance away. Over that tomb, a large structure had likewise been built; but that building is a place of silence, incense, and solemn chanting. It is the tomb of King David's descendant, Jesus of Nazareth. For a moment, I was discouraged that there was no joyful singing at His tomb. But as I reflected on these two very different scenes, I remembered the most significant contrast between the two sites—the tomb of Jesus is empty, and then my heart began to dance.

JUNE 24
Psalms 31-32

"GOD'S HEAVY, HEALING HAND"

It has been said that the deepest theology is the theology of the heart, not the head. There is all the difference in the world between knowing truth about God through *education* and knowing Him through *experience*. The Psalms of David are filled with some of the deepest truths of God in all the Bible, but what gives these songs such power is that they flow from David's *personal experience* in knowing and serving his God. These experiences span every segment of David's life and sometimes bring together both physical and spiritual encounters with God.

Some people believe there is no connection whatsoever between our physical and spiritual well-being, but David knew better than that by experience. "For when I kept silent, my bones wasted away through my groaning all day long. For day and night your hand was heavy upon me; my strength was dried up as by heat of summer. I acknowledged my sin to you, and I did not cover my iniquity; I said, 'I will confess my transgressions to the Lord,' and you forgave the iniquity of my sin" (Ps. 32:3-5).

David felt in his body the spiritual and physical pressure of God's conviction for his sin. Truly God was "heavy-handed" in His dealing with David's sin. Why would the Lord treat His beloved servant this way? Why does He treat *us* this way? Because as the Westminster

Catechism says, He wants us to glorify Him and enjoy Him forever. God knows that in honoring Him, we experience the joy found only in Him. Unconfessed sin short-circuits our joy. Confession restores our joy connection with God, so God presses us to confess. He squeezes our life back into us! He wants us to sing again!

> *"Blessed is the one whose transgression is forgiven, whose sin is covered.*
> *Blessed is the man against whom the Lord counts no iniquity,*
> *and in whose spirit there is no deceit."*
> (Psalm 32:1-2)

JUNE 25
Psalms 33-34

"THE FEAR THAT FREES US"

We keep score on everything from sports, to grades, to investments. President Franklin Roosevelt, as he began his administration in the heart of the Great Depression, famously declared, "We have nothing to fear, but fear itself." In many ways, he was undoubtedly correct. When fear grips people's hearts, many can respond in desperation, and the very fabric of civil society can begin to tear apart. That type of fear is definitely dangerous.

However, there is a different kind of fear that does not cause people to lose control but instead brings us *under* a control that is the ultimate expression of true freedom. I am talking about the fear of God, the same kind of fear that David praised in Psalm 34. When we fear the Lord, we are freed from all other fears because the true fear of the Lord does not cause us to run *from* Him but to run *to* Him. "I sought the Lord, and he answered me and delivered me from all my fears" (Ps. 34:4).

I grew up in a neighborhood that was known to be rough in many ways. I learned very early in life that some "not so nice" individuals lived on those streets and I had to keep my eyes open for them. I also remember that when I walked through those streets and alleys, as I often did, accompanied by my father, I had no fear whatsoever. I had a deep respect for my dad that was rooted in the security I sensed in his love. I also possessed a loving fear for my father, and the knowledge of his love for me and his presence *with* me "delivered me from all my fears."

Our Heavenly Father is an awesome, holy God, but He is our *Father*. We fear him, yet with a fear that flows from reverential love. It is a fear that draws us to Him and frees us from all other fears.

> *"The Angel of the Lord encamps*
> *around those who fear him, and delivers them.*
> *Oh, taste and see that the Lord is good!*
> *Blessed is the man who takes refuge in him!*
> *Oh, fear the Lord, you his saints,*
> *for those who fear him have no lack!"*
> (Psalm 34:7-9)

JUNE 26
Psalms 35-36

"THE FOUNTAIN OF LIFE"

The World's Fair Exposition held in New York City in 1893 highlighted many of the advances that were being made in what we would now describe as the Industrial Revolution. One of the most effective but somewhat deceptive displays that intrigued the patrons was that of the amazing mechanical man. When approaching the display, a person's attention would go to a life-size man made of metal who was furiously pumping a water pump that poured out gallons and gallons of refreshing water. It seemed like a miraculous scientific breakthrough until the viewer finally recognized what was happening. The purpose of the display was to show the possibilities of hydraulic power. The mechanical man was not pumping water; the water was pumping him!

Psalms 35 and 36 are written by David in a time of personal hardship. He laments the deviousness of a false friend who has betrayed and attacked him. Evidently, this traitor has been joined by others who have been relentless in their lies and attacks against David. It is all too much for David, way too much, so David decides to tell somebody. He tells of his anger and anguish to the Friend who has always proven faithful—the Lord his God.

In going to the Lord in his distress, something miraculous takes place; David's pleas turn into praise. His broken-hearted and bitter song in Psalm 35 becomes an anthem of praise in Psalm 36. The wilderness experience in David's life becomes a river of God's flowing grace, and the praise pours out of his soul.

> *"For with you is the foundation of life; in your light do we see light.*
> *Oh, continue your steadfast love to those who know you,*
> *and your righteousness to the upright of heart!"*
> (Psalm 36:9-10)

Our Fountain of Life still flows; may we drink deeply from Him today.

JUNE 27
Psalms 37-38

"Do What You Love"

Every person of a "certain age" reading today's devotion can remember (or wish you could forget) the lighthearted tune made famous by Bobby McFerrin in 1988, "Don't Worry Be Happy." Okay, I apologize to many of you for planting that song in your head again, where it will repeat itself many times over the next few days!

Believe it or not, I actually used those words as a sermon title for a message on Psalm 37:1-4 many years ago. It seemed like a very "cool" idea at the time. Though I would not use that 80's title in this "millennial" culture, the words do serve as bookends for the message conveyed in those verses. "Fret not yourself because of evildoers..." Don't worry. "Delight yourself in the Lord..." Be happy.

David says in this song that you cannot do the first—fret over wicked people, and experience the last—be happy in the Lord. Of course, like most things in the Christian life, this is easier said than done. Most of us have struggled at times with an inability to understand how wicked people can seem to prosper in every way. Also, it is difficult to hear and see the stories of terrible violence around the world and in our own communities and not be overwhelmed with concern.

What is the answer? Faith and faithfulness. "Trust in the Lord, and do good; dwell in the land and befriend faithfulness" (Ps. 37:3). The antidote for the fear of man is faith in God and pursuing Him. Does that mean the world and its evil will change? No, but it does mean *we* will change. When we delight ourselves in knowing God, the Lord begins to change our desires. Our lives begin to find ultimate joy in who He is and what He is doing.

As the Lord becomes our chief desire, the ultimate freedom comes to us. We begin to want what God wants! We can pursue any goal or interest because our values are anchored in God. Bobby McFerrin and his catchy tune, "Don't Worry Be Happy," can then become a catechism for our daily lives.

"Delight yourself in the Lord,
and he will give you the desires of your heart."
(Psalm 37:4)

JUNE 28
Psalm 39

"Tempus Fugit"

"O Lord, make me know my end and what is the measure of my days; let me know how fleeting I am!"
(Psalm 39:4)

The ancient Greeks and Romans had an interesting image for time. They often portrayed time in the figure of a running man whose long forelock of hair was flowing in the wind. The concept behind this image was the idea that time was quickly passing, and you had to catch it by the hair of its head. The Latin phrase "tempus fugit"—"time is fleeting," expresses this.

In our reading from Psalm 39 today, David not only recognized the brevity of time but also prayed that the Lord would cause him to feel it. "Let me know how fleeting I am!" (Ps. 39:4) What an important prayer this is. Our time on earth is so brief, and it is also so unpredictable. None of us has the promise of a long life. Rather than discouraging us, this reality should motivate us. In the New Testament, the Apostle Paul challenges us to make "the best use of time" (Eph. 5:16). His challenge is so instructive; we should not measure our days in their *quantity* but in their *quality*.

Only the Lord is in control of how many days we will live, but we share, through His grace, in deciding *how* we will live those days. Since our time on earth is so limited, it only makes sense that we should invest our time in what is eternal. That narrows the focus considerably because only God and people are eternal. When we prioritize our days around them, our days take on an *eternal significance*.

It should come as no surprise that this is precisely how the Lord has instructed us to live our days on this planet. "You shall love the Lord your God with all your heart and with all your soul and with all your strength and with all your mind, and your neighbor as yourself" (Luke 10:27). It is through worshiping God and working on His behalf for others that the days of our life become more than time. They become timeless. Today is a treasure; let's not squander it but invest it!

JUNE 29
Psalms 40-41

"Rising Above the Clouds"

Several years ago, a major airline expressed a theme in its commercials that I have always thought was not only effective but also inspiring. In each of the commercials, the closing statement was shared in a very encouraging voice, "Where the sun is always shining, just above the clouds." I liked that motto because I have experienced it when traveling by air on so many occasions. The weather would be dark and cloudy early in the flight, but when the plane finally popped through the grey, overcast skies, there was a moment when the sunshine and beautiful blue of the upper atmosphere would surround me.

Psalms 40 and 41 express a season in David's life when he was surrounded by enemies, to the point where he despaired life itself. In fact, much of Psalm 40 is Messianic in nature as it expresses the thoughts and emotions of the Lord Jesus as He carried out His Father's will. Faithfully serving God does not mean we will never struggle with emotional and spiritual gloom and the feeling of being surrounded by it. Believers do not constantly live on the mountaintops emotionally just because they are believers. However, our emotionally dark times neither define our ultimate reality nor our true identity.

We are children of the light, and the Son is always shining above the clouds, *around us*, and on the clouds *within us*. By determining that we will worship God despite our emotional and spiritual fog, we can take in the "high view" and the "long view" of life. That is what David did in both of these Psalms: "But may all who seek you rejoice and be glad in you; may those who love your salvation say continually, 'Great is the Lord!'" (Ps. 40:16) "Blessed be the Lord, the God of Israel, from everlasting to everlasting! Amen and Amen" (Ps. 41:13).

Now, that is a shining light to walk in, no matter how dark our day!

JUNE 30
Psalms 42-43

"Sacred Self-Talk"

"My soul is cast down within me; therefore I remember you..."
(Psalm 42:6)

Few people readily admit that they occasionally talk to themselves, but in reality, most of us do. It has been said that talking to yourself is entirely normal but answering yourself... Now, that's a problem! Self-talk can actually become an expression of healthy self-awareness when practiced with grounding in truth.

David was a big-time self-talker. In many of his psalms, he enters a conversation with himself as he seeks to work out the inner conflict he feels in his soul. Psalms 42 and 43 are perfect examples of David's practice of this spiritual discipline as he asks himself the same question three times. "Why are you cast down, O my soul, and why are you in turmoil within me?" (Ps. 42:5a, 11a; 43:5a) Reading these two psalms together, it is clear that David is going through a season of deep emotional trauma. It appears to be rooted in vicious attacks by people he once considered friends and companions in worship but who have become unrelenting in their lying assaults. David is heartbroken by their betrayal and tearfully pours out his grief to God, "My tears have been my food day and night, while they say to me all the day long, 'Where is your God?' These things I remember, as I pour out my soul" (Ps. 42:3-4a).

David is in the middle of an emotional and spiritual crucible when he does a very wise thing. He starts talking to himself. He is in the dark, but he recalls and repeats the truths he learned in the light, "Hope in God; for I shall again praise him, my salvation and my God" (Ps. 42:5b, 11b; 43:5b). Three times David speaks to himself and speaks against the turmoil within him by declaring the rock of his confidence—*the reality of God, his Savior.*

External events and internal emotions can change quickly and endure persistently, but one thing that cannot change, for any of us who trust in the Lord, is the steadfast love our God pledges to us. He is our ultimate reality, the fixed center of our very existence. When all sources of human security fall away, He remains unchanged, and we still abide in His unconditional love through Christ our Lord. So, go ahead and engage in a brilliant conversation. Talk to yourself about the greatness of your God.

JULY

"The Lord answered me and set me free."
(Psalm 118:5)

JULY 1
Psalms 44-46

"Knowledge in the Stillness"

*"Be still, and know that I am God.
I will be exalted among the nations,
I will be exalted in the earth!"*
(Psalm 46:10)

Psalm 46 is one of several psalms in which David intentionally creates tension by contrasting radically conflicting experiences. He does this to share a message of worship regarding the Lord's character and provision. In this psalm, David writes about events in the world that are described as *a raging among the nations*. The convulsions are so fearful he likens them to *earthquakes that topple the mountains and floods sweeping over the face of the earth*. The *nations totter*, and the *earth melts*. The earth is in chaos. Sound familiar?

This psalm also says that amid all this international upheaval, there is a peaceful stream flowing for God's people that brings joy to their hearts. That stream is the living presence of God Himself. The earth is in turmoil, but He is not, and neither should His people. The simple truth is, God has got this! "Come, behold the works of the Lord, how He has brought desolations to the earth. He makes wars cease to the end of the earth; he breaks the bow and shatters the spear; he burns the chariots with fire" (Ps. 46:8-9). God is in sovereign control of all things. His purposes will be accomplished. We need not fear, "The Lord of hosts is with us; the God of Jacob is our fortress" (Ps. 46:7).

As believers, we know this. The question is, how do we experience this calm in the midst of the clamor of the world? Ready for the answer on what to do? Do nothing. Seriously, don't do anything, but rather *be* something. *Be quiet*. Many of us can't hear the murmuring of the streams that "make glad the city of God" (Ps. 46:4), because we won't sit on the bank and be still. The Lord says, "Be still and know that I am God." If we won't be still, then we really won't know.

In the Lord's purpose for our lives as believers, *being* always comes before *doing*. We are told that when Jesus selected the Apostles, He chose 12 "so that they might be with him and he might send them out to preach" (Mark 3:14). Their first calling was to "be with Him;" it is our first priority as well. Being "still" is the most proactive thing we can do, for it is by being still in God's presence that we come to *know* God more intimately, which is our ultimate purpose. "And this is eternal life, that they know you, the only true God, and Jesus Christ whom you have sent" (John 17:3). The world may rage, but God will be exalted among the nations. When we are still, He is exalted in our hearts.

JULY 2
Psalms 47-48

"Greatly Feared, Greatly Praised"

The psalms of David were the songbook of Israel and the early church. We do not know what these songs sounded like; it may be that the words could be sung to a variety of chord structures or sung a cappella. What we do know is that sometimes the singing was loud, very loud.

Some of the psalms, such as those we read today, were specifically written by David to be sung by the Sons of Korah, a choir of priests numbering in the hundreds as they stood upon the temple walls. Can you imagine several hundred men's voices singing lyrics like these with all their might?

> "Clap your hands, all peoples!
> Shout to God with loud songs of joy!
> For the Lord, the Most High, is to be feared,
> A great king over all the earth." (47:1-2)

> "Great is the Lord and greatly to be praised
> in the city of our God!
> His holy mountain, beautiful in situation,
> is the joy of all the earth,
> Mount Zion, in the far north,
> the city of the Great King." (48:1-2)

Wow. Visualize that scene and hear those sounds in your mind. Can you imagine the people just muttering along with these words? Could you see the congregation standing with blank, expressionless faces as these songs were sung? Hardly. Why? Because the greatness of the Lord, the God of Israel, was being proclaimed! "This is God, our God forever and ever!" (Ps. 48:14)

Jesus told the woman at the well in John 4 that God is seeking worshipers who will worship Him "in spirit and in truth." That means God delights in people worshiping Him with all they are, for all He is. If you have been faithfully reading the words of the Scriptures and the words of these devotionals for several weeks, I think I can safely assume that you have a sincere desire to worship God in truth. But, allow me to challenge you today about worshiping God with your spirit, all you are. Worship is to be emotional; worship means we are to be moved in our spirit by God's Spirit. This does not mean that we are to disengage our *minds* in worship, nor does it mean we are to disengage our *emotions*.

How long has it been since you *joyfully*, and yes, *loudly* expressed your raptured soul in praise to God? There are times we are to be quiet before the Lord (Ps. 46:10), but there are also times we are to be loud. Yes, that might be emotional, but it is also Biblical.

> "Clap your hands, all peoples! Shout to God with loud songs of joy!"
> (Psalm 47:1)

JULY 3
Psalms 49-50

"Worship, Walk, Wisdom"

> *"The one who offers thanksgiving as his sacrifice glorifies me;*
> *to the one who orders his way rightly*
> *I will show the salvation of God!"*
> (Psalm 50:23)

Psalm 50 is a song of worship about worship. In this song, David speaks as a worshiper expressing why the God of Israel is so worthy of the worship. But in this song, David also takes his place as a worshiping listener. David's pen becomes the voice of God, calling the people to an understanding of the requirements and rewards of acceptable worship. God affirms that the nation is offering plenty of burnt offerings and doing so in the prescribed manner, but their sacrifices are not acceptable to God. God did not need the animals they were offering, for "the cattle on a thousand hills" are His, as is the world and all it contains.

What God desires in worship is the *worshiper*—the heart devotion of His people expressed in thanksgiving. The utmost offering is one of thanksgiving for who God is and what He has done for all of His people and each of His people. God is a jealous God. He cannot be bought off with ritualistic religious activities. His people are His people; they belong to no one else and nothing else. God desires to be loved and *deserves* to be loved because He is love and has fixed His love on His people. God is glorified in our loving worship, and He is also glorified in our loyal walk. He is honored as we live our lives in His presence and walk before Him rightly (Ps. 50:23).

Worship is a walk, a way of living as to the Lord. As Paul would say a thousand years after David, our lives are "living sacrifices" and to be presented "holy and without blemish to the Lord" as our spiritual act of worship (Rom. 12:1-2). When the Lord calls us to thanksgiving in worship and dedication in our walk, it is not motivated by what we can give to Him but by what He can give to us. "I will show the salvation of

God" (Ps. 50:23). This promise involves more than the guarantee of eternal salvation. It is the promise of understanding the salvation of God, which means to know God intimately and personally. This is the promise of the "abundant life" that Jesus said He came to give. It means to live life with the highest form of wisdom, which is the knowledge of the Holy One Himself.

"The fear of the Lord is the beginning of wisdom, and the knowledge of the Holy One is insight" (Prov. 9:10). Psalm 50 is a call from the Lord to measure our worship and our walk. It is an offer from God to immeasurable wisdom, a life ever-growing in the knowledge and experience of God. What better way of living could there possibly be?! Let's not miss it.

JULY 4
Psalms 51-52

"A Light to Guide Us Home"

What would it sound like if a man on death row finally decided to confess fully? Not just to a pastor or priest, but to God? What would the confession of a traitor, murderer, and adulterer sound like? It would sound like Psalm 51. This psalm is the darkest song David ever wrote. It is utterly personal and penitential as David sobs out his confession to the Lord.

This song has been months in delay as David has tried to hide his terrible secret. But all that changed when Nathan the prophet pointed his finger in David's face and powerfully condemned his hiding and hypocrisy, "You are the man!" (2 Sam. 12:7). Finally, David was brought face-to-face with the enormity of his sin against Bathsheba, her husband Uriah whom he had murdered, his people whose trust he had betrayed, and most of all against his God who never failed him or withheld anything from him. David fled to the tent where the Ark of the Covenant rested, and there the tears of repentance came in torrents of grief, and the words of confession flowed from his lips:

> "Have mercy on me, O God,
> according to your steadfast love;
> according to your abundant mercy
> blot out my transgressions.
> Wash me thoroughly from my iniquity,
> and cleanse me from my sin!
>
> "For I know my transgressions,
> and my sin is ever before me.

> *Against you, you only, have I sinned*
> *and done what is evil in your sight,*
> *so that you may be justified in your words*
> *and blameless in your judgment."*
> (Psalm 51:1-4)

Nothing could undo what David had done by his sin. But his sin could be pardoned and forgiven, not because he deserved it, but because of the love and mercy in the heart of God. David cast himself entirely on God's redeeming grace and pleaded for forgiveness, and God granted it to him. God still hears the repentant prayers of His people today.

Psalm 51 is recorded in the Bible not just to let us know what David said but to guide us in what to say when we confess our sins to our Heavenly Father. Yes, it is a dark song but bright with promise. The Lord put the psalm in His Word for the darkest hours of our lives to guide us back home to Him.

JULY 5
Psalms 53-54

"Severe Mercy"

> *"Behold, God is my helper; the Lord is the upholder of my life."*
> (Psalm 54:4)

On several occasions, David writes in his psalms about how the Lord blesses him with "songs in the night." Several of David's most moving lyrics were written during the "deep nights of the soul." Reading the psalms is to read a personal journal of almost the entire range of human emotion. David is not writing fiction or history. David is writing from his own personal experiences. In doing so, he is sharing his experiences with God. This is especially true of his experiences with deep, personal pain.

The author C. S. Lewis once described pain as "God's megaphone." By that, Lewis meant that in times of plenty and prosperity, we typically *do not* listen to God's voice. But in times of pain, we are alert to hear from the Lord and the message He has to share with us. Trouble is an excellent mentor for our soul's pursuit of God.

In Psalm 54, David is struggling again with heartache and fear because he has been betrayed by people who made a covenant pledge of protection with him. He feels helpless, and life seems hopeless. That is when the Lord speaks to his heart, in his darkness and pain. The light of

God shelters his darkness. "Behold, God is my helper; the Lord is the upholder of my life" (Ps. 54:4).

Today we might say it this way, "God's got this, and God's got me!" Even in his swirling emotional distress, David was safe in God's hands. No one was in charge of his life but God. God was the "upholder of his life." My friend, what was true of David 3,000 years ago is true for you today. Whatever you are facing, "God's got this, and God's got you!"

Selah.

Trouble is a wonderful mentor for our soul's pursuit of God.

JULY 6
Psalms 55-56

"Making it Personal"

If every member of the congregation did it, it would be a problem. However, sometimes I find it to be personally helpful. On occasion, as the church family sings a song where the word "we" is used, I will change it to "I." I have often experienced added power to the words of exaltation, testimony, or confession when I have made it more personal. Sometimes we need to hear our own voices personally expressing to the Lord the deep issues we feel in our hearts.

This is definitely a Biblical practice as we often hear David speak to himself as he declares his praise or plea to God. Psalms 55 and 56 are perfect examples of this. David is struggling to cope with the traitorous actions of someone he held as a beloved and trusted friend. The pain was just too much for David to carry, but he knew it wasn't too much for God, so David decided to give it to Him.

> "Cast your burden on the Lord, and he will sustain you;
> he will never permit the righteous to be moved."
> (Psalm 55:22)

Having made this personal decision, David followed it up with a personal declaration; in fact, he declared it twice. "In God, whose word I praise, in God I trust; I shall not be afraid. What can flesh do to me?" (Ps. 56:4, 10-11). David is so right. We may have been victimized, but we don't have to be victims; we can be victors. The burden may be too great for *us*, but it is not too great for *God*. Roll it onto His broad shoulders and raise up your voice in a declaration of trust in Him. Go ahead, do it out loud. It may not be pretty, but God will enjoy it.

JULY 7
Psalms 57-58

"The Shadow of the Almighty"

She was a young widow, not yet 32 years old, and mother to a little girl nearing two years of age. She and her husband had spent less than three years together with the brightest of hopes in how God was going to use their lives for sharing the Gospel of Jesus and His love. That all changed horribly one day in January 1956. Her ever-moving, ever-smiling husband, Jim, and four of his friends and missionary colleagues were brutally ambushed and killed by Auca warriors on a jungle riverbank in Ecuador. Elisabeth was devastated beyond words, as were the other young wives and families of these martyred servants of God. In her grief and depression, Elisabeth Elliot sought comfort where she had found it all through her young life— in prayer to God and His Word. One verse from our reading today in Psalm 57 became her comforting prayer and renewing reality:

> "Be merciful to me, O God, be merciful to me,
> for in you my soul takes refuge;
> in the shadow of your wings I will take refuge,
> till the storms of destruction pass by."
> (Psalm 57:1)

"The shadow of your wings" is where Elisabeth found comfort for her breaking heart. And in time, she also found meaning in the sacrifice of her husband's life and those of his friends. Elisabeth committed to writing the things God gave her in His presence. What she wrote became one of the greatest classics of Christian literature, *The Shadow of the Almighty*. Since 1958, millions of copies of this book have been published worldwide. Only God knows how it has been used to call and inspire multitudes in service for Jesus. You and I will probably never write or say anything that millions of people will read for decades to come. However, God is writing a story in each of our lives, and He also has messages for each of us. We hear His voice most clearly when we are alone, quiet, and in the shadow of the Almighty.

JULY 8
Psalms 59–60

"Howling Dogs, Happy Hearts"

Many years ago, when my wife and I traveled to Romania to adopt our son, Stephen, we experienced one of the most unique hotel amenities imaginable. At the main entrance of our hotel was a fashionable container that resembled an umbrella stand. However, this container was not holding umbrellas but large sticks. We noticed that most people who walked out of the hotel picked up a large stick to carry along with them. This seemed just a little strange to us, but on finding out the purpose of the container of sticks, we were even more surprised and, quite frankly, a little alarmed.

The sticks were made available to people who were going for a walk to use them against the packs of dogs that sometimes prowled the streets! That was a definite first for us in our international travels. We have been blessed to return to Romania several times, and thankfully, any walking sticks provided now are just for walking!

In Psalm 59, David refers to those threatening his life as howling packs of dogs—the human kind. They are King Saul's "hired dogs," set on David's destruction. Against these growling enemies, David picks up a "walking stick" to support him during their attacks. It is the walking stick of praise, and David uses it to "beat back" panic that the hate-filled enemies of God can produce in his heart.

> *"But you, O Lord, laugh at them;*
> *you hold all the nations in derision.*
> *O my strength, I will watch for you,*
> *for you, O God, are my fortress.*
> *My God in his steadfast love will meet me;*
> *God will let me look in triumph on my enemies."*
> (Psalm 59:8-10)

Now, that is a big stick we can pick up whenever we need it!

JULY 9
Psalms 61-62

"Preaching to Ourselves"

On a Sunday nearly 150 years ago, the famous pastor of the Metropolitan Tabernacle in London, England, Charles Spurgeon, slipped into the back row of a small, rural church located near the place he and his family were vacationing. That Sunday morning, Spurgeon felt himself to be anything but great. In fact, the purpose of the "vacation" was to find some relief from the relentless stress of his many and widespread ministry responsibilities and some emotional sunlight from the darkness of depression that covered his spirit. As the pastor of the little chapel began to preach, Spurgeon sensed he recognized the minister's message. As the sermon continued to be shared, it dawned on Spurgeon that he was listening to one of his own sermons! After the service, the most famous preacher in the world shook the hand of the understandably embarrassed pastor of the chapel, who said, "Oh, Dr. Spurgeon, it was one of your sermons I preached this morning," to which the famous preacher replied, "Indeed it was; and was it not so gracious of our Lord to use my own words to so encourage my heart as he did today?"

That's a great story. Yes, the best sermon is the one we preach to ourselves. That is exactly what David is doing in Psalm 62. He is preaching to himself the truth he has been declaring to others for years, "For God alone, O my soul, wait in silence, for my hope is from Him" (Ps. 62:5). This is exactly the testimony he shared in verse 1, except now he directs the challenge to himself. David is preaching to himself what he has shared with others about the Lord.

Let's do that today. Right now, reflect on some things you have learned about God and then preach that sermon to the congregation of "you." It will be a powerful worship service!

JULY 10
Psalms 63-65

"The Hope of All the Earth"

It is one of the world's most beautiful yet pathetic works of art today, and it is on prominent display in our nation's largest city. The work is truly beautiful, entitled "Let Us Beat Our Swords into Plowshares." It depicts a man taking his sword and hammering it into an emblem of peace, a plowshare.

The sculpture is stunning. It is based on one of the most touching promises in the Old Testament from the lips of the prophet Isaiah. "He shall judge among the nations, and shall decide disputes for many peoples; and they shall beat their swords into plowshares, and their spears into pruning hooks; nation shall not lift up sword against nation, neither shall they learn war anymore" (Isa. 2:4). That is a truly beautiful image of the peace that will come to the earth when the Messiah establishes His kingdom on the planet.

This amazing work of art is pathetic because the USSR presented the sculpture to the United Nations in December 1959. That nation at that time was the epitome of anti-Christ philosophy and atheistic totalitarianism. The sculpture was presented to an organization that is the epicenter of secular humanism in all the world. Just as the builders of the Tower of Babel declared, "Come, let us build a tower to heaven," so this sculpture declares, "Let us accomplish what God has promised He alone will accomplish."

Mankind cannot change mankind. Leaders of nations may speak words of peace, but war springs from the recesses of the heart, which no power on earth can change. But, praise God. He changes human hearts, and by doing so, He changes the world. He does this one individual at a time by bringing His peace to rebel hearts. Our God is the God of salvation, "The hope of all the ends of the earth and of the farthest seas" (Ps. 65:5b). A new world order is coming, a kingdom in which peace will reign because Jesus will reign. Until then, may we pray that our King will make us instruments of His peace.

JULY 11
Psalms 66-67

"Blessed to Be a Blessing"

"May God be gracious to us and bless us and make his face to shine upon us."
(Psalm 67:1)

News flash. We are selfish. I hope that does not come as a surprise to you. It certainly does not surprise me regarding myself. In my fundamental nature, I am a very selfish man. The struggle with selfishness is that it is so deceptive. We often equate selfishness with being greedy or completely materialistic, which is not at the heart of selfishness.

Selfishness is the natural tendency we all have to view and value life as it relates to us. We can even begin to form a faith that is about us.

The incredible amazing truths of all that Jesus has done for us can lead us to believe that our salvation is ultimately about us. It isn't. The Bible clearly states that the ultimate purpose of our salvation is to display God's glory in this life and the life to come. We have been redeemed to bless God and bless others. Paul tells us we were saved for the praise of God's glory (Eph. 1:6).

Two thousand years earlier, David expressed it this way, "...that your way may be known on earth, your saving power among all nations. Let the peoples praise you, O God; let all the peoples praise you!" (Ps. 67:2-3) It's not about *us*. It's about *Him*, and it's about *them*. We have been blessed to be a blessing to God and others.

This is not natural; it is supernatural, yet it can become the guiding principle of our lives as we make it a matter of focused prayer. David shows us the way in Psalm 67. Please take a few moments to read it out loud. Did you feel it in your spirit? This prayer of David lifts us up from the valley of self-focus and gives us a view of the greater purpose of our lives. Our lives really matter! God has blessed us to make His blessings known to people everywhere. Now, that's a blessing!

JULY 12
Psalms 68-69

"A HOME FOR THE LONELY"

"Father of the fatherless and protector of widows is God in his holy habitation. God settles the solitary in a home."
(Psalm 68:5-6a)

The verses above have a star next to them in my Bible and the date 1995. The notation is there because, in the spring of that year, God used these verses to give my wife, Susan, and me the confirmation we needed for one of the biggest decisions of our life. We were in the process of adopting a child from Romania. All of the many steps in working on the necessary applications, background checks, etc., had been taken, and then it arrived. We received a packet in the mail with the picture of a 2-year-old boy and some personal information regarding him. The adoption agency needed a decision: Do you want to proceed or not? The enormity of the impact of our answer settled heavily on us. Is this the child for us or not? How do we decide?

Susan and I committed to pray about it separately and then talk later that day. That afternoon as I prayed, I was prompted to look again at the passage I had read earlier in the morning. When I opened my Bible to Psalm 68, my eyes fell on verses 5 and 6. In the version I was reading at that time, I saw these words I had read a few hours before, "Father of the fatherless and protector of widows is God in His holy habitation, God makes a home for the lonely." Wow. Okay, start packing for the trip! That was the word we needed that day, but it is also guidance for *every* day. God has made room for us in *His house* and in *His family*, and we need to make room for others in ours. We may not be led to the ministry of adoption, but we are all called to share the Father's love for the displaced, the outcast, and the lonely. Hospitality is the gospel in action. Yes, make a meal for others occasionally, but make room in your life for others *every* day.

JULY 13
Psalms 70-71

"A Lifelong Purpose"

"O God, from my youth you have taught me,
and I still proclaim your wondrous deeds.
So even to old age and gray hairs,
O God, do not forsake me,
until I proclaim your might to another generation,
your power to all those to come."
(Psalm 71:17-18)

Look at the date for today's devotional reading—July 13. Even as I see the date on the page, I am amazed at how quickly this year is passing by! Some of you reading these words can join me in saying that it is true, not only about the days on the calendar but also the years of calendars themselves! We often use the image of grains of sand in an hourglass to express the passing of time, but David, in the verses above, reminds us that our years are not grains of sand to be *counted* but nuggets of gold to be *invested*.

Each year given to us contains experiences with God to "another generation" (Ps. 71:18). This was David's fervent prayer as a man of a "certain age"; he wanted to pass on a legacy of God's renown to the next generation and beyond. By doing this, we, too, can grow older and younger while investing our lives in the lives of those who will remain on earth when we go to heaven.

As I write these words, I am impressed that many reading these words need to pray verses 17 and 18 to the Lord today and then look for ways to invest their golden nuggets of a long life with God into "another generation." Could you be one of them?

JULY 14
Psalms 72-73

"GOOD THINGS TO BAD PEOPLE"

*"I was envious of the arrogant
when I saw the prosperity of the wicked."*
(Psalm 73:3)

It is an age-old issue that has troubled godly people for centuries, even before Priest Asaph wrote this 73rd Psalm about his struggle concerning good things happening to bad people. In these stanzas, Asaph is brutally honest about a crisis of faith he experienced. He was sickened by the continued prosperity of the ungodly and the ongoing oppression of God's people. It seemed to Asaph that the wicked did not have a care in the world. They appeared to get away with sinful living and face no consequences.

To Asaph, it seemed like all his diligence in obedient service to God was in vain (Ps. 73:12-13). The only thing that kept him from declaring his feelings about God's unfairness was a concern about how he might impact the faith of others. Oh yes, he still had faith in God's justice, but he wasn't *seeing* it and definitely wasn't *feeling* it. He had reached the crisis moment, and then everything changed. How did it happen? He *acted* on the faith he did not *feel*.

He went to church, the sanctuary of God, worshiped, and listened (Ps. 73:16-17). There in the presence of God, he received a fresh revelation of what he already knew—the wicked are destined for the terrors of eternal judgment (Ps. 73:18-19). How could he possibly be envious of temporarily carefree sinners who will experience God's righteous justice? (Ps. 73:19) Even more, how could he ever covet the lives of evil people when the real eternal treasures of the Lord Himself are his?

Asaph's self-focused bitterness was transformed into a God-focused blessing: "Nevertheless, I am continually with you; you hold my right hand. You guide me with your counsel, and afterward you will receive me to glory. Whom have I in heaven but you? And there is nothing on earth that I desire besides you. My flesh and my heart may fail, but God is the strength of my heart and my portion forever" (Ps. 73:23-26).

And the people of God said, "Amen!"

JULY 15
Psalms 74-75

"GOD'S TIMETABLE"

"At the set time that I appoint I will judge with equity."
(Psalm 75:2)

The poet Henry Wadsworth Longfellow once wrote this short poem entitled "Retribution."

Though the mills of God grind slowly,
Yet they grind exceeding small;
Though with patience he stands waiting,
With exactness grinds he all.

Another poet, the priest Asaph, nearly 2900 years earlier, often wrote on the same theme. Both Longfellow and Asaph were very aware of the injustice displayed at the highest levels of government and religion. It was discouraging for them in their day, and we are certainly aware of it in our own age. With the advances in communication in this generation, the images and messages of injustice are "constantly in our faces."

Asaph in Psalm 75 reminds us that these things happen in God's face as well. In fact, God is completely aware of what is happening and the hidden agendas and motives behind why it is happening. We must never allow ourselves to believe that God's silence is God's blindness. His promise is "at the set time that I appoint I will judge with equity" (Ps. 75:2).

"The powers that be" are not "the powers that *will be*" forever. "All the horns of the wicked I will cut off, but the horns of the righteous shall be lifted up" (Ps. 75:10). Jesus pronounced a blessing on those who in meekness now are His humble servants, "...for they shall inherit the earth" (Matt. 5:5). The earth belongs to the One who created it. It groans and totters under sin (Ps. 75:3), but things are not out of control, for God declares, "...it is I who keep steady its pillars" (Ps. 75:3).

As Paul said, "For the creation waits with eager longing for the revealing of the sons of God" (Rom. 8:19). The world waits, and we wait too, but we wait in worship of the One who is working all things in His perfect way, and right on schedule!

JULY 16
Psalms 76-77

"Reminding God"

*"Then I said, 'I will appeal to this,
to the years of the right hand of the Most High.'"*
(Psalm 77:10)

We do not know very much about Asaph. We do know that he was a priest serving in the temple. We know that, like David, he was a fantastic poet. We think of the Psalms being written by David, but Asaph wrote many of them, and some are the most beautiful in the entire book of 150 psalms. In Psalm 77, we listen to Asaph speak in another remarkable role as a plaintiff to God.

Certainly, Asaph is a man of deep faith, but the silence of God in response to him and the people of Israel has deeply troubled his soul. His crisis of faith comes to a climactic question in verse 9. Has God forgotten to be gracious? Has he, in anger, shut up his compassion? Asaph is pouring out his heart to God as if he were standing in the courtroom of heaven, filing his complaint before the Judge of the universe. At that moment, standing before Almighty God, an insight comes to Asaph, *I will remind God and I will remind myself of all the powerful deeds of His right hand* (Ps. 77:10). Asaph then begins to list many of the mighty acts God has done for His people with His mighty right hand (Ps. 77:11-20).

Of course, God doesn't need this reminder; but Asaph does, and so do we. God has recorded His mighty deeds in His Word, which are also recorded in our personal memories so that we may bring them to God in worship and to ourselves in encouragement. Asaph did not realize it, but in speaking of God's "right hand," he also spoke as a prophet. At the "right hand of God" is the most gracious and most glorious of all God's marvelous deeds—the Beloved Son, who is the eternal reminder of God's care.

If you are struggling with God's silence today, remember the works of His right hand and, most of all, remember the One *at* His right hand. He has not forgotten you!

JULY 17
Psalms 78-79

"For Your Name's Sake"

"Why should the nations say, 'Where is their God?'
Let the avenging of the outpoured blood of your servants
be known among the nations before our eyes!"
(Psalm 79:10)

Vengeance is an activity that is off-limits to every child of God. The Lord has made it clear that vengeance is His private property, and repaying the wicked for their actions is His responsibility. Nevertheless, praying for the vengeance of God to come on His enemies is not wrong, as long as the prayer is offered with the right motive. The Bible contains numerous prayers to God for His vengeance on His enemies. In the psalms and the Book of Revelation, we hear the people of God crying out for vengeance (Rev. 6:10). When we pray the final prayer of the Bible, "Even so, come Lord Jesus" (Rev. 22:20), we are actually praying for vengeance. The Bible makes it very clear that when our Lord returns in glory, He will be coming in "flaming fire, inflicting vengeance on those who do not know God and those who do not obey the Gospel of our Lord Jesus" (2 Thess. 1:8).

As you read this page today, multitudes of our brothers and sisters in Christ are languishing in prison, enduring torture for the cause of the gospel. God alone knows how many of His children, this day, will be martyred for their faith in Jesus. This grieves us. Yes, this angers us. We speak the words with our spirits, if not with our lips, "How long, O Lord?" It is right to cry out to God for vengeance for His people and cause. However, we must always be sure that our motives are right.

Our desire for God's vengeance must be for the glory of His Name and the vindication of His cause. And even in our prayers for God's vengeance to come, we must also praise Him for the unmerited grace and mercy He has shown to us.

"But we your people, the sheep of your pasture
will give thanks to you forever;
from generation to generation we will chant your praise."
(Psalm 79:13)

JULY 18
Psalms 80-82

"Open and Enjoy"

It always seemed a little weird to me. However, the kids loved it. And I must admit, it was an effective motivation. Anyone who knows my wife, Susan, knows very well that she loves ice cream. Actually, that might be an understatement. The word "adores" comes to mind! She *adores* ice cream, and she loves to cover the bowl of ice cream with whipped cream. All of our children also enjoyed ice cream, but they *really* enjoyed the whipped cream! Susan always made sure that a can or two were kept in the refrigerator.

When "Team Polson" pulled together on household chores, she would line the three of them up and, with mouths wide open, she would reward each with a mouthful of delicious whipped cream! It could get messy, but as I said, it was great motivation!

I have often thought of that image in connection with the Lord's pleas to Israel recorded in Psalm 81:10, "I am the Lord your God, who brought you out of the land of Egypt. Open your mouth wide, and I will fill it." With what did the Lord promise to fill the mouths of His children? "With the finest of wheat, and with honey from the rock I would satisfy you" (Ps. 81:16). What a picture!

The Lord desires to bless His children with the sweetest delicacies for their lives and their souls' satisfaction. God does not want His children to simply *believe* in Him. He wants them to *experience* Him and know the sweetness of His loving provision.

However, God does not force-feed His children. He loves us too much to pry open our mouths against our will. Sadly, Israel proudly refused God's delightful provision, so He "gave them over to their stubborn hearts, to follow their own counsels" (Ps. 81:12). My friends, our Lord has some delicious things to place in our mouths. Are we going to open up or clam up?

JULY 19
Psalms 83-84

"How Beautiful"

"How lovely is your dwelling place, O Lord of hosts!"
(Psalm 84:1)

It is one of my wife's favorite magazines. Over the years, I have seen her read carefully through issue after issue. I'm talking about the magazine *House Beautiful*. Susan has to be one of its "hall of fame" subscribers! I have often teased her about it. But confidentially, I have picked up a copy from time to time when she is not around and enjoyed looking through it. Again, I'm telling you this in confidence!

All the choir members in Israel were men, the sons of Korah, yet they loved to sing the praises of the "House Beautiful," the temple of God. Psalm 84 is a lovely anthem of this priestly choir about the blessing and strength that comes to the people who dwell in God's house. Of course, the house itself, as incredibly beautiful as it was, had no special power to provide help to those who gathered there. The inhabitant of the house, the Lord God Almighty, was the source of all the joy and strength that came to those who regularly entered the courts.

In the New Covenant, there is not a specific spot or particular building that is God's dwelling place on earth. This does not mean there are *not* places that His followers consider very special "houses of God." The "house of God" is whatever location His people gather to worship in the name of His Son and their Savior, Jesus Christ. Paul refers to this gathering as the "house of God" when he instructs one of the young pastors, Timothy (1 Tim. 3:15). The church is the house of God, and the gathering together of the body of believers is the beautiful dwelling place of the Lord, whether it is in a basement, a storefront, or stately sanctuary.

May the preciousness of the gathering of God's people always cause us to feel in our hearts, "My soul longs, yes, faints for the courts of the Lord; my heart and flesh sing for joy to the living God" (Ps. 84:2).

JULY 20
Psalms 85

"A Cry for Revival"

"Will you not revive us again, that your people may rejoice in you?"
(Psalm 85:6)

Growing up as a boy in Immanuel Baptist Church, it seemed like our song leader, Bill Swift, led us in the same song every other Sunday. I can still see him in my mind's eye with his flat-top haircut, horn-rimmed glasses, and smiling face. He would beat his right arm up and down with his index finger extended as he enthusiastically led the congregation in singing. I wondered why we would sing such an old song; after all, it was published in 1863.

Of course, I did not know that the song was based on a hymn of praise sung by the choir in the Temple in Jerusalem nearly 3000 years ago. I just knew Bill Swift enjoyed it, and clearly, our small congregation did as well because they made the sanctuary ring with its words and melody. Over 50 years later, I can still hear it; its memory and message still stir my heart to this day. I have often made it a prayer to God. Perhaps you would like to join me in offering it today in a prayer for revival. "Revive Us Again" by William P. Mackay:

> We praise Thee, O God!
> For the Son of thy Love,
> For Jesus who died,
> And is now gone above.
> We praise Thee, O God!
> For Thy Spirit of light,
> Who hath shown us our Savior,
> And scattered our night.
> All glory and praise
> To the Lamb that was slain,
> Who hath borne all our sins,
> And hath cleansed every stain.
> Revive us again;
> Fill each heart with Thy love;
> May each soul be rekindled
> With fire from above.
>
> Refrain:
> Hallelujah! Thine the glory. Hallelujah! Amen.
> Hallelujah! Thine the glory. Revive us again!

That was beautiful. Bill Swift would be so happy! Now, may the Lord hear and answer our prayer. Amen

JULY 21
Psalms 86-87

"DELIVERANCE AND DEDICATION"

"Give ear, O Lord, to my prayer; listen to my plea for grace. In the day of my trouble, I call upon you, for you answer me."
(Psalm 86:6-7)

Many of David's psalms were "written on the run." That is, he wrote a number of his songs as he was literally under pursuit by his enemies.

Some of the deepest heartaches of his life were that those pursuing him were often some of his closest companions and, in the latter years of his life, even members of his own family.

As you can read in these psalms, they were not the product of a peaceful and meditative season in David's life. You can literally sense the urgency and the desperation in his words as he prays to God. Yet, as I read the psalms like Psalm 86, I am struck by the fact that, in his cries for *deliverance* from his enemies, David also pleads for something more; he pleads for *direction.*

Of course, he prays for rescue, but he also asks for wisdom to learn what God desires to teach him through the ordeal. "Teach me your way, O Lord, that I may walk in your truth; unite my heart to fear your name" (Ps. 86:11). David asks that the Lord use this season to draw him closer in obedience and deeper in understanding. He prays to *walk* in the Lord's truth and *know* the Lord's ways. This is the prayer of a "man after God's own heart." He understands that obeying the Lord in times of trial produces a deeper intimacy with Him.

David's "Greater Son," the Lord Jesus, promised all of us, as His disciples, that if we would *obey* Him, we would really *know* Him. "Whoever has my commandments and keeps them, he it is who loves me. And he who loves me will be loved by my Father, and I will love him and manifest myself to him" (John 14:21).

Amid the pressures of trials in our lives, we must pray as David showed us, and as Jesus taught us, that we "press on" in obedience and "press in" in worship. If we do that, we will know more clearly what our Lord *wants us to do* and more deeply *who our Lord is.*

JULY 22
Psalms 88-89

"WHY?"

Not long ago, I sat with a brother in Christ and was just stunned. Then my tears began to flow (as did his) as he shared some of the things that were transpiring in his life and the lives of those he dearly loved. I sensed myself literally *feeling* some of his pain and heartache connected with earthquakes and successive shock waves of suffering at that moment. I remembered Job and determined that I would not resemble Job's "friends" as they tried to respond to his suffering with challenges about the "hidden sins" that must be in Job's life. Then, I remembered David and the other authors of Psalms and how they expressed their grief and complaints to God.

I reminded my friend, and also spoke to myself, saying that life is sometimes worse than hard. It can be horrible, and it is not fair. I could not, nor would I even attempt to give my brother some glib and easy answers or some pseudo-philosophical reason for why terrible things happen. I also did not try to help him understand the "nature of evil" and the "practical implications of the doctrine of original sin." Those things are true and appropriate in the classroom or the sanctuary, but not when you are sitting in a booth and weeping tears of bewildered pain. A couple of Biblical responses were appropriate, and we both expressed them. First, "Why, God? Where in the world are you?" Yes, that response is Biblical: "O Lord, why do you cast my soul away? Why do you hide your face from me?" (Ps. 88:14)

It is spiritual and healthy to grieve over the terrible agony of emotional pain and the even greater suffering of God's *perceived* absence and indifference. My friend did that, and I agreed with him. But together, we did something else. While we cried together, we also claimed what is true even when we do not "feel" it—the Lord God is good, and He is the God of our salvation (Ps. 88:1). The storms indeed rage; they rage around us, and they rage at times within us, but the anchor holds. God is real, and His steadfast love endures forever.

JULY 23
Psalms 90-91

"The Number of Our Days"

"So teach us to number our days that we may get a heart of wisdom."
(Psalm 90:12)

25,567.5. I'm sorry, but the strange working of my brain wouldn't allow me to *not* do the math. However, 25,567.5 is a very Biblical number. It is the number of days in 70 years. If you are curious, the .5 day comes from factoring in leap years! In this psalm, Moses tells us to number our days, then reminds us that the 70 years of a typical lifetime are soon gone, and then we fly away (Ps. 90:10, 12). We will soon be gone and then fly away, but how quickly do those days fly by even *before* we fly away?! Got a calculator handy? How many days have you lived? Do the math, and you may be amazed at how little is left of those "three score and ten years," or you may realize that in Moses' math, you are already living on "borrowed time!"

Regardless of where you stand on the number of days you have lived, it is never too late to begin devotedly serving the Lord. Take encouragement from Moses himself. The Bible says that Moses was 80 years old when he stood before Pharaoh and demanded, in the name of Jehovah, to let God's people go. Moses lived for 40 more years, passed away, and was buried by God at the age of 120. What an impact Moses made in his "retirement years!" David tells us in Psalm 139 that "all of our days are written in God's book."

Only God knows the number of our allotted days, and He wants us to "number our days that we may get a heart of wisdom" (Ps. 90:12). The greatest wisdom is knowing that eternity is long and our days are few, but *eternity is in our days.* Yes, our lives are very brief indeed, but "whoever does the will of God abides forever" (1 John 2:17). The words of Moses gripped the heart of a young British athlete many years ago. C.T. Studd dedicated his life to living out a truth he wrote in a poem of exhortation, "Only one life will soon be past, only what's done for Christ will last."

JULY 24
Psalms 92-93

"FRUITFUL FOREVER"

Several years ago, a member of our congregation showed me around his property. He was an elderly brother, and he and his dear wife had lived in the small frame house for nearly 50 years. My friend was especially grateful for several immense oak trees that grew in his front yard. He showed me the stump of the biggest oak of all, which had been damaged in a terrible storm a few years earlier and had to be removed. When the tree was cut down, a professor from the school of agriculture at the University of Tennessee came by the property to determine the age of the mighty oak. The professor counted 232 annual growth rings in the base of the tree. That tree was already growing strong when the original 13 colonies became the United States. In fact, it was over 25 years old when Knoxville was founded in 1791! In a unique way, it was humbling to think of the strength of that majestic tree in standing firm for over two centuries.

I thought of that ancient oak as I read about the tree described in our reading today from Psalm 92: "The righteous flourish like the palm tree and grow like a cedar in Lebanon. They are planted in the house of the Lord; they flourish in the courts of our God. They still bear fruit in old age; they are ever full of sap and green, to declare that the Lord is upright; He is my rock, and there is no unrighteousness in Him" (Ps. 92:12-15).

The ancient title for this psalm is "A Song for the Sabbath." It is a beautiful hymn of praise and worship for God's sustaining strength. These cedars have no special endurance in themselves, but they draw their life and strength from the blessed soil of the temple courts. The psalmist sees himself as one of those cedars blessed with strength because he draws his life from the God he worships.

Three thousand years have not changed the truth of this beautiful image. We certainly will not live for 232 years like that oak did in our fellow worshiper's yard, but we can be full of life and bear fruit each year we are given on Earth. Our worship is the root system that connects us with our source of strength, the God of Israel. He is the soil of our souls, and as we press deeply into Him, we flourish and bear fruit for His glory year after year after year.

JULY 25
Psalms 94-96

"The Sheep of His Hand"

"Oh come, let us worship and bow down; let us kneel before the Lord, our Maker! For he is our God, and we are the people of his pasture, and the sheep of his hand."
(Psalm 95:6-7)

As I read the verses above, I recalled a lesson shared by one of my professors in seminary regarding an experience he had while touring Israel. He told us that one afternoon as the tour bus traveled through a rural section of Israel, the group was forced to wait as a gathering of several flocks of sheep blocked the road. As the tour leader, the professor, was irritated at first because this delay could put them behind schedule. However, he did not realize that he was about to experience one of the most essential Biblical insights he would ever gain in his long teaching career.

Hundreds of sheep clogged the roadway, and the professor thought it impossible that these shepherds could separate the sheep into their own flocks. Just then, he watched something incredible take place. Each of the shepherds, having ended their joint conversation, began to walk in separate directions while at the same time humming or singing softly a song. Amazingly, as the shepherds slowly walked away, the sheep in their flocks lifted their heads and began to follow *their own shepherd*. The professor told us he knew he was witnessing the living illustration of Jesus' words, "My sheep hear my voice, and I know them, and they follow me" (John 10:27). We are truly the people of God's pasture and "the sheep of his hand" (Ps. 95:7).

What an amazing reality for us to meditate on during our times of worship. We come before the Lord, the Creator and our Maker, but we have nothing to fear, for we are the sheep of His hand. Our God's hands flung the stars into space, scooped out the seas, and pushed up the mountains. How mighty are the hands of our Creator! But our God's hands also have another quality—they are scarred. Our Maker's hands bear the marks of His redeeming love. We are God's lambs because He became *The Lamb of God*. Now it is the sheep's turn to sing! The Shepherd will listen.

JULY 26
Psalms 97-98

"SEEDS OF LIGHT"

"Light is sown for the righteous, and joy for the upright in heart."
(Psalm 97:11)

The Lord has several guiding principles that are taught throughout Scripture. Of these, there is probably none that is shared more often or upheld more fundamentally than the principle of "sowing and reaping." This principle is not only etched, time and again, into the revelation of Scripture, but the Lord has also made it operational to the existence of life itself on earth. The essence of most of the vegetation around the globe exists in its *seeds*. Life reproduces itself as the seeds are scattered and, in some way, *planted* each year. The harvest is in the nature of the seeds sown in the planting, which takes place months earlier.

The harvest is not accomplished overnight or even in a short period of time, but it is an axiom of God's laws of nature that the harvest will come in proportion to the *type of seeds* and the *number of seeds* sown in the planting season. This law of God guides *biological* life and exists in the guiding principle of *spiritual* life as well, "For whatever one sows, that will he also reap" (Gal. 6:7b).

Our lives are, in reality, a season of sowing and reaping. In the ultimate sense, eternity will be the harvest produced from our lifetime of planting. "For the one who sows to his own flesh will from the flesh reap corruption, *but the one who sows to the Spirit will from the Spirit reap eternal life*" (Gal. 6:8). Eternity will be the harvest of the seeds sown in this lifetime. It will be heaven or hell, but in that place, the proportion of award of righteous living in Christ, or sinful living in the flesh, will be experienced in the *eternal* harvest.

However, this lifetime is also a season of sowing and reaping, planting and harvesting. If we plant negativity and unbelief, we will reap a harvest of darkness and depression. If, on the other hand, we plant seeds of kindness, love, and compassion, then we will experience the harvest described in Psalm 97. We will know the light of joy and the blessing that comes for the righteous. "Light is sown for the righteous, and joy for the upright in heart. Rejoice in the Lord, O you righteous, and give thanks to His holy name" (Ps. 97:11-12). What seeds are you planting?

JULY 27
Psalms 99-100

"Serve the Lord with Gladness"

"Serve the Lord with gladness! Come into his presence with singing!"
(Psalm 100:2)

Abraham Lincoln is known as one of the greatest, if not *the* greatest, of all the presidents in the history of the United States. He holds that level of esteem because he almost single-handedly held together the union of the states during the darkest, bloodiest days our nation has ever known. Lincoln possessed a fantastic gift of verbal eloquence to express the loftiest ideals of the American republic using the simplest of terms. Phrases from his speeches are woven into the very fabric of the symbolism represented in our nation's flag.

What many people do not know about Lincoln is that despite his tendency toward emotional melancholy, he was an avid collector and dispenser of funny stories and witty sayings. One humorous proverb that Lincoln shared often had to do with a person's countenance, "Every man over forty is responsible for his face," he insisted. Now, that might seem unfair, but what Lincoln referred to was the reality that a person's spirit has a way, over time, of etching itself on his face. The modern discovery of "cell memory" lends some scientific support to Lincoln's belief. The issue is not the physiology of facial beauty but the emotionality and spirituality of it.

There truly is, I believe, a physical impact on the face of a person who is filled with the Spirit of the Lord. We are told in the book of Acts that even in his trial and suffering, the people noted of Stephen "that his face was like the face of an angel" (Acts 6:15). The reality of Christ and His presence was displayed on the countenance of that first Christian martyr. Sometimes our faces will be etched with lines of pain and sorrow. However, what spirit is *most commonly* expressed in our countenance?

It has been said of some believers that they probably have Jesus in their hearts, but their faces just don't know about it. Gloominess and pessimism have never been good advertisements for the gospel. The psalmist challenges us to serve the Lord with "gladness," not "sadness" (Ps. 100:2). The Lord may or may not have blessed you with physical beauty, but *if you are a believer in Jesus, the beautiful Spirit of God is within you.* May our desire and prayer today be, "And let the beauty of the Lord our God be upon us" (Ps. 90:17a KJV).

JULY 28
Psalms 101-102

"Unchangeable"

"Of old you laid the foundation of the earth,
and the heavens are the work of your hands.
They will perish, but you will remain;
they will all wear out like a garment.
You will change them like a robe, and they will pass away,
but you are the same, and your years have no end."
(Psalm 102:25-27)

I have never experienced an earthquake, and I am perfectly fine with that. People who have endured that trauma have told me it is probably the most terrifying experience they have ever had. During an earthquake, all you have known as fixed and certain for your entire life suddenly isn't. It is one thing to experience the rising and falling sensation when you are on the water in a boat or the air in a plane, but when the ground beneath your feet rises and falls, reality is completely changed. I can imagine that someone who has experienced an earthquake, to some extent, has had their sense of the stability of the earth forever changed.

In some ways, that might be a good thing. We so easily forget that we are all riding a huge rock covered with shifting plates over a molten core and spinning through space at over 25,000 miles per hour! That doesn't sound exactly predictable. It can change at any moment, and in fact, it will change drastically.

The psalmist reminds us the foundations of our existence, the earth beneath us and the atmosphere above us, will one day perish and be worn out like a garment; but the one who formed them will never change. "But you are the same, and your years have no end" (Ps. 102:27). God never changes. He is immutable and eternal. He had no beginning, and He will have no end. He is "I Am." This Eternal One has formed us in His image and placed eternity in us.

There never will be a time when we are not. God alone is from everlasting to everlasting, but every human being, once given life by Him, becomes eternal. So, what should we live for? The only answer that makes any sense at all is to live for what is eternal, the God of eternity, and those who will live for all eternity. The days of this earth are numbered, and our days on this earth are numbered, but our existences continue forever. Let's live today for the Eternal One and for those who will live forever.

JULY 29
Psalms 103-104

"God's Benefit Plan"

"Bless the Lord, O my soul, and forget not all his benefits, who forgives all your iniquity, who heals all your diseases."
(Psalm 103:2-3)

One thing that concerns people most about a potential employment opportunity is the benefits package. The hourly pay or salary is, of course, really important; but also significant are additional benefits like vacation, retirement plan, health insurance, profit sharing, expense account, etc. Sometimes the benefits package is even more important than the basic salary as people consider their decision. In Psalm 103, David is encouraging himself to bless and worship the Lord and "forget not all his benefits" (Ps. 103:2). No song or volumes of songs could ever express even a fraction of all the benefits God shares with His people. However, just meditating on two of His benefits listed in verse three is enough to thrill any fainting heart, "Who forgives all your iniquity, who heals all your diseases." Those two benefits encompass all the needs we can possibly have, either spiritually or physically.

Spiritually, He forgives all our iniquity. The wonderful word here is "all." God forgives *all* our iniquity. Everything we have ever thought, said or done that was sinful, and all the things *undone* that we should have done. All of these have been forgiven by God for Jesus' sake. Amazing!

Then, all the physical ailments that plague us have been healed. "By his stripes we have been healed" (Isa. 53:5). It might seem that this health benefit is not true; after all, we get sick and experience physical ailments. However, this is not true for our "retirement." The physical distress only extends to this temporary earthly body we inhabit, but the "new and improved version" will never experience sickness or pain. He has healed all our diseases. We will be free from them forever! What a benefit plan we have been given, and we haven't worked for it or earned it! The free gift of God is eternal life through Jesus Christ our Lord (Rom. 6:23). Bless the Lord, O my soul!

JULY 30
Psalms 105-106

"RELENTLESS LOVE"

"Nevertheless, he looked upon their distress, when he heard their cry. For their sake he remembered His covenant and relented according to the abundance of his steadfast love."
(Psalm 106:44-45)

Our reading today from Psalms 105 and 106 is an overview of the history of the nation of Israel, spanning a timeframe of about 1500 years. Psalm 105 begins as a song of God's sovereign love expressed to Abram when he was a pagan idol worshiper living in the Ur of the Chaldees. The song continues through Psalms 105 and 106 until it reaches the time of Judah's defeat and captivity in Babylon, which culminated in 586 BC. These two psalms form an epic, musical narrative of God's relationship with the people of Israel over the centuries.

Two primary themes characterize not only the song but also the character of God and His people over the ages—His *faithfulness* and their *faithlessness*. Time and again, the people would cry out under the oppression brought on them by their own sin, and time and again, they would cry out to God, and He would rescue and restore them. How could God do this to a people so faithless, and how does He still respond this way to us today, as faithless as we often are? The answer is not in His people then or in us now; the answer is in Him. "For He is good, for his steadfast loves endures forever" (Ps. 106:1b).

God is good. He is good in every way. He is good every day. When we are not good, He is. When we are faithless, He is faithful. This is why we, as believers, have any hope at all. "For I the Lord do not change; therefore you, O children of Jacob, are not consumed" (Mal. 3:6). We truly are the "children of Jacob," a man as unreliable and shifty as sand. We love the Lord but love ourselves. We trust Him, but we depend on our abilities. We accept His provision but doubt His promises. We wrestle with Him, and we fight our dearest Friend. What can we do? We can do nothing. He can do anything, even the greatest, most gracious miracle of all—saving us from ourselves.

JULY 31
Psalms 107-108

"TELL IT!"

*"Let the redeemed of the Lord say so,
whom He has redeemed from trouble."*
(Psalm 107:2)

He would say it every time. *Every time.* Pastor Snavely, whom I served with for nearly seven years in Ohio, loved a testimony service. He regularly made them part of the Sunday evening services at Calvary Baptist Church. He always started them and kept them going with the same exhortation, "Let the redeemed of the Lord say so!" He was an intense and devoted follower of Jesus; he talked about the Lord to everyone all the time, and he loved to hear others do the same. Whether it was a sermon, a song, or a testimony, Pastor Snavely delighted to hear the praises of the Lord.

It is incredible how much of the book of Psalms is given over to the same purpose. A vast amount of these songs are testimonials recounting the mighty works of God in the life of the nation of Israel and in the lives of His people individually. The works of the Lord were the oral history of God's greatness and grace recounted from generation to generation for ages before Moses ever recorded a single written word of the first five books of the Bible.

God's Word is the only inspired and infallible expression of God's redemption story. Yet, as believers, each one of us is part of that story; we are "a letter from Christ" (2 Cor. 3:3). The power of God is in His Word in a completely unique way, but His power is also in each of *our stories* as His children. This is the reason we are "witnesses" of Christ. As witnesses, we do not share the story of others. We share what we have personally experienced in Christ and with Christ. I have observed that power so many times.

People usually listen intently when I teach from the Bible, but when I share a personal witness, I can see many people "lean in" to what I am saying. It is not that my stories have anything like the power or authority of God's Word, but they are *my story, my witness.* How often do you speak the witness of your stories? Take a moment to consider that seriously. What are people who interact with you and listen to your conversations, learning about the Lord? Of all the things we can ever share, nothing compares to the significance of our witness. Your life stories have incredible power! Take it from the psalmist and Pastor Snavely, "Let the redeemed of the Lord say so!"

AUGUST

"For the Lord God is a sun and shield."
(Psalm 84:11)

AUGUST 1
Psalms 109-111

"LIBERTY AND SECURITY"

"He sent redemption to his people; he has commanded his covenant forever. Holy and awesome is his name!"
(Psalm 111:9)

One of the most beautiful memorials on the National Mall in Washington DC, is the Jefferson Memorial. It is not as easily accessible as other monuments, but the walk around the beautiful tidal basin to reach the memorial is part of the enjoyable experience. The monument is a columned rotunda that resembles Jefferson's home, Monticello, and the architecture of the first building for the University of Virginia, which Jefferson also designed. Encircling the bronze statue of Jefferson are etched some quotations from his writings. I remember being particularly struck by one of them: *"God who gave us life gave us liberty. Can the liberties of a nation be secured when we have removed a conviction that these liberties are the gift of God?"*

God is truly the giver of life and liberty — physically, nationally, and spiritually. The ultimate of all these liberties is the liberty of *spiritual life*. The psalmist is thinking primarily of the *national liberty* God provided Israel and secured with the covenant at Mount Sinai. Believers in Jesus have been graced with the incredible freedom of redemption confirmed through the New Covenant that our Lord Jesus ratified on Mount Calvary. The people of Israel were redeemed from the destruction of Egypt by the sacrifice of a lamb. We have been rescued from the judgment of God on sin and freed from the slavery of sin by the sacrifice of The Lamb. God "sent redemption" (Ps. 111:9) to us and made us "his people" forever. This relationship is completely due to His gracious work. He initiated it and will preserve it. In fact, He "has commanded His covenant forever."

Our spiritual freedom is secured forever by the commanding word of the all-powerful God. Our freedom and liberty will be maintained as long as God sits on the throne of heaven. Through the circling ages of eternity, our liberty will be secure, for encircling the throne of eternal God shines a beautiful rainbow that symbolizes His covenant-keeping love forever and ever (Rev. 4:3). God is the "Author of Liberty," and He "remembers his covenant forever" (Ps. 111:5).

AUGUST 2
Psalms 112-113

"The Dawn of the Righteous"

"Light dawns in the darkness for the upright;
he is gracious, merciful, and righteous."
(Psalm 112:4)

I once heard a preacher say that five of the most blessed words in all the Bible are these: "And it came to pass." We can all smile at those words because we have been through seasons so difficult that it was an incredible blessing just to have them come to a conclusion. Some people reading this page right now might be taking those five words by faith because this present dark season has lasted so long, and as yet, there has been no glimmer of a new day. The *ability to hope* is such a gift from the Lord.

To have hope is not *to wish*; it is so much more than that. *To wish* is to desire something for which there is no objective basis in reality. Unlike a wish, hope is reality. It is simply a reality that has not yet been experienced. Unlike a wish, hope is based on objective truth, the ultimate truth, the promises of God. Hope is the present experience of faith that takes hold of God's promises and delivers them to His people. "Now faith is the substance of things hoped for, the evidence of things not seen" (Heb. 11:1). It is this objective reality—hope, that is experienced by faith.

Hope is the "light" that "dawns in the darkness" for a believer. Ultimately, the light we have in the deepest trials has its source, not in the "SUN" but the "SON." God's light in His Son has shined and continues to shine in the darkness, and the darkness has not been able to overcome it (John 1:5). By God's gracious salvation, He has shined into our hearts "the light of the knowledge of the glory of God in the face of Jesus Christ" (2 Cor. 4:6).

We, who were once darkness ourselves, have become light in Christ (1 Thess. 5:5). This light is so inextinguishable that, even in the darkest seasons, we can overcome it by being "gracious, merciful, and righteous" (Ps. 112:4). We sometimes walk in the night seasons, but by God's grace, we don't have to let the darkness reign in us. "Light dawns in the darkness for the upright" (Ps. 112:4).

AUGUST 3
Psalms 114-115

"THE WORSHIP MAKEOVER"

"Those who make them become like them; so do all who trust in them."
(Psalm 115:8)

It would be hard to determine where and when the first project was recorded, but today there exists an entire field of communication that could be called "renovation media." The examples are endless, but the process is basically the same: buy a run-down property, fix it up, flip it, sell it, rent it, love it, leave it, keep it... Well, you get the picture. Now, all these programs exist because there is great interest in property renovation. It is interesting and truly amazing to watch the transformation of a house take place through insight, investment, and yes, hard work.

In Psalm 115, we are told about a transformation that is even more powerful than that which can ever take place to a property, and that is the personal transformation accomplished by trust. The psalmist reminds us that people become, in character, what they trust in spirit. In his song, the writer compares the impact of the devotion of idols to the results of trusting in the Lord. Of course, the idols cannot speak, see, hear, feel, or walk (Ps. 115:5-8). But the worship of these senseless and stationary idols is very influential, "Those who make them become like them; so do all who trust in them" (Ps. 115:8).

This is a startling but enlightening revelation. We become like what we worship. That means the primary focus of our lives will form our lives. That is why the psalmists so enthusiastically challenge those who hear this song to trust, fear and praise the Lord. He is entirely worthy of adoration, producing the most wonderful transformation (Ps. 115:8-18).

Our worship not only honors God, but it also changes us. "And we all, with unveiled face, beholding the glory of the Lord, are being transformed into the same image from one degree of glory to another. For this comes from the Lord who is the Spirit" (2 Cor. 3:18). Worship is ultimately, by faith, "beholding the glory of the Lord." It is focusing our minds on Him. When we worship, we "are being transformed into the same image"; we are becoming more like Christ. That is the most "extreme makeover" of all, and its value is priceless and eternal.

AUGUST 4
Psalms 116-118

"THE OUTCAST RETURNS"

"The stone that the builders rejected has become the cornerstone."
(Psalm 118:22)

Many psalms are filled with praise, but Psalms 116, 117, and 118 stand out as a unique trilogy of joyful thanks expressed to the Lord. The cause of this worshipful celebration is centered on David's return to Jerusalem after he was forced to flee because of the treachery of his son, Absalom. David had feared for his own life and those of his loved ones and loyal followers (Ps. 116:3). By God's miraculous intervention and deliverance, David returned to open the "gates of righteousness" (Ps. 118:19) and be like "the stone that the builders rejected has become the cornerstone" (Ps. 118:22).

David wrote these lyrics from his own experience of deliverance, but he also wrote them as a prophet. For over 1000 years after he composed them, his greater Son, Jesus of Nazareth, would proclaim these words as fulfilled in His rejection, crucifixion, resurrection, and glorification. "Have you not read this Scripture: 'The stone that the builders rejected has become the cornerstone; this was the Lord's doing, and it is marvelous in our eyes'?" (Mark 12:10-11) Also, Peter and Paul, along with the early disciples, would cite this psalm of David as proof of Messiah's rejection and exaltation.

The gospel is the message of "Him who for a little while was made lower than the angels, namely Jesus, crowned with glory and honor because of the suffering of death, so that by the grace of God He might taste death for everyone" (Heb. 2:9). For our Savior, it was first the cross, then the crown and coronation. Jesus' path is ours as well, but as the old gospel song reminds us, "The way of the cross leads home." How wonderful to think of arriving at the New Jerusalem and declaring, "Open to me the gates of righteousness, that I may enter through them and give thanks to the Lord" (Ps. 118:19). Then, how wonderful to hear the reply to us from within that glorious city, "Blessed is he who comes in the name of the Lord! We bless you from the house of the Lord" (Ps. 118:26).

AUGUST 5
Psalm 119

"LIGHT FOR THE DARKNESS"

"Your word is a lamp to my feet and a light to my path."
(Psalm 119:105)

I do not like being in the dark. Now, let me be specific. It is not being afraid *of* the dark but more a genuine dislike of being *in* the dark. There is something deeply unsettling about not knowing where you are and where you are going.

Many years ago, as a youth minister in Ohio, I had to take several teenagers home following one of our evening outreach events. The last young man lived many miles out of town on a farm. I got the student safely home, then started making my way back to the city through narrow country roads. It was early fall before the corn had been harvested, so I was literally driving through tunnels of corn, standing thick and higher than my head for acres and acres. That is when it happened. The lights on my car began to dim, the dashboard sensors began to flutter, and the engine started to lurch, then stopped altogether. The alternator had gone out. This could not have happened at a worse time because it was a cloudy night without a moon, and it was dark. And this was before cell phones, so there was nothing I could do but start walking or carefully shuffling because that was the only way I could stay on a road that I could not see.

I shuffled and stumbled along in the dark for what seemed to be a *very* long time until I finally arrived at a crossroad of two country lanes. That is when I saw it. Far off in the distance, a farmhouse had a light shining on the front porch that gave me a sense of direction. I shuffled toward that light, and the closer I came, the more light shined on the gravel road in front of me. I finally reached the front porch and discovered a very nice couple occupied the home with a very mean dog, but that's another story. Since that night, I have never read or heard quoted Psalm 119:105 without a deeper appreciation of the value of a "light to my path" in a time of darkness. God's Word is that for us—*light for the darkness.*

The Bible does not fully illuminate every moment of our lives with a floodlight of complete understanding, but God's Word does keep us headed in the right direction and gives us light to take the next step in dark seasons. The key is not just having God's Word *with* you but having it *in* you. The darkest place the Bible illuminates is our own minds. We don't usually stumble because of the darkness of the world but because of the darkness of our mental pathways. God's Word brightens our lives from the inside out. There is no denying that the darkness in us and around us is real, but God's Word is also real and brighter than any darkness!

AUGUST 6
Psalms 120-121

"LOOK UP!"

"I lift up my eyes to the hills. From where does my help come? My help comes from the Lord, who made heaven and earth."
(Psalm 121:1-2)

Your Bible may include a notation over these two psalms in today's reading that identifies them as "Songs of Ascents." These songs were specifically written to be sung by pilgrims as they made their way toward the temple in Jerusalem to worship Jehovah. In particular, Psalm 121 was written for singing during the final part of the journey to the House of the Lord. If you are familiar with the topography of Jerusalem, you will recall that the City of David was established on Mount Zion, a steep rocky crag surrounded on three sides by deep valleys. So, when people approached the Temple Mount, they were literally making an "ascent" as they came to worship. The pilgrims would first see the spectacular panorama of the Holy City from one of the surrounding hills, but as they descended into the valleys, they would "lift up" their eyes to the hills. Those valleys were incredibly deep-like ravines, and dark shadows would abound there even in the light of day. But as the pilgrims kept walking through those shadows, rising up and shining above them were the gleaming walls and gates of God's Temple. That beautiful sight, as they gazed upward, would remind them of the faithfulness of God and His steadfast love. The One who formed these hills was their Helper. They might be footsore, but He would keep them from falling. It was dark in the valleys, but their God was always wide awake. These mountains and their shadows would remind them that He is their shade of rest and refreshment from the burning sun of long days.

The valleys could be dark and scary, but as they see the Temple gleaming above them, they would find comfort in knowing that the One who dwells there is their Guardian from all evil. They are worshipers of the God who is always with them so that, whether coming from or going to His House, they are never out of His loving presence. Now, that song of ascents is one for the ages! It is a call to us, as today's worshipers, to "Look Up!"

AUGUST 7
Psalms 122-124

"THE POWER OF HIS NAME"

"Our help is in the name of the Lord, who made heaven and earth."
(Psalm 124:8)

Names in the Bible are very significant. They carry with them important information concerning the events surrounding the birth of the child or perhaps an expression of the hope or faith of the parents regarding the child. Names were considered to be very important. That is certainly the case when it comes to the names of God. In one sense, no one could ever name God because God is the *uncaused cause* of all creation. No one ever preceded Him because He had no predecessors. God has always been the eternal first. So, the names of God are the qualities He wants to communicate about Himself.

God does this because He wants us to *know* Him. This does not mean just knowing a title for Him, but *knowing Him in experience.* Our experiences of God become the means by which we truly "know His name." These experiences of God are sometimes known at the physical level in the events of our life on earth. Some of these experiences of God are those we encounter in the realm of faith. By trusting and relying on Him, we experience the life of His Spirit, strengthening our spirit. Either in the spiritual or physical realm, we experience what today's psalm proclaims, "Our help is in the name of the Lord, who made heaven and earth" (Ps. 124:8). Notice it is the "name" of the Lord that is our "help." Sometimes it is very "helpful" to meditate on some of the names of the Lord shared with us in Scripture. Take some time throughout the day to ponder, pray, and praise these names of our God.

> El Shaddai, Lord God Almighty
> El Elyon, The Most High God
> El Olam, The Everlasting God
> Jehovah-Nissi, The Lord My Banner
> Jehovah-Raah, The Lord My Shepherd
> Jehovah-Rapha, The Lord My Healer
> Jehovah-Shammah, The Lord Who is There
> Jehovah-Tsidkenu, The Lord My Righteousness
> Jehovah-Shalom, The Lord My Peace
> Jehovah-Melech, The Lord My King
> Jehovah-Jireh, The Lord Will Provide

AUGUST 8
Psalms 125-126

"SHOUTS OF JOY"

*"He who goes out weeping, bearing the seed for sowing,
shall come home with shouts of joy, bringing his sheaves with him."*
(Psalm 126:6)

In the little church I attended as a boy, two books guided the service—the King James Bible and the blue-backed Baptist hymnal. I can still remember the sound of dozens of those hymn books being pulled out of their wooden holders on the back of the pews simultaneously. Those dear folks at Immanuel Baptist Church sure loved singing those hymns and gospel songs. One of the favorites we sang often and loudly was "Bringing in the Sheaves." As a little boy, I enjoyed singing that song very much.

One day I realized I didn't know what "the sheaves" were and why we were singing about "bringing them in." On the way home in the car, I asked my mom about it. She explained it was a song about the harvest, gathering the wheat, and winning souls into the Kingdom. I don't know if I made the spiritual connection, but I remember learning a little more about agriculture and what those tall and bound stacks in the fields were that I had seen in books. Eventually, I came to recognize that Psalm 126 was the source of the image in that great gospel song.

These verses have often been used with an application toward winning people to Jesus Christ. It is a beautiful thought and an appropriate application. However, the psalm is a song of praise for those who have waited long for deliverance for the people of God and their city of Zion. When God finally brought deliverance, it was like the rain on the mountains of Judah, causing streams to flow in the wilderness. It is a song of steadfast hope. No matter how long it is delayed, the Lord will bring deliverance to His people. Like farmers who have planted their final seeds with tear-stained faces, when the Lord brings the life-giving rain, those who have toiled with tears shall reap in joy. They come home at harvest time with loads of wheat, shouting for their family and friends to rejoice with them. It is a beautiful image.

As you read it today, perhaps you can hear the words of the Apostle Paul as he challenges us about the great harvest of the resurrection.

"Therefore, my beloved brothers, be steadfast, immovable, always abounding in the work of the Lord, knowing that in the Lord your labor is not in vain."
(1 Corinthians 15:58)

AUGUST 9
Psalms 127-128

"SACRED SLEEP"

"It is in vain that you rise up early and go late to rest, eating the bread of anxious toil; for he gives to his beloved sleep."
(Psalm 127:2)

One Sunday morning, just before the worship service began, I was strolling up the aisles of the auditorium, welcoming people. To my surprise and their embarrassment, a couple in the congregation were finding their seats as I approached them, and they were carrying pillows! Well, this provided lots of ammunition for some wonderful banter with them. For the life of me, I can't remember exactly why they had pillows with them. I am confident it had nothing to do with the sermon! Sleeping in service may sometimes be unavoidable (I'm not certain about bringing pillows!), but sometimes sleep is sacred.

Our reading today in Psalm 127 tells us that restful, peaceful sleep is a gift from God (Ps. 127:2). There can be many legitimate reasons for not getting a good night's sleep, but stress, fretting, and worry are not one of them. God has ordained the virtue of work and working to the best of our abilities. But burning ourselves out with no margins for family, friends, and the enjoyment of life is not God's will. The Lord wants us to live at a "pace for grace" (Ps. 46:10). The *law* of the Sabbath is not binding on believers in the New Covenant; however, the *principle of sabbath* is not a law but a gift. Jesus said man was not made for the Sabbath, but the Sabbath was made for man (Mark 2:27). He meant that it was a gift so that rest, reflection, and time with family could be a sacred part of His people's lives.

Sleep is a form of sabbath. It is rest from the toil of the day, but it is also an opportunity to express trust in God's care and watchfulness over His people. "He who keeps Israel neither slumbers nor sleeps" (Ps. 121:4). God can accomplish more while we sleep than we could in a lifetime. When we have done our work and done our best, we can leave the results with Him.

I have yet to have anyone tell me at the end of their life that they wish they had spent more time at work. However, I have had many people tell me they wish they had spent more time with family and friends and trusted God more with their work. So, don't just stand on God's promises; lie down on them! "In peace I will both lie down and sleep; for you alone, O Lord, make me dwell in safety" (Ps. 4:8).

AUGUST 10
Psalms 129-130

"GRACE THAT IS GREATER"

"O Israel, hope in the Lord!
For with the Lord there is steadfast love,
and with him is plentiful redemption."
(Psalm 130:7)

As one of the Songs of Ascent, Psalm 130 was a hymn people sang as they approached the temple in Jerusalem. If you could be transported back in time to stand on the steps of Solomon's Temple or Herod's Temple in Jesus' day, you would have heard groups of pilgrims and individuals singing this psalm as they came to worship. It is a beautiful anthem of contrition and faith. Everything about the magnificent temple reminded the pilgrims of the awesome holiness of the God of Israel and their own awful sinfulness.

They came to worship, bringing the required sacrifice to offer, but how could the blood of their bleating goat or sheep possibly be the basis of their pleas for the forgiveness of their sins? It couldn't. They did not deserve God's forgiveness, and they certainly could not earn it. Yet, it was to this Sovereign God, Maker of heaven and earth, that they must be reconciled, or they would most certainly perish. If they were to be forgiven, it was only on the basis of His "steadfast love" and "plentiful redemption" (Ps. 130:7).

There has always been only one basis for the forgiveness of sin: God's unmerited, undeserved love. "Steadfast love" in Hebrew is the equivalent of the Greek word for "grace" in the New Testament. Paul spoke the gospel truth for all the ages when he said, "for it is by grace that you have been saved" (Eph. 2:8). God's marvelous, infinite, matchless grace has always been the basis of the plea and the praise of the people of God.

Marvelous grace of our loving Lord,
Grace that exceeds our sin and our guilt,
Yonder on Calvary's mount outpoured.
There where the blood of the Lamb was spilt.

Dark is the stain that we cannot hide,
What can avail to wash it away?
Look! There is flowing a crimson tide;
Whiter than snow you may be today.

Marvelous, infinite, matchless grace
Freely bestowed on all who believe;
You that are longing to see His face,
Will you this moment His grace receive?

Grace, grace, God's grace,
Grace that will pardon and cleanse within;
Grace, grace, God's grace
Grace that is greater than all our sin.

("Grace Greater Than Our Sin," by Julia H. Johnston)

AUGUST 11
Psalms 131-132

"REMINDING GOD"

"Remember, O Lord, in David's favor, all the hardships he endured..."
(Psalm 132:1)

By virtue of His very nature, God has no limits whatsoever. He is infinite. Nothing limits God, but *we* are certainly limited in our ability to perceive, in our finite minds, even a speck of all the glory of His infinite greatness. It is evident through the psalms and the other prayers and praises of Scripture that God takes a Father's delight in His infant children communicating with Him in their very limited understanding and vocabulary. If the Lord were not the completely good, gracious, and kind being that He is, He might take offense at some of the things we say to Him during our sincere prayers, like asking Him to "remember." Think about it—us reminding the all-knowing God! However, God loves it so much that He has chosen to record some of these "less-than-theologically-accurate" prayers in His eternal Word. Psalm 132 is a wonderful example of this delight of our Heavenly Father.

The psalmist writes perhaps generations or centuries after the Lord made a covenant with David and declared promises He would keep for all of David's sons who honored Him. In this psalm, one of David's sons lays hold of that covenant and reminds the Lord of what He said. "The Lord swore to David a sure oath from which he will not turn back: 'One of the sons of your body I will set on your throne. If your sons keep my covenant and my testimonies that I shall teach them...'" (Ps. 132: 11-12) We don't know which of David's descendants sent this "prayer mail" reminder to God, but he is an excellent example.

The old gospel song is so encouraging, "Standing on the Promises of God," but we also need to practice often "kneeling on the promises." After all, we can have confidence in our prayers when we are praying God's own promises back to Him! God's Word is filled with hundreds, perhaps thousands, of promises. God did not record these only to inform us of what He had done in the past but also to inspire us about what He will do today. He made an eternal record of these promises so we can reflect on them, respond to them, and remind Him of them. When was the last time you reminded the Lord of one of His promises? Go ahead; He won't mind at all!

AUGUST 12
Psalms 133-134

"The Smell of Unity"

When you think of heaven, what do you think about? No doubt, the Lord Jesus comes to your immediate thoughts, and perhaps the incredible joy of seeing your family and friends there. The sights and sounds of heaven are definitely beyond our wildest dreams, but have you ever thought about what it *smells* like? Since in our glorified bodies, we will have all the physical senses that are part of our existence on earth, I am sure that included in the indescribable and endless joys of heaven will be the absolutely wonderful smells. Imagine that first moment of inhaling the atmosphere of glory!

Truly, we can only imagine for now. However, we do have recorded in Psalm 133 a description of what smells a little bit like heaven on earth—unity among the family of God. The inspired psalmist tells us that unity among the family members of the Lord is amazingly "good and pleasant." It is like the secret, sacred perfume used to anoint Aaron's head as high priest and would drip down upon his beard and saturate his robes. So, as Aaron and the high priests after him went about their duties in the presence of God, the fantastic aroma would waft behind the curtain to God's dwelling place in the Holy of Holies. It would also be carried outside and smelled by the gathered worshipers. It must have smelled amazing!

As New Testament believers, we now understand that everything about the service and worship in the Tabernacle was representative of Jesus. That means it is not saying too much to realize that the reason this unity of the family of God is so remarkable is that it carries with it the fragrance of Jesus. The unity we share in Christ has been provided by the blood of the Son of God. As we preserve this unity by the power of God's Spirit, our fellowship is a fragrance to the Father of His beloved Son. It brings such joy to His heart that where this unity is expressed, the Father has commanded His life-giving blessing. How important the unity among God's people truly is! We must also consider what division and strife among His children smell like to God. If unity smells like Jesus, then division must smell like the Devil! We cannot imagine how distasteful that is to our Lord. In our personal relationships, all of us are expressing an aroma to God. What do your relationships smell like?

AUGUST 13
Psalms 135-136

"REPETITIOUS PRAISE"

"...for his steadfast love endures forever."
(Psalm 136)

He was a fine Christian man, but at that moment he was a little upset. As my friend and brother stood before me in the church auditorium that Sunday morning, he had a sincere complaint he wanted to share with me. One of the songs we had sung in worship that morning included a phrase used many times in the song.

"Pastor, to me, that just sounds like vain repetition in worship," he said.

I appreciated his honesty; as I said, he was a godly man and a good friend. I replied to him, "So what you are saying is that you don't want to hear a phrase repeated over and over again in a song?"

"Exactly," he replied.

To which I responded, "For example, like Psalm 136."

"What do you mean?" he asked.

"Well, you do know that the psalmist repeats the phrase, 'His mercy endures forever,' 26 times in that psalm?"

My dear friend smiled his sweet smile and said, "Well, you've got a point there, pastor."

What a dear man! He's in heaven now, and I'm sure the repetition of "Holy, Holy, Holy is the Lord of Hosts" is not bothering him at all. Vain repetition in worship does not refer primarily to repeating the same words frequently. It refers to the danger of only expressing words when our mind and heart are not actively engaged.

Jesus told the woman at the well in Samaria that acceptable worship is offered "in spirit and in truth" (John 4:23, 24). This describes true worship as "all that we are" responding to "all that He is." Both our thinking and our emotions are to be connected as we worship. This type of worship is so *wonderful* because it is so *portable*. Again, Jesus told the Samaritan woman that the true worshipers would not be limited to a mountain in Samaria or Jerusalem (John 4:21).

Worship is not determined by the location or position of our bodies but by the disposition of our souls to God. When the God of Israel and the Savior of the world has captured our affections, the exalting of His love that endures forever will be our continual refrain. Like the psalmist in our reading today, we will recount the victories the Lord has given and sing over and over again the wonders of His love and the triumphs of His grace. We may not be able "to carry a tune in a bucket," but we will lift up our praises for Him in intentional, worshipful repetition.

AUGUST 14
Psalms 137-139

"THE SANCTITY OF LIFE"

"Your eyes saw my unformed substance; in your book were written, every one of them, the days that were formed for me, when as yet there was none of them."
(Psalm 139:16)

The "right to life" and the "right to choose" is a battle constantly being fought in the political arena and the courts of America. However, in the heart of a Christ-follower, there should be no turmoil on this issue. The Supreme Court has already ruled. *THE* Supreme Court. The judge of all the earth has already issued His decree, "All souls are mine" (Ezek. 18:4).

When do the lives of people belong to the Lord? At birth? No. According to His Word through King David, people's lives belong to the Lord from conception. "For you formed my inward parts; you knitted me together in my mother's womb." (v. 13). "Your eyes saw my unformed substance..." (v. 16). The word for "unformed substance" is only used here; in Hebrew, it means "embryo." God says every life is His from conception, and He Himself forms each human being. Not only does God form us, but He also forms the days of our lives. "In your book were written, every one of them, the days that were formed for me, when as yet there was none of them" (v. 16).

Life is sacred from conception to completion, and each life has purpose to the One who gave it. This means *your* life is sacred. Say this today (out loud if at all possible), "I am *personally* created by God. I am *precisely* created by God. I am *purposefully* created by God." Think on those words: "personally," "precisely," and "purposefully." Your life really matters. This day really matters. *Really matters.*

AUGUST 15
Psalms 140-141

"Painful Kindness"

*"Let a righteous man strike me—it is a kindness; let him rebuke me—
it is oil for my head; let my head not refuse it."*
(Psalm 141:5)

Pain is not enjoyable. Pain can be awful, and some who are reading this page today are in the grip of it. Physically, or perhaps emotionally, it is there and very real. In a season of giving and receiving gifts, certainly, none of us would look forward to unwrapping a gift of pain this year. Pain is not pleasant, but it can be good for us. That is the reason King David, in the verse above, speaks of the "kindness" of being struck by a rebuke from a friend. David's son Solomon, who would be the wisest of men, would say, "A friend loves at all times and a brother is born for adversity" (Prov. 17:17).

A true friend loves and is kind, and sometimes that means loving enough and being kind enough to rebuke us, to tell us not necessarily what we *want* to hear but what we *need* to hear. The experience may not be pleasant, but the expression may be true. Valuing the insight and valuing the individual who loved us enough to give it is wisdom. God uses pain as a kind gift of His severe mercy. The British scholar and author C. S. Lewis wisely said, "God whispers to us in our pleasures, speaks in our consciences, but shouts in our pains. It is His megaphone to rouse a deaf world."

Part of our fleshly nature is that we usually require the shouts of pain before we can hear the whispers of love. We typically do not count our blessings until we have felt our bruises. Some of these bruises are caused by the words of a friend who has found it necessary to rebuke us. If you have such a friend who will give you that kind of *gift* sometimes, count yourself truly blessed! Friends like that are treasures themselves.

In light of today's Scripture, the question to ask is, who can count us as such a friend? If we truly love someone, we will not withhold what is in their best interest, even if it may cause some temporary pain. Paul challenged us, "If anyone is caught in any transgression, you who are spiritual should restore him in a spirit of gentleness" (Gal. 6:1). The word Paul uses for "restore" means "to put back in place" like a dislocated bone. Sure, it will hurt, but if it helps a brother walk straight, how kind is that?!

AUGUST 16
Psalm 142

"The Prayer of a Caveman"

"Bring me out of prison, that I may give thanks to your name!
The righteous will surround me, for you will deal bountifully with me."
(Psalm 142:7)

When visiting Israel, I have been blessed, on many occasions, to stand in a spot of one of the famous scenes of the Bible and imagine the events that transpired there. Viewing the geography makes the description of it in God's Word so much more real and personal. Psalm 142 takes on that added dimension today as I recall walking along the river in the oasis-like surroundings of En Gedi. Looking across the stream and above the tree line, you see the orange-tinted, craggy cliffs of the Judean wilderness. It appears the only inhabitants are the eagles and the groups of ibex, sometimes called gazelles, that somehow survive on the tiny tufts of grass and survive the death-defying leaps they make from rocky crag to crag.

In this wilderness oasis, David and a few of his loyal men hid from the soldiers and the deadly hatred of King Saul. David was considered public enemy number one, and he knew there was only a step between him and terrible death. However, hiding in the darkness of his prison-like cave, David grasped the light that shined in his heart, if not in his surroundings. It was the glowing rays of assurance of the power and faithfulness of his God, Jehovah. His sad lament was true, "no refuge remains to me; no one cares for my soul" (Ps. 142:4).

This was the truth of how he felt, but it was not the truth of the ultimate reality; he was not alone. The invisible but ever-present One was there with him. David's refuge was not in a cave but in the Rock of Ages. David knew this, and he made a choice to declare it, "I cry to you, O Lord; I say, 'You are my refuge, my portion in the land of the living'" (Ps. 142:5). We know the rest of David's story, but we don't know the rest of ours. Perhaps today, you are sitting in your house or your car, but it seems like you are sitting in a dark cave; it feels like solitary confinement. You truly feel alone, but you aren't. He is there. The Lord never leaves nor forsakes His people. This "caveman's psalm" was recorded for times just like this. Sing it today and embrace His light in the darkness.

AUGUST 17
Psalms 143-144

"Streams in the Desert"

*"Blessed are the people to whom such blessings fall!
Blessed are the people whose God is the Lord!"*
(Psalm 144:15)

The opening words to Charles Dickens's classic novel, *A Tale of Two Cities*, are considered some of the finest in English literature, "It was the best of times, it was the worst of times...." Those are great words for the beginning of a great book, but over the years I have come to think that those words are an apt description of where most people find themselves on just about any day. Things are great in some areas, and they are terrible in others. I have often jokingly responded to many people when they ask me how I am doing, "Oh, I'm just living the Tale of Two Cities!"

The truth is that most of us on most days are experiencing situations and even emotions that fluctuate between both ends of "the best of times, the worst of times" spectrum. It's called "life." The critical issue for us as followers of the Lord is to be guided by the absolutely reliable compass during the changing emotional terrain of our days. How wonderful it is that each of us possesses that compass with the "true north" for both our mountaintop and wilderness seasons.

David's words in the two psalms for today's Scripture reading are an excellent example of how to use that perfect compass of God's character and faithfulness in the conflicting experiences of "the best of times and the worst of times." That is where David is living in this season. He is experiencing the protection and provision of God as never before in his life, yet he is also being wrongly accused and pursued by King Saul. David is not in denial, and he shares with God all that is happening and all he feels in his fear.

However, also notice all the times he declares, "I remember," "I stretch out my hands," "I meditate," "I am your servant," "I take refuge," and "I will sing." David knew how to look to his "God compass." True north for him was not what he was feeling at any given moment, but rather the fixed point in his universe was the north star of God Himself. Today is probably "the best of times and the worst of times" for many of us, but in all the times of our life, there is the timeless God who declares, "For I am the Lord, I do not change" (Mal. 3:6 NKJV). Let's keep our eyes on Him in "the best of times and the worst of times."

AUGUST 18
Psalms 145-146

"Infinite, Intimate God"

The nature of God is such that God is not only everywhere, but He is all there everywhere. Theologians refer to this truth as the immanence of God. Because God is omnipresent, He is also wholly present everywhere. God is infinitely simple, meaning He cannot be divided into pieces. God is in every place, and all of God is in every place. It was this infinite and intimate nature of God that David adored and celebrated so often in his songs. David praised the God of Israel as the One whom the heavens could not contain but also worshiped Jehovah as the loving and concerned companion who was aware of his every emotion. This is the God of the ages, who is also the Heavenly Father revealed fully to us by His Son, Jesus Christ.

In these two psalms of David, we are given the opportunity to express worship to our infinite, intimate God in word and deed. In our praise and prayer today, there is nothing too big or too small that we cannot bring to Him. We are speaking to the One for whom nothing is so big that it causes Him the slightest challenge, and there is also nothing so seemingly trivial or insignificant that it is beneath His concern or complete attention.

In Psalm 145, we join David as we praise the Lord saying, "Your kingdom is an everlasting kingdom, and your dominion endures throughout all generations" (Ps. 145:13). We also worship God today as we imitate His concern for the most vulnerable members of society, "The Lord watches over the sojourners; he upholds the widow and the fatherless..." (Ps. 146:9) The Lord of the universe is concerned with those most overlooked in the world.

People who truly love God must express their care for those the Lord cares about. Looking out for the immigrant who may not be a fellow citizen but is our fellow man is God's will for us. Upholding the cause and care for the widows and the fatherless is how we uphold the faith. The Lord is glorified when our minds are filled with His infinite glory and our hearts are full of His intimate loving concern for the most at-risk. May we be people today who worship God well by serving others well in His Name.

AUGUST 19
Psalms 147-148

"HEAVEN AND NATURE SING"

In a few months, all around the world will be songs constantly played and sung that celebrate the messages of Christmas. Sadly, so much of that music in this age leaves the "Christ" out of the "Christmas." The madness of the materialism surrounding the holidays often replaces the wonders of the worship in what should certainly be "holy days." Perhaps the days of this week are a good time for us to refocus our concentrated worship of the One for whom "Heaven and Nature Sing."

David certainly was not familiar with the carol, "Joy to the World," but that could be a title for Psalm 148. This psalm is remarkable in that David sees every aspect of heaven and nature, proclaiming a joyful anthem of praise to God. Notice the progression from the highest to the lowest in David's praise. Heavens, heights, angels, and heavenly host lead the worship (Ps. 148:1-2). Then, the solar system, atmosphere, stars, sun, moon, and skies praise the Lord (vs. 3-4). From the earth, the ocean life and depths, the fire, hail, snow, mist, and wind all obey God (vs. 7-8). The wildlife and geography of mountains, hills, fruit trees, cedars, beasts, livestock, flying birds, and creeping insects all worship and praise Jehovah (vs. 9-10). Then the inhabitants of the earth from the most powerful kings, princes, and all peoples, the old men and young men, the maidens and children all join in praising the Lord (vs. 11-12).

It is a wonderful psalm that tells us much about David's worldview. He clearly saw life through the lens of a worshiper. In all its expressions, life for David was resounding with God's praise. What is most revealing is that David could hear the song because he saw the Lord in all things. He saw God because he was listening. *Heaven and Nature Sing*—they truly do, but are we looking in such a way that we can hear the praise of our God?

> *Joy to the world, the Savior reigns;*
> *Let men their songs employ;*
> *While fields and floods, rocks, hills and plains*
> *Repeat the sounding joy, Repeat the sounding joy,*
> *Repeat, repeat, the sounding joy.*
>
> ("Joy to the World" words by Isaac Watts)

AUGUST 20
Psalms 149-150

"Sound His Praises"

"Let everything that has breath praise the Lord! Praise the Lord!"
(Psalm 150:6)

I dearly love these two final psalms of praise to God. When you read them out loud, you can also hear and feel the exuberance of the throngs of worshipers in the temple as they sing to the Lord with all their might. It is noisy praise, with every type of instrument making melody to God. The worshipers are not still and expressionless, but they are engaged in every part of their being in rejoicing before the Lord. Some of them are so filled with joy that they begin to worship the Lord with dance (Ps. 149:3).

Some people may secretly wish that verse was not in the Bible, but there it is! These two psalms have so helped me to recognize the importance of expressing praise to God with freedom and exuberance. Did you notice how many different and varied instruments are used in these worship songs? Tambourine, lyre, trumpet, flute, harp, strings, pipes, cymbals, and clashing cymbals. This is worship loud and big! What is the inspiration for such worship? A heart overwhelmed and awe-struck at the glory, majesty, and love of God. Most of all, it is the overflow of gratitude and thanks for the personal deliverance and salvation from sin and bondage through God's grace.

Fannie Crosby was an amazing woman. Although blinded by an illness at the age of six, she determined that her disability would never be permitted to limit her zeal for education, musical training, and service to God. She wore Victorian-era dresses and the darkened glasses of the blind, but her poems and lyrics were filled with light and joy. Fannie knew Jesus, and her joy was exuberant and contagious. I often think of Fannie Crosby when I read these final stanzas of the psalms. Clearly, Fanny loved these psalms as well, and they inspired one of her beloved gospel songs, sung loudly by millions of God's people, joyful in their worship.

> *Praise Him! Praise Him! Jesus, our blessed Redeemer!*
> *Sing, O Earth, His wonderful love proclaim!*
> *Hail Him! Hail Him! Highest archangels in glory;*
> *Strength and honor give to His holy Name!*
> *Like a shepherd, Jesus will guard His children,*
> *In His arms He carries them all day long.*

Praise Him! Praise Him! Tell of His excellent greatness;
Praise Him! Praise Him! Ever in joyful song!

Praise Him! Praise Him! Jesus, our blessed Redeemer!
For our sins He suffered, and bled, and died.
He our Rock, our hope of eternal salvation,
Hail Him! Hail Him! Jesus the Crucified.
Sound His praises! Jesus who bore our sorrows,
Love unbounded, wonderful, deep and strong.

Praise Him! Praise Him! Tell of His excellent greatness;
Praise Him! Praise Him! Ever in joyful song!

("Praise Him! Praise Him! Jesus, Our Blessed Redeemer," words by Fanny Crosby)

AUGUST 21
Proverbs 1

"LISTEN UP!"

Proverbs is often described as the book of wisdom. In fact, Solomon, the human author of the book of Proverbs, uses the character Wisdom as the narrator of this book. She walks the earth and "cries aloud in the streets, in the markets she raises her voice" (Prov. 1:20). Wisdom's voice is true. It is the voice of the message of God in a world filled with noise. The world's busyness and noise distract unwise people from the reality that life is unpredictable and deadly serious. Wisdom continues to call; she is the messenger of God's Word, will, and ways. Wisdom calls us, and we can hear her. Her voice echoes through the pages of God's Word. As we read and heed Wisdom's voice, we become wise ourselves. And we become "wisdom speakers," inviting people to listen and apply God's Word so they too "will dwell secure and will be at ease, without dread of disaster" (Prov. 1:33).

AUGUST 22
Proverbs 2

"PRICELESS PROTECTION"

Perhaps some of you reading this page grew up in a community where everyone had locks on their doors but rarely used them. You lived in a secure neighborhood. Sadly, mine was not that. Every home had doors with well-used locks, and most yards had a mean dog just to make sure. Security is necessary because the world is not a safe place.

However, even in a world that is often dangerous and deceptive, the Lord has provided the ultimate protection system we need, and that is to protect us from ourselves. Each of us is programmed in our nature toward dangerous and deadly pursuits. But by God's grace, we are offered a priceless security and guidance system—pursuing Him. Solomon challenges us in this chapter to pursue "wisdom" and seek after "insight," "understanding," and "knowledge." These are the ultimate qualities of security, and they are found in God Himself. "Then you will understand the fear of the Lord and find the knowledge of God" (Prov. 2:5). God, Himself is wisdom, knowledge, discernment, insight, and every other resource for security we need. God, Himself is our security. Seek Him and be safe.

AUGUST 23
Proverbs 3

"GOD'S GPS"

The invention of the GPS has been an unbelievable advancement in providing directions for travel. I'm still amazed (and just a little frightened) that there is a system that can track my exact position with pinpoint accuracy anywhere on the globe. What makes this technology even more helpful is that it cannot only tell me where I am but also show me where I want to go and the best way to get there. Amazing.

However, that guidance system for geography is nothing compared to our Lord's guidance system for every aspect of our life's journey. To me, Proverbs 3:5-6 is the ultimate positioning system: "Trust in the Lord with all your heart, and do not lean on your own understanding. In all your ways acknowledge Him, and He will make straight your paths." This is an amazing promise from God on how clearly He will guide us in His will. There are four coordinates, however, that we must enter if we desire His guidance.

REST
"Trust in the Lord with all your heart." Believe in and depend on God's good intentions for you.

REFUSE
"Do not lean on your own understanding." Don't permit yourself to believe you can make the best decision on your own.

RECOGNIZE

"In all your ways acknowledge Him." If you desire to know God's unrevealed will, then obey Him in all ways in which He has already revealed His will.

RESPOND

"And He will make straight your paths." Don't be an initiator and determined to "make it happen," but walk with the Lord as He opens and makes smooth the way for your next steps.

AUGUST 24
Proverbs 4

"Even Brighter"

It is an incredible thing to watch. The pitch black of night ever so slowly begins to give way on the horizon. At first, only a gray curtain seems to rise in the east. But then the sky starts to glow with an amazing mixture of purple, blue, and orange hues. At last, the beautiful yellow sphere emerges and slowly rises in the sky.

If you are blessed with a schedule that permits a few hours of dedicated focus, you can watch the sun rise higher and higher until the whole sky is blazing with its glory, and you must shield your eyes from its brightness—a new day. Darkness once again gives way to the relentless journey of the sun. Solomon meditated on this scene and made an inspired application, "But the path of the righteous is like the light of dawn, which shines brighter and brighter until full day" (Prov. 4:18). Paul tells us that at "one time you were darkness, but now you are light in the Lord. Walk as children of light" (Eph. 5:8).

Our Lord and Savior illuminated our *spiritual darkness* with the *light of His salvation*. We have no light of our own, but we are bearers of God's light in Christ. Jesus said we are the light of the world. Our journey through this world, by His grace, can brighten the lives of those who live in the shadows. We can warm, with His love, those who are shivering in the darkness. As we daily follow the Son, our path can shine brighter and brighter until we step into the perfect day "and night will be no more" (Rev. 22:5).

AUGUST 25
Proverbs 5

"Out of Bounds"

We griped all the time. We really did. Years ago, when I was actively involved in sports, we complained on a regular basis. We would grumble and complain about the heat, the length of practices, the limited number of balls or bats, the constant exercises and sprints, tacky uniforms, etc., etc. However, with all of our complaints, I never once remember anyone being upset about the lines on the field or court. No one ever complained about boundaries. We didn't think lines that defined inbounds and out-of-bounds were legalistic. The game *required* boundaries. Boundaries made the game fun and kept it from descending into chaos.

Proverbs, Chapter 5 is about the blessing of boundaries, particularly *moral* boundaries. When we live within these God-given boundaries, we experience freedom. Our lives are liberated by "wisdom," "understanding," and "discretion" (Prov. 5:1-2). When we believe Satan's original lie, that real freedom is found in a life without boundaries, what do we experience? Bondage. "The inequities of the wicked ensnare him, and he is held fast in the cords of his sin" (Prov. 5:22). What is freedom? Freedom is not the right to do your own thing; it is the privilege to do the *best* thing.

AUGUST 26
Proverbs 6

"A Mountain from an Anthill"

If you have ever attempted to learn another language, you know it is not an easy undertaking. When the Lord confused the languages at the Tower of Babel, he did an outstanding job! People from other countries have often told me that learning American English is quite difficult because it is a language full of so many idioms. Idioms are figures of speech that convey a concept in a *word picture* that the literal words themselves do not communicate. For example, in America, the phrase, "Don't make a mountain out of a molehill," is a typical, well-known expression. Can you imagine how confusing that could be to a person trying to learn American English? However, most people raised in America clearly understand that this expression means, "Don't make a big issue out of a minor event or situation." That is a good idiom, and it is also great advice.

In Proverbs 6: 6-11, our Lord reverses the message of the molehill idiom by telling us to make a big deal out of a very little hill—the anthill. In fact, God urges us to carefully study the ants on the anthill in order to gain a mountain of wisdom.

We learn from the ants that working diligently is the answer to financial want and emotional worry. The ant does not work under a *slavish* obligation to a master but in a wise response to the opportunity to prepare now for the future needs of the winter season. The ant works in the summer in preparation for the next season of life. That's pretty smart! Let's learn from these little "wise guys," the ants. Life is short. Opportunities abound. Death is certain. Eternity is long. Rewards are promised.

> "Go to the ant, O sluggard; consider her ways, and be wise."
> (Proverbs 6:6)

AUGUST 27
Proverbs 7

"TWO VOICES"

Proverbs, Chapter 7 begins and ends with two startling contrasts:

> (v. 2) "Keep my commandments and live."
> (v. 27) "Her house is the way to Sheol, going down to the chambers of death."

This is a message about the pleading calls of two women. One woman is "Wisdom," who often, in Proverbs, is symbolized as a beautiful woman that calls on people to follow the commandments of God. The other woman is often referred to as the "Adulteress," who pleads with men to forsake God's path, come to her house, and fulfill their desires in sensual pleasure. The warning in these passages is directed toward young men. However, the more profound principle and application is shared with *all* people, whether men or women.

There are constantly two voices calling out to be heeded and followed—the voice of Wisdom and the voice of the World. In reality, the voice of Wisdom is the voice of the Lord, calling us to keep His commandments, follow His ways and experience life. The other voice (and it is alluring indeed) is the voice of the World. This lively voice promises self-fulfillment and pleasures of every kind, but in terrible reality, it ultimately only produces misery and destruction.

How do we hear Wisdom and her voice more clearly, and how can we make the World's voice grow fainter? One word, "Devotion." Devote yourself to Wisdom; pledge your allegiance to her. Make her your closest companion. "Say to wisdom, 'You are my sister,' and call insight your intimate friend" (Prov. 7:4). How do we develop this love relationship with Wisdom? The Father of Wisdom tells us how:

> *"My son, keep my words and treasure up my commandments with you; keep my commandments and live; keep my teaching as the apple of your eye; bind them on your fingers; write them on the tablet of your heart."*
> (Proverbs 7:1-3)

AUGUST 28
Proverbs 8

"THE VOICE"

"Does not wisdom call? Does not understanding raise her voice?"
(Proverbs 8:1)

Songs are some of the most powerful influences on the face of the earth. As the world grows ever smaller because of the advances of telecommunications, so also the power and the influence of songs grow ever larger. The biggest hit songs that used to impact several countries, particularly in the west, are now immediately embraced, loved, and played around the globe. Popular vocalists and groups today have an immediate, worldwide following.

All people love to sing. There has never existed a people group that did not communicate through songs. The Bible informs us that songs existed before mankind existed. We are told that the morning stars, the angels, sang together and shouted for joy at the glories of God's creative acts (Job 38:7). It is not in the least disrespectful of the Lord to refer to Him as the "God who sings," for He describes Himself as a parent who quiets the hearts of His children by lovingly singing over them (Zeph. 3:17).

It is this "singing God" whose voice is referred to as "Wisdom" throughout the book of Proverbs. In our reading today, Wisdom is "The Voice," personified as a woman who cries out (actually sings out) to people everywhere. Proverbs 8 is, in effect, a song from the voice of Wisdom, "The Voice," singing a song of 33 stanzas! (Prov. 8:4-36) And what a voice and song it is! The voice of Wisdom is everywhere—on the mountains, at the crossroads, in the city gates, and in the portals of every doorstep. What is most notable about this omnipresent voice is that it is so pleading and so promising simultaneously.

Wisdom is like a paradoxical, incessant beggar who follows us doggedly, *begging to give us great riches*. Wisdom, "The Voice," singing every day and in every place, offers integrity (vs. 5-9), riches (vs. 10-11), and guidance. (vs. 12-17) Wisdom, "The Voice," sings that she is a treasure for us today and our children in the future (vs. 18-21) and that from the most ancient times, she has been the constant companion of God. (vs. 22-31) Wisdom pleads and promises us that she offers the experience of a fulfilled life and the favor of God. Also, she warns us that all other voices are only siren songs that allure to destruction and death. (vs. 35-36)

Listen carefully to "The Voice" in this chapter, for I think if you do, you will recognize whose voice it is. Wisdom is God's voice. God is wisdom and truth, and understanding. God's voice is a kind voice calling out to His children, just as He did when He walked in the garden in the cool of the day (Gen. 3:8). Whatever causes us to hide from God's voice is evil. When we are not listening, we are hiding, and we are denying ourselves the enjoyment and enlightenment that comes from hearing the most beautiful of all sounds, "The Voice" of unconditional love. Listen today for the love song of "The Voice." The song is for you.

AUGUST 29
Proverbs 9

"GOD'S CURRICULUM"

God, by His very definition and attributes, is the source of all knowledge. What we refer to as the past is the present moment to Him, and what we call the future is to our Lord as certain as things that have already happened. All that can be discovered has always been known to Him. He possesses all knowledge. Therefore, whatever we want to call "education" can only be genuine as it relates information correctly to Him, the God of all truth. In reality, gaining knowledge without connecting it to Him is a journey into foolishness. That is why the wisest man ever to live, King Solomon, rightly declares, "The fear of the Lord is the beginning of wisdom, and the knowledge of the Holy One is insight" (Prov. 9:10). True education, Solomon says, is always spiritual in nature. It involves aligning ourselves and all of life with Him. Apart from Him, human education is only folly.

Being a truly enlightened person is a journey into the Lord. The journey begins with the "fear of the Lord," which means an awe-inspired respect and love that becomes the guiding star of our life. This journey does not end with a graduation or degree but continues into the increasing understanding of who God is and how all of our existence relates to Him. The "knowledge of the Holy One" provides us with insights into life that cannot be provided by the finest of universities. How wonderful that His education is not available for just a few but for all who will hear God's gracious invitation, "Leave your simple ways, and live, and walk in the way of insight" (Prov. 9:6).

For all of us, class is in session today!

AUGUST 30
Proverbs 10

"PRICELESS"

"The blessing of the Lord makes rich, and he adds no sorrow to it."
(Proverbs 10:22)

The two afternoon strolls were separated by only three days, but they seemed to be taken on two different planets. While traveling to a mission ministry in Asia recently, my wife and I were able to include, in our travel schedule, a two-day layover in Paris. On the second afternoon, we hopped off the tour bus to take pictures of the Arc de Triomphe, and then we walked down the famous avenue Champs Elysees. This street is considered the fashion and culture capital of the world, and the prices proved it! The sidewalks were crowded with people from around the world carrying the shopping bags, proudly displaying the logo emblems of the most elite design houses.

Our afternoon stroll seventy-two hours later had a slightly different ambiance. Along with our ministry partner in India, we visited members of his congregation living in one of the slums of Delhi. Words fail to describe the sights, sounds, and smells of countless thousands of people living in what amounts to a garbage dump in America. No one carrying designer bags, no fragrances of Chanel wafting from doorways, no lighted display cases, no diamond-encrusted jewelry, and no designer clothes.

But guess what we did experience there? Children with beaming faces singing praise songs to Jesus, joy-filled believers gladly welcoming us into their dirt-floor shanties, former idol-worshiping people of the pariah caste, now members of the family of God through faith in Jesus. My wife and I walked both of these streets in Paris and Delhi, and in our minds, we remembered God's real estate appraisal, "Listen, my beloved brothers, has not God chosen those who are poor in the world to be rich in faith and heirs of the kingdom, which He has promised to those who love Him?" (Jas. 2:5).

Amen.

AUGUST 31
Proverbs 11

"The Genius of Generosity"

*"Whoever brings blessing will be enriched,
and one who waters will himself be watered."*
(Proverbs 11:25)

For many years, our family lived in a house at the top of a hill on a small cul-de-sac. As a result of our home's location, we experienced a wonderful hilltop view; but we also experienced the impact of southwest winds that would sometimes suddenly rush up the slope of the street. I vividly remember the night our family was traveling back to our house when a strong storm and 60-70 mph straight-line winds swept across the area. All of us were delighted to make it home safely, but as we pulled up our driveway, I noticed our yard was covered with much debris. You can imagine my concern when I recognized that the debris consisted of a large section of our home's roofing! Hundreds of shingles had been blown off the roof by the winds, and to make matters worse, the rain was coming down in torrents.

Desperate times call for desperate measures, so overcoming my dislike for heights (and the fact that I'm allergic to lightning), I grabbed a hammer, some nails, and a plastic tarp and started climbing up a ladder onto the roof. That is when it happened—someone called out, "Let us do that, Sam." Looking down, to my amazement, I saw many of my neighbors bringing ladders, tools, lumber, and tarps. Before I could respond, several men were on my roof in the intense storm and were nailing down tarps to cover all the places where the shingles were missing. Within a matter of minutes, these men had most of our roof covered and no doubt saved our home from a great deal of damage. I was so humbled and so incredibly grateful for their kindness. Later that evening, as my wife and I discussed what happened, she helped me gain perspective and even deeper gratitude for what had occurred. Susan said, "Honey, we have tried over the years to be a blessing to our neighbors in any way we could, and tonight the Lord has returned the blessing to us." As usual, my wife was right, and her discernment about why our neighbors responded so quickly and generously just added to the joy we had received.

Our experience that night, in just the smallest of ways, illustrates the principle King Solomon shares in verses 17-26. Generosity is the gift we can never truly give away because it always comes back to us. This is a principle as sure as the law of sowing and reaping. The one who plants is the one who harvests. The seed guarded and protected in the barn never produces a bountiful harvest from the field. When we withhold from others, we ultimately rob ourselves of true riches—the wealth of joy that comes from influencing others with God's love and then experiencing His love returned to us through them. That is rich, indeed!

SEPTEMBER

"Return, O my soul, to your rest; for the Lord
has dealt bountiful with you."
(Psalm 116:7)

SEPTEMBER 1
Proverbs 12

"Take a Load Off"

*"Anxiety in a man's heart weighs him down,
but a good word makes him glad."*
(Proverbs 12:25)

Many years ago, I heard a speaker say, "If someone ever tells you that he never gets depressed, I have some advice for you—don't buy a used car from him because a man who will tell a whopper like that cannot be trusted!" That may have been slightly overstated, but probably not very much. The truth is that life can sometimes be depressing, and depression tends to be contagious. We catch it occasionally. A depressed spirit is not in itself sinful. We are told in Scripture that some of the greatest people of faith struggled sometimes with depression. Moses, Elijah, David, and Jeremiah experienced the "dark night of the soul." Even the One who was filled with perfect faith knew the weight of a depressed spirit.

Our Lord was in many ways a "man of sorrows and acquainted with grief" (Isa. 53:3), and in the garden of Gethsemane, His soul was burdened down so terribly that He asked His closest friends to stay close by and pray with Him. The disciples were so physically and emotionally exhausted that they could not provide their Master with the encouragement He desperately needed. Yes, we all struggle with depression and anxiety at times, but this spirit does not have to dominate our lives. We can walk in the light because we are children of the light.

One of the ways we can lighten our own spirit is by speaking light into someone else's. "Anxiety in a man's heart weighs him down, but a good word makes him glad" (Prov. 12:25) Our words have power, and other than worship, encouragement is the best use to which our words can be given. Encouraging words lighten a heavy heart and give life to a sagging spirit. Mark Twain once quipped, "I can live two months on a good compliment." Most of us are not blessed with great abilities, but we all have the ability to encourage. This is a true ministry and is very needed in the church and the world as well.

Take a few moments to give this vital calling some thought right now. Who could you visit, call, email, text, or write today and give them a "good word?" It will only take a few moments, but your investment of encouragement will be a treasure in the heart of the person in which it is deposited. "For I have derived much joy and comfort from your love, my brother, because the hearts of the saints have been refreshed through you" (Philem. 1:7).

SEPTEMBER 2
Proverbs 13

"Guarded Mouth, Guarded Life"

*"Whoever guards his mouth preserves his life;
he who opens wide his lips comes to ruin."*
(Proverbs 13:3)

It has been well said that there is great significance in the fact that God created us with one mouth and two ears. It may very well be that He intends us to listen twice as much as we speak. Regardless of whether there is anatomical support for that statement or not, there is certainly much instruction in God's Word regarding the importance of being very careful about our speech. To apply these Bible principles adequately, we must think of our "words" and our "speech" as more than just verbal communication. In our technologically advanced world, communication is now not just from our mouths but also from our fingertips on a keyboard and the camera's lens on our smartphone. Today we communicate in many different ways. So perhaps, more than ever, the incredible importance the Lord places on the control of our communication should be emphasized.

In our text from Proverbs 13:3, we are challenged by Solomon to guard our lives by guarding our words and warned that when we are quick to "say what we think," we are exposing ourselves to ruin. When we are quick to enter into issues that do not directly involve us, we are partners in strife (Prov. 13:10). When we answer a matter before we fully understand the issues, it is folly and shame to us (Prov. 18:13). Ungoverned speech leads God's people into transgression (Prov. 10:19). When a person is hasty in his words, there is no hope that he can avoid bringing guilt upon himself (Prov. 29:20). Uncontrolled speech is indeed so dangerous. However, it is clear that the Lord gave us mouths and wants us to use them for the noblest of purposes, which is for the encouragement and strengthening of others. "Let your speech always be gracious, seasoned with salt, so that you may know how you ought to answer each person" (Col. 4:6).

Paul also challenges us, "Let no corrupting talk come out of your mouths, but only such as is good for building up, as it fits the occasion, that it may give grace to those who hear" (Eph. 4:29). The best way to guard and guide our communication is to use the **T.H.I.N.K.** test.

T Is it **T**rue?
H Does it **H**onor God?
I Does it **I**nspire?
N Is it **N**ecessary?
K Is it **K**ind?

SEPTEMBER 3
Proverbs 14

"THE WISEST WRONG ROAD"

Several years ago, our family vehicle had an early edition of a GPS system that we named "Edna." I'm not sure how we came up with that name, but we did so because the system gave directions in the most crisp and articulate female voice, so we decided to call her Edna. Edna was incredibly helpful on many of the trips we took as a family. She guided us over a good part of the Eastern United States. Edna almost became an invisible part of the family as we traveled together. We would often journey many miles without a word from Edna, but then suddenly, she would speak out in her lovely voice to guide us on our way.

Edna was amazingly accurate *most* of the time, and therein lies the problem. She did not give you correct directions *all* of the time. As a matter of fact, the longer we had Edna, the less dependable she became. More and more often, we would follow her directions given in the lovely voice, only to find she had taken us on the wrong road. Finally, we discovered the problem. Edna's guidance system was based on data that was not being updated as changes were made to the highway infrastructure around the country. Edna was using *outdated* information, and, as a result, she often gave faulty directions. Oh, Edna's crisp, articulate voice sounded just as convincing as ever, but we couldn't trust her anymore.

This is a very similar and sinister issue for us as well when we are guided by our IGS—*Internal Guidance System*. King Solomon, the wisest man who ever lived, warns us, in the strongest terms, not to trust the guidance we receive from our own understanding and insight: "There is a way that seems right to man, but its end is the way to death" (Prov. 14:12). Our internal guidance system is faulty and cannot be trusted because the data on which it operates is corrupted. The impact of our sinful nature on our decision-making system makes it fatally flawed. At times, the guidance we give ourselves can seem so sound and wise, but it cannot be trusted; in fact, it can be terribly deadly. How can we avoid the danger of a flawed internal guidance system? By making our decisions on a guidance system that never relies on corrupted or out-of-date information—the infallible "GPS," *God's Positioning System.*

Our Lord's guidance system, based on His eternal Word and indwelling Spirit, can always be trusted. The road on which He guides us may not always be the easiest or most direct route, but it is always the *best* route! What is your guidance system? Honestly, thoughtfully consider that. Do you trust in the IGS or GPS? Always go with God, my friend. Always.

SEPTEMBER 4
Proverbs 15

"LITTLE IS MUCH"

*"Better is a little with the fear of the Lord
than great treasure and trouble with it."*
(Proverbs 15:16)

As a boy growing up in Indiana, our family faithfully attended a small Baptist church. Our church was never known for excellent Bible exposition because our pastor, although a faithful and good man, was never known as a strong preacher. What our church was known for was music—southern gospel music. It may seem strange to think of a church in Indiana focusing its worship on southern music, but it makes perfect sense when you understand that our small town was full of people from the hills of Kentucky. A significant portion of the population of central Indiana in my youth consisted of people who had migrated from Southern Kentucky. It was popular then to tell a joke about the definition of the word "Hoosier." What is a Hoosier? Answer: A Hoosier is a man from Kentucky who was on his way to get a job in Michigan, but his car broke down in Indiana.

In my youth, I did not enjoy our church's southern music. My brother and I used to smugly refer to our church as "Grand Ole Opry Baptist." Of course, that was before both of us (in our teens) were soundly converted to Christ. Our conversion was due, in many ways, to the gospel message we heard from our youth leaders' teaching and many of the southern-style songs regularly sung in the services. As I read Proverbs 15:16, I recalled the lyrics of one of the southern gospel songs often sung in our worship gatherings:

> *Little is much when God is in it,*
> *Labor not for wealth or fame,*
> *There's a crown and you can win it.*
> *If you go in Jesus' name.*

In my memory, I can still hear the sound of the four-part harmony singing out that message. Today, over 50 years later, I thank the Lord that He used the music I did not really like at the time to plant a timeless guiding principle from God's Word in my soul. It is the blessing of God that makes a person truly rich (Prov. 10:22). In fact,

God has chosen by His grace to make so many of the poor of the world to be rich in faith (James 2:5).

Oh, to be sure, our Heavenly Father is no miser, for He freely, out of His inexhaustible resources, gives us all things richly to enjoy (1 Tim. 6:17). He provides for us as His dear children, graciously supplying all our needs according to His riches in glory by Christ Jesus (Phil. 4:19). God knows and supplies just what we need.

What we do not need are earthly riches. Wealth is not a blessing to the vast majority who achieve it. It is not that money in itself is the source of the troubles. It is the idolatry in our hearts that so easily begins to pursue gold more than God. The *love* of money is the root of all kinds of evil (1 Tim. 6:10). Those who *desire* to be rich fall into the snare of the Devil and, as a result, pierce themselves with much sorrow (1 Tim. 6:9).

Why should we relentlessly labor for that which is ultimately not gold? The most priceless possession is contentment, a satisfied heart in God. A contented heart is full of more true gold than sits in Fort Knox, Kentucky. I heard folks from Kentucky sing about that years ago, and I still believe the message today: "Little is much when God is in it."

SEPTEMBER 5
Proverbs 16

"The Greatest Victory"

"Whoever is slow to anger is better than the mighty, and he who rules his spirit than he who takes a city."
(Proverbs 16:32)

One time, a young couple was in a marriage counseling session. When asked how the couple handled conflict, the young man said, "Well, when I get angry, I may blow up, but it is over in just a few seconds." To this, the counselor replied, "Yes, just like dynamite." Boom.

Getting angry is not necessarily a sin. The Bible says, "Be angry and do not sin" (Ps. 4:4a). Jesus Himself, on occasion, displayed very deep anger. However, self-focused and not self-controlled anger is always sinful and is it ever destructive.

Recently, an angry meeting of some of our nation's leaders in Washington lasted less than two minutes before it concluded in outbursts of anger. That two-minute angry meeting tore down a two trillion-dollar plan for national infrastructure improvements—an expensive meeting.

Solomon was the most powerful man of his age, but he tells us the strongest person is the one who can control themselves. In one sense, we are not capable of bringing our emotions under control. However, the fruit of the Holy Spirit working in our lives is growing in self-control (Gal. 5:23). Ultimately, we cannot live under self-control until we surrender control to our Master, Jesus Christ. We need Master control if we expect to experience self-control.

Anger is usually selfish. It is a learned technique of trying to control others. We can unlearn what we have learned. How does that happen? Talk to Jesus about it continually, and then ask others to tell you how you are doing. Invite the Lord to make you strong in self-control, and then be strong enough to ask others for help. Now that is a powerful step toward victory!

SEPTEMBER 6
Proverbs 17

"Near-sighted Wisdom"

"The discerning sets his face toward wisdom, but the eyes of a fool are on the ends of the earth."
(Proverbs 17:24)

It has been said that the clearest vision is that which causes you to see the beauty that is right in front of you. William Randolph Hearst was a household name in America for decades in the early and mid-twentieth century. He founded the nation's largest newspaper and went on to establish the international Hearst Media empire. He was known as a total narcissist who lived only to own all the people and things he could.

Once, Hearst read of a famous work of art that he was determined to possess, so he sent his personal assistant on a worldwide search to find it and purchase it regardless of the cost. Weeks later, the assistant met with Hearst to inform him that he had located the treasure but that he was unable to purchase it. Hearst cursed in anger and demanded to know why not. To which Hearst's employee replied, "I could not buy it, sir, because you already own it."

Solomon was far wealthier than William Randolph Hearst and far wiser, too. Solomon had imported treasures from around the world beyond calculating, but he realized that the greatest treasure was always at hand and could be stored in his heart—the free and priceless gift of wisdom. Wisdom is seeing life on earth from an eternal and heavenly perspective. How foolish and incredibly sad to wander everywhere seeking something elusive to bring satisfaction when the greatest and most fulfilling existence is to peacefully journey with the Lord, treasuring what He shows you day by day. What a treasure we can find without having to look for it anywhere but up!

SEPTEMBER 7
Proverbs 18

"RUN TO THE TOWER"

*"The name of the Lord is a strong tower;
the righteous man runs into it and is safe."*
(Proverbs 18:10)

There are dates on a calendar that define a generation. For people in America during the past 80 years, three dates come quickly to mind. December 7, 1941, the date President Franklin Roosevelt said "will live in infamy," defined the first 50 years of the twentieth century. It was, of course, the day of the bombing of Pearl Harbor by the Japanese military, which "awakened the sleeping giant" and brought the United States into the global conflict of World War II. As a small child, I vaguely remember the shock and national grief associated with November 22, 1963, when President John Kennedy was assassinated by the sniper Lee Harvey Oswald on a crisp and clear autumn day in Dallas, Texas.

Then, practically all Americans and billions of people worldwide can remember when they first heard the news and saw the scenes of September 11, 2001, in New York City. By means of telecommunications and worldwide social media, the world watched in almost disbelief as the two massive towers of the World Trade Center collapsed and fell from the terrorist-guided weapons of hijacked passenger jets. For so many millions of people like myself and my wife, it was unimaginable that those two towers we had visited on several occasions could fall. Yet, scenes were being televised in real time, showing streets teaming with people running from the smoke, dust, and debris of those iconic structures. The unspeakable evil which caused such death, destruction, pain, and grief was beyond comprehension to any but the most corrupted and debased of minds.

Only the God of all grace and omnipotent power could cause such wrath and evil of wicked men to be used for good, and He did, and He does. Millions of people who watched the horror of the collapse of those two towers turned their hearts and minds toward the only truly secure place of complete, ultimate, and eternal safety—God Himself. Only eternity will reveal the total number of people who, when so graphically confronted with the reality that there exists no assurance of protection on earth, turned to entrust their souls to the safe-keeping found only in God. For the blessed gospel, truth is the opposite of the scenes witnessed on 9/11. In reality, the whole world is crumbling, and there is only one Tower standing firm.

The world we live in is morally and culturally crumbling, and the planet on which we walk is destined to do the same. The system of this age "is passing away" (1 John 2:17), and this earth is destined to be consumed in "the Day of the Lord" and the fire of His judgment (2 Peter 3:10). Yet, there is a place of eternal safety—"eternal," because it is not limited by time and is unaffected by any dangers which exist in the material or spiritual world. This timeless safe place is a "tower," for it truly towers over all the wreck and ruin of this world. This tower is in the shape of the cross, and the voice of the One with the outstretched arms fastened to it by nails calls all of the weak and fearful of mankind: "Come to Me, all who are weary and burdened, and I will give you rest" (Matt. 11:28).

SEPTEMBER 8
Proverbs 19

"Our Plans, His Purposes"

It has been said that "failing to plan is planning to fail." Not only is it unwise to fail to make plans, but it is also unscriptural. The Bible is filled with admonitions to make plans. Solomon challenges us to make plans and to work diligently toward them. Failing to make plans is closely connected with laziness, which Solomon mocks and strongly condemns in this chapter. "The sluggard buries his hand in the dish and will not even bring it back to his mouth" (Prov. 19:24). The wisest thing any human being can do is plan for the only thing that is completely certain in this life. "And just as it is appointed for man to die once, and after that comes judgment" (Heb. 9:27). It is very wise to plan, but it is folly to make our own plans separated from God's purposes.

Human plans only have wisdom and are only really good plans when they are aligned with God's purposes. Certainly, all of God's purposes have not been made clear to us, but God gave us His Word and His Spirit so that we might be guided into all truth (John 16:13). Even when we feel that the plans we make are good and in accordance with God's wisdom, the ultimate act of faith is to submit them to His will. James challenges us, "Instead you ought to say, 'If the Lord wills, we will live and do this or that'" (Jas. 4:15).

Perhaps it is true that we would always choose what God would choose if we were wise enough to choose it. It is always a wonderful thing to plan and dream, but we must never forget that the One who loves us so much that He did not spare His own Son will always have the best plans as His purpose.

SEPTEMBER 9
Proverbs 20

"Preserved by Love"

*"Steadfast love and faithfulness preserve the king,
and by steadfast love his throne is upheld."*
(Proverbs 20:28)

We have all heard the ancient cliché, "Love is blind." Perhaps many of us are grateful that cliché was true for our spouses, for they certainly would not have loved us if they possessed excellent vision! However, the wonderful truth is that love, especially as it is defined and described in God's Word, is not blind. Love sees others with complete clarity and yet, in selfless devotion, *chooses* to love them unconditionally. This is the true meaning of the primary words used to communicate the meaning of love both in the Hebrew of the Old Testament and the Greek of the New Testament. "Hesed" in Hebrew and "agape" in Greek convey a devotion that is not rooted in emotion but rather in determination. Love is "others-focused," love is selfless, and therefore, as we are told by Solomon in the proverb about love, it is "steadfast" (Prov. 20:28).

What is very interesting and helpful to note in Solomon's wise insight is that this *steadfast love* is actually the source of a *steadfast life*. "Steadfast love and faithfulness *preserve* the king, and by steadfast love his throne is *upheld*" (Prov. 20:28). The reality is that steadfast love is the great stabilizer of our lives. It is steadfast love that secures our identity, and it is steadfast love that directs our activity. Our identity as believers is ultimately based not on *what we do* but on *whose we are*. We are image-bearers of God; we are children of the King because of His steadfast love. The reality and the identity of every believer is this: "See what kind of love [steadfast love] the Father has given to us, that we should be called the children of God; and so we are" (1 John 3:1). Notice how John makes it a point to tell us that it is God's love that makes us who we are. Life changes and circumstances are unexpected and certainly unpredictable, but the steadfast reality of who we are is never altered. We are loved, always. We are God's children, always. Now, there is stability, indeed!

But, also, in this steadfast love of God is all the guidance we need. We are loved, so what are we to love? Life as the Lord intends it to be is defined by love. We are loved by God, and we love Him back. We are loved by God, so we love others for Him. *The Great Commandment* becomes *The Great Alignment* of our life: "'And you shall love the Lord your God with all your heart and with all your soul and with all your mind and with all your strength.' The second is this: 'You shall love your neighbor as yourself.' There is no other commandment greater than these" (Mark 12:30-31). In receiving and sharing God's steadfast love, our life is preserved from being wasted. The world is passing away, and so is our allotted time upon it; but steadfast love preserves our lives, for love is eternal (1 John 2:17).

SEPTEMBER 10
Proverbs 21

"The Anvil of the Lord"

We seldom hear the sound in our day, but a few generations ago practically everyone was familiar with the rhythmic singing coming from the local blacksmith shop. What hard work, but what fantastic skill! Years of experience trained a young man how to heat metal in a blazing furnace and then, carefully and relentlessly, pound the moldable metal into the precise size and shape necessary. This trade is often mistakenly considered to have only been connected to the shoeing of horses, but these master craftsmen framed an infinite number of essential objects used daily.

We can hardly imagine the toll such work must have taken on the arms and joints of these strong men over the years, not to mention their hearing! The beating of the hammer on the anvil would produce a decibel level that could be heard for great distances. It was the ringing of the anvil that caught the attention of John Clifford. The chiming of the anvil sounded to him like the bells in the local church steeple calling people to vesper worship. The image of the hammer beating on the anvil reminded Clifford of the relentless hammering of the skeptics over the ages in assaulting God's Word. He used the imagery of that analogy to express the truth shared by the wisest man who ever lived, King Solomon, that we see today in Proverbs 21:30, "No wisdom, no understanding, no counsel can avail against the Lord." John Clifford captured the timeless truth beautifully in this poem from the blacksmith's shop.

> *"The Anvil of God's Word"*
>
> *Last eve I paused beside the blacksmith's door,*
> *And heard the anvil ring the vesper chime;*
> *Then looking in, I saw upon the floor,*
> *Old hammers, worn with beating years of time.*
>
> *"How many anvils have you had," said I,*
> *"To wear and batter all these hammers so?"*
> *"Just one," said he, and then, with twinkling eye,*

"The anvil wears the hammers out you know."

And so, thought I the anvil of God's Word,
For ages skeptic blows have beat upon;
Yet, though the noise of falling blows was heard,
The anvil is unharmed—the hammers gone!

SEPTEMBER 11
Proverbs 22

"Ancient Landmarks"

"Do not move the ancient landmark that your fathers have set."
(Proverbs 22:28)

If you have ever had the privilege of driving in the countryside of any of the mid-Atlantic or New England states in America, you will always remember the beautiful stone walls surrounding the farms and properties in that area. They are stunning but also very functional as those stones picked up and plowed up over the years have been used to mark the boundaries of the owner's land. Moving one of those stone walls was a serious matter indeed.

Likewise, in Biblical times the rocks were collected to make stone walls to mark the boundaries of these fields. Large piles of stones would be erected at the corners of a family's property to designate the portion of the land that the Lord had given as their inheritance in the "promised land." Moving one of these markers was considered a serious offense because it was a form of robbery and a rejection of a decision and boundary that God had revealed.

Solomon is probably referring to the application of both these principles in verse 28. He is sharing the wisdom of a warning against treating a neighbor with selfish disrespect for his possessions. Solomon was also instructing that respecting these boundary markers was expressing honor to God in recognizing that the land was not theirs but His. Going beyond the boundaries God had set was going against His will. These landmarks are not "ancient" and therefore irrelevant, but they are from the "Ancient of Days," God Himself, and therefore always relevant and totally "up to date." The "ancient landmarks" are always trustworthy because they are true, and they are true because they are established by the God of truth.

Truth is not established by mankind's opinions and decisions, which are in a constant state of flux. Truth is determined by the only just and unchanging source in the universe, God Himself. The "ancient landmarks" are not interesting relics of a bygone era. They are the eternal boundaries between right and wrong, good and evil, and truth and lies. Solomon's wise challenge of 3,000 years ago should be on our minds every day of our lives, "Do not move the ancient landmarks that your fathers have set" (Prov. 22:28).

SEPTEMBER 12
Proverbs 23

"Chasing Money"

*"Do not toil to acquire wealth; be discerning enough to desist.
When your eyes light on it, it is gone, for suddenly it sprouts wings,
flying like an eagle toward heaven."*
(Proverbs 23:4-5)

I once heard a comedian say, "Yes, it is true that 'money talks,' but all it has ever said to me is, 'Bye, Bye!'" Many of us may smile at that line, but sadly it is probably a "knowing smile" of personal experience. Yes, our money talks, but there is often so little of it that it only whispers! Solomon knew a lot about money; he was probably the wealthiest man the world has ever known. However, Solomon was also the wisest of men, and although he did not say that money talks, he did warn us that it has the ability to fly away. In verses 4 and 5, he uses the humorous word picture of someone who becomes fascinated with wealth and begins chasing it, only to see the "bird of wealth" suddenly sprout wings and fly away like an eagle.

Solomon is not saying that wealth is, in and of itself, evil or contrary to God's law. It is clear from reading the Bible that many faithful servants of the Lord were quite wealthy. It is the *life pursuit* of wealth that is so dangerous. Jesus said living for money *disqualifies* a person from being a disciple. "No one can serve two masters, for either he will hate the one and love the other, or he will be devoted to the one and despise the other. You cannot serve God and money." (Matt. 6:24) Jesus did not say it was *difficult* to serve God and money; He said it was *impossible*. We have to choose. Also, the Apostle Paul warned that pursuing wealth was a path of *deception and danger*. "But those who desire to be rich fall into temptation, into a snare, into many senseless and harmful desires that plunge people into ruin and destruction. For the love of money is a root of all kinds of evil" (1 Tim. 6:9-10a).

Paul agrees with Solomon that chasing money is foolish. While it may sprout wings and fly away, by chasing it, we find ourselves plunging over a cliff into ruin and destruction. If money "comes to us" as we serve the Lord, we can receive it with gratitude. But if we "chase after it," we are not following Him but pursuing folly, which never has a happy ending.

SEPTEMBER 13
Proverbs 24

"YOU'RE NOT HOME YET"

Over 100 years ago, an elderly missionary was returning to the United States after decades of serving the Lord in the continent of Africa. His health had failed through a battle with a dreadful virus that had also taken the life of his beloved wife. She was buried in Africa, where they had labored faithfully through the years, alongside the graves of two of their children who died decades earlier.

The old man heard music playing as the ship cruised into the New York harbor and approached the pier to dock. Looking below, he saw a large band and an enormous crowd of people holding banners, waving flags, and cheering enthusiastically. The faithful missionary was dumbfounded. He had no idea his friends were aware of his arrival and that they would assemble such a welcome. The old man took off his hat and waved back to the cheering crowds. That is when he recognized that they were not looking at him. This large and joyful welcome celebration was not for him at all.

It just so happened that on that same vessel, Theodore Roosevelt, former President of The United States, was returning from a hunting expedition in Africa. He was the one receiving the hero's welcome. Slowly the old missionary made his way down the ramp, and, as he expected, there was no one on the dock to greet him. Just then, it seemed the Spirit of the Lord brought a much-needed message to His faithful servant's mind. "Cheer up my child; you are not *home* yet."

So often in the book of Proverbs, we are admonished not to envy the prosperity of people who do not seem to know God. We are reminded again that it is the blessing of God that makes a person rich. We know this in our hearts; however, it is sometimes difficult not to find ourselves "envious of the wicked" (Prov. 24:19). It is as we take the long, eternal view that things come into perspective. "For the evil man has no future; the lamp of the wicked will be put out" (Prov. 24:20). The future for us is as bright as the promises of God; and if we listen well, we can hear our Father's voice softly saying, "Cheer up my child; you are not *home* yet."

SEPTEMBER 14
Proverbs 25

"Getting Back or Getting Blessed?"

"If your enemy is hungry, give him bread to eat, and if he is thirsty, give him water to drink, for you will heap burning coals on his head, and the Lord will reward you."
(Proverbs 25:21-22)

The poet Edwin Markham was only a 13-year-old boy in Oregon when Abraham Lincoln died in 1865, but the great president's example and character greatly impacted the young boy and that impact lasted all of his life. When Markham was 70 years old, he was honored to personally read his lengthy poem "Lincoln, Man of the People" at the dedication of the Lincoln Memorial in 1922.

One of the qualities that impacted Markham was how Lincoln treated his enemies. Lincoln once asked a harsh anti-confederacy critic, "Do I not destroy my enemy when I make him my friend?" Historians have noted that Lincoln's gracious and magnanimous treatment of people who opposed him and his policies made him one of the greatest, if not *the greatest*, of all American presidents.

Lincoln's wisdom in doing that was like King Solomon's wisdom recorded in verses 21-22, but the practicing of it is grace in action. It is the most natural thing in the world to seek to punish an enemy, but it is the most divine-like thing to respond to an enemy with kindness and love.

We were all once enemies of God and rebels to His gracious rule. Yet, in His great love with which He loved us, He did not just withhold His wrath, but He gave us His grace and mercy. He made us His friends. We are not responsible for the *actions* of our enemies, but we are responsible for *our* reactions. The key part of that last sentence is "actions." Love does not express itself in what we *feel* but in what we determine *to do* for our enemies. Whether or not our enemies "feel the heat" of a guilty conscience and reconcile with us, we cannot know. But what we can know is the certainty of our Lord's favor and our own freedom. The poet Edwin Markham wrote,

> *He drew a circle that shut me out—*
> *Heretic, rebel, a thing to flout.*
> *But love and I had the wit to win:*
> *We drew a circle that took him in!*

SEPTEMBER 15
Proverbs 26

"THE BOASTING OF FOOLS"

*"Do you see a man who is wise in his own eyes?
There is more hope for a fool than for him."*
(Proverbs 26:12)

Several years ago, a successful businessman sold his company for a tremendous amount of money and decided to fulfill his dream of owning a large ranch out west. After a lengthy search for just the right property, he finally selected his dream homestead. It was located along a lovely river with an incredible view of the majestic mountains. During the construction of his dream home, the man came across several large stones on his ranch. They were a beautiful light gray color with black lines coursing through them. Immediately, the wealthy man decided the rocks would be *perfect* for constructing the immense fireplace that would be the centerpiece of the sprawling mansion. At the completion of construction, the businessman invited a large number of his friends and business associates to attend a celebration party for his massive home. The highlight of the evening was the lighting of the first logs in the fireplace. The flames roared upward in the beautiful fireplace made of the unique stones, and the gathered guests laughed and applauded to the delight of the wealthy and proud host.

Very soon, however, the laughter turned to gasps and screams as flames erupted all around the fireplace and soon engulfed the house. Days later, the inspectors determined that the cause of the fire was the fireplace itself. Those beautiful black lines in the stones were actually oil deposits, so the material of the construction project *fueled* the destruction of the rich man's dream house. That is a true story, but in reality, it was not the oil deposits in the rocks that destroyed the home. It was the pride deposits in the man's heart.

To the rich or the poor, pride always brings the same result—destruction. Pride is the origin of sin because it was the original sin in the heart of Lucifer, who was guided by "I will" rather than "God's will." Whatever we build in life with a spirit of self-will has, within the brick-and-mortar, the proud fuel of its own destruction. It will burn up one day. Humility does not cause a person to work less or produce little; humility causes us to rely on God and realize that all we accomplish is for His glory and the good of others. That spirit produces things that last forever.

SEPTEMBER 16
Proverbs 27

"A Hungry Soul"

"One who is full loathes honey, but to one who is hungry everything bitter is sweet."
(Proverbs 27:7)

Several years ago, I recall listening to a couple describe a "parental showdown" they had experienced with their youngest son. It seems that the boy, about 6 or 7 years old, decided that he only wanted to eat food that he enjoyed. It did not matter that his mother had worked diligently to provide a good and nutritious meal; all the son wanted to eat was junk food. Imagine that! Well, this abstinence led to numerous unpleasant and tear-filled battles of will during the time the family was gathering together for meals.

Finally, the mother and father devised a plan. They would not force their son to eat what was placed on the table for dinner, but that plate of food was all that would be provided at any meal. It would be kept in the refrigerator and reheated for the next meal. Of course, the young man tested this plan. He sat glumly through dinner, looking at the food on his plate while the other family members enjoyed theirs. The next morning, he bounded in for breakfast only to be dismayed that the meal from the evening before was placed in front of him again; all the while, his siblings enjoyed his favorite brand of cereal. At lunch, the warmed-up plate of food was placed in front of him yet again as the other family members enjoyed sandwiches. Guess what? An amazing thing happened at dinner that evening when, after several minutes of watching his family eat their food and enjoy conversation, the boy slowly, gingerly picked up his fork and began eating the meal from 24 hours prior. Scripture was fulfilled at that dining room table, "To one who is hungry, everything bitter is sweet!" I'm not sure if the mom and dad high-fived each other, but I know they did so on the inside!

You see, the boy's sense of hunger performed a miracle on his taste buds. Just as this is true *physically*, it is also true *spiritually*. People hungry for the Word of God aren't too concerned if the teacher's lesson is illustrated cleverly or if the pastor's message is a little long. They just want the food of the Word. Also, hungry people don't get overly concerned about the name of the church or where the leaders attended seminary. When you are starving, the restaurant's name and the cooks' training don't seem to be important as long as there is good food and lots of it. Let's stay hungry, my friends!

SEPTEMBER 17
Proverbs 28

"A Believing Boldness"

"The wicked flee when no one pursues, but the righteous are as bold as a lion."
(Proverbs 28:1)

During the early days of World War II's "Battle of the Bulge" in mid-December of 1944, all available units of the United States Army were rushed forward to stem the tide of the surprise Nazi onslaught. The epicenter of the attack converged on the town of Bastogne, Belgium. Major Richard Winters of Pennsylvania led one of the battalions of the 101st Airborne Division.

As his men prepared to move forward to the front, they were met by a group of shell-shocked soldiers moving back from the lines. One of the men, a lieutenant, informed Major Winters that the road behind them was about to be cut off by a German Ranger division and that it looked like the major and his men would be surrounded. To this information, Major Winters responded, "We're paratroopers, Lieutenant; we're supposed to be surrounded." Great statement.

This was not just bravado on the part of Major Winters; it just reflected a calm acceptance of what their identity and their mission naturally required. At times as believers, we can certainly sense that the evil and hatred of the world system has us surrounded. In those moments, we need to remember our identity and our mission. *We are Christians; we are supposed to be surrounded.* Our identity is *not* of this world, it is *not* our home, and we are foreigners in it. However, our mission is *in* this world. Jesus said He was making us lights for this world, and lights have their mission of illuminating the darkness. It is why we are here.

Indeed, knowing our identity and mission does not mean we are automatically prepared for it. Fear is the most dangerous enemy any military unit faces in times of conflict. Fear can turn even the best-trained soldiers into cowards. What is the quality that produces boldness in battle? It is faith. "The righteous are as bold as a lion" (Prov. 28:1). Righteousness is based on faith; but then, what is the basis of faith? Faith rests on reality. It may be an unseen reality, but it is reality—"the assurance of things hoped for, the conviction of things not seen" (Heb. 11:1). It is true; we are surrounded. But it is also true that those who surround us are also surrounded!

Here is the reality and the basis of our faith—*we are not alone.* Like Elisha's servant, we need our eyes opened "for those who are with us are more than those who are with them" (2 Kings 6:16). Yes, we are surrounded, and praise God for that!

SEPTEMBER 18
Proverbs 29

"The Song of Freedom"

*"An evil man is ensnared in his transgressions,
but a righteous man sings and rejoices."*
(Proverbs 29:6)

Toward the end of his long career, a well-known entertainer in North America would sing at his concerts and performances, "I Did It My Way." The song's music is beautiful, and the singer, with his voice and captivating stage presence, could certainly make it a "show-stopping moment." I can still recall as a young boy being riveted to the screen of the television. However, as I grew up and became aware of the performer's turbulent lifestyle, I remember thinking, "Maybe doing life 'My Way' isn't the best way after all." Over the years since then, numerous artists have recorded the song, each one belting out the lyrics with bravado and the boast of individual freedom. However, the theme of the song does not depict a person who is truly free. Rather, the lyrics describe the self-focused life philosophy which produces the ultimate bondage. King Solomon so wisely warned, "An evil man is ensnared in his transgressions" (Prov. 29:6a).

The righteous man or woman, on the other hand, may have no vocal or musical abilities whatsoever; but they can always sing because "a righteous man sings and rejoices" (Prov. 29:6b). Joy is the song in the soul of a truly free person. Freedom is not "doing your own thing" but "doing the right thing," and joy is the product of "doing what is right" because "you are right" with God. Both freedom and joy are gifts from God, for "if the Son sets you free, you will be free indeed" (John 8:36), and the fruit of the Spirit is joy (Gal. 5:22).

When we are freed from our sins through faith in Christ, we are able to experience and share God's freedom with Him. The Lord is the one completely free being in all the universe, and He is a God of joy. That is why the angels could sing, "Joy to the world" (Luke 2:10) because Jesus would bring the joy of salvation to the people of God. It is not wrong to live for joy. The Lord actually commands us to rejoice in Him (Phil. 4:4) and serve Him with gladness (Ps. 100:2). Can you imagine the unspeakable joy awaiting those who are welcomed by Jesus into heaven and hear Him say, "Well done, good and faithful servant!" (Matt. 25:23)

In effect, what will He be saying? He will be exclaiming, "You Did It My Way!"

SEPTEMBER 19
Proverbs 30

"THE LIE OF LEGALISM"

"Do not add to his words, lest he rebuke you and you be found a liar."
(Proverbs 30:6)

The watershed issue of all Christian faith and practice is the reliability and sufficiency of Scripture. The key words in that statement, which I believe with all my heart, are "reliability" and "sufficiency." Religious liberalism denies the former, and religious legalism denies the latter. They are both evil and deadly. Religious liberalism is based on the denial that there exists a source of absolute truth in the Bible. Of course, this denial is never expressed that bluntly or blatantly, but it is affirmed in innumerable ways.

Religious liberalism is based on the deceptive technique of the Devil in the Garden of Eden—"has God actually said?" The attack subtly put a question mark where God put a period. Satan did not at first deny outright the Word of the Lord. He just questioned whether the Lord had actually been heard accurately. The Devil planted the seed in Eve's mind as to whether the Lord's Word was absolute or relative. He posed the question of whether God's children could be absolutely certain that God had spoken absolutely. After all, times and circumstances change, so it isn't reasonable to think guiding principles do not need to adapt as well.

Nothing is a clearer demonstration of this devilish and diabolical reasoning than simply following what is being written and spoken by the major Christian denominations worldwide today. It is Babylon. Truth is being suppressed so people can have clear consciences to live as they please. The sin of Romans 1:18 and its resultant debased thinking has become the "open-mindedness" set forth as love. It is, in reality, a hatred of God. The lying serpent is still in the garden of God. All that I have just shared has probably been received by most of the readers of this devotional with a response of "Amen." However, we who affirm the *reliability* of God's Word must constantly be on guard against rejecting the *sufficiency* of Scripture.

Legalism is radically different from religious liberalism, but it is just as wrong and just as poisonous. You see, legalism believes that God has spoken; He just hasn't said enough. Legalism is also inherently a denial of God's truthfulness, just as liberalism because it affirms that human beings can determine God's authoritative Word. Again, as with liberalism, this is never actually stated; however, it is validated in countless expressions of saying what God has never said. This is a terrible sin, for to "add to His words" is to "be found a liar" (Prov. 30:6). Our Lord Jesus condemned religious legalism and its deadliness with His strongest words of judgment. He so wanted us as His followers to reject legalism that He gave it a timeless definition: "teaching as doctrines the commandments of men" (Matt. 15:9). This was the sin of the Pharisees and is still the sin of their spiritual descendants today. They are not found in mainline Christian churches but abound in what is often called "fundamental," "Evangelical," or "conservative" circles. Regardless of the label, the label is not the danger. It is the poisonous content that can be contained beneath the label. What is the way to avoid this poison and also the poison of religious liberalism? Say what God says, nothing more and nothing less. Let's not subtract from God's Word, and let's not add to God's Word. That is simple. That is radical. Here endeth the lesson.

SEPTEMBER 20
Proverbs 31

"A Mother's Wisdom"

"The words of King Lemuel. An oracle that his mother taught him."
(Proverbs 31:1)

Abraham Lincoln once said, "All that I am or ever hope to be I owe to my dear mother." Nancy Hanks Lincoln died when her son, Abraham, was only 10 years old, but she made an incredible impact on him and the world *through* him. Any man or woman who has been blessed with a godly mother has been given, from God, a treasure of incalculable worth. I know personally and will always praise the Lord for the good and godly mother He gave to me.

We are not told the specific identity of Lemuel or his mother, but most Bible scholars agree that Lemuel is a spiritual title for King Solomon and that his mother is the famous Bathsheba. She was a very wise woman because she mentored her young son by teaching him oracles, that is, specific instructions of wisdom based on God's Word. Sadly, some of the things she taught Solomon slipped from his grasp later in his life as he failed in some of the same areas she instructed him —focusing his energies on relationships with many women who turned his heart from the Lord. Also, Solomon pursued a life of parties and pleasure for a season that undermined his faith and integrity. When anyone, especially a leader, is distracted by self-focused living, they cannot be the advocate for the poor and destitute who desperately need the focused concern and efforts of God's servants.

Solomon's mother spoke to him with wisdom as a youth, and in later years, he spoke of her with the highest affection and admiration. In fact, the remainder of this last chapter of Proverbs is an oracle on the character and conduct of a godly woman, wife, and mother. Solomon describes the qualities of a virtuous woman from his own mother's life. The Lord inspired his words and inscribed them in the Bible for all ages. What a testimony of grace and redemption is given in these words from Bathsheba and Solomon's words about her. As a young woman, she knew abuse by King David in his lust and the loss of her dear husband by David's deception. But in the grace and strength of the Lord, she overcame the abuse and became a blessing to her family and an example for the ages of a woman who fears the Lord. The same God and the same grace are available for every abused and used person today.

SEPTEMBER 21
Ecclesiastes 1-2

"Preacher of Vanities"

"Vanity of vanities, says the Preacher, vanity of vanities! All is vanity."
(Ecclesiastes 1:2)

That is a lot of "vanities." Five of them, to be exact. And there are 29 more in the chapters that follow. In order to understand the book we will be reading over the next few days, it is vitally important to understand a few critical pieces of information. Let's start with this word "vanity," which appears in some form, 34 times in 12 chapters. The word has a different meaning than it is typically used in our day. "Vanity" has, at its core, the idea of "mist," "vapor," or mere "breath," and so metaphorically, it came to express something fleeting or elusive. So, the author is proclaiming as a theme in his "sermon" (I will explain that momentarily) that so much of what is valued in this world is without lasting, satisfying substance. It is vanity, "...a striving after wind" (Ecc. 1:17), having been grasped, there is found to be nothing of lasting substance and satisfaction to it.

Secondly, it is important to understand the title, "Ecclesiastes," for it is an understanding of the author's identity and the concept of his message and mission. "Ecclesiastes" has a familiar sound to us in English as we hear in it the concept of something "ecclesiastical," or having to do with church or religion. That is precisely the connection we need to make as we read this section of God's Word. "Ecclesiastes" is connected with the Hebrew word for "assembly," especially a gathering of the community to hear the Word of the Lord. So, we begin to see the image the author has in mind as he writes. He is "the Preacher" (Ecc. 1:1) who has an important message to declare to the gathered assembly, God's people.

Now, who is the Preacher who believes he is uniquely called and qualified to deliver this lengthy sermon of wisdom? We are not directly told the Preacher's name, but from internal evidence and the ancient Jewish and Christian witness, there is almost uniform agreement that this minister is Solomon, "the son of David, king in Jerusalem" (Ecc. 1:1). And what a qualified witness Solomon is to the vanity of mankind's relentless pursuits for satisfaction and purpose through earth's pleasures! From the beginning of his "sermon," Preacher Solomon lets us know by personal testimony he had tried it all—education (1:13), pleasure and laughter (2:1-2), philosophy (2:3), architecture (2:4), landscape design and development (2:4-6), all the while amassing wealth such as the world had never known before (2:7-8). Having grasped for it all, the Preacher tells us what he found in his grip:

> "Then I considered all that my hands had done and the toil I had expended
> in doing it, and behold, all was vanity and a striving after wind,
> and there was nothing to be gained under the sun."
> (Ecclesiastes 2:11)

That sounds depressing, doesn't it? However, a tiny beam of light shines through those three last words, "under the sun." Pleasure and fulfillment do exist and can be experienced on this earth. However, we can never find satisfaction by focusing on what is *"under the sun."* Fulfillment can only be found when our life's focus is *"above the sun."*

SEPTEMBER 22
Ecclesiastes 3-4

"CHRISTIAN HEDONISM"

> *"I perceived that there is nothing better for them than to be joyful*
> *and to do good as long as they live."*
> (Ecclesiastes 3:12)

Some things don't seem to go together. We have even developed an idiom in American English to express irreconcilable differences. We say, "oil and water," and immediately, people recognize that whatever subjects are being discussed, it is impossible to bring them into alignment or agreement. Evidently, the Lord does not understand this "oil and water" concept because, throughout the revelation of His will and ways in Scripture, He constantly unites things that we (in our great wisdom) would believe are irreconcilable. The poor are rich, the servants are leaders, the meek are mighty, the weak are strong, etc., etc. It is actually the understanding, accepting, and embracing of these "foolish assertions" that leads to not only enlightenment but also fulfillment.

King Solomon, the wisest of all people on the earth, came face to face with the reality that it is in humbly embracing these seemingly contradictory realities that life ceases to be a vain "chasing of the wind." The ceaseless activity of his brilliant mind and relentless pursuits of his hyper-frenetic life never brought him the ultimate accomplishment—joy. He was amazed by the beautiful, brilliant simplicity of joy: "I perceived that there is nothing better for them than to be joyful and to do good as long as they live; also that everyone should eat and drink and take pleasure in all his toil—this is God's gift to man" (Ecc. 3:12-13).

Solomon is telling us that the ultimate meaning of life is found in joy—joy in a life lived as a gift from God. In fact, it is a life centered on the enjoyment of God that alone can fill the "God-sized" hole in the human heart. "He has made everything beautiful in its time. Also, he has put eternity into man's heart, yet so that he cannot find out what God has done from the beginning to the end" (Ecc. 3:11). The idea Solomon communicates here is that it is futile, impossible to comprehend all the ways of God, for no human being can. However, God can and will fill that "God-sized hole" in the heart of every person who rests in Him. The fourth century church father, Augustine, expressed this truth in his famous words of prayer: "You have made us for Yourself, O Lord, and our hearts are restless until they rest in You."

Augustine and Solomon share the same revelation that humbled and enlightened both their incredibly brilliant minds—the great pursuit of life is in not *running* at all; it is in *resting*, living at rest in the joy of life with God. Life is about the pursuit of joy-filled pleasure, and that pleasure is found today, tomorrow, and for all eternity in God Himself.

> *"You make known to me the path of life; in your presence there is fullness of joy; at your right hand are pleasures forevermore."*
> (Psalm 16:11)

SEPTEMBER 23
Ecclesiastes 5-6

"Financial Failure"

"He who loves money will not be satisfied with money, nor he who loves wealth with his income; this also is vanity."
(Ecclesiastes 5:10)

When I was young, a series of well-known commercials aired on television over a period of several years. The commercials were an advertising campaign for the then-famous financial brokerage firm E. F. Hutton. The ads consisted of a basic plot repeated in a similar scene. Two people would be talking about finances in a crowded space, and then one of the characters would say, "Well, my broker is E. F. Hutton, and E. F. Hutton says...." The sentence was never finished. In each commercial, when the actor made that statement, the activities in the room would come to a complete stop, and every conversation would immediately cease. Total silence filled the room while all the people waited to hear what E. F. Hutton had to say. With the two actors surrounded by the crowd waiting to hear the financial advice, the announcer's voice would close the commercial with the same statement, "When E. F. Hutton talks, people listen." That was a great ad campaign.

Who could possibly have better financial advice than E. F. Hutton? Well, how about the wealthiest and wisest man who ever lived, King Solomon? When Solomon gives financial advice, we should certainly listen, especially when we know his advice is inspired by the all-wise owner of all things, Jehovah. What is Solomon's "satisfaction guaranteed" money advice? That money is guaranteed never to satisfy. The person who chooses money is chasing the wind. We are often told today that money can buy you anything, but we are being told a lie. In fact, the truth shared by Solomon regarding money was also shared by a rock group from the same era of many of those E. F. Hutton commercials. The Beatles sang the truth, "Money can't buy me love."

People who try to find fulfillment in their funds will experience the harsh reality that another rock group, the Rolling Stones, declared: "I can't get no satisfaction." Our currency in the United States has printed or minted upon it the motto, "In God We Trust." Although that motto is certainly not true in our nation as a whole, it conveys a truth that each of us should trust God to fill the "God-sized hole" in our hearts. Within us is a space that is not "gold-sized" but "God-sized." No amount of gold can ever fill a space the size of God. God alone can fill our lives with a treasure that no amount of money can ever provide, and that treasure is contentment.

> "But godliness with contentment is great gain, for we brought nothing into the world, and we cannot take anything out of the world. But if we have food and clothing, with these we will be content."
> (1 Timothy 6:6-8)

SEPTEMBER 24
Ecclesiastes 7-9

"A FUNERAL OR A FEAST?"

> "It is better to go to the house of mourning than to go to the house of feasting, for this is the end of all mankind, and the living will lay it to heart."
> (Ecclesiastes 7:2)

If you read the verse above with only a surface consideration or read through it quickly, you might think it is a strange statement. You would feel that way because it *is* a strange statement. It is completely counter-cultural, or as we might describe it, "a shock and awe message." Solomon intended it to be shocking because it deals with a topic of the utmost importance and therefore needs to grip our attention.

I can attest that what Solomon said nearly 3000 years ago still retains the ability to startle an audience. That is one reason I began many years ago including this verse in most funeral services I conduct. Every time, eyes widen just a bit when, standing above or next to the coffin or urn containing the remains of their departed relative or friend, I share with them that the wisest man who ever lived said attending a funeral is more profitable than going to a party. After a moment's pause, I tell the audience why that wisest man's statement is neither stupid nor insensitive to our time of grief, "for this is the end of all mankind, and the living will lay it to heart" (Ecc. 7:2).

A funeral brings us face to face with our finality; we have a meeting with our own mortality. Even if our life is one long party, that party has a moment when it will be over. Every person's life has an expiration date, known only to God, but it is a definite date. In a completely uncertain world, acknowledging and preparing for the one absolute certainty is the most significant expression. "And just as it is appointed for man to die once, and after that comes judgment… (Heb. 9:27) Once in a while, by the grace of God, attending a funeral at the end of one person's life becomes the illuminating event that marks the beginning of another person's spiritual life. I thank God that He used a funeral in a life-giving way to bring me to Himself.

When I was 17, the most shocking event of my high school years occurred. My cousin, Jill, who lived just three blocks from me and who I had known most of my life, one sunny fall afternoon collapsed and died on the football field as the marching band practiced for the half-time performance. I was not there because I was a member of the football team. But I can never forget the shock I felt when a friend ran to tell me what had happened. Neither can I ever forget the stunning awareness of my own mortality as my girlfriend, Susan (now my wife), and I looked at Jill's lovely teenage face in that coffin. I thought, "Where is Jill now?" and "Where would I be now if this had happened to me?" I did not have a confident answer to that question, and that doubt was a seed used by the Holy Spirit to bring me to faith. Thank God, a few months later, He brought both Susan and me to assurance of eternal life through trusting in Christ alone.

The most incredible wisdom in this life is being prepared for the greatest certainty—death. Life, death, and eternity. Are you living in the light of your funeral and your resurrection?

SEPTEMBER 25
Ecclesiastes 10-12

"LIVING FOR JOY AND JUDGMENT"

"The end of the matter; all has been heard. Fear God and keep his commandments, for this is the whole duty of man. For God will bring every deed into judgment, with every secret thing, whether good or evil."
(Ecclesiastes 12:13-14)

Solomon ended this essay of life perspective with a hard stop—"The end of the matter." That is a brief conclusion indeed, but it is also very effective. He is definitely following his own advice that nothing productive comes from superfluous speech (Ecc. 5:7). Solomon has said a lot and has said it with directness and clarity. In many ways, Solomon and Ecclesiastes in the Old Testament correspond to James and the epistle that bears his name in the New Testament. Both were gifted and wise men who could have dazzled their listeners and readers with the scope of their intellect. However, the goal of both these men was not to impress their audience's sensibilities but to make a lasting impression on their minds and, therefore, their entire lives. We need that. We really do.

So, Solomon the Wise brings us to the summation of his lessons, and, Lord willing, his summation becomes our life's goals. In brief, Solomon says the guiding poles of our lives should be *Joy* and *Judgment*.

GUIDED BY JOY

What Solomon says in his final phrases about judgment seems quite clear, but joy? Where is the joy in "fear God and keep His commandments"? It is found by people like missionary, author, and teacher Elisabeth Elliot. She knew and taught—"the joy of surrender." It is by recognizing and responding to the lordship of God that we come to understand His love. "God is love" (1 John 4:8, 17). Therefore, in truth, the wisest, most fulfilling, and the most joy-saturating thing we can do is reverence and obey Him. Expressing the confident assurance of loving obedience allows us to experience the joyful awareness of His living presence. We walk in the light as He is in the light, and then we experience fellowship with Him (1 John 1:7). We are "surprised by joy" in finding that His commands are commands of love and that they are not grievous (1 John 5:3). No, the "way of the treacherous is their ruin" (Prov. 13:15), but walking with God brings the pleasures of His presence (Ps. 16:11).

GUIDED BY JUDGMENT

Martin Luther said he lived his life focused on this day and *THAT* day, and in saying "that day," he meant Judgment Day. How little we think of Judgment Day in comparison to its importance. Part of our fallenness is not being as remotely guided by it as we should be. A definite day, a personal day, a probing day, an evaluating day, a day to meet our Maker—Judgment Day. Could anything guide us, guard us, and govern us more? But does it? Solomon wants us to sit with that day as he closes his lesson. Let's do that. Before we rush to start, restart, or bring this day to a close, let's sit with *THAT* day before us.

Never forget. Enjoying this day *with* God is the best preparation for that day when you will be standing *before* God.

SEPTEMBER 26
Song of Solomon 1-3

"HIS BANNER OF LOVE"

"He brought me to the banqueting house, and his banner over me was love."
(Song of Solomon 2:4)

When our pastor's wife taught us a praise song in junior church on the verse above, I can assure you she had no idea she was teaching us a sexy song, but in reality, she was. The words of that phrase from the children's song, "His Banner Over Me is Love," come directly from a book in the Bible that celebrates the joys of passionate, sexual love between King Solomon and his wife, identified only as the Shulamite. A book in the Bible that celebrates marital sexuality?! Absolutely. God is not prudish over something He created and called "very good."

Sex and sexuality are God's idea, and it is beautiful, satisfying, and holy when it is treasured for what it is—the wedding gift God gives to two of His children He has joined together in the covenant of marriage. Only the perversion of this gift by the world, the flesh, and the Devil twists the gift of sexual love into selfish self-gratification that is sinful and unholy. This corrupted thinking has made the Song of Solomon off-limits literature for even some "super saints."

I remember well when I was reading the Song of Solomon as a senior in college, and another ministerial student told me in no uncertain terms that a godly young man should not read that section of the Bible before he was engaged. I know I shouldn't have responded as I did, but I couldn't help myself as I laughed out loud when I realized he was serious. Not read the Song of Solomon as a 22-year-old man? Thank the Lord; I was engaged to be married! My friend and fellow ministerial student did not appreciate my incredulous laugh. Perhaps three years later, he could understand my sad sigh when I learned he had left his wife (also a college classmate) for another woman. "If then the light in you is darkness, how great is the darkness!" (Jesus, Matt. 6:23)

There is a reason this portion of God's Word is not a source of temptation (as if the Word of the Lord could be!) and why preachers and pastors through the ages have expounded it. In particular, the Puritans (yes, those prudish Puritans!) delighted in teaching from the Song of Solomon. Charles Spurgeon, "the last of the Puritans," preached from it hundreds of times and published 58 of those sermons. Since the days of the apostles and early church leaders, people of God have seen the Song of Solomon as an exquisitely beautiful allegory of God's love for His people. Prophetically, The Song portrays the devotion of Christ, the Heavenly Bridegroom, who shares with His Bride the Church. A careful reading of the images used by Jesus in His public ministry and the writings of His apostles, such as Paul and John, reveals that they use the intimate love between a husband and wife as an earthly expression of spiritual union between the Lord and His people.

Wade Robinson, a follower of Jesus during the Victorian era, was gripped by the passionate declaration of love by the Shulamite for her bridegroom as she declared, "My beloved is mine, and I am his..." (Song 2:16) Deeply moved as he meditated on that phrase, Robinson wrote these words flowing in devotion from his heart for his Beloved:

> *Heav'n above is deeper blue,*
> *earth around is sweeter green,*
> *that which glows in ev'ry hue*

> Christless eyes have never seen.
> Birds in song his glories show,
> flow'rs with richer beauties shine
> since I know, as now I know,
> I am his, and he is mine.

("I Am His, and He is Mine" by Wade Robinson)

SEPTEMBER 27
Song of Solomon 4-5

"THE PURSUIT OF LOVE"

"This is my beloved and this is my friend, O daughters of Jerusalem."
(Song of Solomon 5:16)

Several of the most moving and intense stanzas found within the love song of the Song of Solomon are scenes depicted in a garden, describing the joys of love in the allegory of a beautiful garden. That imagery of love, the pursuit of a beloved one, and a beautiful garden are not without significance. Interestingly, throughout the ages and among all types of people groups, the pursuit of a beloved person and the delight of fulfillment in love is compared to a garden. God understands that the power of the imagery of a beautiful garden and the joy of complete love is etched in the human soul.

It is not overemphasizing this love-in-the-garden imagery too much in saying it is connected very closely to the love story of redemption revealed as God's eternal plan for mankind. Think about it. *God created and blessed mankind to know and enjoy His love in a garden.* The Bible opens with God making the man and the woman in His image. They alone of all His creation have the ability and the privilege to know the Father, spirit to Spirit, in a relationship that is one of unhindered, unlimited love. In the beautiful Garden of Eden, Adam and Eve could sing of their love relationship with their Creator.

> And He walks with me, and He talks with me,
> And He tells me I am His own,
> And the joy we share as we tarry there,
> None other, has ever, known.

("In the Garden" by C. Austin Miles)

The Son of God in love devoted Himself, in a garden, to the Father's plan of redemption. Tragically, the perfect relationship the man and the woman enjoyed with their loving Father was ruined by their unfaithfulness. Listening to the serpent, they sought greater fulfillment and pleasure in love of self and betrayed their Beloved. They were expelled because of their rebellion and betrayal from the garden of life with the Father. Thousands of years later, the second Adam, the dearly Beloved Son, entered a beautiful garden one spring night in Jerusalem and, in the agony of soul, poured out His heart to His Beloved Father. In that beautiful garden, in awful struggle, the Son sought and found His Father in prayer. In the Garden of Gethsemane, the Son of God, in complete and obedient love, pledged Himself by saying, "Not my will, but Your will be done." It was in the garden that the Son won His victory.

The Son of God displayed and declared His victorious love in a garden. Joseph of Arimathea had prepared a beautiful new tomb for himself and his family within a lovely garden. It was there in the garden that the body of the Beloved One was laid to rest. It was in the garden that angels announced His resurrection to a few of His disciples. And in that garden, to a weeping Mary Magdalene, her Beloved Master revealed Himself and announced the victory of His sacrifice and resurrection.

The love story of redemption concludes in the garden of eternal love. The Bible begins and ends with scenes of perfect love in a beautiful garden. In the New Jerusalem, the trees of life grow beside the ever-flowing river of salvation that streams from the throne of God. Paradise lost is paradise regained. The Beloved Bridegroom and His beloved and redeemed Bride, the Church, are united never again to be separated in the garden of the Father's eternal love.

SEPTEMBER 28
Song of Solomon 6-8

"The Flame of the Lord"

"Set me as a seal upon your heart, as a seal upon your arm,
for love is strong as death, jealousy is fierce as the grave.
Its flashes are flashes of fire, the very flame of the Lord."
(Song of Solomon 8:6)

There is nothing in heaven or on earth quite like it. There is no end to its existence; there is no measurement of its power. It is a priceless treasure available to all, yet no one fully comprehends it. What is this enigma of which I write? Love. Yes, love. It is a word we use so flippantly—we love our family, our pets, our sports teams, our church, we love pizza, the beach, and yes, come to think of it, we love Jesus.

Of course, I am not advocating that we stop using the word "love" to express our devotion to many things, but I do think it is helpful for us to take a few moments to consider the meaning, source, and priority of love regarding our identity and mission as disciples. The Song of Solomon is a perfect portion of Scripture in which to do this because the pages literally drip with love. The emotional and devoted love expressed by Solomon and his Shulamite bride is burned into these pages of their love song. Yet, even they understand that the source of their passion and devotion to each other is beyond them; it is "otherworldly," if you will. Love is as "strong as death" with a "jealousy [ardor] as fierce as the grave. Its flashes are of fire, the very flame of the Lord" (Song 8:6). In fact, no amount of water is able to quench this fire (Song 8:7).

As I meditate on what God reveals in His Word about love, I am amazed that love is "the flame of the Lord" and that love is the guiding light by which to understand all that God has chosen to reveal about Himself, His people, our mission, and our destiny. Volumes could be written on what our Father has revealed about love and not scratch the surface of its depths. However, please take a little extra time right now to consider the following insights and prayerfully meditate on these selected passages about the greatest thing in the world—love.

- Love has God's heart as its source (1 John 4:7).
- Love was the basis of God's choosing of a people to be His Son's Bride (Eph. 1:4-6).
- Love was the compelling motivation for God sacrificing His Son and for the Son sacrificing Himself (John 3:16, Gal. 2:20).
- Love is the ultimate requirement God calls His people to fulfill (John 13:35).
- Love for God is expressed in a love for all people, for all people bear His image (Luke 10:27).
- Love is the identifying quality of a person who has been born again (Rom. 5:5).
- Love is the most unmistakable witness to the reality of the gospel (John 17:23).
- Love is the ultimate fruit of God's Spirit (Gal. 5:22-23).
- Love is the supreme quality that Jesus desires to bind His people to Him (Rev. 2:4).
- Love is the greatest of all gifts, and its absence invalidates all other gifts (1 Cor. 13:1-3).
- Love is the greatest of all the Christian graces: "So now faith, hope, and love abide, these three; but the greatest of these is love" (1 Cor. 13:13).

SEPTEMBER 29
Isaiah 1-2

"WHITE AS SNOW"

"Come now, let us reason together, says the Lord: though your sins are like scarlet, they shall be as white as snow; though they are red like crimson, they shall become like wool."
(Isaiah 1:18)

With our Scripture reading today, we arrive at another of the great divisions of the Old Testament. So far on our *Pathways* journey, we have traveled through the Law, the historical books, the Psalms, and the wisdom literature. The rest of the days ahead will cover "the prophets." This final section of the Old Testament has two subsections—the major and the minor prophets. These titles do not mean that some prophets are more important than others. All the books of the prophets are equally inspired by God and, therefore, equally authoritative. The titles "major" and "minor" are used because of the size and scope of the prophetic messages they contain.

Having said that, it is very fitting that Isaiah stands at the gateway into the prophetic books of the Old Testament. The message of Isaiah is unique in so many ways. The breadth of what Isaiah covers has caused this book to be called "the Bible within the Bible." It encompasses the entire spectrum of God's redemptive plan. No book in the Bible reveals more clearly and poetically (for it is an epic poem) the depths of the depravity of sinful man and the infinite heights of God's redeeming love. Like no other prophet, Isaiah warns of the terrors of worldwide judgment and the glories of global redemption. Isaiah is filled with the bad news of sin and the good news of the gospel. Isaiah, in many ways, can be called the "Gospel according to Isaiah." He cries out for people to flee from the destruction coming as judgment on their sin and run to the welcoming embrace of a merciful, saving God. Isaiah is not God, but he speaks for God. He calls people to repent of their sins and trust in the love and mercy of Jehovah. Isaiah proclaims the gospel, so his long prophetic message of 66 chapters is filled with invitations.

There are two beautiful invitations in the opening verses of Isaiah: one is *from* God Himself, and the other is *to* God Himself. In the first invitation, Jehovah calls people to experience the most dramatic of all transformations: sins as dark as scarlet and crimson washed clean like wool or snow. This is the invitation to free grace and full salvation. It is the offer of so much more than a reformed life but a regenerated life. The new life will not be one of denial and servitude but one overflowing with blessing and feasting on "the good of the land" (Isa. 1:19).

The people who respond to the invitation *from* God will one day be blessed to share and receive an invitation *to* God. "Come, let us go up to the mountain of the house of the Lord, to the house of the God of Jacob, that He may teach us His ways and that we may walk in His paths... O house of Jacob. Come, let us walk in the light of the Lord" (Isa. 2:3, 5). This is the vision that stretches into eternity. People who once were filthy and dwelling in darkness now and forever washed clean and living as God's beloved children walking in His loving light.

God's invitation is freely offered today for all who will hear and turn to Him. Listen, the God of Israel is calling. "Come, now." May that be our invitation we share with others today.

SEPTEMBER 30
Isaiah 3-4

"THE SHADE OF THE BRANCH"

"Then the Lord will create over the whole site of Mount Zion and over her assemblies a cloud by day, and smoke and the shining of a flaming fire by night; for over all the glory there will be a canopy."
(Isaiah 4:5)

Since the prophecies of Isaiah are, for the most part, shared in poetic form, it is important to understand the imagery that Isaiah uses in communicating the messages Jehovah places on his heart. A common example of an image used by Isaiah is that of a branch, and in our reading today, Isaiah employs this image for the first time. "In that day the branch of the Lord shall be beautiful and glorious, and the fruit of the land shall be the pride and honor of the survivors of Israel" (Isa. 4:2). As we journey through the book of Isaiah, it will become evident that "the Branch" is an image and also a title for Messiah.

As "the Branch," the Messiah grows out of the root and the stump of Jesse (Isa. 11:1, 10). "Jesse," here, is the father of David, and the Messiah is the descendant of the kingly line of David. The Messiah will be "cut off," yet from this apparently "dead stump" will come the new life in the beautiful and glorious "branch of the Lord" (Isa. 4:2). God will bring life and beauty out of the horrors of death.

This promise is made to the "survivors of Israel," a remnant who have been chosen for life (Isa. 4:2, 3) and will be rescued out of death to experience the blessed life of God's care and protection, "a booth for shade by day from the heat, and for a refuge and a shelter from the storm and rain" (Isa. 4:6). This prophecy of Isaiah was repeated over 800 years later as Paul, in Chapters 9-11 of the book of Romans, assures believers that God has not utterly rejected the nation of Israel. A remnant of Jewish believers in Messiah Jesus will endure until the great season when vast numbers are brought to repentance and faith.

These prophecies of Isaiah and the Apostle Paul will one day certainly come to pass. God cannot and never will forsake the promises He has made, whether to a people or an individual. God, in His providence, permits great trials to come to believers. Sometimes, as was the case with Israel and Judah, the terrible trials are consequences of terrible transgressions. Yet, God never forgets or forsakes His own.

You, too, are not forgotten today if you are Jehovah's child by faith in Jesus. Your life circumstances may not reflect that, but your identity in Christ is not based on your current situation but on His eternal revelation. If you cannot escape the desert of your present landscape, you can choose to once again rest in the cool shade found in the shadow of the cross. Faith is the substance and reality of the things we are assured of even when we do not presently see them (Heb. 11:1).

The day of rest is most definitely coming, but today for a few moments, sit quietly beneath "the Branch" of Jesus and His love, "a booth for shade by day from the heat, and for a refuge and a shelter from the storm and rain" (Isa. 4:6).

OCTOBER

"They rejoice before you as with joy at the harvest."
(Isaiah 9:3)

OCTOBER 1
Isaiah 5-7

"A VOLUNTEER VISION"

"And I heard the voice of the Lord saying, 'Whom shall I send, and who will go for us?' Then I said, 'Here I am! Send me.'"
(Isaiah 6:8)

Two of my most cherished possessions are the Bibles belonging to my mother and father. Thank God, they bear the marks of how much my parents read them. I once heard someone say, "A Bible that is falling apart is owned by someone who isn't." My mom and dad passed away, worn out by many years of life and labor, but their worn-out Bibles reflect the fresh faith and trust in God and His Word that they both demonstrated to their final days. From time to time, I leaf through pages of their Bibles and read the passages they highlighted and the items they stored within the pages.

When I open the copy of my dad's Bible, I always get moist eyes and a lump in my throat as I turn to the Book of Isaiah. There next to the verse cited above, Isaiah 6:8, my dad had taped a small picture of me from my college days. I can still recall his beaming smile when I told him that after much struggle and prayer, I was convinced the Lord was calling me to the ministry and that I was planning to change my major in college to ministry training. From that day on, Dad often jokingly called me "Isaiah" because I had said, "Here I am, send me!" Well, I wish I had been more of a volunteer, but the truth is I struggled for many months before I, in a sense, "surrendered" to God's call. My "volunteering" was more like that of Moses, "Here I am, send Aaron!"

What made Isaiah so quick to respond to the Lord's question, "Whom shall I send, and who will go for us?" The answer to the reason for Isaiah's immediate response is found in volunteering a *vision* God gave to Isaiah and a *provision* God made for Isaiah. It was in the year that one of the greatest and longest-reigning kings of Judah, Uzziah, died that Isaiah was granted to see the true King. Isaiah was granted a vision of almighty, sovereign, holy God, seated on an exalted throne and constantly worshiped by the adoring, angelic Seraphim. Heaven and earth shook with their shouts of "Holy, Holy, Holy!" Then, Isaiah, smitten by the awful reality of his sinfulness and the Lord's holiness, pronounced judgment upon himself. "Woe is me! For I am lost; for I am a man of unclean lips..." (Isa. 6:5) To this cry from his repentant heart, the Lord in this vision sent an angel carrying coals from the altar, the place of sacrifice, and ringing the gospel message, "Your guilt is taken away, and your sin atoned for."

That was motivation enough for Isaiah. The gratitude of his heart to God for the assurance of his sin forgiven could permit only one response to whatever God desired. "Yes!" Is that motivation enough for us today?

OCTOBER 2
Isaiah 8-9

"THE LIGHT OF THE WORD"

"The people who walked in darkness have seen a great light; those who dwelt in a land of deep darkness, on them has light shone."
(Isaiah 9:2)

The Book of Isaiah contains allegories and symbols to convey the message the Lord shares with all who will hear His divine revelation. A recurring symbol used by Isaiah is the contrast of "light" and "darkness." As in the entire Bible, light is an image of God, His nature, and His truth, while darkness is regularly presented as an image representing all that is contrary to God and, therefore, inherently evil. The Psalmist David, 200 years before Isaiah, sang a petition to God, "Send out your light and your truth" (Ps. 43:3). Isaiah picks up that same theme when he pronounces the judgment of God on the false sources of light and yet also declares the promise from God of a perfect light that will come to the world. What is this light source from God, and where do we find it? We encounter God's light in God's Word—the *inspired Word* and the *incarnate Word*.

In Chapter 8, Isaiah asks an apparently foolish question, "Should not a people inquire of their God? Should they inquire of the dead on behalf of the living?" (Isa. 8:19) Judah's apostasy was so great in Isaiah's day that many people resorted to mediums and necromancers to bring messages from the dead for the living. Isaiah's rhetorical question is intended not only to condemn but also to mock such foolishness—can the dead give light to the living? Then, Isaiah shares a litmus test to apply to those who profess to be sources of light. "To the teaching and to the testimony! If they will not speak according to this word, it is because they have no dawn" (Isa. 8:20). Isaiah's declaration is decisive and timeless. It is wisdom for us today to evaluate "sources of wisdom." If any prophet, counselor, teacher, or author does not align their message with God's Word, there is no "dawn," no light, in them. Any source of guidance regarding truth that is not intentionally and clearly anchored to Scripture is not a source of light at all.

Thank God for the light found in His *inspired word*, and praise His name forever for the Light of the World that has shined into the global darkness—*the incarnate Word*! The writer of Hebrews tells us that Jesus is God's "final word." "Long ago, at many times and in many ways, God spoke to our fathers by the prophets, but in these last days he has spoken to us by his Son" (Heb. 1:1-2). As John the apostle shared, Jesus is "the Word become flesh" (John 1:14). In Jesus of Nazareth, the invisible God became visible for time and eternity. Jesus is God's Word, God's final Word. To seek a message from God, disconnected from the inspired Word and the incarnate Word, is to seek for light where there is no light.

We must regularly ask ourselves, "What is my source of light?" "Where do I turn for directions for the maze of this world system?" We need to be careful. We need to listen to Isaiah, who is still warning God's people today: "To the teaching and to the testimony! If they will not speak according to this word, it is because they have no dawn" (Isa. 8:20).

OCTOBER 3
Isaiah 10-12

"MESSIAH AND HIS KINGDOM"

"They shall not hurt or destroy in all my holy mountain; for the earth shall be full of the knowledge of the Lord as the waters cover the sea."
(Isaiah 11:9)

Isaiah continues his incredible, epic prophecy using the most amazing symbols, symbols that seem to be the ultimate mixing of metaphors. I was always surprised in college when professors noted the mixing of metaphors in many of my essays and deducted from my score because of them when both the Old and New Testaments overflow with them. I suppose it reflected that they considered the quality of my work just a little bit less than "inspired." Indeed, Isaiah delighted in mixing metaphors as he conveyed the glories of Messiah and His kingdom. A stump-bearing fruit, (Isa. 11:1) a delight in fear, (11:3) a rod of iron and a world of peace, (11:4-7) a mountain that covers the earth like the waters cover the sea. (11:9) It is fortunate for Isaiah that he did not submit his poetry to my English Literature professors. But, how fortunate for us that Isaiah reached for every beautiful metaphor in his imagination to give us a glimpse of the Heavenly King and His earthly Kingdom!

Notice, now, this "new world order" rises like a shoot from a stump and a branch from roots (Isa. 11:1). The stump speaks of a tree being cut down, and the roots are a picture of the part of the tree that is buried. Likewise, it will appear that the kingly line of the family of Jesse is cut off. A branch will bud, but then it will be buried. Yet, this "branch," the buried "root of David," *will stand*—rise like a living tree, a "signal for the people," and they will find the shadow of His resting place to be glorious (11:10). These are images of life from the dead and life for the dead through the death and resurrection of Messiah. The cross, a symbol of death, and the empty tomb, a symbol of resurrection, become the "mixed metaphors of Messiah," testifying to all the peoples of the world regarding the King and His Kingdom. The dispersed people of Israel will flow from the nations and return to the Holy One of Israel (12:6). And, the nations themselves, from every corner of the earth, will also join the pilgrimage to the Lord and, through Him, joyfully draw water from the wells of salvation (12:3). What a promise!

Also, what a privilege and a purpose! This procession to the King and His Kingdom has already begun. We are not just spectators; we are participants in the pilgrimage. In fact, we are "recruiters" for this "Kingdom caravan." How do we invite people to join us? What can we do to increase the number of our fellow travelers? Share the gospel, the "good news." Our celebration is their invitation: "And you will say in that day: 'Give thanks to the Lord, call upon His name, make known His deeds among the peoples, proclaim that His name is exalted" (Isa. 12:4). Celebrate the King; the King will do the rest. Who have you joyfully invited recently to join you on the journey home?

OCTOBER 4
Isaiah 13-15

"The Devil Gets His Due"

"How you are fallen from heaven, O Day Star, son of Dawn!
How you are cut down to the ground, you who laid the nations low!"
(Isaiah 14:12)

Christopher Marlowe was a well-known playwright from the late sixteenth century, a contemporary of the greatest of all European playwrights, William Shakespeare. Marlowe is perhaps best known for his posthumously published work, "The Tragical History of the Life and Death of Doctor Faustus." This tragedy is based on a collection of German legends and stories about Doctor Faustus, a man of science who foolishly makes a bargain with the demon, Mephistopheles in return for 24 years of supernatural power. It was a terrifying play in its day and still is, especially the scene when the "Devil collects his due," and too late, Faustus recognizes the tragic and eternal price he must pay for his foolish and prideful ambition. "The Devil gets his due" is an expression that has come down through Marlowe's play and from those ancient legends to our present day.

In reality, the Devil will one day "get his own due" through a just and everlasting punishment for his betrayal and rebellion against God. This is the "back story" to the prophetic doom that Isaiah announces upon the "king of Babylon" in Chapters 13 and 14. It is a remarkable prophecy because Babylon was a minor kingdom in Isaiah's lifetime compared to the contemporary world power of Assyria. However, by revelation, the Lord permitted Isaiah to share that it would be Babylon and its proud king that He would raise up and use to punish Judah for its terrible idolatry and disloyalty. However, God will ultimately use the Medes (another kingdom that does not exist in Isaiah's day) to bring His judgment on the wickedness of Babylon (Isa. 13:17-22). God is indeed sovereign over the nations!

In Chapter 14, as Isaiah prophesied the judgment on the evil king of Babylon, he draws back the curtain of earthly events and reveals the original treachery of the Devil and his ultimate destruction (Isa. 14:12-15). Isaiah proclaims the downfall of "Day Star, son of Dawn" (v. 12). This is also translated as "Lucifer, son of morning." Before he was Satan or the Devil, the angel Lucifer was an exalted being within God's heavenly host. Yet, being so close to God was not enough for Lucifer; in pride, he plotted to "make myself like the Most High" (v. 14). For his rebellion, Lucifer was expelled from his position, and his doom was set, "But you are brought down to Sheol, to the far reaches of the pit" (v. 15). The Devil is not yet destroyed, but he has been defeated by the Son of the Highest, Jesus Christ. The Lord, in His death, crushed the head of Lucifer and, in His glorious resurrection, conquered the Devil's domain of death. One happy day, the arch-deceiver will, at the command of Jesus, be cast into the Lake of Fire.

So, how should we fight the Devil today? By doing what he *refuses to do*—submit ourselves to God and *resist the Devil in faith* (James 4:7-10). And the next time the Devil reminds you of your *past*, remind him of *his future*! Yes, most assuredly, "The Devil will get his due."

OCTOBER 5
Isaiah 16-18

"FRIEND TO THE OUTCAST"

"Let the outcasts of Moab sojourn among you;
be a shelter to them from the destroyer."
(Isaiah 16:4)

Reading this verse of Scripture from a distance of 2800 years, it is hard to understand just how startling Isaiah's admonition would have been for the people of Israel in his day. The kingdom of Moab was the ancient foe of the people of Israel. From the days of the Exodus, the Moabites repeatedly opposed and attacked the Jews. Many of the greatest moments in the history of Israel and Judah were the crushing defeats they had inflicted on Moab. We can imagine with what glee Isaiah's pronouncements of God's coming judgment on Moab were received. Unitedly, the citizens of Judah would say of the terrible things predicted by Isaiah, "Well, they have it coming to them!" Yet, God in His just wrath remembers to be merciful, and He calls on His people to do the same toward the remnant of Moab, saying, "...let the outcasts of Moab sojourn among you; be a shelter to them..." (Isa. 16:4)

As unpopular as this message from Isaiah was to many, maybe most of the residents of Judah, perhaps a few took time to recall that there was another "outcast of Moab" who, centuries earlier, had come to live in Israel. And also remember that a kind-hearted Boaz had shown mercy to, and eventually fell in love with, the young Moabite widow, Ruth. From this "love your enemy" relationship came a son. "They named him Obed. He was the father of Jesse, the father of David" (Ruth 4:17). Yes, *that* David! The greatest King in the history of Israel was the great-grandson of one of "the outcasts of Moab."

Being a friend to the outcasts is more than a "nice thing to do." It is the *gospel* thing to do. Treating enemies as friends is the heart of the gospel, for it is what God has done for us in Christ. We were not born, nor did we ever live as "friends" of God. As guilty sinners, we were by nature, attitude, and action the enemies of God. Not one thing did we have to commend us to God. We were, in truth, enemies of God, yet the Lord, in His amazing grace, determined to overcome our enmity by making us friends.

"Remember that you were at that time separated from Christ, alienated from the commonwealth of Israel and strangers to the covenants of promise, having no hope and without God in the world. But now in Christ Jesus you who once were far off have been brought near by the blood of Christ" (Eph. 2:12-13).

"Aliens," "strangers," people "having no hope and without God," now "brought near by the blood of Christ." What a way to overcome an enemy with relentless love! That was done to us. Now today, let's go do that to others.

OCTOBER 6
Isaiah 19-21

"Striking and Healing"

"And the Lord will strike Egypt, striking and healing, and they will return to the Lord, and he will listen to their pleas for mercy and heal them."
(Isaiah 19:22)

An amazing advance of missionary involvement occurred among a number of churches in America during the late 1940s and early 1950s. A special focus of this global mission advance was in Western Europe, the islands of the South Pacific, and the country of Japan. This surge of missionary efforts in these regions was unexpected, and the cause of the interest in the fields of service was shocking—war. World War II opened the spirited eyes of countless United States armed services members to the great gospel need worldwide. Even more unprecedented were the numbers of Christian servicemen and women who felt deeply compelled to take the message of Jesus and His peace to people who had previously been bitter enemies during the war. How can people, once ready to kill their enemies, be prepared to die for them, in such a short amount of time? Answer—the grace of God. The grace that is in the heart of God for His enemies.

Our reading today stuns us with the depths of God's grace. Every single time I read two of these verses from Isaiah, Chapter 19, I read them carefully again and consider the context to make sure I am not misinterpreting them: "In that day Israel will be the third with Egypt and Assyria, a blessing in the midst of the earth, whom the Lord of hosts has blessed, saying, 'Blessed be Egypt my people, and Assyria the work of my hands, and Israel my inheritance" (Isa. 19:24-25). Egypt, Assyria, and Israel. Which one of these is not the same? I know, right? Yet there it is in black and white in God's Word, sharing God's Words: "Egypt...my people, Assyria, the work of my hands." Now, that is grace upon grace! Egypt, who enslaved the people of Israel for over 400 years, and Assyria, who would destroy and carry off the survivors from Twelve Tribes of Israel, now named by God as part of His people.

When the Lord said to Abraham, "In you all the nations of the world will be blessed" (Gen. 22:18), He really meant that. When God said through David, "Let the nations be glad and sing for joy" (Ps. 67:4), He really meant that. Any yes, when Jesus said, "For God so loved the world, that he gave his only Son, that whoever believes in him should not perish but have eternal life" (John 3:16), He really meant that as well. God's love is a redeeming love deeper than all sin, and God's love is a reconciling love wider than all alienation. This amazing mercy of the Father gripped the heart of Frederick Faber and caused Frederick to grip a pen. May his words and the message of God's mercy be written on our lives for others to observe:

There's a wideness in God's mercy, like the wideness of the sea.
There's a kindness in God's justice, which is more than liberty.
There is no place where earth's sorrows are more felt than up in heaven.
There is no place where earth's failings have such a kindly judgment given.

For the love of God is broader than the measures of the mind.
And the heart of the Eternal is most wonderfully kind.
If our love were but more faithful, we would gladly trust God's Word,
And our lives reflect thanksgiving for the goodness of our Lord.

("There's a Wideness in God's Mercy" by Frederick William Faber)

OCTOBER 7
Isaiah 22-24

"AN EPICUREAN EXIT"

"In that day the Lord God of hosts called for weeping and mourning, for baldness and wearing sackcloth; and behold, joy and gladness, killing oxen and slaughtering sheep, eating flesh and drinking wine. 'Let us eat and drink, for tomorrow we die.'"
(Isaiah 22:12-13)

Epicurus was not the founder of a food site on the web. If you do a search, the algorithms of the internet will direct you to web pages that inform you about "the best in food, wine, and culture." If Epicurus were alive today (he died in 270 BC), he would be upset by that association. He taught that the purpose of life was the enjoyment of the simple pleasures of food and friendship shared with others and to strive for tranquility in a life characterized by the freedom of fear, especially the fear of death, which Epicurus taught was the end of all consciousness. However, it was not long until Epicurus's name became the basis of a lifestyle focus that emphasized the satisfaction of all the human senses and desires—Epicureanism. Epicurus should not have been surprised, for once a people or a person believes this life is all there is, the restraint that comes with the belief in *personal accountability to a Creator* will usually remove all moral and ethical guardrails. Five hundred years before Epicurus was the "party-hearty" spirit in Jerusalem. God had called for national and personal repentance and mourning for sin, and the response of the leaders and most of the population was, "Let us eat and drink for tomorrow we die" (Isa. 22:13).

Several years ago, author and educator Neil Postman wrote, "Amusing Ourselves to Death," a work showing how media influences the mind and provides the constant mental stimulation that, in reality, desensitizes the ability of people to think critically and participate in public discourse. Postman wrote his book before the existence of most of the forms of current social media even existed. Imagine what his evaluation would be today!

We certainly do live a "philosophy of life" that guides our lives, regardless of whether we consider ourselves to be the farthest thing from a philosopher. It is possible that we could be practical Epicureans, amusing ourselves to death. The reality is that to live for ourselves and our amusement is to live in death before we die. To live for self is only to "exist" and not to "live" at all. Only the Giver of life can tell us what life really is. God is the "Giver" of life, not the "Taker" of life. Jesus said, "I came that they may have life and have it abundantly" (John 10:10). We are told that the Heavenly Father breathed into the nostrils of Adam "the breath of life." Life comes from God and is only found in God. Think about that for a moment. God is life, He gives us life in His Son, and He promises abundant life now and for all eternity. In a sense, God calls us to "sacred epicureanism." He invites us to "amuse ourselves to life," to truly live for the joy of life found in Jesus. "And this is eternal life, that they know you, the only true God, and Jesus Christ whom you have sent" (John 17:3).

OCTOBER 8
Isaiah 25-27

"FREE AT LAST!"

*"He will swallow up death forever;
and the Lord God will wipe away tears from all faces,
and the reproach of his people he will take away from all the earth,
for the Lord has spoken."*
(Isaiah 25:8)

A few hours before his assassination in Memphis, Tennessee, Dr. Martin Luther King, Jr. delivered what would prove to be his final public remarks. As he addressed that gathering on the evening of April 3, 1968, his closing words now seem prophetic: "Well, I don't know what will happen now. We've got some difficult days ahead. But it doesn't matter with me now. Because I've been to the mountaintop. And I don't mind. Like anybody, I would like to live a long life. Longevity has its place. But I'm not concerned about that now. I just want to do God's will. And He's allowed me to go up to the mountain.

And I've looked over. And I've seen the promised land.... I'm not worried about anything. I'm not fearing any man. Mine eyes have seen the glory of the coming of the Lord." Prophetic indeed.

When we catch a view from the mountaintop, the shadows in the valley lose their ability to cast their darkness over the coming glories we have beheld from the heights. Our reading today is undoubtedly a view from a mountaintop. It is a view of a mountain that will cover and spread over the ultimate shadow that darkens the whole earth—death itself. Death is an intruder into God's creation. Death was never included in what the Lord declared at the end of creation week to be "very good." It was the sin of man that brought death into the world (Rom. 5:12). Death has reigned in this shadowland of the earth since the days of Adam and cast its dark pall upon all his descendants. But God took Isaiah to the mountaintop and allowed him to see the "glories of the promised land."

The second Adam, the Lord from glory, has conquered death and illuminated the tomb with eternal light. Death has been swallowed up forever (Isa. 25:8). The veil of mourning has been rent in two. (25:7) The bodies of God's people, for a brief time, rest behind the doors of their tombs and dwell in the dust (26:19-20). However, with the dew of the resurrection morning, the earth will release them to a new birth (26:19). What a view it is! One that is referenced by the apostles Paul and John (1 Cor. 15:54, Rev. 21:4) and cherished by believers through the ages. This mountaintop view is a light of peace flooding the darkest valleys of our lives. "You keep him in perfect peace whose mind is stayed on you...." (Isa. 26:3)

When was the last time you climbed to the mountaintop and looked beyond your dark valley? This would be a good time to do that. Savor the view in praise-filled worship. Speak the glories of the view to your soul. "I'm not worried about anything. I'm not fearing any man. Mine eyes have seen the glory of the coming of the Lord." Amen, Brother Martin!

OCTOBER 9
Isaiah 28-30

"WAITING TO BE WANTED"

*"Therefore the Lord waits to be gracious to you,
and therefore he exalts himself to show mercy to you.
For the Lord is a God of justice;
blessed are all those who wait for him."*
(Isaiah 30:18)

The Lord is the perfect gentleman. He does not barge in where He is not wanted. It is an amazing truth, yet one which is affirmed throughout Scripture. The Almighty, the Maker of heaven and earth who commands and controls all things, does not force Himself upon those who do not desire Him. "Behold, I stand at the door and knock. If anyone hears my voice and opens the door, I will come in to him and eat with him, and he with me" (Rev. 3:20). The Lord waits to be wanted.

It is hard to imagine the Lord standing outside the closed door of His own church, yet that is exactly how He described His relationship to the church of Laodicea—the door shut to Him, and He, patiently knocking. Sadly, that scene is reflective of so many churches today. The Lord's name is often referenced there. He is mentioned in songs, prayers, and messages, but the living Lord of the church is not desired there. He knocks, and He waits to be wanted...*by anyone*. And that is the patient Lord's invitation—*anyone?*

The Lord speaks to individuals, for what is the church but a community of individual Christians. It is vain and even hypocritical to lament the state of the church if the Lord is conveniently excluded from our own lives. I say *conveniently excluded* because that is often the situation regarding Jesus with His people. They love Him, but hosting Him in their lives is rather inconvenient. Jesus just tends to be.... Well, He's just always *there*. He does not tend to be a very good "guest" because He constantly opens the doors in the house or stands and knocks on the doors that are locked.

As naturally selfish people, we tend to cherish our closed and locked doors but any door we close or lock to Jesus, we do at our own loss. You see, Jesus, as the gracious guest He is, always brings a gift with Him, the gift of His gracious self. "Therefore, the Lord waits to be gracious to you, and therefore He exalts Himself to show mercy to you" (Isa. 30:18). Our Lord waits to be wanted. And when He is wanted, He works "to show mercy." We have nothing to fear from the One who knocks on any door in our lives. Our Lord is not a thief determined to rob us. He is our Redeemer, desiring to restore us. So when Jesus knocks and calls, the wisest thing we can do is return our Lord's greeting and rush to open the door. "He will surely be gracious to you at the sound of your cry. As soon as he hears it, he answers you" (Isa. 30:19).

> *Who at my door is standing,*
> *Patiently drawing near,*
> *Entrance within demanding?*
> *Whose is the voice I hear?*

> *Refrain:*
> *Sweetly the tones are falling;*
> *Open the door for me!*
> *If thou wilt heed My calling,*
> *I will abide with thee.*

("Who At My Door Is Standing" by M.B.C. Slade)

Listen carefully. Is it His knock? Is it His voice?

OCTOBER 10
Isaiah 31-33

"KING, LAW-GIVER, JUDGE"

"For the Lord is our judge; the Lord is our lawgiver;
the Lord is our king; he will save us."
(Isaiah 33:22)

No doubt most of you reading this devotional today are Americans. I am sure you are thankful for that; I know I certainly am. We love our country. We also need to remember that billions of people around the world love their countries too. I must admit embarrassment now because, for some time, I did not understand or appreciate that. I just thought everyone in the world naturally wanted to be Americans, but sadly most were not fortunate enough to have that privilege. In time, I came to understand that patriotism is a quality possessed by people throughout the world.

Patriotism is a wonderful character trait. It is truly a virtue unless, by pride and self-focus, we allow it to become a vice. Patriotism becomes incredibly dangerous when we define ourselves by our earthly citizenship before our heavenly citizenship. "But our citizenship is in heaven, and from it we await a Savior, the Lord Jesus Christ" (Phil. 3:20). Paul wrote those words to the church of Philippi as a gentle reminder. The city of Philippi was an imperial city, which meant that every citizen of Philippi was also a fully enfranchised citizen of Rome. Most of the people in the empire did not possess that status. In his letter, Paul reminded the citizens of Philippi about their ultimate citizenship and their ultimate emperor, King Jesus.

Perhaps a helpful way to evaluate our understanding of our primary citizenship is to honestly ask ourselves, "Am I an American Christian or a Christian American?" Your response to that question might be, "Well, aren't they the same thing?" No, in reality, they are not. One of the words is the object, and one is the modifier. One word, the modifier, adds information to the other, the subject, but they are not equal. There is a world of difference in thinking of yourself as "an American who happens to be a Christian" versus "a Christian who happens to be an American." The words "American" and "Christian" cannot be co-equal; one has to come first. Which comes first in our thinking, focus, loyalty, and devotion?

As Christians in America, we have dual citizenship. We are citizens of an earthly country, and we are citizens of a heavenly kingdom. We have dual citizenship, but we do not have equal *allegiance*. We are sons and daughters and servants of the King. In King Jesus resides the Executive, Legislative, and Judicial branches of His Kingdom. By the grace of God, we have been born again into a government "of the King, by the King, and for the King." What a privilege!

For so many of us, I'm sure a lump rises in our throats as we stand to sing the National Anthem, but may we always remember we only "take a knee" for Jesus.

OCTOBER 11
Isaiah 34-36

"Singing for Sighing"

"And the ransomed of the Lord shall return and come to Zion with singing; everlasting joy shall be upon their heads; they shall obtain gladness and joy, and sorrow and sighing shall flee away."
(Isaiah 35:10)

Israel is a modern miracle in every way. For centuries, the landscape of much of the country was desolate. Over the centuries, this "land of forests" had been stripped of all trees and depopulated of its people to whom it had been given. By 1900, it was estimated that only 25,000 Jewish people lived in the Holy Land. The homeland of the descendants of Abraham, for a centuries-long wilderness season, was primarily a landscape barren of its people and its forests. During the twentieth and early twenty-first centuries, misery and miracles occurred among the people of Israel and the land if Israel. Six million Jewish people were annihilated for the "crime" of being Jewish. The holocaust from hell wiped out 60% of the Jewish population in Europe, representing nearly 40% of the worldwide population. From this unspeakable holocaust came the unimaginable exodus.

Beginning with the devastated and despised remnant from Eastern Europe, Jewish people from around the world returned to their ancient homeland. As they planted themselves on the land, they also planted hundreds of millions of trees. Slowly, the Jewish people irrigated the wilderness and covered the landscape with forests, farms, and vineyards. Today, nearly four million Jewish people live in the state of Israel. And in so many areas, the dry land blossoms like a rose (Isa. 35:1).

It is inconceivable to read Isaiah and the other prophets and fail to recognize the sovereign work of God. What He said would happen has come to pass, but the best is yet to come! The promise given to Isaiah is that one day, "The ransomed of the Lord shall return and come to Zion with singing; everlasting joy shall be upon their heads" (Isa. 35:10). This is the song of the redeemed, not just those of Israel but all the peoples of the earth. In the Messiah, King Jesus, all the nations of the earth are blessed. The promise of the Old Covenant is the promise of the New Covenant. "And it shall come to pass that everyone who calls upon the name of the Lord shall be saved" (Joel 2:32; Acts 2:21; Rom. 10:13). Believers in Jesus are not just marching through time. We are all "marching to Zion." Only God knows how much longer or how much farther we have to travel. But what awaits us is certain: "...they shall obtain gladness and joy, and sorrow and sighing shall flee away" (Isa. 35:10).

OCTOBER 12
Isaiah 37-39

"Lay it Before the Lord"

"Hezekiah received the letter from the hand of the messengers, and read it; and Hezekiah went up to the house of the Lord, and spread it before the Lord."
(Isaiah 37:14)

Many years ago, as a student in seminary, I heard a veteran pastor make this statement in a message to all the assembled ministerial students: "Men, every pastor needs two essential qualities, a tender heart, and a Teflon hide." Most of us as "pastors-to-be" laughed at that unique expression—"a tender heart and a Teflon hide." I heard that over 40 years ago and have never forgotten it. However, it did not take many years in ministry until I fully understood it! The truth is that all of us, as servants of the Lord, need the "tender heart" and "Teflon hide," and only the Lord can provide us with both.

As believers in Jesus, we will face accusations. Sometimes they are deserved, and many times they are not. The culture brings countless charges against Christians and the church. Of course, our enemy, Satan, is "the accuser" who constantly reminds us what miserable failures we are. Most painful are the assaults shouted right in our faces or, more commonly, whispered behind our backs by those who claim to be brothers and sisters in Christ. Regardless of the source of the accusations, how can we respond when condemning words "stick to the Teflon" and threaten to toughen our hearts that need to be kept tender? I think the example of Hezekiah is amazingly helpful.

Hezekiah was denounced and threatened by a public proclamation and a private letter from Sennacherib, the king of Assyria. Beyond that, this wicked invader blasphemed the God of Israel and declared Hezekiah's Lord to be powerless to resist him, just like all the gods of the other nations (Isa. 37:8-13). What did Hezekiah do with such a fearful and hate-filled accusation? He "spread it before the Lord" (37:14). I love that Hezekiah's response was his personal answer to the ridiculing question the royal ambassador had earlier thrown in his face, "Say to Hezekiah, 'Thus says the great king, the king of Assyria: On what do you rest this trust of yours? Do you think that mere words are strategy and power for war?'" (36:4-5a) The enemy's ridicule was exactly the right recommendation for Hezekiah. He would "rest his trust" in the Lord his God, and he would believe that "mere words" offered in prayer "are strategy and power for war" (36:5).

For Hezekiah, God would be his trust, and words of prayer would be his warfare! What a timeless example for us whenever we are accused or attacked! Let the temple of God be our refuge and words of trusting prayer be our weapons. "For the weapons of our warfare are not of the flesh but have divine power to destroy strongholds" (2 Cor. 10:4).

OCTOBER 13
Isaiah 40-42

"THE BIBLE OF ISAIAH"

"Comfort, comfort my people, says your God."
(Isaiah 40:1)

If you have ever viewed copies of the ancient Hebrew or Greek passages in Scripture, I'm sure it made you grateful for chapter and verse divisions of the texts we read today. No numbered chapters or verses, capitalization, periods or commas, or spacing between sentences exist. And perhaps most challenging of all, there are no cross-references in the columns or study notes at the bottom of the page! We are truly blessed today by the excellent efforts of Bible scholars and publishers through the centuries to provide many aids for reading and studying the Word of God.

Having said that, sometimes it seems that the Author of the Book Himself has providentially guided the chapter and verse divisions provided by translators. The Book of Isaiah is a perfect example of this providential printing. Many Bible teachers have noticed how the division of the text of Isaiah, in many ways, causes it to become a "miniature" Bible written within the Bible. Notice that the prophecy of Isaiah is presented in 66 chapters, and we have 66 books of the Bible. (The Bible contains 39 books consisting of the Old Testament and 27 books forming the New Testament.) Our Isaiah reading today has reached the transition point for the "Bible in Isaiah."

The first 39 chapters, similar to the 39 books of the Old Testament, have focused on the pronouncements of judgment by holy God on evil and rebellious people and the warning of an ultimate day of God's wrath against all nations. Yet, Isaiah has also shared glimpses in these 39 chapters of a coming age of peace and restoration with God, which extends throughout the whole earth. How can such a return to paradise be provided in this rebellious, polluted world? The answer is revealed in "the New Testament of Isaiah," Chapters 40-66, 27 chapters that, like the 27 books of the New Testament, convey a worldwide gospel message of redemption.

The transition from the "Old Testament" to the "New Testament" begins with a startling declaration and challenge of good news: "Comfort, comfort my people, says your God" (Isa. 40:1). This New Testament section of Isaiah opens with, "A voice cries: 'In the wilderness prepare the way of the Lord, make straight in the desert a highway for our God'" (Isa. 40:3). These are the exact words of John the Baptist as he called people to repentance for a visitation from the Lord. Focusing their attention on Him, John declared of Jesus, "Behold, the Lamb of God, who takes away the sin of the world!" (John 1:29) Likewise, Isaiah opens this "New Testament" section of his prophecy with the same announcement of God's gospel intervention. "Behold your God!" The Lord comes, Isaiah says, as the Good Shepherd. "He will tend his flock like a shepherd; he will gather the lambs in his arms; he will carry them in his bosom, and gently lead those that are with young" (Isa. 40:11).

As we read the coming chapters, take some time (beginning right now) to savor the gospel promises in the "New Testament" of Isaiah.

"He gives power to the faint, and to him who has no might he increases strength. Even youths shall faint and be weary, and young men shall fall exhausted; but they who wait for the Lord shall renew their strength; they shall mount up with wings like eagles; they shall run and not be weary; they shall walk and not faint."
(Isaiah 40:29-31)

OCTOBER 14
Isaiah 43-45

"LOOK AND LIVE!"

During the night and early morning hours of Sunday, January 6, 1850, a blizzard covered the southern section of England with a deep blanket of snow. Since it was a Sunday, the streets of Colchester were empty of traffic, and almost all the citizens were huddled indoors near the stoves and fireplaces to keep warm. The churches were closed, and the scheduled services were canceled. Regardless, one young man of 15 dressed as warmly as possible and, against the bitter wind, trudged the city's lanes looking for a place to worship. His slumped shoulders and downward gaze mirrored the posture of his spirit, for he was under a deep burden and heavy conviction regarding his spiritual condition and relationship with Almighty God. He believed himself to be lost, and try as he might in Bible reading and prayer, he was without peace and confidence in the love and mercy of God. He was desperate for a word from the Lord to brighten his darkness with the hope of salvation.

Wandering the deserted streets, the young man heard the faint sound of singing and, following those voices, soon found himself standing in a tiny Methodist church where a few faithful members had gathered for the service despite the dreadful weather. After some hymns were sung and Scriptures read, it was apparent the minister would not be arriving to bring the message. Not wanting the faithful few to go home without a word of encouragement and exhortation, an elderly deacon stepped into the pulpit and read a verse that was on his heart, "Look unto me, and be ye saved, all the ends of the earth: for I am God, and there is none else" (Isa. 45:22 KJV).

The deacon then, clumsily but with great conviction, exhorted the people to look in simple and sincere faith to God for the salvation provided through Christ. Then, with his eyes falling on the sad countenance of the youthful guest in the back row, the deacon shared with him a personal challenge, "Young man, you look very miserable today, and miserable you will remain for all your life and all eternity unless you look to Christ for salvation. Look...look to Christ!" It was that simple but sincere exhortation that God used to shine His light of salvation. In the years to come, that young man would testify that on that wintry morning, he did look; he looked with all his heart. With spiritual illumination, by God's grace, he saw the beautiful face of His personal Savior, Jesus Christ. He looked by faith to God, and he was gloriously saved.

Over the coming decades, and, yes, until this day, the voice and pen of that "very miserable young man" has brought the joyful good news of God's salvation to "the ends of the earth." His name? Charles Haddon

Spurgeon, the "Prince of Preachers." Very few people, if any, have been able to preach the gospel better than Spurgeon. But none has had a better gospel to preach than the gospel declared that day by the faithful Methodist deacon. It is the same gospel for each of us, and it is our privilege to share it with others:

> *"Look to Me, and be saved,*
> *all you ends of the earth!*
> *For I am God, and there is no other."*
> (Isaiah 45:22, NKJV)

OCTOBER 15
Isaiah 46-48

"INFINITE, INTIMATE GOD"

"Listen to me, O house of Jacob, all the remnant of the house of Israel,
who have been borne by me from before your birth, carried from the womb;
even to your old age I am he, and to gray hairs I will carry you.
I have made, and I will bear; I will carry and will save."
(Isaiah 46:3-4)

As a young boy, I recall approaching my mother and asking her my first theological question, "Mom, where did God come from?" I am not exactly sure why I asked her that question, and I don't remember the specifics of her answer. I do recall not being entirely satisfied with the response but also thinking it might be best *not* to let her know I was not satisfied. Somehow my mind had awakened to the idea that God was eternal, but in my childish literalness, I just couldn't understand. After all, I had a mom and dad, they had a mom and dad, and everyone has a mom and dad, but who were God's mom and dad? I clearly remember lying in my bed one night and trying to understand that God was the one person who did not have parents. I turned the idea over and over in my mind until it felt like my brain was spinning and aching from trying to understand what it meant for God to have no beginning.

Thankfully the infinite, eternal Lord does not expect us, as finite beings, to "wrap our minds around" His unknowable nature. However, the infinite God does want us to find rest and peace in His intimate care and concern for us as His people. To communicate just how personal, deep, and lasting His love is, the Lord, in one of the most remarkable Bible passages, describes His relationship to us as both our mother and father (Isa. 46:3-4). Jehovah says His people, the house of Jacob, "have been borne by me from before your birth, carried from the womb." What a startling image! Like a mother, God bears and gives birth to a baby, and then, like a delighted father, God carries the infant in His arms. The baby, the child of God, grows up and eventually grows old, yet ageless God, the ever-strong Father, promises, "even to your old age I am he, and to gray hairs I will carry you" (Isa. 46:4). How sweet is that promise!

In my mind's eye, I can still see the little blond-haired boy asking his mom, "Where did God come from?" Now the little boy has grown old, and his blond hair is gray and thin. With decades of learning and study, he still cannot comprehend the answer to the question he asked his mother so long ago. Yet, as he writes these words today, the little boy grown old can share a witness, as no doubt many who are reading this page can. God has kept His promise: "I have made, and I will bear; I will carry and will save" (Isa. 46:4).

OCTOBER 16
Isaiah 49-51

"THE WORLDVIEW OF JESUS"

"It is too light a thing that you should be my servant to raise up the tribes of Jacob and to bring back the preserved of Israel; I will make you as a light for the nations, that my salvation may reach to the end of the earth."
(Isaiah 49:6)

One of the most beautiful and yet startling of all the statements made in Scripture is shared by the anonymous author of the book of Hebrews. Concluding and applying the brief history of the "heroes of the faith" in Chapter 11, the inspired writer challenges the present generation of believers with these timeless words: "Therefore, since we are surrounded by so great a cloud of witnesses, let us also lay aside every weight, and sin which clings so closely, and let us run with endurance the race that is set before us, looking to Jesus, the founder and perfecter of our faith, who for the joy that was set before him endured the cross, despising the shame, and is seated at the right hand of the throne of God" (Heb. 12:1-2). Read those words again and especially note the phrase *"who for the joy that was set before Him endured the cross..."* The writer is telling us that even though Jesus despised the cross and all that it would mean, He endured it for the sake *"of joy... a joy that was set before him."* That is a *future joy.*

This stunning realization begs the question, what did Jesus see that filled His heart with a joy greater than the detestable horror of the cross? The answer is that Jesus could see a purpose in His suffering that would fulfill the Father's promise shared through the message of Isaiah. Lifted up on the cross, Jesus could see beyond the crowd beneath Him and beyond Jerusalem before Him. He could see beyond the horizon of time and know that because of His suffering on this darkest of days, He would rise "as a light for the nations," bringing the Father's salvation "to the end of the earth" (Isa. 49:6). It was this mission that brought Jesus from heaven to earth. Jesus knew in His heart that it was the completion of the mission which would ultimately bring heaven and earth together in Him. The view from the cross was a worldview for Christ, and His eyes could see untold billions of exiled sons and daughters of Adam returning to paradise and life with the Father. Jesus saw this and rejoiced in His spirit.

Now, heaven and earth enter into His joy. "Sing for joy, O heavens, and exult, O earth; break forth, O mountains, into singing! For the Lord has comforted His people and will have compassion on his afflicted" (Isa. 49:13).

This message of "comfort and joy" is for us who believe in more than just a phrase from a Christmas carol. It is the joy of the Lord that we share in Jesus. The incredible reality is that we are the joy of Jesus. He saw us from the cross and, in joy, purchased our salvation with His own blood. He bears in His glorified body today the scars of His love for us, "Behold, I have engraved you on the palms of my hands..." (Isa. 49:16) Little children often sing the song, "He's Got the Whole World in His Hands," and that is truly a wonderful thought. Jesus, with outstretched arms on the cross, took the whole world in His hands. Look closely at His hands, Christian friend, for your name is engraved there.

OCTOBER 17
Isaiah 52-54

"THE GREAT EXCHANGE"

"But he was pierced for our transgressions;
he was crushed for our iniquities;
upon him was the chastisement that brought us peace,
and with his wounds we are healed.
All we like sheep have gone astray;
we have turned—every one—to his own way;
and the Lord has laid on him the iniquity of us all."
(Isaiah 53:5-6)

A locomotive passenger train was slowly pulling away from the station many years ago. Frantically, a young man rushed to catch it. He had run for miles through the city streets to speak personally with the renowned evangelist Dwight Moody, who had concluded a series of gospel services the previous evening. Dr. Moody stood on the passenger car platform, waving farewell to the large crowd as the train pulled from the station. Just then, the young man emerged from the crowd chasing after the evangelist. "Dr. Moody! Dr. Moody!" he cried, "I heard you preach last night, and I am so lost! What shall I do, what shall I do?" Unable to step off the train as it increased in speed, the evangelist raised both hands, forming a megaphone for his voice, and shouted to the young man, "Isaiah 53, verse 6! Go in at the first 'all,' come out at the second 'all,' and you will be all right!"

The troubled young man did not understand what Dr. Moody meant, but he quickly searched through the Bible he had clutched in his hand as he ran to find the evangelist that morning. Locating verse 6 in Isaiah, Chapter 53, as the evangelist had challenged, the young man located the first "all"—"all we like sheep have gone astray." That is certainly true of me, thought the young man. Then reading on, he found the second "all"—"and the Lord has laid on him the iniquity of us all." Those words almost leaped off the page with light for the young man's darkness, "My sins have been laid on Jesus. Jesus died for me!" Faith and joy flooded his soul, and in sobs of surrender, the young man gave his life to Christ.

Isaiah 53:6 could be called the John 3:16 of the Old Testament. It is the heart of "The Gospel According to Isaiah." In Isaiah's words, we are told of the "great exchange" accomplished by our Shepherd on behalf of us, His sheep. "Like a lamb, He is led to the slaughter," and our Shepherd did this for us who "like sheep have gone astray." He took "our iniquities," our "stripes" were lashed out on Him, and our chastisement fell on Messiah. What did He give us in exchange? Peace with God through our Lord Jesus Christ (Rom. 5:1). We often speak of "free grace" and thank God that is true. Free for us, but at what a price for our Lord!

What an exchange! The "all" of our sin for the "all" of His atonement. Hallelujah! What a Savior!

OCTOBER 18
Isaiah 55-57

"Royal Residences"

*"For thus says the One who is high and lifted up,
who inhabits eternity, whose name is Holy:
'I dwell in the high and holy place,
and also with him who is of a contrite and lowly spirit,
to revive the spirit of the lowly, and to revive the heart of the contrite.'"*
(Isaiah 57:15)

You can tell a lot about people from where they choose to live. Perhaps I should rephrase that to say you can tell a lot about *some* people by where they choose to live. Billions of people on the earth live in such abject poverty that the very thought of having *a choice* about where they live is inconceivable to them. However, where people choose to live when they can make that choice reveals a great deal about their values and self-identity.

A few days ago, during a family discussion, the conversation turned to the lifestyle choices of some very prominent Christian leaders. The focus eventually shifted to two individuals who rose from very humble circumstances and achieved national and international notoriety at about the same time several years ago. These two pastors and authors wrote books that sold staggering numbers of copies. One sold over 8 million copies and the other an astounding 30 million copies. How the two pastors responded to their new-found riches revealed much about them. The author of the "8-million-copies" moved from his house valued at nearly $3 million to a sprawling estate valued at nearly $11 million. The pastor who authored the "30-million-copies" responded a little differently. He continued living in his modest home and driving his SUV, which was several years old. In addition, the pastor paid back to his church all the salary he had received throughout his entire ministry. Finally, the pastor and his wife committed to becoming "reverse tithers," giving 90% of their income to the Lord's work and living off the remaining 10%.

It is not my place or my intention to judge the motives behind either of these pastors' choices regarding their sudden wealth. However, it is clear to see with *whom* these men chose to identify by *where* they chose to live. One decided to move and live among the palatial mansions of the uber-rich, while the other chose to remain among the middle-class neighbors his family had known for years.

The Bible tells us that God is the ultimate and rightful owner of all, "The earth is the Lord's and the fullness thereof, the world and those who dwell therein..." (Ps. 24:1). Beyond that, the entire creation and all of time itself is God's "home." Isaiah shares in the verse cited above, "For thus says the One who is high and lifted up, who inhabits eternity, whose name is Holy: 'I dwell in the high and holy place...'" (Isa. 57:15) Our great God's dwelling place is the eternal heaven, and His address is eternity. Yet, where is God's *home*? Where is His *residence*? God chooses to live among and identify with people of a "contrite and lowly spirit" (Isa. 57:15). Our infinite God identifies with the humble... those whose spirits are broken and contrite over their spiritual condition.

This extraordinary truth about God challenges us to consider a few questions personally and carefully. First, is my heart attractive to real estate for my God? Does the God of heaven who loves to dwell among the humble find in my heart a "humble abode"? Also, how at home do I feel among the "lowly" of the world? My Lord identifies with the broken places and broken people. Do I?

OCTOBER 19
Isaiah 58-60

"The Story of Hope"

"Arise, shine, for your light has come, and the glory of the Lord has risen upon you. For behold, darkness shall cover the earth, and thick darkness the peoples; but the Lord will arise upon you, and his glory will be seen upon you. And nations shall come to your light, and kings to the brightness of your rising."
(Isaiah 60:1-3)

Following an evening city-wide evangelistic service, an active member and leader in one of the participating churches approached the preacher. "Brother," he said, "I don't care at all for the way you are presenting the gospel." "Well, I am very sad to hear that," replied the minister. "Might I ask how *you* share the gospel?" "That's just the point," answered the frustrated church leader, "I don't share it." "Well, I must say, I like my way better than your way!" replied the evangelist.

In reality, there are innumerable "methods" taught and presented in print and social media about how to engage people with the gospel. I have been personally helped and encouraged by several of these training seminars over the years. In fact, I have been a teacher and trainer of several of them. While I have seen many people equipped as witnesses for Christ, I have also noted that many people are more focused on the *presentation* than on the *person* to whom they are speaking.

Another weakness I have observed in some of the evangelism training courses is that they often assume a basic understanding of Bible information by the person receiving the witness. The harsh reality is that the vast majority of people in other parts of the world, and now a majority of the people in our own culture, have practically no understanding of the Bible or how Jesus fits into and fulfills that story. "Story" is a great place to begin, adjusting our gospel methods for witnessing to a biblically illiterate world. The "story" is clear and straightforward: God, creation, mankind, rebellion, curse, Christ's crucifixion, resurrection, grace, return, judgment, and eternity. These are the key points of the "meta-narrative," the "big story" of the Bible. It is the story of hope, and the "good news" of the gospel. There are many presentations of this gospel in the Bible; each is unique, but they all share the "one gospel."

In our reading today in Isaiah, we hear Isaiah share prophetically the "story of hope." Mankind is separated by his sins from God and from fellowship with Him (Isa. 59:1-8). No one is capable of changing their nature or doing what is right in God's eyes (Isa. 59:9-15). However, in His infinite, marvelous grace, God has taken it upon Himself to provide salvation for lost and hopeless sinners, accomplishing a new covenant that creates a new heart and brings new life (Isa. 59:16-20). This "story of hope" in Messiah is to shine through the darkness covering the peoples of the earth and bring them to the light of eternal salvation and His kingdom, which in its fullness, darkness will be banished forever. The Lord Himself will be the light eternal. "The sun shall be no more your light by day, nor for brightness shall the moon give you light; but the Lord will be your everlasting light, and your God will be your glory" (Isa. 60:19).

What a story of hope! Is it *your* hope? If so, share this story of your hope whenever and with whomever you can. Just tell the story, and watch God work!

OCTOBER 20
Isaiah 61-63

"The Text of Jesus"

"The Spirit of the Lord God is upon me, because the Lord has anointed me to bring good news to the poor; he has sent me to bind up the brokenhearted, to proclaim liberty to the captives, and the opening of the prison to those who are bound; to proclaim the year of the Lord's favor, and the day of vengeance of our God; to comfort all who mourn."
(Isaiah 61:1-2)

Nazareth was a very small town in Jesus' day, probably having no more than 300-400 citizens. Everyone in the community knew everyone else, and in one way or another, all the citizens' lives were interconnected. It had always been that way for as long as anyone could remember. It was to this community Joseph, Mary, and their little son, Jesus, settled after their return from Egypt, where they had migrated shortly after the baby's birth. As the years passed, Jesus became known as an excellent and dependable carpenter, a faithful provider for his widowed mother, Mary, and an incredibly gifted teacher of God's Word.

He had been noted for His amazing knowledge and understanding of the Torah since childhood. So it was not uncommon for Him to be selected for reading and teaching the Scriptures at the weekly sabbath services. In fact, Jesus was most assuredly the favorite among all those who instructed the community when the people gathered for worship. It seemed like Jesus always brought some new insight to the congregation from the Word.

However, nothing could have prepared the audience for what Jesus said one sabbath morning. He had requested from the officer of the synagogue the scroll of Isaiah for public reading at the service. Having found the passage cited above in the scroll, Jesus distinctly read from the text; but then, unexpectedly for those familiar with Isaiah's prophecy, Jesus stopped the reading mid-sentence "to proclaim the year of the Lord's favor." Without concluding the sentence, Jesus rolled and closed the scroll, and handed it back to the attendant. Then, waiting until every eye in the synagogue was fixed upon him, Jesus astounded the audience with this statement, "Today this Scripture has been fulfilled in your hearing" (Luke 4:18-21).

There could be no doubt about it. Jesus, the local carpenter, their favorite teacher who had recently begun to preach in nearby communities as well, was declaring to be the Messiah, the fulfillment of the dreams of Israel for hundreds of years. Jesus continued teaching that morning, but His sermon was rather rudely interrupted as the audience dragged him from the pulpit, through the streets, and to the nearby cliff in an attempt to execute him for blasphemy. Jesus stopped them with the same simple authority with which He had stopped His reading from Isaiah.

Jesus never finished his sermon in Nazareth, but one day He will finish the remainder of His text from that day. The pause in His reading of Isaiah 61:2 has lasted for over 2,000 years as "the year of the Lord's favor," that is, the season of the good news of the Kingdom and the King has been "proclaimed" to all the people groups of the world. Perhaps soon, the "year of the Lord's favor" will conclude, and Jesus will finish his text—"and the day of the vengeance of our God; to comfort all who mourn" (Isa. 61:2). The Day of the Lord will come as Jesus the King returns, bringing judgment for His enemies and eternal comfort for His people. What a day that will be! What a privilege to be included in Jesus' reading of His text! What a joy to be present one day when He finishes His sermon!

OCTOBER 21
Isaiah 64-66

"WAITING AND WILLING"

"Oh that you would rend the heavens and come down,
that the mountains might quake at your presence—[1]
But now, O Lord, you are our Father;
we are the clay, and you are our potter;
we are all the work of your hand."[8]
(Isaiah 64:1, 8)

I like to think of myself as a patient man. It is my opinion that I am patient will all types of people except those who refer to me as impatient. This can make things challenging in my home because the only person who ever calls into question my patience is my wife. Of course, as much as I hate to admit it, she has ample evidence to prove the case that I do struggle with patience. Guilty as charged. My personal expression of impatience is unusual because it is generally directed at situations and circumstances rather than people. With this evaluation, even my wife agrees! Perhaps at times, you share my forms of impatience. If that is the case, let me share what I have come to understand about my impatience with situations and circumstances in my life. In reality, my impatience is ultimately with God. As challenging as it is to admit that, and as long as it has taken me to recognize that flaw in my character, the truth is I have a very strong tendency to want life to follow my well-made plans and carefully crafted timetables.

I am learning that waiting is a big part of my growth in faith and spiritual formation. Waiting reminds me that *life* is not about *me*. Waiting also rebukes my selfish bent to believe *my life* is about *me*. It isn't. My life is all about *Him* and *them* (other people). That is why I (and you) are on this planet—*Him* and *them*. Jesus put it this way, "You shall love the Lord your God with all your heart and with all your soul and with all your mind... You shall love your neighbor as yourself" (Matt. 22:37, 39). The Apostle Peter reminds us that this love for others should cause us to patiently embrace God's patience in His timetable of redemption. "The Lord is not slow to fulfill his promise as some count slowness, but is patient toward you, not wishing that any should perish, but that all should reach repentance... And count the patience of our Lord as salvation" (2 Peter 3:9, 15).

While we are waiting and *awaiting* the Lord, He is always at work in the world globally and in us personally. We should be patient with God's work in both. With regard to *waiting* as He "works on us," our waiting can become *worship*. Isaiah shows us the way. "But now, O Lord, you are our Father; we are the clay, and you are our potter; we are all the work of your hand" (Isa. 64:8). The wheel spins at the Potter's rhythm and the pressure of His hands is determined by Him. May we never forget as we wait that His hands are nail-scarred by His perfect love for us.

> *Have thine own way Lord!*
> *Have Thine own way!*
> *Thou art the potter,*
> *I am the clay.*
> *Mold me and make me*
> *after thy will,*
> *while I am waiting,*
> *yielded and still.*

("Have Thine Own Way, Lord" by Adelaide A. Pollard)

OCTOBER 22
Jeremiah 1-3

"ON PURPOSE"

> *"Before I formed you in the womb I knew you,*
> *and before you were born I consecrated you;*
> *I appointed you a prophet to the nations."*
> (Jeremiah 1:5)

Over the last several years in America, when controversial subjects such as climate change or dealing with the COVID virus have been discussed on social media platforms, a common challenge that has been issued is "follow the science." Generally, this statement has been made to communicate that the truth about these two issues should be separated from personally held values. "Just follow the science" has been the statement made time and time again to communicate that decisions should be made on "objective data" and not on personally held opinions, and most certainly not on the basis of personal faith.

Interestingly, I have found it strange that the "just follow the science" challenge has not been used by the advocates of a woman's "right" to obtain an abortion. On that issue, the "champions of reproductive rights" never promote the cause by appealing to science but by declaring unequivocally that every woman has a right to determine what she does with her own body. Why is there never, it seems, a plea to "follow the science" on the issue of abortion? The reason is simple. Science leads to the conclusion that the baby forming in a woman's womb is actually not her body at all. It is a different human being. Science has made very clear what God has informed us in His Word through the ages. Every baby is a unique individual specifically created by Him. To deny this is to deny science, deny conscience, and deny God.

What God told Jeremiah about his own existence, each of us can also claim, and we desperately need to trust, regarding the reason we are on this planet at this specific time. None of us is an accident. There ultimately is no such thing as an "illegitimate baby." The parents may not have been "legitimate" in their actions, but no person created by God can be called illegitimate because each one of us is a legitimate creation by Him. Each of us was created *on purpose* and *for a purpose*. We may often ask what that purpose is, but we usually do this in questions regarding specific situations or decisions we face. I have found that the answer to the specific questions is generally answered by acknowledging and following the "bigger truths" about my life on this planet.

You and I have been made in God's image (Gen. 1:27), and through the power of His Spirit, the Lord's purpose is to form us more and more into the image of His Son, Jesus (Rom. 8:29). We also share with Jeremiah another great purpose in our lives, which is to share the message of God. We may not be prophets, yet we are all messengers for the Lord, ambassadors for Jesus (2 Cor. 5:20). Like Jeremiah, the Lord has "put my words in your mouth" (Jer. 1:9). Made by God, made in His image, and made for His message. Now, that is quite a purpose!

OCTOBER 23
Jeremiah 4-6

"Painless Poison"

"They have healed the wound of my people lightly, saying, 'Peace, peace,' when there is no peace."
(Jeremiah 6:14)

Neville Chamberlain, the prime minister of England, stood smiling into the crowd of news reporters and photographers as he held up a piece of paper that fluttered gently in the breeze, saying that he believed it represented "peace for our time." The paper was a promise made in "good faith" by the leader of Germany that with the acquisition of Czechoslovakia, he would make no more territorial demands in Europe. Of course, as we know now, the value of that promise was less than the paper Mr. Chamberlain joyfully held in his hand and the cost of believing it would be millions of lives over the next few years. Too late, the prime minister and the majority of leaders in Great Britain learned that in dealing with Adolph Hitler, they were dealing with a devil. Devils cannot be trusted, whether they be political devils or religious devils. They speak words of peace from their lips, but war is in their hearts.

Throughout his ministry for God, Jeremiah was opposed by the religious leaders. This, on the surface, would seem strange indeed; after all, was not the religion of Judah the worship of Jehovah? However, it is in religion that the Devil does some of his best work. Satan recognizes that the need to worship is inherent in all people, so he uses that desire for religion to his perverse advantage. Behind the soothing works of peace, he carries out war. He did this in Jeremiah's day through "prophets for profits," saying, "'Peace, peace,' when there is no peace" (Jer. 6:14). The Devil carried out this same strategy in Jesus' day when the religious leaders were "teaching as doctrines the commandments of men" (Matt. 15:9). Apostle Paul warned believers in his day about "peace-speaking preachers" who would, in reality, be ministers of Satan, disguising themselves as ministers of righteousness (2 Cor. 11:15).

Our day is no different from the days and ages that have preceded us, but the dangers are the same. All of us have a natural tendency to be drawn to the path of least resistance and least distance. The smooth words of writers, teachers, and influencers can draw us to the smooth and easy way of a comfortable Christianity. We take that journey at the peril of our souls, forgetting that our Savior warned us of the "broad, easy road" that leads us to destruction. Our Lord bids us to take the "crossroad"—"take up his cross and follow me" (Matt. 16:24-26). The way of the cross, the way of following Jesus, is never the easiest path to take. However, it is the true path of peace—peace of mind and soul. Listen to the voice of the ever-truthful Prince of Peace today: "Come to me, all who labor and are heavy laden, and I will give you rest" (Matt. 11:28).

OCTOBER 24
Jeremiah 7-9

"Harvest Past, Summer Ended"

"The harvest is past, the summer is ended, and we are not saved."[20]
Is there no balm in Gilead? Is there no physician there?
Why then has the health of the daughter of my people
not been restored?"[22]
(Jeremiah 8:20, 22)

A few years ago, my wife and I were invited to speak at a training conference in Romania for pastors, wives of pastors, and women in ministry. It was an amazing privilege to spend several days with some of the most humble and devoted servants of the Lord we have ever had the privilege to meet. As I write these words, Susan and I look forward to seeing our friends in Romania again and spending several more days in fellowship around the Word of God and prayer. An added blessing during our trip to Romania a few years ago was the opportunity to enjoy a layover in Paris and spend a few days exploring and experiencing that beautiful city. As a certified history geek, I made sure that part of one day was spent touring the famed Cathedral of Notre Dame. It was magnificent, but perhaps even more beautiful and also intriguing to me was the historic Cathedral of St. Denis.

This ancient church, located just north of Paris, is famous for its breathtaking stained-glass windows and the fact that it has been the final resting place of almost all France monarchs for 1,000 years. The tombs of some of the most powerful men and women surround the beautiful altar and fill the royal vaults beneath. While I walked among these royal tombs, I learned a startling fact. No one knows whose bones are resting within the various tombs. During the Reign of Terror marking the French Revolution of the 1790s, the general assembly passed a law calling for the desecration of the royal tombs. As a result, the burial vaults at St. Denis were pried open, the treasures pillaged, and the bones of royalty were dumped into the pits dug outside the cathedral's walls. By order of Napoleon years later, the bones were regathered from these mass graves and restored to the vaults, yet there was no way of knowing which bones went into which vaults.

It is hard to imagine the bones of kings and queens treated this way. Yet, we read in our passage today that God declared the bones of kings, priests, and prophets to "be brought out of their tombs. And they shall be spread before the sun and the moon and all the hosts of heaven, which they have loved and served..." (Jer. 8:1-2) It is hard to imagine the beloved city of Jerusalem being the site of such desecration. Yet, in His justice, the Lord rendered to the idol-worshiping rulers and leaders of Judah precisely what they loved in life.

The greatest tragedy is that it did not have to come to such a revolting result. For generations, God, as the Great Physician, offered to heal the nation and restore the health of His beloved people. Through the years, the Lord offered mercy, pardon, and forgiveness. Yet, the people "Heaping oppression upon oppression, and deceit upon deceit, they *refuse to know me*, declares the Lord" (Jer. 9:6). Now, the consequences of their rebellious choices have come. "I will scatter them among the nations whom neither they nor their fathers have known, and I will send the sword after them, until I have consumed them" (Jer. 9:16). The harvest always comes. "Do not be deceived: God is not mocked, for whatever one sows, that will he also reap" (Gal. 6:7).

OCTOBER 25
Jeremiah 10-12

"SCARED OF THE SCARECROWS?"

*"Their idols are like scarecrows in a cucumber field,
and they cannot speak; they have to be carried,
for they cannot walk. Do not be afraid of them,
for they cannot do evil, neither is it in them to do good."*
(Jeremiah 10:5)

My wife and I were exhausted after a very long day and night of travel to participate in a Bible conference and were almost asleep on our feet as we waited in a hotel lobby to check into our room for the night. You can imagine our frustration as we stood in line at the counter and waited for the two men at the head of the line to stop arguing with the desk clerk. It was impossible not to overhear the conversation as the men became increasingly loud and agitated, demanding that they be given another room. Our fatigue was eventually overcome by amazement about why the men were so adamant about not accepting the room that had been reserved for them. The men were determined not to stay in that room and demanded another one because *the room number was unlucky.* You read the last phrase correctly; the two men were afraid to stay in that room (and they succeeded in transferring to another one) because the combination of the numbers on the room door would bring them bad luck.

I must admit that my initial reaction to their objection was one of exhausted anger at their ridiculous superstitions. However, it was not long until both Susan and I sensed deep sadness that these two clearly successful businessmen could be under the domination of such spiritual fear. They were not atheists; no, their religion actually enslaved them. Whatever "god" they worshiped did not have enough power to free them from the perceived power of random numbers on the door of a hotel room. The tragedy of such a "faith" should never be lost on us, for it is certainly not lost on God. Human beings made in His image surrender their birthright freedom to images they themselves construct and often carry from place to place. The governing principle of their lives is founded on items they create, move, build, or destroy. Is there a bondage more dreadful than religious bondage, a faith that does not overcome fear but pledges allegiance to it?

The ancient world was completely engulfed in the superstitious fear produced by idolatry. Sadly, that expression of fear-based worship still exists today and is often deceptively displayed in what passes for Christianity. It is not of God. Fear is not of God, for God is love and the love of God in our heart conquers fear. The apostle John tells us that the person who lives in fear has not yet become strong in love (1 John 4:18). As believers, we fear the Lord; that is, we reverence Him for His greatness and glory (Prov. 9:10). Yet, we live in godly fear (1 Peter 2:17), which is awe-inspired love for the One who has loved us with an everlasting love (Jer. 31:3). What God commands more than anything else in His Word is this, "Fear Not." Your Father is the everlasting, all-powerful, ever-present God of heaven and earth. Fear not indeed!

OCTOBER 26
Jeremiah 13-15

"Sweetness for our Sorrows"

*"Your words were found, and I ate them,
and your words became to me a joy and the delight of my heart,
for I am called by your name, O Lord, God of hosts."*
(Jeremiah 15:16)

Judah had passed that point, not necessarily a date on a calendar or a specific national moment, but Judah had passed the point of no return. The country continued to carry out daily government activities, the population practiced the various rhythms of life as families and communities, and even the religious leaders fulfilled the prescribed temple worship rituals; but it was over. There was no hope for the nation because God had made His decision to bring judgment on Judah, and that decision was final. "Then the Lord said to me, 'Though Moses and Samuel stood before me, yet my heart would not turn toward this people. Send them out of my sight, and let them go!'" (Jer. 15:1) What a dreadful condition for any people or any person when the Lord says, "I'm Done!" Hope is truly gone when God no longer offers it.

We can only imagine the heartache the reality of this hopeless situation brought to the heart of Jeremiah. No wonder he is called "the weeping prophet." He knew in his heart that his beloved nation was destined for destruction. Yet, in these darkest of times and most bitter of seasons for his country, Jeremiah bears witness of a sweetness he personally experienced in the Word of God. The Word of the Lord became a feast for his soul amid the spiritual desert of the culture surrounding him. God's Word became a source of joy and delight for Jeremiah, constantly reminding him that he was called, known, and loved by the Lord (Jer. 15:16).

It is impossible to read through the chapters of Jeremiah and not consider the condition of our world and, specifically, the moral darkness in the United States. Recently, my heart was grieved as I listened to a 100-year-old veteran of WWII in broken-hearted tears say that what he and his comrades fought and died to save was not the America that now exists. Has our nation crossed that same line as Judah did in rebelling and turning from God? Has God given up on America? Is it too late for a return to God? Only God knows when a nation has crossed that line. Still, when we compare our government's sinful, godless values with those of ancient Israel and Judah, it is impossible to think that the United States is not headed for a similar Divine judgment. However, we must always remember that revival is not a blessing the Lord brings to governments. Revival and spiritual renewal are always a blessing to God's people. The question is not whether America will have revival but will the church have revival. And beyond that is the question, "Will *I* experience revival?"

The rebellion of our country can never rob us of revival. That experience of renewed faith, joy, and peace is freely offered to every person who will turn to God, the Giver of life, and the Reviver of the doubters, the depressed, and the discouraged. Jesus still shares in the present darkness the promise He made to His disciples that final Passover night. "So also you have sorrow now, but I will see you again, and your hearts will rejoice, and no one will take your joy from you" (John 16:22).

OCTOBER 27
Jeremiah 16-18

"SHRUBS OR EVERGREENS?"

> *"Blessed is the man who trusts in the Lord,*
> *whose trust is the Lord.*
> *He is like a tree planted by water,*
> *that sends out its roots by the stream,*
> *and does not fear when heat comes,*
> *for its leaves remain green,*
> *and is not anxious in the year of drought,*
> *for it does not cease to bear fruit."*
> (Jeremiah 17:7-8)

Arizona is beautiful. The fact that both of my visits to that state have been in January rather than July has much to do with my impression. No place is beautiful when it is 112 degrees in the shade! However, Arizona is truly remarkable to visit in the harshest weeks of winter. Warm sunshine, low humidity, and spectacular sunsets are everyday occurrences during that season. On one visit to the Phoenix area several years ago, my wife and I had the opportunity to take a hike on a nature preserve. The path was just a little different from what we experience in

Eastern Tennessee! The trail was along a barren rocky path that meandered through a sparse grove of cacti and shrubs, and there were signs at regular intervals warning hikers to watch for rattlesnakes! It did not take Susan and me very long to be satisfied with our experience of the Arizona wilderness and make our way back to the vehicle. Though our hike was brief, I still remember how amazed we were at how those desert shrubs eked out enough water in that wilderness ecosystem compared to the lush green vegetation that easily thrives along the mountain streams in our area. Water changes everything; water means life.

It is beautiful how many times in the Bible, the Lord compares Himself to life-giving water. He flows with life, and like a nourishing, limitless stream, God promises to abundantly sustain all who trust in Him. Regardless of the desert-like environment of this world, those who trust in Jehovah are planted like a tree next to a stream—rooted, strong, ever-green, always bearing fruit. No drought can harm us, for there is no limit to the "streams in the desert" that flow from the Lord. "All who are thirsty, come to me and drink," is the invitation of Jesus (John 7:37-38). This world offers no life-giving water. People who seek satisfaction in the world's provision will find that this world only provides "broken cisterns that can hold no water" (Jer. 2:13). The "oasis-like" lifestyle promised by the world turns out to be a mirage. The person who pursues this deception will find, "He is like a shrub in the desert, and shall not see any good come. He shall dwell in the parched places of the wilderness, in an uninhabited salt land" (Jer. 17:6). Why live a shrub-like existence when living water flows for all who trust in the Lord? Put your roots of trust down deep today into His flowing life. Fear no heat and be anxious about no drought.

OCTOBER 28
Jeremiah 19-21

"SIMMERING SILENCE"

"If I say, 'I will not mention him, or speak any more in his name,' there is in my heart as it were a burning fire shut up in my bones, and I am weary with holding it in, and I cannot."
(Jeremiah 20:9)

I can distinctly recall the sound of my mom's pressure cooker chattering away in the kitchen of the small house where I was raised. I admit I was a little afraid of that cooker, especially after asking my mom what would happen if the round metal valve on top ever stopped clattering and spinning. "Well, it would blow up because all that pressure has to be released continually," was my mother's answer. From then on, I kept a safe distance from that cooker.

Jeremiah would have identified with that pressure cooker. In many ways, life was like a pressure cooker inside and out for him. Jeremiah lived in a pressure cooker culture that continually exerted its force upon him and his ministry. To say that Jeremiah was not popular in Judah would be the epitome of understatements. He was generally castigated and condemned by the general population. He was considered a troublemaker by the ruling officials and despised by the "ministerial association" of religious leaders. People just wanted Jeremiah to shut up, and he certainly desired to accommodate them. In fact, on occasion, he would try his best to keep silent, but he could not do it. Why? Because he was a man on a mission with a message, and neither the mission nor the message was his. Jeremiah had been ordained and appointed a prophet before he was born (Jer. 1:5), and as a prophet for Jehovah, his mission was to share God's message. When Jeremiah attempted to remain silent with God's message, he became like a pressure cooker without a release valve, "I am weary with holding it in, and I cannot" (Jer. 20:9).

We live in an era often described as a "cancel culture." Faithful Christian witnesses, if not outright canceled by the "media masters" who control most forms of social communication, often find themselves overwhelmed by an avalanche of online scorn and abuse for sharing God's Word. So, what is a Christian to do? Simply shut up? Sadly, some have done so. But how can "ambassadors for God" cease speaking for the King? We fail our Master and His mission if we do so.

Yet, we must never allow the external pressure of the culture to cause us to "blow up in anger." The only thing worse than submissive silence is a religious rant. Jesus was "the Word become flesh," and His words were full of "grace and truth" (John 1:14). "The spirits of prophets are subject to prophets" (1 Cor. 14:32). As the Lord's messengers, we are never to be out of control; but, controlled by the Spirit, we *must* speak for God. We cannot keep silent. If persecution is the price we pay, then let us praise the Lord for the privilege. "Rejoice and be glad, for your reward is great in heaven, for so they persecuted the prophets who were before you" (Matt. 5:12). Listen. I think I just heard Jeremiah say, "Amen!"

OCTOBER 29
Jeremiah 22-24

"The Righteous Shepherd"

*"In his days Judah will be saved, and Israel will dwell securely.
And this is the name by which he will be called:
'The Lord is our righteousness.'"*
(Jeremiah 23:6)

Sheep without a shepherd are entirely helpless. There is no animal more incapable of defending itself than a sheep. The most dangerous and despicable situation imaginable for sheep is to be willfully scattered by wicked shepherds. Sheep without a shepherd are helpless, but sheep with wicked, divisive shepherds are a guaranteed disaster. However, this is just the image the Lord shares through Jeremiah regarding the condition of His people. Judah and Israel have not just gone astray from Him like wandering sheep. They have *been driven from Him* by wicked political and religious leaders.

As awful as that image is, it was the reality in Jeremiah's day, and it is the reality in *our* day. Government and religious leaders who are the servants of God to care for His sheep, human beings created in His image, by their wicked decisions and false messages drive the sheep of the Lord away from His paths. What a dreadful account these leaders will give to the Chief Shepherd one day! Yet, wickedness and wrath of ungodly people cannot thwart the council of the Lord or set aside His determined plans.

The day draws near when the Lord will raise up His Faithful Shepherd, another David who, as the Messiah, the "righteous Branch," shall "reign as king and deal wisely, and shall execute justice and righteousness in the land" (Jer. 23:5). This Shepherd will be called "Jehovah-Tsidkenu," "The Lord is our righteousness"(Jer. 23:6). He will gather a flock from all the corners of the earth. The exiles of Israel and Judah scattered to the nations will hear the voice of the Great Shepherd and return to the Lord their God. This flock will not just include the physical descendants of Abraham, Isaac, and Jacob because the Lord promised that all the nations of the earth would be blessed through them (Gen. 26:4). In Christ the Savior, there is no longer Jew or Gentile, for all who believe are the sons and daughters of God through faith (Gal. 3:26).

Through faith in our Shepherd, we, the scattered sheep, not only discover that He is righteous, but His righteousness actually becomes *our* righteousness. "For our sake he made him to be sin who knew no sin, so that in him we might become the righteousness of God" (2 Cor. 5:21). What a marvelous exchange! The Shepherd receives our sins, and we receive His righteousness. Our Shepherd has a name, Jehovah-Tsidkenu, and what a name it is, "The Lord is our righteousness"(Jer. 23:6). Not *almost* righteous, or *mostly* righteous, but *completely* righteous through Him. Our wandering days are over. "For you were straying like sheep, but have now returned to the Shepherd and Overseer of your souls" (1 Peter 2:25).

OCTOBER 30
Jeremiah 25-27

"STAND AND DELIVER"

> *"Thus says the Lord: Stand in the court of the Lord's house, and speak to all the cities of Judah that come to worship in the house of the Lord all the words that I command you to speak to them; do not hold back a word."*
> (Jeremiah 26:2)

It was a moment and an image never to be forgotten. On the morning of February 3, 1994, the National Prayer Breakfast, sponsored by the United States Senate and House of Representatives and attended by President Bill Clinton, Vice-President Al Gore, and their wives, Hillary and Tipper, was held in Washington, DC. Before the gathered audience, including some of the most powerful people in the nation and the world, stood a tiny lady of 4 foot 6 inches in height and dressed in the white and blue trimmed habit of the Missionaries of Charity order of Roman Catholic nuns. If ever there was a setting in which a person would be expected to fit their comments carefully, it would certainly be one such as this. And the speaker that morning, Mother Teresa of Calcutta, did just that. She made her remarks with complete regard to her audience, but the audience she addressed that day was not the crowd *before her* but the "Crowned One" *above her*. Mother Teresa was mindful that winter morning that she spoke *before God* and that she spoke *for God*. With that awareness, Mother Teresa spoke movingly for the most vulnerable and at-risk people in America, the unborn babies in their mothers' wombs.

Her heavily accented voice spoke prophetically in English on behalf of the unborn children. A search can easily find her address in its entirety on social media platforms, but what follows is just a small part of her powerful message of truth and love: "Please don't kill the child. I want the child. Please give me the child. I am willing to accept any child who would be aborted and to give that child to a married couple who will love the child and be loved by the child." The spacious hall was utterly silent as this tiny woman pleaded for the lives of children. The room was quiet, but heaven's applause reverberated in the King's presence and throughout His kingdom. What a moment!

Very few, if any of us, will ever know a moment of such significance as came to Mother Teresa, but we all *do choose* our audience. It is that choice that determines what we say and how we say it. If ultimately, we believe our audience is on earth, we will at some time amend our message to make it pleasing to the ears of men and women. However, if in our hearts we believe we speak to a heavenly audience, we will speak to please the King who listens from His throne. This mindfulness of a Divine audience should guide not only our public statements but our private conversations as well. Wherever we are, whether it be in a public setting or the most secluded, "The Lord is at hand" (Phil. 4:5). If we could but remember "the Divine audience" in every conversation, how much more profitable our words would be! So today, let us remember.

OCTOBER 31
Jeremiah 28-29

"Living in Exile"

"But seek the welfare of the city where I have sent you into exile, and pray to the Lord on its behalf, for in its welfare you will find your welfare."
(Jeremiah 29:7)

The Lord was very clear with His timetable. He had made His plans definite and specific. The people of Judah would live in exile from their homeland for 70 years. God had commanded the Israelites centuries before that they were to let the land rest every seventh year and trust that the Lord, in six years of blessing, would provide more than enough food to care for the nation during the sabbath year. The people had never obeyed the Lord regarding the sabbath years, so the Lord determined that the land would experience the rest for 70 years while the people were exiles in Babylon (2 Chr. 36:21).

However, a very popular prophet with a very positive prosperity message, Hananiah of Gibeon, was proclaiming a "word from the Lord" that the exiles would return to Judah in less than two years (Jer. 28:1-4). This message reached the exiles living as captives in faraway Babylon, and we can only imagine how excited they must have been to learn that they would soon "be going home." Perhaps the only phenomenon that comes close to this type of empty "word of revelation" in modern times is the many occasions "end time prophets" have revealed dates on specific seasons in which the return of Christ and the Rapture of His church would occur. Regardless, the results were the same among the exiles in Babylon. They had been among the "true believers" regarding those rapture promises. The focus of their daily lives moved from active participation in kingdom living to idle euphoric anticipation of deliverance.

Jeremiah was given a message for those sixth century BC exiles from Judah that applies to us today as twenty-first century AD exiles from the New Jerusalem. The promise is definite; we are going home! The Lord will miraculously intervene in the affairs of the nations and, with His all-powerful voice, call His people home. But, until then, as author and theologian Francis Shaeffer asks in the title of his renowned work, *How Shall We Then Live?*—how are exiles of the faith expected to live by faith in a pagan, godless world?

Should we live in protest of the oppressive government? Should we stop participating in or supporting such a Christless culture? No. That is not God's will and plan, either for His ancient people living as exiles in literal Babylon or for followers of Jesus living "away from home." God wants His exiles *engaged. Engaged in promoting the common welfare* —"But seek the welfare of the city where I have sent you." *Engaged in intercessory prayer*—"and pray to the Lord on its behalf." *Engaged in supporting God's people by living as good citizens*—"for in its welfare you will find your welfare" (Jer. 29:7). Hard work, virtue, and virtuous living pleases the Lord, advances His kingdom, and blesses His people. By the grace of God and His goodness, we can "settle down" and live active, productive lives, even as we "set our affections on things above" and things to come (Col. 3:1-4).

NOVEMBER

"I will magnify him with thanksgiving."
(Psalm 69:30)

NOVEMBER 1
Jeremiah 30-31

"Everlasting Love"

*"I have loved you with an everlasting love; therefore
I have continued my faithfulness to you."*
(Jeremiah 31:3)

My wife and I have enjoyed visiting New York City several times over the years, and the same thing happens on practically every trip. As we walk along one of the busiest streets, we will come upon a small crowd gathered around a vehicle with an opened trunk. The vehicle owner "is open for business" and is selling various items at "greatly reduced prices." My wife loves to listen to the salesman's pitch and enjoys, even more, entering into the banter about the quality and price of the merchandise. I only recall her buying a few souvenir items during these exchanges, but I vividly recall one "sales presentation" in which a man offered "genuine Rolex watches" at bargain prices. I was amazed to watch as several tourists purchased these treasured timepieces, and I was amused to listen to the verdict of a police officer who walked up to close up the "open trunk operation" and clear out the congestion. Someone on the street asked the officer, "How can you tell if it is a counterfeit Rolex?" "Simple," replied the policeman. "The real ones last."

Over the years, I have thought of the officer's words concerning the genuineness of the profession of faith by many who claim to follow Jesus—"the real ones last." It is important to remember why any person perseveres in saving faith. The basis of that durability of belief is in the ever-enduring love of God for His people. "I have loved you with an everlasting love; therefore I have continued my faithfulness to you" is the Lord's pledge to each one of His children (Jer. 31:3). What a gleaming promise this is on the dark background of Jeremiah's message of judgment! God reaffirms His covenant promises to the descendants of Abraham in the most powerful imagery. If "the fixed order" of the sunlight by day and the moon and the stars by night cease, only "then shall the offspring of Israel cease from being a nation before me forever" (Jer. 31:35-36).

God's covenant relationship with Israel is so absolute that He promises to reconfirm it one day with a "new covenant" in which "I will put my law within them, and I will write it on their hearts. And I will be their God, and they shall be my people" (Jer. 31:33). Thank God that new covenant has been ratified by the Messiah, and we who trust in Him are included in its promises! "Therefore He is the mediator of a new covenant, so that those who are called may receive the promised eternal inheritance" (Heb. 9:15). There is no longer an old covenant and a new covenant. The old was torn in two with the dying, victory shout of Jesus. Now, the New Covenant will endure as long as the heart of Jesus beats with love for His people—in other words, forever and forever.

NOVEMBER 2
Jeremiah 32-33

"The Time of Faith Capsule"

"'Thus says the Lord of hosts, the God of Israel: Take these deeds, both this sealed deed of purchase and this open deed, and put them in an earthenware vessel, that they may last for a long time.'"
(Jeremiah 32:14)

God instructed His prophet, Jeremiah, to do a very strange thing. In fact, in light of the circumstances surrounding the instructions and also the specific directions, it could be said that the Lord *commanded* Jeremiah to do a very foolish thing. It was absolutely the worst imaginable market for a real estate purchase in the land of Judah and that surrounding area Jerusalem had ever known. The Babylonian army had already conquered the entire land and now encircled Jerusalem with siege mounds in preparation for a final and devastating assault. In a somewhat comical response, Jeremiah reminds the Lord that the real estate market was just a little "volatile," to say the least (Jer. 32:24-26). Yet, that is precisely what God instructed Jeremiah to do—buy the field he was being offered by his very sly relative, Hanamel.

The Lord then directed Jeremiah to bury both copies of the title deed, the private personal copy and the public one, in the field he purchased. This was also an unusual form of real estate guidance. Usually, the public document was posted at the city gate and then kept in the government archives, and the personal copy was kept by the family as proof of ownership. Why would the Lord turn these copies of the deeds of ownership into the contents of a time capsule?

First of all, for Jeremiah and his family, who were soon to travel as refugees to Egypt, these documents would be evidence of their family's ownership of the land in years to come. Secondly, these documents were a continuing witness to the Lord's rhetorical question/answer response to Jeremiah's reminder that this real estate purchase might not be wise. "Behold, I am the Lord, the God of all flesh. Is anything too hard for me?" (Jer. 32:27).

Finally, and most importantly for the Jewish people in Babylonian exile and the scattered descendants of Abraham in the centuries to come, this purchase of land by Jeremiah would be a reminder of the

Lord's unalterable promises to Israel. "Behold, I will gather them from all the countries to which I drove them in my anger and my wrath and in great indignation. I will bring them back to this place, and I will make them dwell in safety. And they shall be my people, and I will be their God" (Jer. 32:37-38).

Whether the earthenware jar which Jeremiah buried 2,700 years ago has ever been discovered or not, we do not know. However, one thing we do know is that the promise of God it represented will be completely fulfilled. God's promises are seeds that never die but, like Him, are eternal and full of life. The contents of that 2700-year-old time capsule are ours to claim now through faith in Messiah Jesus. "I will make with them an everlasting covenant, that I will not turn away from doing good to them. And I will put the fear of me in their hearts, that they may not turn from me. I will rejoice in doing them good, and I will plant them in this land in faithfulness, with all my heart and all my soul" (Jer. 32:40-41). Let's bury those promises deep in our hearts today.

NOVEMBER 3
Jeremiah 34-35

"FAITH OF OUR FATHER"

"Therefore thus says the Lord of hosts, the God of Israel: Jonadab the son of Rechab shall never lack a man to stand before me."
(Jeremiah 35:19)

Some passages of Scripture in the Old Testament share information so foreign and disconnected from our current understanding that we "speed-read" our way through them, if we read them at all. When we give in to that tendency, the personal loss we sustain can be significant. Not all the gold in the Bible lies open on the surface for the casually walking pilgrim to pick up quickly! Some of the Lord's most priceless treasures must be discovered by faithful, diligent miners of God's Word. Jeremiah, Chapter 35 is certainly a passage that contains rich veins of gold that yield priceless nuggets of truth for those who dig.

In this chapter, Jeremiah records an "upper room" conversation he shared with the leaders of the family of the Rechabites. These people were not direct descendants of Jacob but were part of the family group of the Kenites (also known as Midianites) who were related in marriage to Moses. The Rechabites lived among the people of Israel for hundreds of years. The most noted of these people, Jonadab, 200 years before Jeremiah's day, had assisted Jehu in ridding Israel of Baal worship in the reign of wicked King Ahab (2 Kings 10:15-27).

To maintain their family identity and values, Jonadab commanded his descendants to live in tents as shepherds and never to plant vineyards or even partake of wine. For 200 years, his descendants kept their promise to their esteemed leader and patriarch. Now at the command of God, Jeremiah invites the leaders of this clan into an upper chamber of the house of God and sets before them huge bowls of wine. To this offer from Jeremiah, they responded, "We will drink no wine, for Jonadab the son of Rechab, our father, commanded us, 'You shall not drink wine, neither you nor your sons forever" (Jer. 35:6). For their faithfulness in passing this test, the Lord spoke the promise of blessing from 35:19 shared above! God used these Rechabites' faithfulness to their earthly father's commands as contrast and testimony against the faithlessness of Judah to their God and Heavenly Father (Jer. 35:15-17).

Over the years, I have been blessed to observe the lengths people have gone to honor the memory and legacy of parents, grandparents, and other family members. Sometimes at great cost to themselves and even in the face of opposition, they have determined to honor the wishes of their loved ones. This is so commendable. How much more than (and this is the Lord's principle shared through Jeremiah) should we be committed to honor and obey our Father and God? It is undoubtedly wise for us as believers to be students of the culture in which we live so that we might most effectively bear witness to Christ within it. However, we must always be careful that in studying the culture, we do not fall into it. Cultural awareness does not mean cultural assimilation. The descendants of Rechab maintained their identity and integrity in a culture overflowing with disobedience and disloyalty. May we do the same in honor of our Heavenly Father.

NOVEMBER 4
Jeremiah 36-38

"INDESTRUCTIBLE, INEXTINGUISHABLE"

"Now after the king had burned the scroll with the words that Baruch wrote at Jeremiah's dictation, the word of the Lord came to Jeremiah: 'Take another scroll and write on it all the former words that were in the first scroll, which Jehoiakim the king of Judah has burned.'"
(Jeremiah 36:27-28)

In his epistle to the Romans, Apostle Paul writes of the perverse foolishness that results in the minds of people who intentionally attempt to suppress the truth of God (Rom. 1:18). Ultimately, their attempts to destroy the Word result in the destruction of their own ability to perceive truth. Choosing not to retain God in their thinking, they produce in themselves a "foolish heart" that is morally and intellectually darkened (Rom. 1:21). Our reading today provides a historical yet timeless example of mankind's futile attempts to destroy the Word of God. The King of Judah ordered that the copy of God's message of judgment, delivered by God to Jeremiah and then presented to him by Baruch, be destroyed by fire in his presence (Jer. 36:33). The blatant and evil arrogance of King Jehoiakim in this action is breathtakingly wicked. But the calm, controlled response of the Lord is marvelous—"write another copy" (Jer. 36:28).

We are familiar with the adage, "Fight fire with fire." But, we learn from absolute truth in this account that no one can destroy God's Word with fire because *God's Word IS the fire*! "Is not my word like fire, declares the Lord, and like a hammer that breaks the rock in pieces?" (Jer. 23:29) God's Word is a fire that burns with everlasting truth, and no flames of earthly attacks on it can do anything but make His truth burn brighter. Like His own holy nature, the fire of God's Word burns with inextinguishable flame. God's Word burns like stubble the resistance of man, and shatters like a hammer all evil opposition.

Many years ago, I heard a children's chorus joyfully singing a song they had learned in a Bible club. I remember thinking how the music, though it sounded a little dated, was perfectly suited for the children to easily learn and sing so enthusiastically. It was only later when I read the story of the song's origin. I learned that the composer, Haldor Lillenas, wrote the song as a response to the attacks of critics on the Bible, fueled by the same hatred that filled King Jehoiakim centuries earlier. The song is a celebration of the indestructibility of God's Word, for through the centuries, despite the relentless opposition of unbelievers, "The Bible Stands."

> *The Bible stands like a rock undaunted*
> *'Mid the raging storms of time;*
> *Its pages burn with the truth eternal,*
> *And they glow with a light sublime.*
>
> *Chorus:*
>
> *The Bible stands tho' the hills may tumble,*
> *It will firmly stand when the earth shall crumble;*
> *I will plant my feet on its firm foundation,*
> *For the Bible stands!*

That may be considered a children's song, but it shares a very grown-up theme and a promise that will never grow old!

NOVEMBER 5
Jeremiah 39-41

"The Safest Place in the World"

"Nebuchadnezzar king of Babylon gave command concerning Jeremiah through Nebuzaradan, the captain of the guard, saying, 'Take him, look after him well, and do him no harm, but deal with him as he tells you.'"
(Jeremiah 39:11-12)

Many years ago, a young couple dedicated their lives to serving the Lord as missionaries in central Africa. These young adults and their little children were deeply loved by their parents and all the members of both families. The zeal of this young couple to serve the Lord wherever He devoted was an incredible influence on so many people. Yet, the idea of the dangers they would face and the distance they would travel from home was overwhelming to many members of their families. Finally, the mother of the young woman took her aside to challenge the plans of her daughter and son-in-law for service in that faraway region. With tears in her eyes, the mother pleaded with her daughter, "Darling, how can you leave us and take your little ones, our grandchildren, to be buried in Africa?" "Mother," the daughter responded, looking tenderly into her eyes. "You are mistaken; we are not going to Africa to be *buried* but *to be planted.*"

The difference in those two words, "buried" and "planted," were not lost on the worried mother, and they should not be lost on us. The seed that remains in the barn is certainly secure, but the potential of an exponential harvest also remains in the barn. Likewise, it is in the trying to clutch and protect our lives that we lose them, and only in releasing our lives to our Master do we truly find them (Matt. 16:25). Our Lord said, "Truly, truly, I say to you, unless a grain of wheat falls into the earth and dies, it remains alone; but if it dies, it bears much fruit" (John 12:24).

Following our Lord produces a radical redefining of many concepts, and one of the foremost of these is the meaning of "safety." As we grow in the grace and knowledge of the Lord, we also advance in the understanding that our Lord never promised that serving Him would be a "safe thing." Jesus' call, "Follow Me," is not a summons to a life of playing it safe, but rather one of following His lead. We must sometimes talk ourselves through faulty logic, causing us to consider somehow that following our Lord is "safer" than choosing our own path. Could there possibly be a safer place than walking with the Lord?

Jeremiah did not "play it safe" when he spoke for God to the rulers of Judah. He most certainly did not "play it safe" when he prophesied of the Lord's coming judgment on the kingdom of Babylon. Yet, who specifically directed Jeremiah to be treated with the utmost kindness and respect after the fall of Jerusalem? Yes, the King of Babylon, Nebuchadnezzar himself, commanded that Jehovah's prophet be protected! What earthly king should we fear when we walk with the King of kings?

> *"The Lord is on my side; I will not fear. What can man do to me?"*
> (Psalm 118:6)

NOVEMBER 6
Jeremiah 42-43

"TRUTH OR CONSEQUENCES"

> *"Then they said to Jeremiah, 'May the Lord be a true and faithful witness against us if we do not act according to all the word with which the Lord your God sends you to us. Whether it is good or bad, we will obey the voice of the Lord our God to whom we are sending you, that it may be well with us when we obey the voice of the Lord our God.'"*
> (Jeremiah 42:5-6)

Several years ago, a team of volunteer firefighters was battling a surging forest fire sweeping through the mountains of Northern California near Reno, Nevada. A sudden shift in the wind turned the deadly flames upon the firefighters and a small group of campers they had managed to reach. With no chance of outrunning the windswept flames, the personnel decided to deploy the fire-resistant tents they each carried in their packs. Some of the campers listened to the pleas of the firefighters and squeezed into the aluminum-looking tents with them. Soon, the wall of flame swept over the huddled people in the frantically deployed tents. Several people in the tents suffered severe burns, but every person who listened to the firefighters' directions survived the ordeal.

Sadly, in our Scripture reading today, we learn of a large group of Jewish people who, rather than listen to the offer of safety promised by God if they remained in Judah, chose to flee to Egypt and find protection in this "superpower nation." The people asked for the truth and promised to obey whatever the Lord spoke, yet when God's truth required them to surrender their plans, they exchanged truth for consequences.

When it comes to the Word of God, the decision we face is never a multiple-choice regarding *truths* and consequences. There never exists a plurality of truths from which we choose our personal favorite flavor. According to its very definition and the specific and definite statement of Jesus, truth is absolute. "Sanctify them in the truth; your word is truth" (John 17:17). Notice Jesus did not say God's Word is *true*, but that God's Word *is truth*. Truth is not something we decide. Truth is permanently defined—God's Word is truth.

We have nothing to fear as we come under the protective covering of God's truth. God's truth is a place of *safety*. "He who dwells in the shelter of the Most High will abide in the shadow of the Almighty. I will say to the Lord, 'My refuge and my fortress, my God, in whom I trust.' For He will deliver you from the snare of the fowler and from the deadly pestilence. He will cover you with His pinions, and under His wings you will find refuge" (Ps. 91:1-4). It is in God's truth we experience the consequences of safety. Likewise, it is within the boundaries of God's truth that we find *freedom*. "Then you will know the truth, and the truth will set you free" (John 8:32 NIV).

Our Lord does not save us to enslave us, for the truth is we are already slaves to sin and its consequences of death. The Lord is our Redeemer, the One who liberates us from the bondage of lies by the truth of His gospel. May we all recognize the privilege of experiencing "truth and consequences," the *truth* of His Word, and the *liberty* of living it.

"It is for freedom that Christ has set us free. Stand firm, then, and do not let yourselves be burdened again by a yoke of slavery."
(Galatians 5:1)

NOVEMBER 7
Jeremiah 44-46

"The Eye of the Storm"

"But fear not, O Jacob my servant, nor be dismayed, O Israel, for behold, I will save you from far away, and your offspring from the land of their captivity. Jacob shall return and have quiet and ease, and none shall make him afraid."
(Jeremiah 46:27)

Although I have never personally experienced the phenomenon, several friends and acquaintances have described being in "the eye of the storm." This phrase describes an area of fascinating calm and tranquility in the center of a tropical storm's vortex. The storm bands may extend for several hundred miles, and the wind velocity in the outer walls of the hurricane may approach or even exceed 200 mph. Yet, in the very center of the storm, there is a space and a time period of utter calm.

The events God prophecies and Jeremiah records in these chapters are truly a multi-national hurricane of historic and epic proportions. Jehovah shares this prophetic word in response to the expressions of confidence by refugees from Judah who have fled to Egypt and are boasting they will be completely safe there. They mock Jeremiah's denouncements of their continued idolatrous practices and boast that they and their families will continue making offerings to the "queen of heaven" just as they had done in Jerusalem and Judah (Jer. 44:15-19). Jehovah responds by saying that because of their continued idolatries, "All the men of Judah who are in the land of Egypt shall be consumed by the sword and by famine, until there is an end of them" (Jer. 44:27). Moreover, the "superpower," Egypt, in whom they place their trust, will march north to destroy the armies of Babylon and King Nebuchadnezzar, but they will be utterly annihilated.

In 605 BC, this is exactly what took place at the Battle of Carchemish near the modern Syria and Turkey borders. Nebuchadnezzar's armies destroyed Egypt's kingdom and the Assyrian empire's remnants, and Babylon rose to dominate all of the Middle East (Jer. 46:26). Amid this cataclysmic hurricane-like conflict lived the remnants of the tiny nation of Judah and also the Jewish refugees dwelling in Babylon. These people are like terrified crew members and passengers gripping onto a small sinking boat while a few survivors float together in the waves. Bearing down on them is the most gigantic storm ever recorded. What possible hope is there for these defenseless people? Plenty. Infinitely more incredible than this dreadful storm is the Master of all storms, and He speaks to these imperiled people as the "Prince of Peace." "But fear not, O Jacob my servant, nor be dismayed, O Israel, for behold, I will save you from far away, and your offspring from the land of their captivity. Jacob shall return and have quiet and ease, and none shall make him afraid" (Jer. 46:27).

The Lord never told us we would not experience storms in our lives. In fact, on some occasions, He sovereignly guides us into hurricane-like seasons. Yet, He did promise He would be with us in the storms. Our Prince of Peace is the "*Prince of Peace.*" He is never alarmed and always in control. Our little boat may enter terrible storms, but the Master of the storms is always in our vessel. He speaks during our storms to the storm of fear raging in our hearts, "Peace, be still." Fear not, my brothers and sisters, the eternal calm is just ahead, and there on that bright shore, none make you afraid.

NOVEMBER 8
Jeremiah 47-48

"Mourning for Moab"

*"Therefore my heart moans for Moab like a flute,
and my heart moans like a flute for the men of Kir-hareseth.
Therefore the riches they gained have perished."*
(Jeremiah 48:36)

Recently, one of the preachers in our church reminded and warned us as a congregation about the danger of the "revenge culture" in which we live. We are constantly encouraged through social media, movies, television shows, and, sadly, even our political leaders, that, "payback," "eye for an eye," and "bury you" are not just *a way* to deal with your enemies, but the *right way* to deal with them. The mantra of our age has become a phrase from the Bible taken out of context and personally claimed—"vengeance is *mine*, I will repay" (Deut. 32:35).

This is not surprising because when the philosophy extolled is continually one of "*personal empowerment*," people eventually begin appropriating power to themselves, the authority that belongs to God. However, this murderous Lamech spirit (Gen. 4:23-24) can never be accepted or tolerated among the people of God. How can we speak to the world in witness if we permit the revenge spirit of the world to be displayed in our lives? How can we, followers of the One who wept in tears over the judgment rightfully coming to Jerusalem, be characterized by glee and gloating with the downfall and destruction of those we have judged worthy of the consequences of their evil actions or attitudes?

A revenge-seeking heart does not seem to align with these words, "Beloved, never avenge yourselves, but leave it to the wrath of God, for it is written, 'Vengeance is mine, I will repay,' says the Lord." On the contrary, "If your enemy is hungry, feed him; if he is thirsty, give him something to drink; for by so doing you will heap burning coals on his head" (Rom. 12:19-20). We must constantly examine our attitudes and actions to see if we reflect these qualities of mercy and grace.

Our God is Holy, Holy, Holy, and despises evil with all of His perfect nature. God's justice burns and builds against all the unrighteousness of evil people (2 Thess. 1:8). Yet, our God, in His just wrath, remembers mercy (Hab. 3:2). He delights to forgive and to restore those who many would believe are beyond redemption. In our reading today, we have highlighted in a brief statement the amazing grace and redemption of God. If ever there existed a nation and a people who were hate-filled, insolent, and relentless enemies against God and His people, it was the Moabites. From their lofty and impenetrable mountain fortresses, these people for centuries worshiped their vile god, Chemosh, and attacked the followers of Jehovah at every opportunity. Finally, the full cup of God's wrath poured out upon them through the devastating assault of Nebuchadnezzar in 582 BC. God's vengeance was just and terrifying. Yet, what was God's attitude? "Therefore I wail for Moab; I cry out for all Moab; for the men of Kir-hareseth I mourn" (Jer. 48:31). The Moabites have been destroyed and disbanded for 2700 years, but are they forgotten by God and without hope? Absolutely not, "Yet I will restore the fortunes of Moab in the latter days, declares the Lord" (Jer. 48:47). "Where sin increased, grace abounded all the more" (Rom. 5:20). God's greatest triumphs are the triumphs of His grace. May His victory of grace in our lives conquer our vengeful spirits this day.

NOVEMBER 9
Jeremiah 49-50

"THE STRONG REDEEMER"

"Their Redeemer is strong; the Lord of hosts is his name.
He will surely plead their cause..."
(Jeremiah 50:34)

Not long ago, a photographer on assignment for a media company took a series of photos capturing the utter devastation resulting from a forest fire that swept through a community in a western state. Practically all the buildings, within the small town and surrounding area, were utterly destroyed. This included the small, wood-frame chapel that had been a place of worship for generations. The photographer snapped away with his camera as he took dozens of shots of the rubble which had once been the center of the town. However, as he looked through the lens of his camera, the photographer suddenly stopped, amazed at the scene framed for his view. At the spot that had once been the altar for the little church stood a small, fire-singed table and, resting upon it, a soot-covered cross. Lying open in front of the cross was a Bible with its pages slightly darkened but miraculously unconsumed by the raging fire. Some people thought it merely an interesting phenomenon, but others saw it as a clear and comforting sign from the Lord that He was with them throughout the fiery ordeal.

The chapters we read today in Jeremiah describe a fire of complete devastation that swept through the region of the Middle East during the sixth century before Christ. We read the pages today as history, but we must remember when the prophet wrote these words they were prophecy. In Jeremiah's day, it would have seemed ridiculous, if not insane, to declare that all these nations would be destroyed. The most ridiculous of all would have been the idea that the mightiest empire of its age, or perhaps any age, Babylon, would be completely overwhelmed and inhabited only by wild animals and birds (Jer. 50:39-40). Yet, within 100 years, this is exactly what took place. Babylon, the destroyer of these nations, would herself be destroyed in the sweeping inferno of God's judgment.

Babylon, the terror of the nations, would be burned and forsaken, but not the people of Israel and the people of Judah. God would remember them, and in repentance for their sins, they would remember Him. "In those days and in that time...the people of Israel and the people of Judah shall come together, weeping as they come, and they shall seek the Lord their God" (Jer. 50:4). They are only a scattered and weak people, but "their Redeemer is strong" (Jer. 50:34). God has never yet, never will, and in fact, cannot forsake His people. "I will never leave you or forsake you" is His promise (Josh. 1:5).

It may be that a fire rages around you today. It may be that complete and total destruction is upon you. In the fire of this testing, don't forget that your Redeemer is strong. He hears the prayers of those who call upon Him, and always remembers the promises He has shared in His Word and confirmed by the cross of His Son. God's promises in the Bible and on the cross are never consumed in the fires we experience.

When through fiery trials thy pathways shall lie,
My grace, all sufficient, shall be thy supply;
The flame shall not hurt thee; I only design
Thy dross to consume, and thy gold to refine.

("How Firm a Foundation," by John Rippon)

NOVEMBER 10
Jeremiah 51-52

"BABYLON HAS FALLEN!"

"Then the heavens and the earth, and all that is in them, shall sing for joy over Babylon, for the destroyers shall come against them out of the north, declares the Lord."
(Jeremiah 51:48)

The commission that Jeremiah gave to his assistant, Seraiah, could hardly have seemed more ridiculous and the carrying out of it more preposterous. Seraiah was commanded to carry the judgments against Babylon, pronounced and then written down on a scroll by Jeremiah, and take them with him as he accompanied a group of refugees to that vast city. Standing before the walls of Babylon that loomed into the sky and were so thick the Greek historian recorded two chariots could travel side by side upon them, Seraiah was directed to open the scroll and read aloud the judgments of God pronounced upon that city and its kingdom. Having read the words, Seraiah was commanded to tie a rock around the scroll and throw it into the Euphrates River flowing around the walls. Any uninformed bystander would have laughed with derision at Seraiah's speech and concluded he was utterly deranged.

However, time is a great revealer of the difference between foolishness and faith. "Time will tell," and in very little time, we are told of the amazing and literal fulfillment of God's Words of judgment. It was not without significance that Seraiah was told to sink the scroll of God's Words into the river. History records that in 539 BC, Cyrus the Persian diverted the Euphrates from its flow under the massive walls of Babylon, marched into the city, and captured it. Immediately, couriers were sent riding throughout the empire's provinces and the surrounding nations declaring, "Babylon is fallen!" Millions of people dreading that kingdom's ruthless power began to rejoice, and the hosts of heaven joined them in the celebration (Jer. 51:48).

The historic celebration of Babylon's destruction is a prophetic one as well. We are told in the Book of Revelation that in the final days of this earth, the glad shout will once again ring through heaven and across the planet, "Fallen, fallen is Babylon..." (Rev. 14:8) We must remember that in the Bible, Babylon is not just a city but a system. It was at Babylon that, in ages past, rebellious mankind, in betrayal of God, rejected His command and erected a tower in defiance of Him and His authority (Gen. 11:1-9). In Babylon, the worship and ways of the Lord were rejected, and a demonic, man-focused mixture of religion and political power united in rebellion against God. Babylon represents the spirit of anti-Christ, the philosophy of 666, exalting the "glory of man" above the only true glorious One—God Almighty, Maker, and Ruler of heaven and earth.

This is the spirit of the age in which we live—Babylon, the exaltation of man's "enlightenment" and the suppression of God's light and truth. We grieve at such glorification of darkness, but we must also rejoice in anticipation. One day, once again, the host of heaven and the righteous on earth will rejoice, "Babylon is fallen, is fallen!" The ridiculed and rejected Lord will return in all His power and great glory, once and for all destroying the system and spirit of Babylon. Then the world's kingdom will become the Kingdom of our Lord and His Christ! (Rev. 11:15) Get ready to shout. It won't be long!

NOVEMBER 11
Lamentations 1-3

"Great is Your Faithfulness"

"But this I call to mind, and therefore I have hope: The steadfast love of the Lord never ceases; his mercies never come to an end; they are new every morning; great is your faithfulness."
(Lamentations 3:21-23)

For centuries, Jeremiah has been referred to as "the weeping prophet." This is not unwarranted, for this man of God experienced much personal hardship and pain that would break the heart of any person. However, it was not the suffering that Jeremiah endured *personally* that brought him the title "weeping prophet" because his tears were not shed for his *own* trials. Jeremiah weeps for his people and the beloved city of his God, Jerusalem, and the devastation the citizens and the city experience in divine judgment for centuries of idolatry and rebellion. With a broken heart, Jeremiah laments over the destruction of Jerusalem and the captivity of his people by the Babylonians. "Lamentations" in our Bible is a collection of five poems recording the grief of this good and righteous servant of God over the calamities that have befallen his beloved nation.

Today, a very misguided message proclaims it is wrong for believers in the Lord to ever lament. While the motive of those who share this challenge may be sincere, it is not a message that is helpful to hurting people and it is not biblical. God has given us an entire book in His eternal Word that bears the title "Lamentations." God tells us there is a "time to mourn" (Ecc. 3:4). We are told that the Lord Jesus wept and mourned over Jerusalem (Matt. 23:37). The Bible does not say as Christians, we will not or should not express deep sorrow, yet we do not sorrow "as others do who have no hope" (1 Thess. 4:13). In fact, there exists a "godly sorrow" that is radically different from the worldly sorrow that produces death—the sorrow over sin that expresses the priceless gift of repentance (2 Cor. 7:10).

As believers, we will occasionally experience and express lamentation. As we do this, however, we must not allow our grief to become faithless. We must not forget in our grief the faithfulness of our God. We must lament and grieve in faith. "Weeping may tarry for the night, but joy comes with the morning" (Ps. 30:5). Into the life of every believer comes many "dark nights of the soul." This is part of the path before us that was walked by our dear Savior, a "man of sorrows and acquainted with grief" (Isa. 53:3). The Lord endured His Gethsemane, and so must we if we truly desire to be conformed to His image and experience the "fellowship of His sufferings" (Phil. 3:10 KJV). Through the experience of sorrow, we are equipped by God's comfort to encourage others with the comfort we have received (2 Cor. 1:4).

There is a purpose and a plan in our sufferings, and it is in that confidence we must be sure that our seasons of lament are also accompanied by praise. No tragedy, no sorrow, regardless of how overwhelming it may be, can alter the truth of God's steadfast love. Our Lord's love is constant and unchanging, yet fresh with every sunrise. "The steadfast love of the Lord never ceases, his mercies never come to an end, they are new every morning; great is your faithfulness" (Lam. 3:22-23). The world turns, darkness comes, and the night seasons fall upon our hearts. Yet, the sun never ceases to shine, and eventually, the dawning of a new day slowly emerges. We must remember as we lament in the dark nights of our souls to sing by faith the truth that never fails.

> Great is Thy faithfulness, O God my Father;
> There is no shadow of turning with Thee;
> Thou changest not, Thy compassions, they fail not;
> As Thou hast been, Thou forever will be.
> Great is Thy faithfulness!
> Great is Thy faithfulness!
> Morning by morning new mercies I see.
> All I have needed Thy hand hath provided;
> Great is Thy faithfulness, Lord, unto me!

("Great Is Thy Faithfulness" by Thomas O. Chisholm)

NOVEMBER 12
Lamentations 4-5

"KING FOREVER"

"But you, O Lord, reign forever; your throne endures to all generations."
(Lamentations 5:19)

It is hard for us to imagine what the eyes of Jeremiah looked upon as he lifted his pen to record this heartbroken lament over the destruction of Judah and Jerusalem. Some of the brutal images he describes regarding the wicked and beast-like atrocities carried out by the Babylonians against his people are hard for us to read. Imagine what it must have been like to witness them firsthand! Everywhere Jeremiah looked was a ceaseless landscape of brokenness, grief, devastation, and death.

Only people who have survived the horrors of ethnic cleansing and wars of annihilation can even begin to identify with what the people of

Judah and Jerusalem experienced during and after that final invasion by the armies of Nebuchadnezzar in 586 BC. In every direction, there is nothing that inspires hope, so Jeremiah turns his gaze to look in the one direction, untouched and unmoved by the tragedies of this world—*he looks up*. What physical eyes cannot see, the eyes of the soul can view by faith—God Almighty, eternal and immutable, sits on His royal throne. God still reigns. The temple in Jerusalem has been utterly destroyed, yet in heaven, "The Lord is in his holy temple; let all the earth be silent before him" (Hab. 2:20). Jeremiah recognizes this truth, but he cannot keep silent. The reality that the God of Judah, the Lord of all creation, is seated on His throne in heaven keeps Jeremiah from remaining silent. He simply has to pour out his heart to his Heavenly King!

In the dreadful scenes Jeremiah describes, his response is a timeless example for our seasons of despair. He looks to God; he laments to God. Our place of lament should not be social media. Our Father on the throne of heaven and not our "friends on Facebook" should hear the message of our misery. A lamentation is not an "online rant" but divinely directed worship when we cast our burdens on the Lord and call on Him to sustain us (Ps. 55:22). It is not sinful to bring our complaints to the Lord. We learn this from Jeremiah, who learned it from King David, who learned it from the Spirit of God. "Evening and morning and at noon I utter *my complaint* and moan, and he hears my voice" (Ps. 55:17). "Hear my voice, O God, in *my complaint*; preserve my life from dread of the enemy" (Ps. 64:1). "I pour out *my complaint* before him, I tell my trouble before him" (Ps. 142:2). The Lord is guiding us in His Word regarding how to respond when it seems that in every direction our lives are surrounded by sorrow. *Look up...lament...then listen.*

> *When darkness veils His lovely face,*
> *I rest on His unchanging grace;*
> *In every high and stormy gale,*
> *My anchor holds within the veil.*
> *On Christ, the solid Rock, I stand;*
> *All other ground is sinking sand,*
> *All other ground is sinking sand.*

("The Solid Rock" by Edward Mote)

NOVEMBER 13
Ezekiel 1-3

"A Prophet Among Them"

There is no higher privilege on this earth than to be a servant of the God of heaven. We use the term "servant" so frequently in connection with our faith and our relationship to the Lord, the world, and each other that I think we often fail to recognize what a radical concept it is to view ourselves as servants. The Lord has turned the role of servanthood upside down, or perhaps it is more accurate to say, "right side up." Apart from the grace of God's work in a person's mind, no one would ever aspire to the calling or position of a servant. In the values of this world's system, no place is more demeaning than that of a servant. It carries with it, we are told, the loss of identity and self-esteem. Nothing could be further from the truth! Living as a servant of God is the way to finding our true life and ultimate freedom (Matt. 16:24-26).

This does not mean that serving the Lord will always be an easy or even pleasant responsibility. Ezekiel will make that clear as we follow his service for God in our Scripture reading over the next several days. Ezekiel was called to a simple yet arduous task, to a difficult people in a difficult time. Ezekiel lived as a priest among the refugees of Judah held captive in Babylon. In effect, Ezekiel was a minister of God in a huge refugee camp established by King Nebuchadnezzar near Babylon. Most Bible scholars believe Ezekiel was included in the second deportation of Jewish people in 597 BC. The final deportation occurred in 586 BC with the destruction of Jerusalem. So in effect, Ezekiel had a "double audience," including refugees already in exile and the other comprised of people in Judah who continued in their rebellious ways and would soon join them.

Neither of these audiences were receptive to the ministry and message of Ezekiel. The Lord told Ezekiel that he was being sent as God's servant-messenger to a willful and stubborn people. No promise of "success" was given to Ezekiel by the Lord (Ezek. 2:1-4). However, what *was* given to Ezekiel was a very clear mission and mandate. "I send you to them, and you shall say to them, 'Thus says the Lord God'" (Ezek. 2:4). Ezekiel had one supreme ministry, to say what God said. He was not to create a message; he was to deliver a message. Ezekiel's call was not to be an orator but an ambassador. He was not accountable for responding to God's message; he was responsible for delivering God's message. And just what would be Ezekiel's reward? The reward of knowing he had faithfully fulfilled his calling as God's messenger, "And whether they hear or refuse to hear...they will know that a prophet has been among them" (Ezek. 2:5).

As believers in the Lord, we may not be called to the *office* of a prophet, but we do have the ministry of a prophet. We are to faithfully "say what God says." Our primary message is not sharing our opinion but our Lord's revelation. It is not an easy thing. In a culture significantly based on falsehood, the truth is not often a highly valued commodity. But, we must *highly value* the responsibility and the reward of being our Lord's servant-messenger. We must be *faithful*.

> *"Moreover, it is required of stewards that they be found **faithful**."*
> (1 Corinthians 4:2)

> *"Well done, good and **faithful** servant... Enter into the joy of your master."*
> (Matthew 25:23)

NOVEMBER 14
Ezekiel 4-6

"Payday Someday"

> *"And I will stretch out my hand against them and make the land desolate and waste, in all their dwelling places, from the wilderness to Riblah. Then they will know that I am the Lord."*
> (Ezekiel 6:14)

Thomas Jefferson is remembered for many things (not all of them for a noble character). However, if he did nothing but write the words and phrases recorded in the Declaration of Independence, he certainly gave an invaluable gift to the citizens of the original 13 colonies and, ultimately, to the world. They are truly timeless. Yet, in his long life, Jefferson authored an innumerable amount of correspondence, some of which continue to inform us in this present time within our nation.

Some of Jefferson's most powerful words, (we could also describe them as *prophetic*), are inscribed on the stone panels within his memorial in Washington, DC. Perhaps none more sobering and in need of careful consideration in this day than these: "God who gave us life gave us liberty. Can the liberties of a nation be secure when we have removed a conviction that these liberties are the gift of God? Indeed I tremble for my country when I reflect that God is just, that His justice cannot sleep forever."

Jefferson made those statements concerning the dreadful evil of slavery. We could wish that the great man had personally heeded his own words regarding his part in perpetuating that horrible evil. Regardless, Jefferson's words carry with them a message prophetic and as true of God today as in Ezekiel's day. "God's justice cannot sleep forever." Ezekiel described in words and dramatic actions how truly terrible it is when God's justice is awakened and applied to a nation. For over 800 years, Jehovah had patiently endured the rebellion and the idolatry of His people, Israel. After repeatedly disciplining judgments for their sin through the generations, the full wrath of His "awakened justice" would now fall upon the people of Judah and Jerusalem.

One of the most celebrated orators in America during the first half of the twentieth century was Dr. R. G. Lee, longtime pastor of Bellevue Baptist Church in Memphis, Tennessee. His most noted sermon and oration was entitled "Payday Someday." The message focused on the wrath of God that ultimately fell upon wicked King Ahab, Queen Jezebel, and the people of Israel. However, Dr. Lee's application, shared in his inimitable expressiveness, warned people everywhere of the ultimate "payday" that will come "someday" to unrepentant sinners.

In that sobering truth of inescapable judgment against unrepentant sinners, we also find an absolute and certain hope. It is the *hope of repentance*. Jesus said, "...unless you repent, you shall also likewise perish" (Luke 13:3), and His words contain the unexpressed but unequivocal promise if you repent, you shall not perish. Jesus' message to His own generation is His timeless message shared by His ambassadors to every generation, "Repent and believe the gospel" (Mark 1:15). The gospel is the good news promising that we can all avoid the "payday someday" for the wages of our sin, and instead receive *this day* the "free gift of God," eternal life, through Jesus Christ our Lord (Rom. 6:23). Thank God, through faith in Jesus, our "payday someday" is past. *Jesus paid it all!*

NOVEMBER 15
Ezekiel 7-9

"A Desecrated Temple"

"Then he said to me, 'Son of man, dig in the wall.' So I dug in the wall, and behold, there was an entrance. And he said to me, 'Go in, and see the vile abominations that they are committing here.'"
(Ezekiel 8:8-9)

During my senior year in college, I served as a hall leader in one of the dormitories. In that role, I was responsible for maintaining basic discipline and "law and order" among about 100 college-age men. Not an easy task, I can assure you, even at a Christian university! At the close of the school year, one of my responsibilities was to recommend room leaders who would serve in the dormitories the following semester. One man who greatly impressed me was a sophomore named

James. When James learned of my nomination of him to serve the following school year, he sought me out and said he was somewhat nervous regarding the position. As I recall, he shared those concerns with me, saying, "Sam, I'm just not sure. What if I get someone in the room who has real issues?" "James," I said, "I know you are up to the job; you will be just fine."

Four months later, as I walked across campus during my first semester in seminary, I heard someone loudly calling my name. Turning, I saw James running toward me on the sidewalk, emphatically saying, "I told you so! I told you so!" "What are you talking about, James?" I asked as he caught his breath. "I told you last spring that I was concerned about being responsible for someone with serious issues!" When I asked James to explain what he meant, he shared an experience that stunned me. Earlier that week, he had returned to the dorm unexpectedly and, entering his room, discovered one of his roommates kneeling in the dark before a lighted candle shrine, chanting prayers to a pagan god. To say I was surprised by what James recounted would be the understatement of my life! Having lived in that dorm and involved in prayer meetings, ministry planning, and great times with Christian friends, I simply could not imagine a room becoming, for a moment, a shrine for pagan worship!

What James saw pales in comparison to what the Lord revealed to Ezekiel regarding what was taking place in the temple of God on Mount Zion. Pagan worship by the priests in their chambers, weeping by women at the temple gate in the worship liturgy for the fertility god, Tammuz, and the elders of the nation with their backs to the temple sanctuary worshiping the sun god. Unspeakable idolatry, hidden from the eyes of the people but not from the all-seeing eyes of God.

This Old Testament revelation should remind us personally of a New Testament exhortation. "My little children, keep yourselves from idols" (1 John 5:21). The aged apostle John wrote these words to believers living in the idol-filled culture of the first century. Still, we must not believe that John's nor Ezekiel's revelation exhortation has no bearing for us as believers in this twenty-first century. For anything we honor or cherish more than Jesus is an idol. John Calvin warned us that apart from the means of God's grace, our hearts become "factories of idols." Yes, we must be relentless daily in rooting out of our hearts any competitors for the love and loyalty that belong only to Jesus. "What agreement has the temple of God with idols? For we are the temple of the living God..." (2 Cor. 6:16)

NOVEMBER 16
Ezekiel 10-12

"ICHABOD"

"And the glory of the Lord went up from the cherub to the threshold of the house, and the house was filled with the cloud, and the court was filled with the brightness of the glory of the Lord...4 And the glory of the Lord went up from the midst of the city and stood on the mountain that is on the east side of the city."23
(Ezekiel 10:4; 11:23)

Ichabod is a strange word for those of us who speak English, for it is not an English word. In reality, very little of the English language has its roots in England or America. However, people who speak American English are usually only familiar with the term "Ichabod" as the name of the main character Ichabod Crane in the story by Washington Irving, "The Legend of Sleepy Hollow." The word "Ichabod" is of Hebrew origin, meaning "without glory" and communicating "departed glory." It is first used in 1 Samuel 4:21 when the dying wife of Phinehas utters it as the name for her newborn son upon hearing that the Philistines have captured the Ark of the Covenant, and her husband and her father-in-law, Eli, have died.

Our reading in Ezekiel today records the terrible spiritual realization of "Ichabod" as the glory cloud of God's presence, the "Shekinah," rises up from the place it descended nearly 400 years earlier at the dedication of the temple by King Solomon. We are told the glory cloud departed by way of the temple's eastern gate and then moved further east to temporarily manifest the presence of God over the mountain to the east of Jerusalem, the Mount of Olives. Eventually, the glory cloud of the Lord lifted up from that mountain crest and disappeared from the earth altogether. No event could have been more indicative of God's removal of His presence from Jerusalem and the temple than this, "Ichabod," the glory of God departing.

However, within our reading today is also the promise that God's glory will not be lost forever. Jehovah promises through Ezekiel that in the latter days, He will bring spiritual, redeeming life to the people of Israel. "And they shall be my people, and I will be their God." (Ezekiel 11:19-20) As believers in Jesus, we are given a fuller revelation about the return of God's glory and His salvation to Israel. We are told that Jesus was welcomed at his birth as the "glory to your people Israel" (Luke 2:32). Jesus prayed to His Father the evening before His crucifixion that His followers might experience "the glory" He had known and shared before the world began (John 17:24). When Jesus ascended to heaven, He was taken up in a cloud of glory (Acts 1:9).

When Jesus returns to earth, He will come with "power and great glory" (Luke 21:27). In fact, it is to that same small mountain to the east of Jerusalem that Jesus will return (Zech. 14:4). Then, in fulfillment of the ancient prophecy and psalm of David, the shout will rise as Messiah enters in all His glory to establish His Kingdom that will never end:

"Lift up your heads, O gates! And lift them up, O ancient doors, that the King of glory may come in. Who is this King of glory? The Lord of hosts, He is the King of glory!" (Ps. 24:9-10)

"Ichabod," no more, forever. Amen.

NOVEMBER 17
Ezekiel 13-15

"CAREFUL WHAT YOU SAY"

"Because you have disheartened the righteous falsely, although I have not grieved him, and you have encouraged the wicked, that he should not turn from his evil way to save his life..."
(Ezekiel 13:22)

Many who are reading these pages heard as a child, or possibly spoke yourself, the cute "comeback" when engaged in a childhood "word fight" —"Sticks and stones may break my bones, but words will never hurt me." That sounded like a fantastic response as a child, didn't it? Yet, we know now, all too well, that it was childish and untrue. Words can hurt, and they can hurt deeply. The truth is that there is tremendous power in words, both for good and for evil. The Bible tells us that "death and life" are in the power of words (Prov. 18:21). According to Jesus, people will one day give an account to God for "every careless word" they have spoken (Matt. 12:36). Our words are incredibly important, especially when they are employed in speaking for God.

Many years ago, I was invited to participate with two other pastors on a local television program focused on issues related to faith and the practice of faith in our community. As expected, several of the host's questions had to do with what we, as pastors, believed the Lord had to say about some subjects that are often considered "culturally" sensitive. In response to one of my statements, a fellow pastor-panelist of what could be described as a theologically liberal persuasion thumped his fingertips together and, looking to the ceiling (though directing his words toward me), said, "Well, we must be careful not to come across as if we speak for God." I freely admit it took more self-control than should have been necessary to keep me from responding, "Well, Reverend, I don't think you have to worry about that because it is very obvious *you don't!*"

Perhaps a better question for me to have asked the pastor, and in doing so also to have asked myself, would have been, "If we do not speak for God, then for whom do we speak?" As ambassadors for God, we are called and commissioned to speak for Him. However, we must never allow ourselves to think we only speak for God in public gatherings. We are to speak in all situations with an awareness that our words are to align with God's Word. Only God can author the Word of God, but in all our conversations, we need to be mindful that our words either draw people to God's truth or deter them from it. How can we fulfill that assignment most faithfully? First, by knowing the Word of God ourselves. How can we speak from our minds what is not in our minds? Secondly, by relying on the Holy Spirit to make our words reflect the character of Jesus, "...full of grace and truth" (John 1:14). Thirdly, by giving space and freedom to others to speak into our own lives.

Perhaps when it comes to *our* words, there are no words more important than these to commit to our memory for controlling our present and future conversations: "Let your speech always be gracious, seasoned with salt, so that you may know how you ought to answer each person" (Col. 4:6).

NOVEMBER 18
Ezekiel 16-18

"Turn and Live"

"For I have no pleasure in the death of anyone, declares the Lord God; so turn, and live."
(Ezekiel 18:32)

I will call her "Janet," though that is not her name. She now lives in another state and continues to enjoy the "new life" she entered one evening so many years ago. Her story is one of the most unique examples of the plea and promise that God made through His prophet Ezekiel 2600 years ago. Janet is an example of a person who, by the grace of God, "turned and lived."

I remember the first time I saw Janet; however, it was not until the following day that I had the opportunity of hearing and becoming part of her amazing story. One Wednesday evening, while I was teaching a Bible study class in our church auditorium, I saw a woman slip in late to the service and take a seat in the back row. When the gathering concluded, I looked for the lady to speak to her and invite her to another service, but she left as soon as the class ended. The following afternoon, my administrative assistant informed me that someone was at the reception desk and would like a few minutes of counsel. When Janet entered my office, I immediately recognized her as the late-arriving guest from the previous evening. I asked her how I could be of help, and that is when she told me her unique story.

"Yesterday afternoon," she said, "I decided that when I got home from work, I was going to commit suicide. My life has been nothing but heartache and pain for years." Janet continued, "As I drove down the road on my way home to carry out my plans, I followed the cars ahead of mine in making what I thought was a detour around an accident. I was amazed when I discovered the cars were turning into a parking lot, and I suddenly found myself sitting in front of your church." What Janet said next astounded me then, and these many years later thrills my soul. "I thought maybe this was a sign from God or something, so I decided to follow the people into the church and sit in the sanctuary. You were teaching from the Bible and sharing how God says He will give people a brand-new life. Somehow, I knew this was what I was supposed to hear. I prayed along with you at the end of the class, and from that moment and all through the night and all day, I have been filled with joy and peace. Pastor, I just had to come to see you today. Can you tell me what has happened to me?" I paused for several moments, taking in what I had just heard, and then amazed at God's grace, I answered, "Yes, Janet, I most certainly can tell you what has happened to you."

What a joy it was to share the good news of God's love with Janet and see her, over the months ahead, publicly profess her faith at her baptism, grow in the Lord, and enter the community of our church family. You can imagine my joy when, a couple of years later, I was blessed to officiate at her wedding and watch her and her husband serve the Lord together. Janet is a living example of the Lord's invitation, "turn and live" (Ezek. 18:32). Whenever any person turns to the Lord, it is a "right turn" because it is a "life turn." I am so glad for those people who, that Wednesday evening, led Janet to make a "right turn!" I wonder, if people followed us today, where would our turns lead them?

NOVEMBER 19
Ezekiel 19-21

"A Fool's Judgment"

"Then I said, 'Ah, Lord God! They are saying of me,
'Is he not a maker of parables?'"
(Ezekiel 20:49)

One Sunday evening in the late 1960s, a missionary spoke in a small church to an even smaller congregation in West Texas. Over the previous weeks, he had traveled hundreds of miles visiting churches and Sunday schools to share his burden for bringing the gospel to a poor and needy country in South America. A young couple attended the service that evening who had come to hear the missionary and see his slide presentation about his "field of dreams." The couple was very poor as well and had recently purchased some barren acres of land in an attempt to build a small cattle ranch. That evening, their hearts were touched as they learned of the needs of that far away, impoverished, unreached country. In an act of faith, the young couple joined with others in supporting the missionary with a small monthly pledge of financial support. As the years passed, the couple succeeded in developing a small ranch, and faithfully they continued to give to the missionary and to the mission agency with which he served.

This couple was never blessed with children, so as they planned for their last will and testament, they decided to bequeath their small ranch to the mission agency they had first learned about in that Sunday evening service long ago. Eventually, the man and his wife passed away. Still, due to administrative failures at the local savings and loan company, the mission agency was not notified about the property bequeathed to it. Eventually, an oil and natural gas company began to dig some very successful wells in that area of West Texas. They inquired about the small ranch's ownership and discovered it legally belonged to the mission ministry. After receiving permission from the mission to conduct initial testing on the land, the oil and gas company made a financial offer to the mission for the rights to drill on the property—$12,000,000! Yes, count those zeroes carefully—12 million dollars! Those funds were eventually used for planting churches and training gospel workers on several continents. The "foolish decision" of the young couple and the "foolish travels" of the missionary appointee long ago did not seem so foolish anymore!

Ezekiel was considered a fool by most of the people in his day. Paul was called a fool by most of the sages and philosophers as he shared the gospel in Athens. Through the ages, believers in Jesus regularly find themselves considered "fools for Christ's sake" (1 Cor. 4:10). No one enjoys being thought a fool. Still, we must always remember that God has "made foolish the wisdom of this world" (1 Cor. 1:20). Foolishness can only be measured by the passing of time. Investing our lives in the service of the Lord may seem foolish in the value system of this world, but in the eternal ages to come, we will recognize it as the wisest investment we have ever made!

NOVEMBER 20
Ezekiel 22-24

"Filling the Gap"

*"And I sought for a man among them who should build up the wall
and stand in the breach before me for the land,
that I should not destroy it, but I found none."*
(Ezekiel 22:30)

Most historians and Civil War scholars agree that the Battle of Gettysburg, fought July 1-3, 1863, was the turning point of the Civil War. Previous to Gettysburg, the war, especially in the eastern theater, had been a continual chain of Confederate victories over the Union Army. To bring the war to a close, General Robert E. Lee made the bold decision to invade the North, believing a major victory on northern soil would force President Lincoln to offer terms for a settlement and recognition of the Confederacy as an independent nation.

The stakes could not have been higher as the massed armies of the north and south, over 125,000 men, converged on the small but strategic crossroads town of Gettysburg, Pennsylvania. Over those three humid summer days in July, the largest and bloodiest battle ever fought in North America took place, producing over 50,000 causalities. There were many turning points in the battle as the two armies assaulted and tore at each other. Still, perhaps the ultimate and decisive moment occurred on the afternoon of July 2, when the left-center of the Union forces began to crumble, and a huge gap emerged in the lines. Surging into the hole charged over 1,500 Mississippi volunteers.

At that critical moment, one of the corps commanders for the Union, General Winfield Scott Hancock, perceived the crisis and mounted his horse. He then looked around for any troops available to plug the gap in the crumbling Federal lines. Nearby, he saw 250 men from Minnesota under the command of Colonel William Calvin. General Hancock shouted from his horse while pointing at the surging line of Confederate troops, "Colonel, do you see those flags? Capture them!" Without hesitation, Colonel Calvin ordered his men to fix bayonets and personally led the charge of the small band headlong into the vast Confederate force. The wave of southern soldiers surged around the Minnesotans, and their attack was slowed for about 10 minutes, but it was enough. Ten minutes was just enough time for General Scott to bring up reinforcements from the reserve and, through bloody conflict, stop and turn back the Confederate advance.

Those 10 minutes saved everything, but at a terrible cost. Eighty-two percent of the 250 who filled the gap that day were either killed or wounded. It is not a stretch to say the obedience of those 250 men and the blood of the 205 who became casualties changed the lives of over seven million people held in slavery, changed the lives of 30 million people living in America, and changed the lives of hundreds of millions of people yet unborn.

"Filling the gap" through intercessory prayer during spiritual warfare has the same incredible power. Intercession means "to go between," and when it is connected to prayer, it expresses "going to God on behalf of another." There is a mystery in how intercessory prayer is part of God's sovereign plans, yet there is no mystery about its power. Also, there is no mystery as to the terrible loss when there is no one to intercede (Ezek. 22:30). God said He looked for an intercessor in Ezekiel's day and found none to pray to Him on behalf of people who were in dreadful danger. God still looks for and *listens to* intercessors. Does He find an intercessor? Does He hear an intercessor in you and me? Who will we "kneel down to" and "stand up for" in prayer today?

NOVEMBER 21
Ezekiel 25-27

"Pre-Written History"

"They shall destroy the walls of Tyre and break down her towers, and I will scrape her soil from her and make her a bare rock. She shall be in the midst of the sea a place for the spreading of nets...."
(Ezekiel 26:4-5)

"**R**ewriting the history books" is a phrase often used to describe the accomplishments of people who have succeeded in their field to such an extent that all the previous records of achievement have been completely shattered. That is something that should be rightly applauded. However, when "rewriting the history books" refers to the practice prevalent in academia today of reinterpreting historical records through the lens of present-day political values, that is, at best, dishonest and potentially dangerous. Thankfully, by God's grace, the attempts to rewrite the historical accounts of the Bible have been proven, time and time again, to be total failures in hindering the testimony of God's mighty acts and eternal truth. For our eternal God, the future is as clear as the past. We see this demonstrated in the fulfillment of the Lord's prophetic messages concerning future events. In fact, for our timeless God, His prophecies are so certain we could describe them as *"pre-written history."*

Our reading today in Ezekiel regarding God's prophetic judgment against the city of Tyre is an amazing example of this "pre-written" history. God declared that Babylon and many other nations would be involved in the destruction of Tyre. The Lord went into such descriptive detail of this judgment that he declared this ancient and renowned city to be scraped to the rock and that it would become a place where fishermen would dry their nets. Just a few years after Ezekiel communicated this coming woe on Tyre, King Nebuchadnezzar and his Babylonian armies laid siege to the city in 586 BC. For 13 long years, Tyre was encircled and starved, finally falling in 573 BC. However, during those long years, the leaders of the coastal city of Tyre built another fortress on a rocky island located about half a mile from the shore.

Eventually, the leaders of Tyre and a sizable part of the population escaped to this new island city, which boasted landward walls built to a towering height of 150 feet. Tyre survived and continued to flourish for over 200 years. Then in 333 BC, Alexander the Great requested that, as an expression of peace, he might be permitted to worship in the great temple of Tyre. Doubting Alexander's trustworthiness, the leaders of Tyre insolently rejected his request, believing their island fortress was impregnable. In response to their rebuff, Alexander spent months building a causeway from the shore to the walls of Tyre. Interestingly, Alexander scraped up the rubble of the previous city of Tyre to construct this highway into the sea. Finally, in July of 332 BC, the walls of Tyre were breached, the leaders executed, and over 30,000 citizens were sold by Alexander as slaves.

If you conduct a media search on the web for pictures of the ancient site of Tyre, you will view some amazing photos. Take your time, and you may find some of my favorites—pictures of fishermen drying their nets on the rubble that was once the great city of Tyre! God's prophecies are certain, and so are every one of His promises to you and me.

NOVEMBER 22
Ezekiel 28-30

"The King Maker Crushed"

"Your heart was proud because of your beauty; you corrupted your wisdom for the sake of your splendor. I cast you to the ground; I exposed you before kings, to feast their eyes on you."
(Ezekiel 28:17)

"When the head of a snake is cut off, the rest of his body is an ordinary rope," so says the wisdom of an ancient African proverb. Many snakes can shed their skins, and some have the ability to reproduce sections of their bodies, but no snake can regenerate its head. "Cut off the head of the snake, and the snake dies," states another African proverb. Since the Garden of Eden, our planet has endured the hissing lies and the venomous evil of the original serpent, Satan. To be certain, this vile creature has the uncanny ability to camouflage himself, sometimes in the form of ruling powers and governmental authorities, as is described in our Scripture reading today in the ancient kingdoms of Tyre, Sidon, and Egypt. Amazingly, and perhaps most deceptively, this serpent, the "father of lies" (John 8:44), has the ability to masquerade, disguising himself as a minister of the gospel (2 Cor. 11:15). This supreme deceiver transforms into an angel of light (2 Cor. 11:14), which is what he once was.

Satan once existed in heaven as Lucifer, "the shining one," and the Lord refers to him in our Scripture reading today as "an anointed guardian cherub" (Ezek. 28:14) who served for ages before the throne of God. Because of his pride-filled rebellion and unrighteousness, Satan was cast "as a profane thing from the mountain of God" (Ezek. 28:16). Since that moment, this arch-deceiver, the Devil, has worked relentlessly to turn the image bearers of God from the blessing of obedience to the destruction that comes through his deception. This one who once served faithfully before the throne of God in heaven still rules behind so many thrones here on earth. He leads an innumerable demonic host of rulers, authorities, cosmic powers, and spiritual forces in this present darkness (Eph. 6:12). Yes, Satan, the god of this world, is powerful (2 Cor. 4:4), but he is not all-powerful. We must not run from him but resist him steadfastly in humble submission to God (1 Peter 5:9).

The fate of this wicked serpent is already set by God and sealed in His Word. "The devil who had deceived them was thrown into the lake of fire and sulfur where the beast and the false prophet were, and they will be tormented day and night forever and ever" (Rev. 20:10). This is the doom awaiting the Devil. So, the next time the Devil reminds you of your past, don't argue; *just remind him of his future!*

> *And though this world, with devils filled,*
> *Should threaten to undo us,*
> *We will not fear, for God has willed*
> *His truth to triumph through us:*
> *The Prince of Darkness grim,*
> *We tremble not for him;*
> *His rage we can endure,*
> *For lo! his doom is sure,*
> *One little word shall fell him.*

("A Mighty Fortress is our God" by Martin Luther)

NOVEMBER 23
Ezekiel 31-33

"A Watchman's Warning"

> *"But if the watchman sees the sword coming and does not blow the trumpet, so that the people are not warned, and the sword comes and takes any one of them, that person is taken away in his iniquity, but his blood I will require at the watchman's hand."*
> (Ezekiel 33:6)

For several years, I served on staff with a fellow pastor who believed he should keep his office desk so well organized that if something happened to him, the person who succeeded him would know exactly what projects he was working on. My ministry colleague faithfully cleared and organized his desk at the end of every day. While I admired my friend's dedication, as anyone who has been in my office can attest, I never followed his example! Any person tasked with deciphering the papers on my desk or the objects in its drawers has their work cut out for them!

Although the things in my desk may not be well organized, each object has a definite meaning and purpose to me. For example, there is an unusual item in the center drawer that I have kept for many years. It has a powerful mission in my life. If you looked there, you would find an obituary I cut from our local newspaper that includes the picture of a man in his late 30s. Years ago, the man was diagnosed with a terrible and terminal muscle disease. His doctor, who was also my physician, asked the man if he would be willing to talk with me. He said he would, so shortly after the doctor reached out to me, I made an appointment to visit the man in his home.

On the day of the visit, his wife answered the door and invited me to come in. Entering the family room, she introduced me to her husband, who was practically unable to walk because of the disease's progression. As you can understand, the man who had been so active and strong a few months earlier struggled emotionally to cope with the terminal diagnosis he had recently received from our mutual physician. During the visit, we developed a level of trust that allowed him to share his fears. I spoke with him about the hope found in Christ, and he listened carefully; however, he tired quickly and needed to rest. I asked to come again, and over the next few weeks, I made several visits to talk and pray with him. On my last visit, I brought him a Bible and promised to return in a few days to talk more about the Lord and eternal life. You will notice I wrote, "my last visit," but I did not know then that it would be our last time together. Somehow, through a busy schedule and a busy life, I did not make that return visit when I had planned. He was in my thoughts and prayers, and I definitely *planned* to return, but my good intentions never materialized. Then one day I received a phone call from the man's brokenhearted wife telling me he had passed away. The feeling that swept over me that afternoon I cannot describe.

Did my friend come to faith in Christ? Is he in heaven? I do not know the answers to those questions, but I never want to forget him or forget the urgent, eternal responsibility that is mine. It is shared by all of us who know the truth of the coming day of God's judgment and the certain hope in this present day of God's salvation: "Therefore, knowing the fear of the Lord, we persuade others" (2 Cor. 5:11).

NOVEMBER 24
Ezekiel 34-36

"SHEPHERD OF ISRAEL"

"And I will set up over them one shepherd, my servant David, and he shall feed them: he shall feed them and be their shepherd. And I, the Lord, will be their God, and my servant David shall be prince among them. I am the Lord; I have spoken."
(Ezekiel 34:23-24)

As we have made this journey along the *pathways* of the Old Testament, no illustration of the people of Israel and the God of Israel has been shared more often than that of sheep and their shepherd. What could be more tragic than wandering and scattered sheep who have worthless and faithless shepherds? Yet, through the recorded history of the descendants of Abraham, that has been the reality of their condition—wandering sheep whose spiritual shepherds have been faithless in lovingly and truthfully caring for the sheep. For this reason, God denounces the behavior and character of the spiritual leaders who failed to care for His flock (Ezek. 34:1-10). And because they are His flock, the Lord, in His love and mercy, takes the responsibility to shepherd His people. What God shares through His prophet Ezekiel, and records in Chapters 34-36, are some of the most beautiful and powerful statements of the Lord's love in all the Word of God.

Even more remarkable is what our Lord declares He will do for His chosen sheep of Israel, those who have been called by His grace to be part of His flock. Take to your own heart these truths about the Shepherd of Israel, our Shepherd.

God is the Sovereign Shepherd...

Read Chapters 34-36 carefully and note the number of times God declares, "I will." These wandering sheep are completely and hopelessly lost and have no claim on the Shepherd's mercy. "It is not for your sake that I will act, declares the Lord God; let that be known to you. Be ashamed and confounded for your ways, O house of Israel" (Ezek. 36:32). God will act because of *grace alone*, His sovereign grace that is an expression of His sovereign will. "I am the Lord; I have spoken, and I will do it" (Ezek. 36:36).

God is the Seeking Shepherd...

It is the "Good Shepherd" who seeks the lost sheep. "For thus says the Lord God: Behold, I, I myself will search for my sheep and will seek them out" (Ezek. 34:11). There are no sheep who are "seekers of the Shepherd." "All we like sheep have gone astray; we have turned—every one—to his own way" (Isa. 53:6). There is none who seeks after God (Rom. 3:11). God is the seeking Shepherd, and He seeks through the whole world to find His sheep that are lost. "As a shepherd seeks out his flock when he is among his sheep that have been scattered, so I will seek out my sheep... And I will bring them out from the peoples and gather them from the countries..." (Ezek. 34:12-13)

God is the Saving Shepherd...

The Shepherd of Israel is on a mission to seek and save the lost sheep (Luke 19:10). He will be the one Shepherd, David, the Prince over the flock. They will be one people, and He will be their one God (Ezek. 34:23-24). God will not only be the Shepherd *over* them; He will be the Shepherd *within* them. The Shepherd and His sheep will be bound forever in a new covenant of peace (Ezek. 34:25) that gives a *new spirit* and *new heart* that produces a *new relationship*. "You shall be my people, and I will be your God" (Ezek. 36:25-28).

What a Shepherd—sovereign, seeking, and saving! What a blessing. "The Lord is *my shepherd!*" (Ps. 23:1)

NOVEMBER 25
Ezekiel 37-38

"ALIVE FROM THE DEAD!"

"And I will put my Spirit within you, and you shall live, and I will place you in your own land. Then you shall know that I am the Lord; I have spoken, and I will do it, declares the Lord."
(Ezekiel 37:14)

Over the years that I have served as pastor, there have been many occasions on which people have become excited or "concerned" that the "last days" prophesied by the Lord have arrived or are highly imminent. On most of these occasions, the impetus has come from the teaching or writings of a prophet who has "discovered" a timetable that can "absolutely verify" that the return of the Lord is at hand. All of these teachings and revelations have had one common denominator: they have all been proven wrong!

Date-setters and end-time prophets have been disrupting and distracting believers since the days of the apostles. Still, it is surprising that, despite our Lord's emphatic statements that no one knows the day of His return (Matt. 24:36) and that His followers are always to be watching and ready for His appearing (Luke 12:40), so many believers spend so much time and money on these "prophetic teachings." No doubt "money" is the true motivation for these "end-time messengers." They are "prophets for profit."

The Lord long ago declared the secret things belong to Him but that the truths He has revealed belong to His people through all generations (Deut. 29:29). God has told us all we need to know to assure us of His plans for the future and what He has told us is amazing! Perhaps few passages in Scripture testify to God's power to accomplish His promises than today's two chapters of our reading. Many are familiar with the words or tune to the old spiritual "Dem Dry Bones," taken from Ezekiel 37. Still, they fail to realize that it is also one of the most miraculous passages concerning the end times and the people of Israel.

Some of us in our lifetimes have seen the amazing words of God's message being fulfilled. After hundreds and hundreds of years in which the scattered Jewish people were "buried" among the nations and against all the possible obstacles and opposition of devils and men, the descendants of Abraham have returned, survived, and thrived on the "mountains of Israel." There has never been such a "resurrection" of a vanquished, despised, and dispersed people in the recorded history of the world.

Yet, nearly 600 years before the birth of Christ, the Lord prophesied and pledged this immigration would occur. The Lord promised that the return of the Jewish people would take place in the "latter days" and that it would precede a life-giving work of the Spirit uniting Judah and Ephraim under the rule of "My servant David," the Messiah who "shall be king over them, and they shall all have one shepherd" (Ezek. 37:24).

What is the timing of the events we have witnessed in the birth and growth of the modern nation of Israel regarding the message in these chapters of Ezekiel? Well, we certainly should not interpret them through the writings of the sensational "end-time experts" available everywhere in print and on the web. However, it is not going too far to say that the "dry bones of Israel" scattered and buried for ages are now assembling in the land promised by God for the nation and that "the stage is set" for the "Return of the King!" Until He comes, let us be faithfully serving our Savior, sharing the good news of His salvation with all people everywhere and praying with expectancy, "Come, Lord Jesus!" (Rev. 22:20)

NOVEMBER 26
Ezekiel 39-40

"The Coming Judge"

"And I will set my glory among the nations, and all the nations shall see my judgment that I have executed, and my hand that I have laid on them. The house of Israel shall know that I am the Lord their God, from that day forward."
(Ezekiel 39:21-22)

Many years ago, two men were spending their last day locked in individual cells on death row in a prison in the Western United States. The hands of the clock on the wall slowly moved, marking the passing of the final hours these two men would spend on earth. Just down the hall, preparations were being made, and the processes were carefully checked and rechecked by the guards designated to carry out the executions. The last meal was eaten by the doomed men. Their family members visited and shared their final, fearful words of farewell. A local pastor arrived to read Scripture, pray with both men, and help them prepare their souls for their departure into eternity in just a few earthly minutes.

The warden alternately looked at the clock on the wall and the phone on the desk, which had a secure line to the governor. How the warden's eyes widened with amazement when the phone did ring only a few minutes before the final preparations for the executions began. The warden's conversation with the governor was brief, but what an impact it made on that death watch. The warden handed the receiver to one of his lieutenants and walked to the front of the prisoner's door in the first cell. With true joy on his countenance, he informed the stunned convict that the governor, upon receiving further evidence regarding his case, was granting the convicted man a complete pardon. Hearing the news, the pardoned man looked toward the ceiling and, with outstretched arms, danced for joy. The warden then walked a few steps further to the next cell, where the convicted man, having heard his fellow inmate's celebration, waited with a face bright with hope and anticipation. Fixed on the face of the warden was a sad and furrowed brow while he silently shook his head and spoke a wordless doom to the guilty man. Hope was extinguished, and judgment had arrived.

Imagine how differently the warden appeared to these two men. To one, his face was like that of a heavenly angel; to the other, he was like the angel of death. The same official, but with two very different judgments to render. So it will be on the day and hour described in Ezekiel, Chapter 39, and in many passages within the Word of God. It is the Day of the Lord, the day of Divine intervention, the day of Christ's return, a day of deliverance, and a day of doom. For the people of the Lord, it is the day of "the appearing of the glory of our great God and Savior, Jesus Christ" (Titus 2:13). For the unrepentant, it is the day when Christ returns "in flaming fire, inflicting vengeance on those who do not know God and on those who do not obey the Gospel of our Lord Jesus" (2 Thess. 1:8). The same coming Judge, yet how different the judgments!

In light of this inevitable approaching day, we must ask ourselves if we are ready. Are we prepared to meet the Lord as our delivering judge? Are we certain? Also, are we ready and willing to be perceived in radically different ways by different types of people? To some, what we believe and live and share smells of a life-giving fragrance. To others, our life and message are like the stench of death (2 Cor. 2:16). Regardless of how we are perceived, will we, with faithfulness, share the message? Time is short; call upon the coming judge!

NOVEMBER 27
Ezekiel 41-42

"THE COMING TEMPLE"

"Now when he had finished measuring the interior of the temple area, he led me out by the gate that faced east, and measured the temple area all around."
(Ezekiel 42:15)

The second time my wife and I were privileged to lead a tour group to Israel, a well-known Bible teacher in America was the trip's organizer.

This man's ministry had grown significantly after he was featured as a guest teacher several times on a nationally broadcast Christian television program. With his skills as a communicator and his area of expertise regarding Israel in Bible prophecy, this brother quickly gained a significant following in both the United States and Israel. In fact, through his teaching, our tour leader became friends with a number of the orthodox rabbis in the city of Jerusalem. This friendship gave him access to places that most tour groups from America had never visited.

Of course, we were delighted to follow our teacher to several of these exclusive sites. Some of them included access to normally restricted areas on the Mount of Olives, and others were allowed access to recently excavated areas under the Temple Mount. It was certainly exciting to visit these sites, but perhaps the most unique was a building we saw located in the old city of Jerusalem. At this location, financial gifts from Jewish people around the world were being used to create garments, tapestries, musical instruments, bowls, censors, tongs, knives, etc. All these objects and more were being prepared for one purpose—for use in the service and worship of Jehovah in the next temple. It was amazing to recognize that many Jewish people took the description of the Third Temple in the Book of Ezekiel quite literally and were preparing the items necessary to reinstitute the worship when that temple was erected.

I recall a member of our group asking the aged lead rabbi how he thought the temple would be constructed on Mount Zion when the site was also claimed by millions of Muslims. With a twinkle in his eye and a shrug of his shoulders, the rabbi responded, "I don't know, but Messiah will take care of the details when He comes." You could not help but be touched by his sincere and trusting faith, but sadly the Messiah for which he looked and longed for was not Jesus.

Bible scholars are divided regarding the nature of this temple described by Ezekiel. Some take it as symbolic of the building of God's Kingdom. Yet, it is hard to imagine that to be the case, given the number of details regarding its dimensions and the references in other Old Testament and New Testament passages regarding a temple standing in Jerusalem in the latter days. Bible teachers who hold to the literal interpretation of the Millennium (the thousand-year reign of Christ on earth) believe Ezekiel is probably receiving a vision of the Millennial Temple. Regardless, this vision of the temple should not be interpreted as the temple located in the New Jerusalem. We are told quite clearly that the heavenly city will not need a temple for a very wonderful and blessed reason: "And I saw no temple in the city, for its temple is the Lord God the Almighty and the Lamb" (Rev. 21:22).

Oh yes, there will be a church in heaven—the Church of the Firstborn (Heb. 12:23). The Bride of Christ will be gathered there. "No longer will there be anything accursed, but the throne of God and of the Lamb will be in it, and his servants will worship him" (Rev. 22:3).

NOVEMBER 28
Ezekiel 43-44

"The Eastern Gate"

"Then he led me to the gate, the gate facing east. And behold, the glory of the God of Israel was coming from the east. And the sound of his coming was like the sound of many waters, and the earth shone with his glory."
(Ezekiel 43:1-2)

Very few spots on earth move the heart of the believer with its view more than that from the top of the Mount of Olives looking down upon the Temple Mount and the city of Jerusalem. If you walk far enough up the hill, your view of the city is unobstructed by the lines of tour buses that bring thousands of people each day to have the great "photo op" moment with the holy city in the background. Honestly, the view of Jerusalem from the summit of the Mount of Olives is worth the hike and the cost of the trip.

In the center of the great wall, which dates from medieval times, is a large ornamental gate that has been walled up for ages. This gate is not the gate from the time of Jesus, but this walled entrance stands directly above a gate discovered only a few decades ago that was part of King Herod's wall. It is the gate through which Jesus and His disciples entered the temple courts as they descended from the Mount of Olives on the Sunday before Passover—Palm Sunday. Jesus entered the temple through the eastern gate and once again cleared the courts of the money changers. He then left the temple by another gate, and during the coming final days, He prophesied to the religious leaders that they would see His face no more until one day they would proclaim, "Blessed is He who comes in the name of the Lord" (Matt. 23:39).

Ezekiel prophesies in our reading today of the return of the glory cloud of God's presence by way of the eastern gate (Ezek. 43:4). It was through this same gate that the prophet had watched, as during an earlier vision, the cloud of Jehovah's presence lift up from His temple and leave Jerusalem in rejection of the nation's hypocritical and idolatrous worship (Ezek. 11:23). Now, the Lord returns, His judgment past, and His throne of grace and mercy is in the midst of His covenant people forever and ever. What a vision! What a promise! One day, the eastern gate of Jerusalem, the beautiful gate of God's temple, will open wide to receive the conquering King, the Lord of glory, Jesus Christ (Ps. 24:8). That is an unconditional, absolute promise that one day the doors of the city and temple will open to the King of the ages.

Dear friend, may I remind you of a promise from the King Himself, a promise just as glorious and even more intimate and personal regarding His entrance through an opened door? "Behold, I stand at the door and knock. If anyone hears my voice and opens the door, I will come in to him and eat with him, and he with me" (Rev. 3:20). The King of Glory knocks at the gate of our lives offering the deepest friendship and fellowship. Oh, may our hearts be wide open to Him this day!

NOVEMBER 29
Ezekiel 45-46

"THE BALANCES OF JUSTICE"

"Thus says the Lord God: Enough, O princes of Israel! Put away violence and oppression, and execute justice and righteousness. Cease your evictions of my people, declares the Lord God. You shall have just balances, a just ephah, and a just bath."
(Ezekiel 45:9-10)

The Apostle Paul, in his famous instructions on the grace of love in 1 Corinthians 13, calls on us all to humbly acknowledge the limitations of our wisdom and insight when it comes to the mysteries of God's ways. "For now we see in a mirror dimly, but then face to face. Now I know in part; then I shall know fully, even as I have been fully known" (1 Cor. 13:12). I have always loved the way Paul's words are rendered in the King James Version, "For now we see through a glass, darkly..." At our most enlightened, there are yet so many things that we do not understand about God's ways and also some of God's Words.

Some parts of the Bible, especially those addressing prophetic issues, are not easily understood. Peter tells us that the prophets often did not understand all of the messages the Lord gave them to proclaim and record (1 Peter 1:10-12). Peter freely admits that his dear fellow Apostle Paul wrote some things in his epistles that were hard to understand (2 Peter 3:15). I have always taken some comfort in Peter's admission. Mark Twain, the famous writer and humorist, once said it was not the things in the Bible that he did not understand that troubled him most, but the things which he *did understand*. Many of us can identify with that evaluation!

Our reading today in Ezekiel (as in several other passages he recorded) expresses things we read as "through a glass darkly." It is obvious from the context that Ezekiel is describing a future temple in which "the prince" joins in worship with his people. Yet, we clearly know from the New Testament that the sacrificial system was fulfilled in the sacrifice of the perfect Lamb, Jesus Christ (Heb. 10:14). How does reinstituting this system align with the wonderful truth? The honest answer, for me, is I am not exactly sure.

These sacrifices are not redemptive. Our salvation is only secured by grace through faith in Jesus alone. Perhaps, as many Bible scholars suggest, during the Millennium, these sacrifices will fulfill a memorial expression of worship of the Lamb of God, similar to the ordinances of the Lord's Supper for believers in this dispensation of the church. Again, the reality is that we are looking ahead in time "through a glass darkly." Yet, in the midst of what is admittedly a more obscure section of the Word, we are challenged by an exhortation from the Lord that is crystal clear and timeless in application, "You shall have just balances..." (Ezek. 45:10).

As believers who have been justified by God's grace, we should demonstrate that by being just in all of our relationships. Just balances are a symbol of equality and honesty. We must treat all people in a manner that reflects the fact that *we value all people*. The expression of favoritism or devaluation toward any person is utterly contrary to the character of our Heavenly Father. He is good to all and shows His kindness to "the just and the unjust" (Matt. 5:45).

Our God is just, holy, gracious, and kind, and how we praise and bless Him that He is! Now, as His children, may we "go and do likewise" (Luke 10:37).

NOVEMBER 30
Ezekiel 47-48

"Jehovah Shammah"

"And the name of the city from that time on shall be, The Lord Is There."
(Ezekiel 48:35)

Over the years, My wife and I have found it so encouraging to travel to other countries and be identified as citizens of the United States. So many times, we have been greeted with bright smiles and affirmations expressing how much the person or group of people admire and are thankful for the influence of America. On a few occasions, however, I recall when Susan and I, while participating on a foreign missions ministry or leading a tour to the Middle East or Europe, were approached by citizens of other countries and asked about political struggles or controversies taking place within the United States. Even more interesting is how people in other countries have reacted when learning that we are from the state of Tennessee. Their expressions have often brightened in recognition, and they have said, "Oh yes, country music!" or "Yes, Elvis!" Sadly, we have heard more than any other response—"Jack Daniels, love it!" While Susan and I are most certainly grateful to be United States citizens and feel blessed to live in

Tennessee, occasionally, we have recognized that the qualities we associate with our nation and our state are not always and not necessarily the impressions made on some people in other parts of the world.

What is true of nations and states is also true regarding cities. There are major metropolitan areas around the world that, as soon as the city is mentioned, most people have one of a few overarching mental images sparked by the name. Try this yourself—what immediately comes to mind as you think about London? How about Rome? Tokyo? What about Washington DC, or Delhi? Granted, as I shared earlier, some individuals might have a response to the names of those cities that is unique to their experience. However, in a survey of a significant number of people, some predominant qualities would be expressed.

Now, take a moment to think of the city of Jerusalem. What comes to your mind when you hear the name of that location? No doubt, for many, the immediate thought goes to the ministry of Jesus, in particular His crucifixion, resurrection, and ascension. Six hundred years earlier, in the days of Ezekiel, Jerusalem was known for infidelity, spiritual idolatry, judgment, and devastation. Jerusalem was beloved by millions and despised by millions more. Yet, Ezekiel, led by the Spirit of God, ends his prophetic messages by declaring that Jerusalem will actually be renamed. It would not bear the name the Roman emperor gave to it in 129 AD, "Aelia Capitolina." The city of Jerusalem will be called "Jehovah-Shammah," for "The Lord Is There."

Does this mean we will never use the name Jerusalem during the coming ages? No, that is not the message for us with this marvelous "name change." "Jehovah-Shammah" expresses the fulfillment of the promise of the ages that paradise has been restored. God and His people are reunited forever, never to be parted again. The curse is lifted as waters of eternal life flow from the throne of God, renewing all creation. There is no darkness in that city, no more silent tears, no cries of grief or pain. Peace reigns because the Prince of Peace rules over all. "The Lord Is There" is what the city means. And best of all, it will be our hometown forever!

December

"For to us a child is born, to us a son is given."
(Isaiah 9:6)

DECEMBER 1
Daniel 1-3

"THE POWER OF PURPOSE"

"But Daniel resolved that he would not defile himself with the king's food, or with the wine that he drank. Therefore he asked the chief of the eunuchs to allow him not to defile himself."
(Daniel 1:8)

Daniel was a remarkable man in his day. With the passing of the centuries, his witness in example and words, duty and devotion, faithful service and faith-filled civil disobedience seems only to grow. Of all the great servants of God whose laws are recorded in Scripture, Daniel certainly must be considered one of the greatest.

He was a redeemed sinner, but other than the Lord Jesus, only Daniel and Joseph have no recorded act of disobedience in their long and eventful lives. Like Joseph, while a young man probably in his middle teen years, Daniel was ripped from his loved ones and home in Judah and carried away captive by the orders of King Nebuchadnezzar after his first invasion of Judah. Daniel, along with other young people, were taken as a hostages and kept as "living leverage" to guarantee that the government in Jerusalem, now vassal, would cooperate with the directives of Nebuchadnezzar.

This terrible event in young Daniel's life gives us some background in which to frame the story of his remarkable life over the next 70 years. Daniel was a member of one of the leading families in Judah; he may even have been a member of the royal family. As just a teenager who already had demonstrated himself to be noteworthy in physical appearance and excellent knowledge combined with a strong character (Dan. 1:3-4), Daniel suddenly found himself a captive in a distant and pagan culture. Everything in his daily life within the King's palace compound was not just foreign but against the core principles of Daniel's life.

The Babylonians took away practically everything—his family, his name (calling him Belteshazzar after one of their gods), his dreams; but the one thing they could not take from Daniel was *his faith*. He was willing to yield to the authorities, but he refused to yield his faith. Daniel's resolve regarding the line he would not cross was not rash or emotionally made, instead "Daniel resolved that he would not defile himself..." (1:8) The issue was not simply about his diet; it was based on obedience to the faith of his fathers and his father's God.

What a brave young man! However, Daniel was not a brash young man; "...he asked the chief of the eunuchs to allow him not to defile himself" (1:8). Don't miss that. Daniel "asked" to be "allowed." His decision was total and irrevocable, but he was polite and respectful. Daniel determined to hold his faith position with the right disposition. Daniel would not lose his faith, but he also would not lose his temper. The result of Daniel's good testimony was a testimony for his God.

What an incredible example this young man from ancient history truly is for believers of all ages in our present age! We, too, live in a culture that contradicts our faith and values. Yet, with the strength of Daniel's God, our God, we can hold our personal faith positions with pleasant, faithful dispositions. "Lord, grant us this grace in our days."

DECEMBER 2
Daniel 4-6

"A KING CONVERTED"

*"Now I, Nebuchadnezzar, praise and extol and honor the King of heaven,
for all his works are right and his ways are just;
and those who walk in pride he is able to humble."*
(Daniel 4:37)

It is difficult for us to imagine what Nebuchadnezzar looked upon as he strolled on the roof of his royal palace in Babylon. He could see tens of thousands of homes, shops, temples, government buildings, and stadiums stretching all the way to the city's walls and beyond. There may have never existed in antiquity, or all history, a city to compare to the splendor of Babylon.

This one great metropolis contained at least three architectural wonders of the world at that time. The Ishtar Gate, the primary entrance to the heart of the city, was noted by many writers of the day as the most magnificent structure their eyes had seen. From a distance, it appeared that the town surrounded a huge tropical mountain, lush with exotic and beautiful vegetation. These were the Hanging Gardens of Babylon—a vast, terraced, earthen pyramid Nebuchadnezzar ordered, designed, and constructed to honor one of his favorite wives. And then, there were the walls of Babylon—three concentric circles encircling the city. The Greek historian Herodotus records that these walls stretched for 50 miles over 80 feet in places and reached 90 feet into the air. The walls were so wide that chariots would race around the tops of them. It is not surprising that with such a view before him, in pride at his accomplishments, King Nebuchadnezzar would boast, "Is not this great Babylon, which I have built by my mighty power as a royal residence and for the glory of my majesty?" (Dan. 4:30) This may have been in his mind the most significant moment of his life, but it wasn't.

The greatest experience of the greatest king on the earth would come much later, following his encounter with ultimate greatness, the glory, power, mercy, and grace of the King of the universe. In His great *mercy*, Jehovah brought Nebuchadnezzar to true sanity by causing him to experience insanity. The horrible psychological disorder of boanthropy seized Nebuchadnezzar, and he began to crawl on the earth like an animal and behave and eat grass like a beast of the field.

We are not told how long Nebuchadnezzar suffered from this affliction, but it was a lengthy period of time. Clearly, it was very effective in accomplishing the Lord's purposes. It is in this purpose that the greatness of God is most displayed, the greatness of His grace to redeem and restore the life of one who would have been considered the least likely person on earth to become a humble worshiper of the God of Israel. By the severe mercy of all-gracious God, this proud leader became a praise leader, "Now I, Nebuchadnezzar, praise and extol and honor the King of heaven, for all His works are right and His ways are just; and those who walk in pride He is able to humble" (Dan. 4:37).

It has been said that our Lord is able to save "from the guttermost to the uttermost." Sometimes in His great mercy, our Lord brings people to the gutter so He can bring them to glory. I'm sure Nebuchadnezzar, gazing upon the glories of heaven, would say, "Thank you! It was worth it all!"

DECEMBER 3
Daniel 7-9

"Historic Prophecy"

"And the kingdom and the dominion and the greatness of the kingdoms under the whole heaven shall be given to the people of the saints of the Most High; his kingdom shall be an everlasting kingdom, and all dominions shall serve and obey him."
(Daniel 7:27)

Perhaps your Thanksgiving Day schedule this year included, as it did for millions in America, watching the famous Macy's Thanksgiving Day Parade. This great event has been celebrated every year since 1924 (except for the years 1942-44 during WWII). I have often thought about how exciting it would be to stand on the sidewalk in New York City and watch the bands, floats, entertainers, etc., one by one go passing by. I admit to a tinge of jealousy when some friends were once able to attend the parade and, several days later, over dinner together, told Susan and me all about it. What a view that must have been watching the parade pass, with each group providing a new scene to view. How differently that same famous Macy's parade would have looked from high above, from the vantage point of the also famous Goodyear Blimp. Hundreds of feet in the air, a person could view, with the help of binoculars, the entire parade from start to finish, all in a moment.

In Daniel, Chapter 7, the Lord, in a similar sense, lifts Daniel up from the vantage point of his time period, in the late sixth century BC, and gives him a view of the parade of empires that stretches to the inauguration of the final, eternal empire. Daniel records all the Lord shows him in the "parade of man" by describing several world-dominating kingdoms that are to rise on the earth. For Daniel, what he sees and records is prophecy, but most of it is history for us now. For the all-knowing Lord, prophecy is just pre-written history because the future is as clear as the past for our God. What Daniel records is so precise that scholars of "the liberal persuasion" have said these prophecies must have been written years after by someone other than Daniel and then were collected and added to Daniel's previous writings. That explanation of the incredible accuracy of these prophetic visions makes perfect sense if you don't believe in God—the God who knows at once all things past, present, and future.

God reveals to Daniel, and to all who read this book that bears his name, that "four great beasts" (Dan. 7:3), four world empires are to arise on the earth. One resembled a winged lion whose wings are plucked off and then given two feet like a man and a mind like a man (7:4). This is Babylon, the kingdom of the humbled and the restored Nebuchadnezzar. This is followed by a bear that leans to one side as it devours flesh (7:5). This is the Medo-Persian empire established by Darius, the Mede (5:31), and then far expanded by his successors from Persia. Next springs up a flying leopard with four heads (7:6). This is the lightning-fast conquering Greek empire of Alexander the Great, whose kingdom was divided among four of his generals after his death at the age of 33. Then arrives "a fourth beast, terrifying and dreadful..." (7:7) This beast with the crushing power is the Roman empire that would rise to conquer nations and people groups from North Africa to Germany and from Britain to the borders of India. Out of one of the horns, that is, one of the kingdoms of the former Roman empire will arise a treacherous ruler who will vainly and blasphemously proclaim his power. (7:8) The self-exalting ruler of the final human kingdom is the Anti-Christ (Rev. 13:1-8), whom the Son of Man coming in the clouds, the Messiah, will overthrow as He receives from the Ancient of Days, God the Father, the Kingdom over which He will reign forever and ever (Dan. 7:13-14).

The passing parade of world powers can sometimes be dreadful, discouraging, and dark. However, as we go deep into the Word, our view of life goes higher and sees farther and clearer. Truly, what the great missionary to India, William Carey, wrote, is what we see: "The future is as bright as the promises of God."

DECEMBER 4
Daniel 10-12

"Beloved in the Silent Seasons"

"At the beginning of your pleas for mercy a word went out, and I have come to tell it to you, for you are greatly loved. Therefore consider the word and understand the vision."
(Daniel 9:23)

I remember as a middle schooler sitting with my older brother and listening to his favorite albums of music. To be honest, I did not get his taste in music. He enjoyed meditative folk-rock songs, and my taste ran more toward the style of the Beach Boys. I recall him telling me several times that I had no taste at all! I remember one duo my brother especially enjoyed—Simon and Garfunkel. (I know I'm dating myself.) Eventually, I did come to enjoy some of their songs; in particular, I remember thinking carefully about the lyrics of one of their ballads, "The Sound of Silence." The primary meaning of the song generally laments how lack of communication between people produces loneliness that, in turn, creates a culture where people feel unloved. The title, "The Sound of Silence," expresses the idea that silence communicates loudly a message of isolation and unconcern.

Perhaps no silence is more difficult for a believer to experience than silence from God, especially when one of His children earnestly pleads to receive a message of guidance or wisdom in a dark and challenging season. We can only imagine how Daniel must have felt after receiving a frightening vision that contained a message for the exiles of Israel and praying with confession and fasting for three weeks. All he heard in answer was "the sound of silence." Thankfully, the messenger angel, Gabriel, finally arrived with an explanation of the vision, an enlightenment regarding the reality of spiritual warfare, and, perhaps most meaningful to Daniel, a moving confirmation that he was "greatly loved" by the Lord (Dan. 10:11).

What a relief and comfort the message of Gabriel must have been to Daniel's soul. And how his mind must have reeled at the thought of Gabriel being involved in conflict with the demon prince of the kingdom of Persia until Michael, one of the chief angels, arrived to help Gabriel in the struggle! (Dan. 10:13) Even today, reading this spiritual warfare among the princes of God's heavenly host and the leaders of Satan's dark forces can astound us.

Our struggle is not "against flesh and blood, but against the rulers, against the authorities, against the cosmic powers over this present darkness, against the spiritual forces of evil in the heavenly places" (Eph. 6:12). Thank God, the battle is the Lord's (2 Chr. 20:15), for we are no match in our strength against such diabolical powers. In reality, our greater battle is often against the fortress in our own minds as we struggle to "take every thought captive to obey Christ" (2 Cor. 10:5). The greatest weapon against doubt is the immutable truth of God's love.

We would not compare ourselves to Daniel, but like him, we are people "dearly loved." God's seasons of silence are not His absence "for He has said, 'I will never leave you nor forsake you'" (Heb. 13:5). May we not allow ourselves to forget in the darkness what we have learned in the light—God is speaking; He is not really silent at all. Listen to His gracious voice today and rejoice. "I have loved you with an everlasting love; therefore I have continued my faithfulness to you" (Jer. 31:3).

DECEMBER 5
Hosea 1-2

"RADICAL LOVE"

"And I will betroth you to me forever. I will betroth you to me in righteousness and in justice, in steadfast love and in mercy. I will betroth you to me in faithfulness. And you shall know the Lord."
(Hosea 2:19-20)

In most cultures around the world, the concept of courtship that leads to marriage is very different from the typical concept in the west of dating, love, and then marriage. Young people from Europe and North America are often aghast to learn about the practice of "arranged marriages" where the parents or legal guardians take responsibility for selecting a mate for their daughter or son. I am not advocating this practice, as I have been very, very satisfied with the decision Susan and I made to spend our lives together. However, in general, when it comes to the success and satisfaction of arranged marriages compared to those made by the couples themselves, the data consistently indicates that parents and guardians make better matchmakers.

We have a cliché that expresses the love, joy, and compatibility of a great marriage—"a match made in heaven." Indeed, there is no better matchmaker for His children than the Heavenly Father. In fact, in the Garden of Eden, we see Him plan all the details and even conduct the service for the first marriage. So, it is incredibly difficult to wrap our minds around the opening statement from God as recorded by Hosea and directed to him, "Go, take to yourself a wife of whoredom and have children of whoredom, for the land commits great whoredom..." (Hos. 1:2) God's directive here is so startling and inconsistent with all we know of His character that what He commands Hosea confounds us. Either the Lord is telling Hosea to marry a woman in full recognition and understanding that she will be unfaithful to him, or God is commanding His prophet to marry a woman, Gomer, who is already in a lifestyle of prostitution.

Added to this awful assignment is the command for Hosea to have children with Gomer. And then, after each of the baby girls is born, the Lord tells Hosea to name one Lo-ruhama, meaning "No mercy," and the other, Lo-ammi, "Not my people." Why in the world would Jehovah do this? Because the Lord wanted to reveal a love that is truly not of this world and is eternal—His love for His people. This marriage is to represent the "romance of redemption." This is a love story of God by His relentless love for a nation that has been faithless to the covenant of their union before it was ever ratified, and has continually prostituted themselves to other gods throughout the years since Mount Sinai. God's holy and righteous anger has been constantly provoked, yet He has been faithful in the nation's unfaithfulness. Now, the ten tribes of the Northern Kingdom will experience the consequences of their spiritual adultery as one of their wicked suitors, Assyria, returns to ravage the nation and traffic her among the nations. Yet, God cannot and will not give up forever His people, His precious bride.

The Lord will call to her, "...allure her, and bring her into the wilderness, and speak tenderly to her" (Hos. 2:14). He will redeem her with His love: "And in that day, declares the Lord, you will call me 'My Husband,' and no longer will you call me 'My Baal'" (Hos. 2:16). God's love always wins. "I will betroth you to me in faithfulness. And you shall know the Lord" (Hos. 2:20).

DECEMBER 6
Hosea 3-4

"WOODEN WISDOM"

"My people inquire of a piece of wood, and their walking staff gives them oracles."
(Hosea 4:12)

In Romans, Chapter 1, Apostle Paul describes the consequences of sin that are often overlooked by non-believers but, strangely enough, also by those who have trusted in Jesus. Most people have a basic understanding that wrong actions, either morally or ethically, will often result in punishment. For example, a man who robs banks is not surprised when he is arrested, tried, judged guilty of those crimes, then placed into a prison cell due to his illegal actions. Yet, what is overlooked by so many people, believers, and unbelievers, is that the consequences of sin are also mental in nature. To practice sin is, in reality, to self-inflict brain damage.

Paul warned that by rejecting the light of God and His truth, some people "became futile in their thinking, and their foolish hearts were darkened" (Rom. 1:21). This means their ability to receive truth is adversely diminished because the truth has been rejected. Ultimately, rejecting the truth can result in a mind that is foolish and guided to foolish values and behaviors.

Hosea lived in that culture in Israel nearly 800 years before Christ. The nation rejected the counsel of the living God, so now they worshiped gods of stone and wood formed by their own hands. The Israelites would cut down a tree, fashion part of it into a god, pray to it, and then take another part of the same tree and shape it into a walking stick. "My people inquire of a piece of wood, and their walking staff gives them oracles" (Hos. 4:12). The very idea sounds ludicrous. But in their rebellion, the people of Israel had become so darkened in their thought processes that this is what they practiced, and "their foolish hearts were darkened," as Paul would say.

How can this prophetic word given 2800 years ago provide us with wisdom today? I hope no one reading this page is carving objects and then praying to them! However, we must hear the challenge that is in Hosea's warning about the "walking staff" that gives "oracles." The walking staff is an emblem of a journey, and an oracle is a prophetic word of guidance.

The timeless application from Hosea for God's people to consider today is the answer to this question: "Where do we receive our wisdom for the journey?" Does the Bible we purchased or was given to us guide our steps? Or, did we buy a laptop or iPhone, and now we find the truth on social media and allow that "truth" to shape our values and decisions? Are we more impacted in our thinking by Facebook or by having our "faces in *The Book*?" Nothing is wrong with any item we purchase or use that can enlighten our understanding, but unless the Lord and His Word enlighten our steps, we most certainly will lead ourselves onto a dark path.

DECEMBER 7
Hosea 5-6

"Press On!"

"Come, let us return to the Lord; for he has torn us, that he may heal us; he has struck us down, and he will bind us up...that we may live before him."[1-2]
"Let us know; let us press on to know the Lord..."[3]
(Hosea 6:1-3)

Of all the wonderful gifts the Lord has so graciously given me over the years of my life (and indeed, there have been many), one of the most priceless treasures the Lord gave me was the gift of my father. My dad married my mom later in life, and since I was the youngest of the three boys born to them, Dad was already middle-aged before I was born. Perhaps because of that, our relationship was more akin to a "grandfather-dad" and son.

The pace of his life seemed to be a little slower than that of my friends' dads. As a result, he seemed to have more time to focus and spend with me. He did the same with my two brothers as well, and, looking back, I quite frankly don't know how he managed it. To be clear, it was more than just time that my dad gave me; he also gave me his heart. By that, I mean he gave me his voice and his thoughts.

As an older child, I already knew my dad's heart—what he valued and that *he valued me*. I never for a moment ever doubted my father's love. In his words, his actions, his touch... I just instinctively knew that my dad was devoted to me. For that reason, I could trust that he would respond to me with his love, even when I had acted in ways he disapproved of and that deeply disappointed him. I knew, I just knew, I could always go in my tears and shame to find him and that his arms would be wide open. That kind of steadfast and devoted love from my dad was a priceless treasure indeed.

Hosea pleaded with Israel and, by the Spirit, pleads with us today to trust the Heavenly Father's heart, proven in so many and varied ways, and return to Him. Listen to Hosea's confidence—"...he will bind us up," "...he will revive us," and "...he will raise us up" (Hos. 6:1-2). Nothing in all creation is more certain of His tender heart and steadfast love. "...his going out is sure as the dawn; he will come to us as the showers, as the spring rains that water the earth" (6:3).

With that confidence in God's love, Hosea calls, "Let us know; let us press on to know the Lord" (6:3). So, we must let nothing, no sin, weakness, or doubt, cause us to question that our God desires us to know Him and experience His love. We must "press on," not stand as idle spectators in religious observance. We must "press on" to know the Lord, who to know is life eternal (John 17:3). With confidence in His love, we must "press on" to "grow in the grace and knowledge of our Lord and Savior Jesus Christ" (2 Peter 3:18). Even if we have strayed far from the Father's house, like the father of the prodigal, our loving Heavenly Father longs for our return. "Come, let us return to the Lord..." (Hos. 6:1)

> *I've wandered far away from God,*
> *Now, I'm coming home;*
> *The paths of sin too long I've trod,*
> *Lord, I'm coming home.*

("Lord, I'm Coming Home," by William J. Kirkpatrick)

DECEMBER 8
Hosea 7-8

"FATAL ATTRACTION"

"They made kings, but not through me. They set up princes, but I knew it not. With their silver and gold they made idols for their own destruction."
(Hosea 8:4)

Rarely does a week pass that we learn in the news of a repeat of the same awful tale of "Fatal Attraction." The tragedy is far more terrible than the plot of a movie in Hollywood. A couple has been involved in an illicit relationship, and one of the people involved desires to bring it to an end. Or, perhaps, the spouse of one of the individuals decides it is time to end the relationship once and for all. By reading this far, you could go ahead and fill in the details of the terrible story. It ends in violence and death. What was considered sowing some wild seeds in a passionate romance often results in a harvest of broken lives, destroyed families, and indescribable grief. In recklessly sowing the wind, they reap the whirlwind of their unfaithfulness (Hos. 8:7).

Just as tragically as this selfish scenario is carried out in human relationships, it occurs even more often and with more destructive consequences in spiritual infidelity. That is how the Lord describes the faithlessness of His mate, Israel, in our reading today.

Israel has long been practicing spiritual adultery by worshiping the gods of other nations. In Hosea's day, Israel has gone after a "new lover" in pursuing security in alliance with Assyria. Little does Israel know that this exciting young lover will kidnap her in just a few years and traffic her among the nations. "Israel is swallowed up; already they are among the nations as a useless vessel" (Hos. 8:8).

What is at the root of this disaster, how did it start, and how can we learn to avoid such ruin? The answer to those questions is one which we should always *remember*—Israel *forgot*. "For Israel has forgotten his Maker..." (Hos. 8:14) The word "forgotten" here is not just a lapse of memory; it is a lack of devotion. Loving self, more than our Savior, is to actively, intentionally forget God.

One of the most powerful words that can guard our hearts against infidelity and unfaithfulness to the Lord is "remember." Take some time right now to reflect on these words from God's Word and "remember."

- "Remember the wondrous works that He has done..." (Ps. 105:5)
- "Remember me when you come into your kingdom" (Luke 23:42).
- "Remember that you were at that time separated from Christ..." (Eph. 2:12)
- "Remember Jesus Christ, risen from the dead..." (2 Tim. 2:8)

- "Remember therefore from where you have fallen; repent, and do the works you did at first" (Rev. 2:5).
- "Remember Me…" (Luke 23:42)

DECEMBER 9
Hosea 9-11

"First, the Plow"

*"Sow for yourselves righteousness; reap steadfast love;
break up your fallow ground, for it is the time to seek the Lord,
that he may come and rain righteousness upon you."*
(Hosea 10:12)

Some time ago, Susan and I were driving through our home state of Indiana on our way to visit our relatives. It was July, and as we intentionally took some of the state and county roads, we often found ourselves in a sea of corn and soybeans! For miles in every direction, we were surrounded by endless rows of crops that glistened in the bright sunshine. It was a beautiful scene to behold. However, we have occasionally traveled those same roads in the dead of winter, and what a radically different scene captures your eyes in January or February. All the lush crops are gone. There is nothing green except the occasional barn or farmhouse roof. The general color is the dark charcoal gray of the frozen, hard dirt. It is difficult to imagine that you are looking at the same fields you gazed upon just a few months earlier. Yet, in just a few more months, this same hard and frozen soil will once again be producing a lush and abundant harvest—*but first, the plow*. Without the plowing of the hardened soil, there will be no harvest. The breaking and upturning of the dirt encourages the soil to receive the planted seeds and the soaking rains in the spring. The seed is ready in the barn for planting, the rains are coming, and the harvest can abound, but the hardened soil must be plowed. *No plowing, no harvest.*

God has established the laws of sowing and reaping to govern not only the physical world but also the spiritual realm of the soul. The prophet Hosea was either a farmer or very knowledgeable of agriculture because his messages are filled with allusions and symbolism connected to the fields. Even after decades of rebellion and idolatry, he shares the promise of a miracle of forgiveness, restoration, and blessing from the Lord. *But first, the plow*. The people of Israel must break up the hardened soil of their hearts, they must repent, and their hearts must be turned up and open to God in repentance to receive the refreshing rain of His Spirit. *It is time to plow*; "it is time to seek the Lord" (Hos. 10:12).

Sometimes we don't see the hard, fallow places in our lives. That is why praying must precede plowing. We need the Lord to reveal the hard, cold dirt in our hearts because spiritual blindness is part of that spiritual hardness. That is why praying and plowing are part of the constant rhythm of our lives. We should always be praying, asking the Lord to show us the fallow soil in our souls, and then praying for His help to plow with repentance, opening those stiff, immovable places to Him. Sowing, reaping, and plowing should never end for us. In fact, we are in each of those seasons all at the same time. So whatever season this is for you as you read this today, "Sow for yourselves righteousness; reap steadfast love; break up your fallow ground, for it is time to seek the Lord, that he may come and rain righteousness upon you" (Hos. 10:12).

DECEMBER 10
Hosea 12-14

"FIRST LOVE"

*"But I am the Lord your God from the land of Egypt;
you know no God but me, and besides me there is no savior."*
(Hosea 13:4)

Recently, I was notified of a Facebook page for my elementary school, Hernly Elementary, in New Castle, Indiana. The building was very old when I attended and has been gone for decades, but the memories remain and are "forever young." When I visited the page a few days ago, I was instantly transported across a half-century and became very young again. There I found pictures of all the teachers and many classmates I knew in those wonderful years of 1st through 6th grade.

I especially enjoyed looking at the class group photos; some of you must remember those. In these photos, your individual picture was grouped with those of the other students and at the top were the images of your teacher and the principal. It seemed like every person's face triggered a recall of forgotten experiences we shared in class, the lunchroom, or on the playground. As I viewed photos posted on the group page, I couldn't help but chuckle out loud as I saw the pictures of my childhood "first love," or I should say "first loves," as there were several of them. Dorothy in the 1st grade, Pamela in 2nd through 4th, and then there was Kim, my "main crush" in my "much more mature" years of grades 5th and 6th. Indeed, "the wonder years," and how golden they seem now after over 50 years have passed!

Paul tells us in Scripture, "When I became a man, I gave up childish ways" (1 Cor. 13:11). In that context, he speaks of mature love and devotion. I'm sure many of you reading this page know, as I do, the incredible joy of finding "the one true love of your life" and sharing "the grace of life" together in marriage (1 Peter 3:7). Even that love is a little experience on earth because there is no love and devotion on this earth that can compare to the "first love" we experience from heaven in our Lord.

Our first love is really not ours at all. It is His love that is the first love. "We love because he first loved us" (1 John 4:19). God loved us when no one knew us, and we did not even know ourselves. For He loved us and foreknew us in Christ before the foundation of the world (Eph. 1:4-5). God loved us, not at our best but at our worst, for "while we were still sinners, Christ died for us" (Rom. 5:8). Jesus loved us as He began His ministry on this earth, and having accomplished all His mission "having loved his own who were in the world, he loved them to the end" (John 13:1).

Jesus loved us all the way to the cross so that each one of us can say, He "loved me and gave himself for me" (Gal. 2:20). He loves us still and has forever etched on His hands and feet the scars that testify of His love for us. Jesus is our first love, which is what He expects in return—our first love. Our love is His *first command*, "You shall love the Lord your God with all your heart and with all your soul and with all your mind and with all your strength" (Mark 12:30). Our love is His *first concern*, and it is His *first question*. Our Master asks, "Do you love me?" (John 21:15)

What is our answer?

DECEMBER 11
Joel 1-3

"THE DAY OF THE LORD"

*"Multitudes, multitudes, in the valley of decision!
For the day of the Lord is near in the valley of decision."*
(Joel 3:14)

One summer when I was just a boy, our area in the Midwest experienced the emergence from the ground of the 17-year cicadas, technically identified as brood X but commonly referred to as the "17-year locust." Their arrival is absolutely predictable, and their number is unfathomable. I once read an article from Purdue University that an estimated 1.5 million per acre of these cicadas burrow up from their holes. They are harmless for all practical purposes, but when billions of them join to "sing" together, it is a terrifying sound. They certainly gave me cause for concern, and my dad did not help ease my fears when one day, standing out in our backyard, he said to me, "Son, can you hear what they are singing?" I responded, "Dad, what are you talking about?" "Can't you hear what the locusts are singing? They are saying, 'Pharaoh!' 'Pharaoh!'" I was almost certain my dad was teasing, but still, it did cause a boy to struggle just a little with his imagination. Years later, with the emergence of cicadas, I shared the same story with my kids and their friends, too!

The plague of locusts was one of the ten plagues Jehovah brought upon Egypt. These were not cicadas but true locusts, and they stripped the land bare. Six hundred years later, in the judgment of the idolatry of the people of Judah, the Lord brought similar vast armies of locusts that swept across the land, devouring every form of vegetation in their path. Joel, whose name means "Jehovah is God," referred to this judgment as the "Day of the Lord," the season of God's intervention and judgment on Judah. Yet, it is also a "scourge of mercy" in which the Lord humbles the nation and extends the promise of deliverance and restoration if Judah repents and returns to Him. With a pleading voice, the Lord calls to his people with an invitation and a promise, "'Yet even now,' declares the Lord, 'return to me with all your heart, with fasting, with weeping, and with mourning... Return to the Lord your God, for He is gracious and merciful, slow to anger, and abounding in steadfast love...'" (Joel 2:12-13) Also, God promises miraculous restoration, "I will restore to you the years that the swarming locust has eaten..." (2:25) Thank God, Judah did hear this call from God, and the nation was saved.

As we read further in Joel's prophecy, it becomes clear that his message is also one that refers to the great "Day of the Lord" in which He will draw the nations to the "Valley of Decision" (Joel 3:14). This is not a symbolic valley because it is carefully identified in the context as the "Valley of Jehoshaphat" (3:12). This long valley that stretches from Mount Carmel to Mount Tabor is also called in Scripture "the Valley of Jezreel," or "the Valley of Megiddo" after the ancient crossroad city, sitting in the center of the valley atop a hill. The word for hill in Hebrew is "Har," so this site is "Har-Megiddo," or in Greek, "Armageddon." The Day of the Lord comes to its final climatic moment when Jesus returns to defeat the massed armies of the world and the Anti-Christ (Rev. 16:16; 19:11-21). Then will come "the Valley of Decision," the time of God's judgment with the people of earth. It is an awful, awe-filled day, but for believers, it is our "Day of Deliverance."

Yet, before that day comes, this is also the "Day of the Lord," the day of His salvation. Peter quoted Joel on the Day of Pentecost to gathered representatives of the nations of the earth, proclaiming the glorious message that today is a Day of Salvation. God's invitation and promise still goes out today, and we are all to share it. "Everyone who calls on the name of the Lord shall be saved" (Joel 2:32; Acts 2:21). Now, that is good news! Let's freely share it.

DECEMBER 12
Amos 1-3

"MY TRUTH OR MY LIE?"

"Thus says the Lord: 'For three transgressions of Judah, and for four, I will not revoke the punishment, because they have rejected the law of the Lord, and have not kept his statutes, but their lies have led them astray, those after which their fathers walked.'"
(Amos 2:4)

Many Bible scholars believe that Amos may have been the first of the "writing prophets," that is, prophets whose messages to Judah and Israel were not only spoken by them but also recorded and included as part of God's written revelation. Amos and his ministry date to the days of Uzziah, the king of Judah, and his contemporary ruler, Jeroboam II, the king of Israel. As is so common with our God, He selects Amos from the common class of people; he was a shepherd and farmer. Yet, what Amos may have lacked in pedigree or education was more than compensated by the power of God's Spirit that filled him and energized his messages.

Amos spoke God's truth and shared it without regard to the recipient's nationality or ethnicity. Amos's audience included Judah, Israel, Edom, Syria, Philistia, Moab, and Ammon. The people of his day would have considered Amos "an equal opportunity offender." What was it about this simple man's message that upset the people of such diverse countries and cultures? The answer is quite simple, quite revealing, and quite relevant today—*Amos spoke the truth*. That's it. It is that simple and yet profound because nothing is as simple and profound as truth, and nothing has been more intolerant universally and historically than truth. It was truth that Satan first attacked in Eden. The serpent said to Eve, "Did God actually say?" (Gen. 3:1), a subtle undermining of God's truthfulness, and then at the optimal moment, the direct assault on truth, "You will not surely die" (Gen. 3:4).

Jesus referred to the Devil as "a liar and the father of lies" (John 8:44). Lying is the heart language of Satan and the cursing of his kingdom. The Devil builds his realm with the bricks of lies, and his greatest deception is that these lies appear rock solid. People build their lives on powerful principles, but tragically their "truth" is the fuel of their destruction. They are like the man who, many years ago, dreamed of building a retirement home on the perfect location—a ridge along one of the most spectacular mountains in the Western United States. He planned every aspect of this fabulous ranch home with painstaking detail over many years.

The views from practically any location in the house would be breathtaking. Several people challenged him to conduct a careful geological study on the site before he began the project. There had been concerns expressed in recent years regarding underground seismic activity in that region. The man ignored his friends' recommendations and pursued his vision to build the retirement home of his dreams. His vision became a reality as he finished the mountaintop residence. It truly was a dream home until it vanished instantaneously in a complete nightmare. The mountaintop home the man planned and built was truly spectacular, but it was no match for the irresistible truth beneath the ground on which it stood—a high ridge on Mount St. Helens erupted with cataclysmic force on May 18, 1980.

Two thousand eight hundred years earlier, the trust of the people of Judah in their own "truth" was their ruin. "They have rejected the law of the Lord, and have not kept his statutes, but *their lies have led them astray*" (Amos 2:4). Note that "their lies," that is, the *lies they told themselves*, have kept them from the way of truth and led them down the path of deception. It is awful to be deceived, but deceiving ourselves by the lies of our own making is tragic beyond the telling. And it is so unnecessary. Jesus said, "You will know the truth and the truth will set you free" (John 8:32).

Liberty is found in truth; slavery resides in lies. So where are we to find the trustworthy stones of truth with which to build our lives? Listen to the answer from truth incarnate, our Master: "Sanctify them in the truth; your word is truth" (John 17:17). Jesus *did not* say God's Word *is true*, although it most certainly is; Jesus said God's Word *is truth*.

As children, we sang in Sunday school, "The wise man built his house upon the rock." Yes, we must always build on the rock, but also, we must be sure to build *with rocks*—the rocks of truth.

DECEMBER 13
Amos 4-6

"SUPERHEROES"

"They hate him who reproves in the gate, and they abhor him who speaks the truth."
(Amos 5:10)

"But let justice roll down like waters, and righteousness like an ever-flowing stream."
(Amos 5:24)

I was reading an article, recently, about the biggest box office money-making movies of the last ten years. I was amazed to see that, by far, most of them were superhero action movies. Taken as a whole, this category of films was so far beyond the others it wasn't even close. Likewise, the highest-paid actors were not those who had won academy awards for their ability to interpret a character and bring them to life. No, the actors dressed in computer-linked outfits jumping across green screens made the "big bucks."

Please don't take my words as rejecting the superhero genre because I was raised on it. Superman's black and white reruns in my childhood kept me transfixed for hours in front of the little box with the rabbit-ears antenna (a.k.a. the television set). Batman was cool when he, Robin, and the Joker arrived in living color, but they could not compete with Superman, who, with arms crossed and cape blowing in the wind, fought for "truth, justice, and the American way." Sadly, those childhood illusions are often ruined by the reality of experience and maturity. The "American way" was driven by greed behind the superhero show. The actor who portrayed Superman, George Reeves, died under very suspicious circumstances that were ultimately ruled a suicide.

However, I also learned that "truth and justice" exist in America. Yet, they are not "the American way." They are the qualities in the lives of people who know and serve the God of truth and justice. Truth and justice are beyond superhero attributes. They are "Sovereign qualities," the character truths of God Himself, and His plan is for the people of His Kingdom to display them in their lives.

In the movies, superheroes have their adversaries, and so do people who advocate for God's truth and justice in this world. "They hate him who reproves in the gate, and they abhor him who speaks the truth" (Amos 5:10). Notice where these true "superheroes" stand for truth and pay the price—"in the gate," in the place of government and power. People are not rejected when they "keep their faith to themselves." It is bringing God's truth from the pew to the pavement that the accusations of religious intolerance and bigotry are hurled.

However, for people of the truth, truth is not just the tenets of our faith or *what* we believe. It is *who* we are. Likewise, justice is more than an ideal to which we aspire. Justice is the working clothes of our faith. Having been "justified by faith" (Rom. 5:1), we should now, by our faith, seek and promote justice in our world. The "streams of living water" that Jesus says flow from His Spirit into ours should also flow through us, causing us to be streams in the desert. "The fountain of living waters" (Jer. 2:13) flows through His people, so "let justice roll down like waters, and righteousness like an ever-flowing stream" (Amos 5:24).

We are not superheroes, but we do have superpowers—the power of the living God at work in us. Truth and justice may not always be the "American way," but they are the King's way, which is *Super Powerful*!

DECEMBER 14
Amos 7-9

"EXPECT GREAT THINGS, ATTEMPT GREAT THINGS"

"'In that day I will raise up the booth of David that is fallen and repair its breaches, and raise up its ruins and rebuild it as in the days of old that they may possess the remnant of Edom and all the nations who are called by my name,' declares the Lord who does this."
(Amos 9:11-12)

At the first, second, or third reading of the verses above, you probably would not connect what Amos shares from the mouth of the Lord as having any connection whatsoever with the fulfillment of the Great Commission and world evangelization (Matt. 28:18-20). I freely admit that I did not see the connection for so many years. Still, two men of God did see it and shared it. The result was a redefining and clarification of the Church's mission that brought millions of people worldwide to faith in Jesus, motivated tens of thousands of others over the centuries to take the message of the gospel to the nations of the world, and continues to do so today.

The first of these two men was James, the half-brother of Jesus, who, as leader of the church in Jerusalem, listened as Apostle Paul explained to the church council how the Lord had been pleased to bring by his ministry, numbers of Gentiles to trust in Messiah. This unexpected gospel advance had completely surprised many leaders, and now the question arose about the relationship of those Gentiles to Judaism. Did these people have to become practicing Jews, including keeping the traditions of Judaism and observing the sacred rite of circumcision in order to be saved?

Acts, Chapter 15 describes some of the discussions that took place in a meeting of the church leaders in Jerusalem called to discuss this issue and others related to Gentile followers of Messiah. Amid a long, loud, and sharp debate, Peter reminded the assembly of God's first Gentile converts under his preaching (see Acts 10:44-48). After Paul and Barnabas related further what God had done among the people of Asia Minor in His saving grace, James rose and spoke to the crowd, quoting the prophecy Amos cited above (Acts 15:15-17). James understood that the raising up and restoring of the booth [tent] of David would bring an expansion of the kingdom to include "all the nations who are called by my name" (Amos 9:12). It is impossible to overestimate the significance of the decision reached that day in Jerusalem about 50 AD, as it defined in the early days of the Church that through it, God would heal the breach between Jews and Gentiles, uniting them by faith in Messiah.

We move forward 1,742 years to a small gathering of Baptist pastors at Friar Lane Baptist Chapel in Nottingham, England. Speaking to the ministers that day was a fellow pastor, William Carey, a cobbler by trade, who had received an unmistakable call from the Lord to take the saving message of Jesus to the lost and idol-worshiping masses of India. His urgency to go as a missionary from the Baptist churches of his association met with some stiff opposition. A few pastors of the hyper-Calvinist persuasion (who rejected the use of man's efforts to accomplish the salvation of God's elect) rebuked William saying, "Young man, God will save 'the heathen' when He purposes to do so."

To persuade the pastors from the Scripture, Carey shared in a sermon what he had discerned from the prophecies regarding the expansion of "the tent of David." In addition to the words of Amos, he referenced specifically the prophecy from Isaiah that immediately followed what is recorded in Chapter 53—the promise of the yet-living-again Messiah. William Carey's text that day was taken from Isaiah 54:2-3, "Enlarge the place of your tent, and let the curtains of your habitations be stretched out; do not hold back; lengthen your cords and strengthen your stakes. For you will spread out to the right and to the left, and your offspring will possess the nations and will people the desolate cities." Thank God the pastors listened to God's prophetic promise! The world was changed on that day in the little Baptist chapel in England.

What was William Carey's sermon title? "Expect Great Things, Attempt Great Things." May we do the same for the sake of souls and the glory of our Savior.

DECEMBER 15
Obadiah

"THE EAGLE'S NEST"

"Though you soar aloft like the eagle, though your nest is set among the stars, from there I will bring you down, declares the Lord."
(Obadiah v. 4)

Hitler should have read Obadiah. Who knows, perhaps he may have at some point in his twisted life. Of course, filled as he was with sociopathic hatred for all things Jewish and dominated by his narcissistic megalomania, he would have never regarded the prophecy against Edom, the ancient foe of Israel, as having any bearing on him.

So, the Fuhrer went forward with the plans to live in the "clefts of the rocks" and "build his nest among the stars" (Oba. vs. 3-4). A clear deadline was given to his "go-to guy," Martin Borman, to build a vast conference center ("The Eagle's Nest," as the Allies later dubbed it) and have it completed in time for Hitler's 50th birthday in 1939. Thousands of trusted men (only those of pure "Aryan blood") worked around-the-clock shifts to construct a fortress on a rocky crag towering above the Berchtesgaden in the mountainous region of Bavaria.

To reach the mountaintop complex, which would serve as the diplomatic crown jewel of Nazism, Borman's engineers created a 400-foot elevator shaft inside the mountain. Through the massive entrance to this shaft, it was planned the diplomatic leaders of other countries would be brought up to stand before the leader of the Third Reich and, of course, be rightly awe-struck by the grandeur of his lofty palace. Neither Hitler nor his lieutenants thought to make sure these "lofty plans" were approved by the Allies and, in particular, the 101st Airborne Division, who ascended to the "Eagle's Nest" in the early days of May 1945. Of course, by then, "the eagle" was no more, as he spent his last days not on the mountaintop but in his bunker deep below the Reich Chancellery in Berlin, where he took his own life with a pistol on April 30. At that moment, the soul of Adolph Hitler fell into the hands of the God of Abraham, Isaac, and Jacob.

Hitler did not listen to Obadiah, the servant of Jehovah, nor did the rulers of the Edomites, the descendants of Esau. For generations, they not only refused to assist their relatives, the people of Israel, but time and again, this nation allied with the enemies of God's people. In the final invasion of Judah by the Babylonians, the Edomites wickedly assisted in the bloodshed by capturing Jewish refugees who had escaped, returning them for a fee to certain slavery or extermination. However, as the Lord predicted, while fire would come upon Judah in the coming days, He would preserve a remnant of His people. On the other hand, Edom would be like stubble in that coming fire, and "there shall be no survivor of the house of Esau, the Lord has spoken" (Oba. 18). This sentence was fulfilled with the destruction of Jerusalem by the Romans in 70 AD. The Jewish people were devastated, but the Edomites were utterly annihilated. Millions of Jewish people live in Israel today; the Lord has brought them back, and the nation flourishes, but not one descendant of Esau can be found anywhere.

So it will always be. God keeps His Word. "The Lord preserves the faithful but abundantly repays the one who acts in pride" (Ps. 31:23).

DECEMBER 16
Jonah 1-2

"A Prophet-able Story"

"But I with the voice of thanksgiving will sacrifice to you; what I have vowed I will pay. Salvation belongs to the Lord!"
(Jonah 2:9)

Most people who grew up attending church cannot even remember the first time they heard the story of Jonah, usually because they listened to the story before the age of their first conscious memories. I'm sure this has been true for thousands of years. Before the days of the New Testament churches, you can imagine little groups of Jewish children sitting wide-eyed as the rabbi in the synagogue recounts, with excitement in his voice, the fantastic story of Jonah to another class of mesmerized pupils. Jonah is a wonderful story for children, but it is a terrible mistake to think the message is *only* a story for children. God did not think so since He determined to include it as one of the 66 books in His eternal Word. There are critical, timeless lessons included in these four chapters of *Jonah*.

We know very little about the man of God, Jonah, other than the name of his father, Amittai (Jon. 1:1), and also that he is referenced as ministering during the reign of Jeroboam II, king of Israel, who ruled 40 years, from approximately 793-753 BC. Jonah, whose name means "dove," lived during a season of national strength for Israel but also one which saw the people of the 10-tribe kingdom increasingly turn from the worship and service of Jehovah to covering the land and filling their homes with shrines to the gods of the Canaanites. Likewise, Jeroboam, in order to secure his kingdom, established diplomatic relations with foreign governments, even with the fast-expanding and ruthless kingdom of Assyria.

It was to the capital of this dangerous and rising world power, Nineveh, that Jonah was summoned by God for a ministry of public preaching, announcing their imminent and total judgment. Not an easy assignment, but clear and definite, and Jonah wasn't having it. He had several reasons for not wanting to go (we will discuss the primary one in the next devotional). Jonah so loathed the prospect, he fled and obtained passage on a ship sailing as far in the other direction as possible—to Tarshish, identified by many Bible scholars as located on the coast of modern-day Spain. Jonah traveled in the exact opposite direction of his assignment, but what is even more significant about his decision is that his heart desired to flee *"away from the presence of the Lord"* (Jon. 1:3).

We can recognize from this statement that, apart from submissive prayer, our intellect can cause us to *attempt* and even *desire* what is *impossible* and *unprofitable* for us—to flee from the "presence of the Lord." First of all, it is *impossible*. God, being omnipresent, is in all places at all times. This means that wherever we run, we are running into God. Two things are true, and we must remember both when we are under emotional duress. Wherever we go, *there we are;* and wherever we go, *there God is*. We cannot run away from ourselves or our God.

Secondly, why would we *really* want to run from the presence of God, our Heavenly Father, dearest friend, and greatest Advocate? Running from God is always the wrong direction. God may allow us to do it temporarily, but ultimately, He will reveal that relentlessly "pursuing" us, He has been there all along. We may come to that recognition after a long and stormy journey, overwhelmed by the waves of our selfish decisions or swallowed up by a "whale of a problem" that is beyond our capacity to solve. He is there, He always has been, and He will hear our cry from the deepest, darkest place we have ever been. "But I with the voice of thanksgiving will sacrifice to you; what I have vowed I will pay. Salvation belongs to the Lord!" (Jon. 2:9)

DECEMBER 17
Jonah 3-4

"For God So Loved the World"

"And should not I pity Nineveh, that great city, in which there are more than 120,000 persons who do not know their right hand from their left, and also much cattle?"
(Jonah 4:11)

As I said in yesterday's devotional, it is a serious error to think of the story of Jonah as only an excellent story for children. It is an excellent story, but not just for children. It shares a message for all believers regarding the redemption that God has provided in Jesus and how incredibly far His grace and mercy extend. Jesus Himself referenced Jonah as an illustration of His own death and resurrection in bringing salvation to the world. "For just as Jonah was three days and three nights in the belly of the great fish, so will the Son of Man be three days and three nights in the heart of the earth" (Matt. 12:40).

However, Jonah is also a reminder for us as followers of Jesus that in our religious selfishness and pride, we can attempt to limit, or at least define, the boundaries of our Lord's mercy and grace. It is not without significance that Jonah went to the port city of Joppa to sail away from God's call on his life. You may recall that it was in Joppa, 800 years later, that Peter received the vision of the large sheet let down from the heavens containing varieties of non-kosher animals and heard the voice from heaven saying, "Rise, Peter; kill and eat" (Acts 10:13). After initially resisting the command, it became clear over the next two days that Jesus was indeed sending Peter to share the gospel with Gentiles in the home of Cornelius, a Roman centurion. God's heart and His forgiveness in Christ embraced the whole world, including Israel's foreigners and adversaries.

Jonah was a *reluctant* prophet who became a *repentant* prophet in the belly of the whale regarding His disobedience to God. Jonah then became a *rewarded* prophet as the success of his ministry saw one of the largest cities in the world repent and seek God's forgiveness. You would expect to read that Jonah praised and exalted the Lord for His great work. But no, we see Jonah as a *resentful* prophet, actually complaining to the Lord about Nineveh's repentance and God's incredible mercy. Listen to Jonah and his bitter prayer: "And he prayed to the Lord and said, 'O Lord, is not this what I said when I was yet in my country? That is why I made haste to flee to Tarshish; for I knew that you are a gracious God and merciful, slow to anger and abounding in steadfast love, and relenting from disaster'" (Jon. 4:2). Incredibly, Jonah did not want to preach to Nineveh because he believed God, being the kind of God He is, might forgive them. Here is the sobering reality and how we need to carefully consider this—Jonah was expressing the view of a *rage-filled, racist* prophet. He did not really want these people to be forgiven; they deserved God's punishment, and in his heart of hearts, he wanted to see them get it. [Selah]

Stop, pause, and reflect for a moment honestly before God. Are there people we desire to be judged more than we desire to see them justified? The Holy Spirit can and will reveal our hearts to us. Is our heart like our Father's? "For God so loved *the world...*"

DECEMBER 18
Micah 1-2

"Proclaiming Prosperity & Peace"

"'Do not preach'—thus they preach—'one should not preach of such things; disgrace will not overtake us...' If a man should go about and utter wind and lies, saying, 'I will preach to you of wine and strong drink,' he would be the preacher for this people!"
(Micah 2:6, 11)

I'm sure you've heard the famous statement, "Those who do not learn from history are doomed to repeat it." When it comes to the message of Micah in today's Scripture reading, it seems that many believers are not only fulfilling that adage but also demonstrating the accuracy of another: "The only thing we learn from history is that people don't learn from history." Micah makes it very clear that the "prosperity preachers" and the "seeker-sensitive" messengers that many people in America have embraced in the last part of the twentieth century and the first decades of the 21st were actively undermining the Word of God in Israel and Judah 2800 years ago. Sadly, there is always a market for a messenger telling people what they want to hear.

The Bible makes it clear that one of the characteristics of the last days is that so many people "will not endure sound teaching but having itching ears they will accumulate for themselves teachers to suit their own passions" (2 Tim. 4:3). This is the theology of "God's favor" regardless of whether or not the person's behavior is favorable to God. This is the promise of "your best life now," which is the self-focused deception that whatever I believe to be "best for me" is God's will for me. The idolatrous message of "my will be done" replaces the humble, trusting heart of God's Son who prayed, "not my will, but yours, be done" (Luke 22:42).

How can we discern whether a messenger and their message are from the Lord? Well, the answer is not complicated; we *measure* the *message*. We measure the message by the only infallible standard of measurement that exists—the Word of God. The early church leaders referred to the Scriptures as "the canon." This term is derived from the Greek word "kanon," which meant a reed or straight rod and eventually came to mean a measuring rod. The Bible is the measuring rod for any message. It is only a true message if it "measures up" to what is written.

Listen to the words of Micah's colleague and contemporary, Isaiah. "To the teaching and to the testimony! If they will not speak according to this word, it is because they have no dawn" (Isa. 8:20). "No dawn" means there is no true light coming from them because they are of the darkness. The only way to test the ministry of any messenger is to measure the message to the standard of the Word of God—not only what they *say* but, just as importantly, what they *will not say*. A faithful preacher, teacher, or writer will always share "the whole counsel of God" (Acts 20:27), not just part of it. We must not be hyper-critical people, but we must be highly discerning. By God's Spirit and His Word, we can be numbered among the wise ones who are exceptions to the rule—we learn from history and, by doing so, don't repeat it.

DECEMBER 19
Micah 3-4

"JOY TO THE WORLD"

"He shall judge between many peoples, and shall decide disputes for strong nations far away; and they shall beat their swords into plowshares, and their spears into pruning hooks; nation shall not lift up sword against nation, neither shall they learn war anymore."
(Micah 4:3)

One of the most beloved carols we sing during this season of the year is the beautiful "Joy to the World." It would be hard to imagine how many millions of people around the world sing or at least hear this wonderful song of praise each Christmas season. What is so interesting about the Christmas tradition that has surrounded the song for at least 200 years is that it is not, at its core, a message about the birth of Christ at all. It celebrates in its lyrics not the joy of Christ's first advent but His second —"the Lord has come, let heaven and nature sing," expresses the liberations of the earth from the curse of sin at His return. "He rules the world with truth and grace" declares the worldwide dominion of Jesus and His rule of justice that will be established when He comes in power and glory. In Christ's Second Coming, He "makes the nations prove, the wonders of His love." Wonders indeed, when peace comes with the Prince of Peace and the ancient and constant hostilities between nations and people groups are obliterated in His reign of grace!

It is interesting to consider that even the development of "Joy to the World," to the version with which we are so familiar today, is a tribute to the "wonders of His love," uniting collaborators from modern countries so long and so often at war. The original words to "Joy to the World" were written by the English Protestant pastor, theologian, and writer of hymns, Isaac Watts (1674-1748). Watts initially framed the words for the hymn from a loose translation of David's theme in Psalm 98:4-9. He entitled the work "The Messiah's Coming and Kingdom."

A contemporary of Watts, George Frederic Handel (1689-1759), wrote the famous oratorio, "Messiah," and portions of the music for his chorus, "lift up your heads," were united with the words of Watts by a third collaborator, American music educator Lowell Mason (1792-1872). Mason combined the text and tune from Watts and Handel into the version of "Joy to the World" we so love to sing today. How appropriate—an Englishman, a German, and an American all uniting in their giftedness to provide a song that is truly a "joy to the world." This is truly the "wonders of His love" provided through Jesus' first coming that will be fully and eternally displayed in His second. Only in Jesus and His unifying Spirit are the dividing walls of national, ethnic, racial, and socio-economic differences torn down. All believers in Christ are members of the same body (Eph. 3:6). Praise God that this spiritual union will one day be global.

This union will not be provided by the United Nations but by the grace and power of the *"Uniter of Nations."* "And many nations shall come, and say: 'Come, let us go up to the mountain of the Lord, to the house of the God of Jacob, that he may teach us his ways and that we may walk in his paths'" (Mic. 4:2). Now, that is something to sing about!

DECEMBER 20
Micah 5-7

"Little Town of Bethlehem"

"But you, O Bethlehem Ephrathah, who are too little to be among the clans of Judah, from you shall come forth for me one who is to be ruler in Israel, whose coming forth is from of old, from ancient days."
(Micah 5:2)

It is a fantastic thing to stand at the spot where BC became AD. It has been my privilege to go there on several occasions and take others. Now, it is impossible to say the exact location, but in the year 326 AD, following lengthy investigations, Helena, the mother of Emperor Constantine, with his approval, constructed a church over the cave near Bethlehem, which for generations preceding had been recognized as the spot of Jesus' birth. Of course, over the past 1700 years, plenty of religious artifacts have been added to the site, yet the cave's ceiling and walls are clearly visible.

When you walk with others into that cramped space, there is something about the mystery and majesty of what took place there that always brings a hush to even the quiet conversations. The idea that the God of heaven and earth was born in this dark cave is almost inexpressible. Who could conceive or imagine such a thing? The One who has sat on the eternal throne is now laid in a feeding trough in this cave? How can it be that God and man are met together in one child, and that child is born in a place as lowly as this?

The truth is God never asks us to understand the miracle of the incarnation; that would be to ask the impossible. Our finite minds cannot contain the infinite truth of God becoming man, which is a mystery. Thankfully our responsibility is not to *comprehend* but to *depend* on this truth. The invitation regarding Jesus is the same as was announced to the shepherds by the angels that night in the fields outside Bethlehem, "For unto you is born this day in the city of David a Savior, who is Christ the Lord" (Luke 2:11).

The message of the angels, "The First Noel," is the message of the gospel, the glorious news that the Lord has undertaken to accomplish for Himself the salvation of His people. By taking on our humanity, the Lord, as Boaz for Ruth centuries before in Bethlehem, became the kinsman-redeemer for His beloved bride, the Church. Our Lord, through His birth, became a member of the human family so that through His perfect life and substitutionary death for our sins, we could be born again and become members of the family of God. Bethlehem means "house of bread," and that night its name was fulfilled, as the Bread of Life arrived, the true manna from heaven, Who satisfies the spiritual hunger of all who believe in Him (John 6:32-35).

So, this season, as we sing or hear "O, Little Town of Bethlehem," let us remember this prophecy from Micah and offer "big worship" to our Kinsman-Redeemer, our Good Shepherd, our David, our Lamb, our Bread of Life, our Savior, Christ the Lord!

DECEMBER 21
Nahum 1-3

"THE STORM & THE SHELTER"

"Who can stand before his indignation? Who can endure the heat of his anger? His wrath is poured out like fire, and the rocks are broken into pieces by him. The Lord is good, a stronghold in the day of trouble; he knows those who take refuge in him."
(Nahum 1:6-7)

We know very little about the prophet Nahum other than the name of his town—Elkosh, and the exact location of that place is not certain. What is certain is that God blessed Nahum with an amazing poetic gift, and he used that gift in an amazing way to deliver with a force unmatched by any other prophet in declaring God's vengeance and wrath against His enemy, Nineveh, the capital of Assyria. Just 100 years earlier, the Lord revealed to this exceedingly wicked population that He truly is slow to anger (Nah. 1:3) when He overcame the reluctance of a resistant, obstinate prophet, Jonah, and through his preaching of impending judgment brought the entire city to repentance. God graciously spared the town at that time, but now the limit of His patience had arrived. Assyria renewed its idolatry and murderous abuse of Israel and other nations, and the day of God's wrath has come.

As Nahum describes it, the devastation God brings upon Nineveh and Assyria is astounding. Perhaps no other passage in God's Word is as graphic and detailed in expressing the chilling truth. "The Lord is a jealous and avenging God; the Lord is avenging and wrathful; the Lord takes vengeance on his adversaries and keeps wrath for His enemies" (Nah. 1:2). Yes, "It is a fearful thing to fall into the hands of the living God" (Heb. 10:31) and "our God is a consuming fire" (Heb. 12:29). Take note of those two Scriptures from Hebrews, for they remind us that the God of Nahum in the Old Testament is the God of the New Testament. We must remember to embrace all God reveals of His nature in the Word. The God who "so loved the world" (John 3:16) is the God who will "by no means clear the guilty" (Nah. 1:3).

    I once heard the story of a farmer who, in the pioneer days of the Nebraska territory, looked up from his work in the fields and was horrified to see in the distance a huge funnel cloud racing toward his small farmhouse and barn. Just then, the cloud touched down, and a tornado began pulling everything up into its vortex. Running back to his homestead as fast as he could, the farmer screamed for his family to flee to the root cellar behind the house. No sooner had the man bolted the cellar door, after getting himself and his family inside, that the terrible cyclone struck and obliterated every building and wiped out every piece of equipment. Nothing remained of the farm, yet huddled in the rough root cellar, the family was unharmed. Nahum reminds us that God is the whirlwind and the stronghold. His holy wrath is terrible, and His mercy is wonderful. This is the gospel in Nahum—the wrath of Holy God fell upon His Holy Son, and those who trust in Jesus discover "The Lord is good, a stronghold in the day of trouble; he knows those who take refuge in him" (Nah. 1:7).

DECEMBER 22
Habakkuk 1-3

"INEXHAUSTIBLE JOY"

"Though the fig tree should not blossom, nor fruit be on the vines,
the produce of the olive fail and the fields yield no food,
the flock be cut off from the fold and there be no herd in the stalls,
yet I will rejoice in the Lord; I will take joy in the God of my salvation."
(Habakkuk 3:17-18)

Habakkuk lived in a time that was like a deep valley between two steep mountains. He was a prophet to God's people just before the downfall of Assyria and the rise of Babylon. In the valley between these two empires, lived the people of Israel and Judah, who were overwhelmed by these two dark kingdoms. Perhaps because of his experiences and those of his people, Habakkuk had many questions of the Lord, and he asked them. The Lord uses Habakkuk's sincere questions as the basis for His answers, and this exchange becomes the message He uses to encourage His people's faith in this book of the Bible.

The key phrase in Habakkuk, which can be easily overlooked, is conveyed in just seven words, "The righteous shall live by his faith" (Hab. 2:4). Tucked away in this book of questions is the answer to the ultimate question "How can a person who is a sinner be right and acceptable to a holy God?" The answer is "the just shall live by his faith" (Hab. 2:4 KJV). It was this phrase that became the great message, the Gospel message of Jesus and His apostles. People are not declared right before God, justified by works, but based on faith alone. This has always been the basis of salvation. Abraham believed the Lord, and He counted it to him as righteousness (Gen. 15:6). The basis of faith is always on the Lord and His promise. Faith is *not faith in faith*. Faith rests on God's promises, which are supported by the character of God. Faith is more than believing in God. It is *believing into God*.

Just as our *faith* has its source in God, our *joy* also has its source in God and His salvation. Based on faith in the Lord, His people not only find their salvation, but they also experience the *joy of His salvation*. This joy in our Savior is a gift that nothing or no one on earth can take from us (John 15:11).

On the day I wrote these words, I heard a testimony of God's inexhaustible joy. A fellow pastor and a friend, just a few days ago, awakened early in the morning to find his house filling with smoke. He instantly woke his wife, and the two escaped the flames that immediately engulfed the home. Standing in the yard, my friend and his wife watched as all their possessions from 30 years of life together were destroyed. What did they do? They held hands and thanked God for protecting them and praised Him for all the memories of the wonderful experiences He had graciously given them there over the years. What a testimony to their faith, and what a testimony to their God and His inexhaustible, indestructible joy! *Joy is real because Jesus is real.* "Yet I will rejoice in the Lord; I will take joy in the God of my salvation" (Hab. 3:18).

DECEMBER 23
Zephaniah 1-3

"LORD OF THE DANCE"

"The Lord your God is in your midst, a mighty one who will save; he will rejoice over you with gladness; he will quiet you by his love; he will exult over you with loud singing."
(Zephaniah 3:17)

Not long ago, I surprised my wife a few days before her birthday by taking her to dinner at one of the nicest restaurants in our city. It was a delicious meal in a delightful environment, and she was as happy as could be. But, the evening was not complete because following dinner, I had planned for another surprise that I knew she would love—tickets in the third row, center section, to the tour performance of *Riverdance*.

Along with millions of "Baby Boomers," Susan and I remember 1994, when that spectacular show, developed by dancer Michael Hatley, took Europe and then America by storm. From the first televised performances, my wife was hooked. I could tell you how she had our two children, Ruth and Stephen, ages 7 and 4, join her in Irish dancing all around our family room, but that's another story altogether! Of course, success often breeds more success, and a few years later, Michael Hatley created and starred in another, even more creative and dynamic show entitled *Lord of the Dance*. In my humble (but very accurate) opinion, although the show is undoubtedly full of energy, it does not compare to the mix of sad and soulful ballads and the joyful and exuberant dancing of *Riverdance*.

Irish music and culture have been characterized for centuries by a surprising mixture of sadness, joy, struggle, and celebration. This emotional combination is rooted in the history of the people of Ireland, but it is also connected to their faith. Ireland's culture has been significantly impacted by the presence of the Christian faith and the church. Both have infused Irish life since the ministry of the missionary Patrick in the fourth century. The land and the people have known many and varied trials over the centuries. Yet, the Irish people have always had an abiding sense of joyful hope.

Genuine joy and hope are founded on God. Without Him, no power can keep and fulfill the promises that produce abiding joy and steadfast hopefulness. For the children of Judah, commonly called for over 2000 years "the Jews," the basis of their underlying hope and constant faith during centuries of unspeakable hardship and persecution has been founded on faith in Jehovah. This hope lays hold on the promises of God's steadfast love despite His severe judgment of their sin. As Zephaniah prophesied to them, the Day of the Lord, which is the time of God's final judgment, would also be a day of deliverance. Their hope is in a love from God so deep in His heart that He delights in their restoration to Him. This hope of Israel is also the hope of all believers, all ages, and for all times because it is a hope realized in the Messiah. In the Messiah, Jesus, all the promises of God are "yes, and amen!" (2 Cor. 1:20)

One of those promises of God's love is so tender and beautiful that if the Lord Himself did not share it, we would be hesitant to apply it to Him. It is the image of God singing softly to His children, His people, to comfort their fears and soothe their hearts. If that image of the singing God is not amazing enough, then we are told, "He will exult over you with loud singing" (Zeph. 3:17). The Hebrew words here are striking; they convey joyfully singing and whirling about with dance. God Almighty dancing? That is the only way our Heavenly Father can convey the depths of His joyful love for us, His little children. He sings and twirls in His love for us. Our God is the ultimate and eternal *Lord of the Dance!*

DECEMBER 24
Haggai 1-2

"THE PROMISE OF CHRISTMAS"

"I am with you, declares the Lord of hosts, according to the covenant that I made with you when you came out of Egypt. My Spirit remains in your midst. Fear not."
(Haggai 2:4b-5)

For millions of people, this day, or perhaps even more specifically, this night, is the most wonderful and encouraging time of the entire year. Yet, for many others, December 24 is the most difficult and challenging date on the calendar. When we stop to give that contradiction some careful consideration, it is not hard to understand. In a unique way, Christmas Eve connects people—bringing past, present, and future all onto the same day. In that way, we are a little like Ebenezer Scrooge, the main character in Charles Dickens's classic, *A Christmas Carol.*

On Christmas Eve, the hard-hearted, miserable miser Ebenezer is visited by the ghost of his "former partner in greed," Jacob Marley. Terrified at first by the encounter, Scrooge eventually dismisses the experience as "Humbug." However, later that night, as Marley foretold, Ebenezer is visited by three spirits—the spirit of Christmas past, present, and future. Because of these three visitations, the result in Dickens's tale is that Scrooge is completely reformed in his character and, from then on, lives with the joy of Christmas in his heart 365 days a year. It's a great story, but it is just that—a story.

The reality is that the *spirits* of countless people are *visited* each Christmas Eve with *memories* of the past, *experiences* in the present, and *dreams* of the future. The character of those memories, experiences, and dreams is determined by innumerable life events, people, circumstances, and emotional associations with Christmas that are as different as the individuals themselves. The phrase "Merry Christmas" rings as true as a bell to one person, while to another, it is as empty and hollow as a dead tree.

So, what makes Christmas Eve ultimately a day worthy of its unique place and recognition that it receives around the world? The answer to that question is in the Spirit of Christmas. Surprisingly, Haggai shares that promise from the Spirit Himself. Five hundred years before the first "Christmas Eve," the remnant of the people of Judah, who had returned from their exile in Babylon, was challenged by the Lord regarding their self-focused materialism (an attitude which sadly so often still undermines Christmas) as they had busied themselves in building their own homes. Still, they had neglected to finish rebuilding God's House, which began several years earlier under Ezra (Hag. 1:2-7).

God challenges His people through faithful servants and messengers to honor Him and trust Him to provide for their needs since all the resources of the earth are His (Hag. 2:8). Also, and most importantly, the Lord reminds them of the greatest treasure they possess, which has always been their security and always will: "My Spirit remains in your midst. Fear not" (Hag. 2:5). God's Spirit ultimately had never departed from Judah for they were forever His people by covenant promise. They had experienced many trials and judgments as a nation, but God would remain steadfast to His promises even in the ultimate shaking of the entire earth that was yet to come. This House, which they were to rebuild entirely, would one day be filled with His Spirit, glory, and peace. This was God's promise, and now through further revelation, we can understand that it was indeed His "Christmas Promise." The One whose birthday we celebrate this night, will one day, by His life, death, and resurrection bring peace with God for all who believe. And will one day reign in this House as the Prince of Peace. Listen to the promise of Christmas: "My Spirit remains in your midst. Fear not" (2:5).

DECEMBER 25
Zechariah 1-3

"GOD WITH US"

"Sing and rejoice, O daughter of Zion, for behold, I come and I will dwell in your midst, declares the Lord."
(Zechariah 2:10)

Zechariah, along with Haggai and Malachi, is the one of the three prophets who served as messengers to the people of Judah, after they returned and settled again in their homeland after their long captivity in the provinces of Babylon. These three men not only shared in the Lord's work during the same timeframe (520-480 BC), but they also shared similar themes in their messages regarding God's principles for the current days and His great promise for the day soon to come. In unison, these three prophets, whose writings form the last three books of the Old Testament, exhort God's people to conform their hearts and prepare their lives in expectation of the great promise soon to be fulfilled. Together, these three final prophecies of the Old Testament share the message proclaimed by John the Baptist: "Repent...and prepare the way of the Lord" (Matt. 3:1-3).

Sometimes we perceive the call to "repent" as a negative and legalistic message. In reality, nothing could be further from the truth. The exhortation to repent is a challenge to prepare now for what is coming, or more accurately, to prepare for *Who* is coming. "Repent" means to change our mind and, as a result, change our direction in expectation for an appearing of the Lord. It means to turn in order to meet the greatest of all gifts, the Giver Himself. This is not just a prophecy of a prophet; this is the promise of the One who is coming and who sends the prophets ahead of Him to prepare His people.

The promise that the Lord shares is the greatest of all gifts and is the true gift of Christmas. "Sing and rejoice, O daughter of Zion, for behold, I come *and I will dwell in your midst*, declares the Lord" (Zech. 2:10). This is the promise made over 200 years before Zechariah by Isaiah. The promise would be made again as the angel of the Lord visited Joseph 500 years later. "'Behold, the virgin shall conceive and bear a son, and they shall call His name Immanuel' (which means, God with us)" (Matt. 1:23).

"God with us" is the promise of Advent and also the truth, without which Christmas is no more than a gift-giving and receiving day that comes around every year. To lose the miraculous truth of "God with us" in the birth of Jesus is to lose everything Christmas truly means. God told the people of Judah He was coming to dwell in their midst, and He kept that promise in His son's life, Jesus Christ. What Zechariah could not see, nor could any other of the prophets or sages of Judah, was that the promises of "Immanuel, God with us," would be "prefilled" at the first advent of Jesus but perfectly and eternally "fulfilled" in the 2nd advent of the Lord.

This is the "Promise of Christmas" that we should prepare for and joyfully expect each day until the "crowning day," that day of all days when our God comes again and remains forever. "For the Lord himself will descend from heaven with a cry of command, with the voice of an archangel, and with the sound of the trumpet of God. And the dead in Christ will rise first. Then we who are alive, who are left, will be caught up together with them in the clouds to meet the Lord in the air, and so we will always be with the Lord" (1 Thess. 4:16-17). May it be soon! Merry Christmas!

DECEMBER 26
Zechariah 4-6

"LITTLE IS MUCH"

"Then he said to me, 'This is the word of the Lord to Zerubbabel: Not by might, nor by power, but by my Spirit, says the Lord of hosts.'"
(Zechariah 4:6)

The older I become and the more years I spend in ministry, the more I am convinced that the significant things in this world are things that would be considered less than significant, not even noticed in the world's evaluation. The most impactful events are probably not even recognized that way by most of the people involved. The original Christmas was only really recognized by two very humble people from the village of Nazareth spending a night in a cave near another village, Bethlehem.

Only two people, Mary and Joseph, knew that night, in the lowliest of locations, the world had been changed forever. Within their sleeping little son resided the power that would change everything. The fullness of God's Spirit indwelt that newborn's frame. It would be the Spirit of God, within and upon the child, causing Him to grow in wisdom and stature and favor with God that would make Jesus the Servant of Jehovah. He would accomplish all the Heavenly Father's will to be born on earth as it is in heaven (Luke 2:40, Matt. 6:10).

The presence and power of the Spirit of God takes the ordinary and accomplishes the extraordinary. This was exactly the message of enlightenment and encouragement that not only the prophet Zechariah but also the high priest Joshua and the governor of Judah, Zerubbabel, needed to hear from the Lord. In their eyes, neither they nor the small Temple, still incomplete after many years, was sufficient for the purpose for which they existed. Neither they nor the Temple measured up to the purpose. However, God knew these doubts and sent a heavenly, angelic messenger informing them that God determines "capability" with a very different evaluation. In effect, God said, "Not so fast, just wait and see what I am able to do in this season of 'small things' that will make your hearts full of big joy!" (Zech. 2:10)

It was true that Zerubbabel and Joshua were not sufficient in themselves for the tasks assigned to them. But, like a man who would follow 500 years later, a man whose name means "little," Saul of Tarsus, they would experience that their sufficiency was not in themselves but in the Spirit who indwelt them (2 Cor. 3:5). Zechariah's message for the Lord is so timely for us today. Our greatest strength is to realize that we have none, and to find in our weakness that His strength is demonstrated. We are not strong when we are strong. We are strong when we are weak (2 Cor. 12:9-10).

Over 50 years ago, I remember sitting transfixed as a young boy in church and watching as a small blind man, a guest musician, was led to the piano on our platform. Finding his place on the keys, he began to play and, looking up with blind eyes, began to sing about the Lord and to the Lord. I don't remember all the songs, but this one gripped my child's heart and planted a seed of faith that maybe even I might somehow be used by God. I can still see him in my memory and hear his clear, tenor voice:

> *Little is much when God is in it!*
> *Labor not for wealth or fame;*
> *There's a crown, and you can win it,*
> *If you go in Jesus' name.*

("Little Is Much When God Is In It" by Kittie L. Suffield)

DECEMBER 27
Zechariah 7-9

"The Feast for the Fast"

"Thus says the Lord of hosts: The fast of the fourth month and the fast of the fifth and the fast of the seventh and the fast of the tenth shall be to the house of Judah seasons of joy and gladness and cheerful feasts. Therefore love truth and peace."
(Zechariah 8:19)

Over the years, a subject that has been asked many times of me as a pastor is what is the right way to fast. As followers of Jesus, people have asked if we should fast at all since He condemned the fasting practices of the religious leaders in His day. These and others like them are excellent questions, for there are certainly *right* and *wrong* ways of fasting. Fasting is not a divine diet plan for losing weight, it is not an act of penance to earn forgiveness for sins, and most assuredly, as Jesus did make clear, fasting is *never* the performance of a religious ritual to be noticed for being holy. That is hypocrisy.

In the Bible, fasting is always accompanied by and connected to prayer. Fasting always includes prayer. It is possible and permissible to pray without fasting, but it is impossible to truly fast without praying. Fasting is a hunger and a longing for God. For that reason, fasting is always a helpful and holy way of seeking God. Our Lord Jesus took it for granted that His disciples would fast, for He instructed us, saying, "you fast" (Matt. 6:16).

However, in answer to the question regarding why His disciples did not fast, Jesus explained that it was not appropriate for the "friends of the bridegroom" (today, we would say the "groomsmen") to fast when the bridegroom is with them. The day of the wedding, the beginning of the wedding feast, and the days of joyful celebration with the bridegroom were not the season for fasting. There would be appropriate seasons for fasting when the feast was over and the bridegroom was gone (Mark 2:18-20).

Jesus' words fully explain God's answer to leaders in Judah, 500 years earlier, about how to fast now that the people had returned to their homeland. God told Zechariah to share two answers—one was a principle and the other a promise. First of all, the people of Judah should be careful not to repeat their fathers' vain and hypocritical fasting practices, which brought the Lord's judgment on them. The sincere fasting to seek Him should result in His character of justice, kindness, mercy, and peace expressed to all people (Zech. 7:9; 8:16). This type of fasting honors the Lord. We should exhibit the same character as followers of the Lord, and the more we seek Him, the more these qualities should be found in us. Secondly, a marvelous promise is included in Zechariah's answer from the Lord. Fasting will one day be replaced forever. Fasting will be overwhelmed by feasting. The day will come when the Lord Himself will dwell in the midst of Jerusalem. "And they shall be my people, and I will be their God, in faithfulness and in righteousness" (Zech. 8:8). Then, fasting will cease forever, because the presence of God will satisfy the hunger of the Lord's people for eternity. This promise from God to His people is His promise to us today.

One day, our fasting will be overwhelmed by feasting. We, the Bride of Christ, will sit with our Heavenly Bridegroom at the marriage supper of the Lamb (Rev. 19:6-9). We will never hunger in our souls again in His presence and the eternal comfort of His love.

DECEMBER 28
Zechariah 10-12

"Mercy for the Murderers"

"And I will pour out on the house of David and the inhabitants of Jerusalem a spirit of grace and pleas for mercy, so that, when they look on me, on him whom they have pierced, they shall mourn for him, as one mourns for an only child, and weep bitterly over him, as one weeps over a firstborn."
(Zechariah 12:10)

Over the years, Bible scholars have helped to recognize that in evaluating prophetic passages, we should see that there is a "prefillment" contained within the "fulfillment." This means that by the additional revelation from God in the New Testament, we can see that many prophecies, especially those related to the Messiah and the nation of Israel, have been partially fulfilled but not yet fully fulfilled. For example, many prophecies in the Old Testament foretell a Messiah who will conquer evil and bring peace and prosperity to Israel. Yet, many other statements, sometimes even connected with passages about this mighty Messiah, speak of His suffering and death. Now, we can see by further revelation in the New Testament that some prophecies were "prefilled" by the first appearing of Messiah, but those same ones will be "fulfilled" at His second appearing.

In our reading today, and specifically in the verse cited above, we are given one of the most remarkable prophecies regarding the Messiah. Zechariah told the remnant that had returned to Judah that one day Jehovah would gather the scattered tribes of Israel through their descendants and cause them to return to the land. The nation would be blessed by God and would prosper. Yet, at the same time, Jerusalem and the Jewish people in the land would cause turmoil to many nations surrounding the land. (This should seem as current to us as the daily news!) Ultimately, the nations will unite and seek to destroy Israel (Zech. 12:9). It is at this moment, which appears to guarantee the annihilation of Israel, that God brings spiritual and national salvation to the people as they "look on me, on him whom they have pierced," they will "weep bitterly over him, as one weeps over a firstborn" (Zech. 12:10) This is astounding! How could the Jewish people be brought to national repentance over their guilt in the "piercing" and death of the nations' "firstborn"? The answer to that incredulous question is that it has already happened, partially.

The prophecy by Zechariah has had a "prefillment." When Jesus stood before Pontius Pilate, having presented for three years and declared Himself that night as the Messiah, Pilate called for a verdict on Jesus' claims. "What shall I do with Jesus who is called the Christ?" The immediate answer from the crowd was, "Let him be crucified!" (Matt. 27:22-23). Seeking to take further responsibility away from himself and the nation's leaders, Pilot said, "Shall I crucify your King?" Definite, horrible, and clear was the immediate renouncement by the people, "We have no king but Caesar!" (John 19:15) Then, John records the awful responsibility for Jesus' death, "So he delivered *him* over to *them* to be crucified" (John 19:16). What terrible guilt! Yet, just 50 days later, what wondrous grace! Peter, on the Day of Pentecost, speaking to a huge assembly of Jewish people from around the world, charged them with Messiah's murder, "This Jesus, delivered up according to the definite plan and foreknowledge of God, *you crucified and killed* by the hands of lawless men" (Acts 2:23). What was the response of thousands of Jewish people that day? "Now when they heard this they were cut to the heart, and said to Peter and the rest of the apostles, 'Brothers, what shall we do?' And Peter said to them, 'Repent and be baptized every one of you in the name of Jesus Christ for the forgiveness of your sins, and you will receive the gift of the Holy Spirit'" (Acts 2:37-38).

Praise God! That is how murderers received mercy, a "prefillment," and we can only imagine the glorious day when there will be a national "fulfillment!" Never forget this, we are *all* murderers of Messiah. It was our sin that caused His suffering and death. Are you a saved or a lost murderer? Today, repent, believe the gospel, and rejoice!

DECEMBER 29
Zechariah 13-14

"When the King Cleans House"

"And every pot in Jerusalem and Judah shall be holy to the Lord of hosts, so that all who sacrifice may come and take of them and boil the meat of the sacrifice in them. And there shall no longer be a trader in the house of the Lord of hosts on that day."
(Zechariah 14:21)

The central theme of Zechariah's prophecies is "the Day of the Lord." This term, used throughout the writings of the prophets, refers to the direct and personal intervention of the Lord God into the life of Israel specifically, and includes all nations, generally. The nation of Israel has been called "the timepiece of prophecy" because the prophecies that are yet to be fulfilled, for the most part, center on the events taking place among the Jewish people. It is shared by the Apostle Paul in Romans that a spirit of hardness and unbelief will remain on the Jewish people nationally, continuing "until the fullness of the Gentiles has come in" (Rom. 11:25). The key word is "until," which means this spiritual hardness is temporary, and that through the sovereign providence of God, the rejection of Messiah by Israel has sent the gospel of the Messiah for all people throughout the whole world.

That *"until"* will continue up to "the Day of the Lord," when during national crisis and invasion, the Messiah will appear suddenly in His return to the place from which He departed—the Mount of Olives. He comes to bring judgment to the invaders and salvation to His chosen ones. "And in this way all Israel will be saved, as it is written, 'The Deliverer will come from Zion, He will banish ungodliness from Jacob'; 'and this will be my covenant with them when I take away their sins'" (Rom. 11:26-27; Isa. 59:20-21).

When He returns, Messiah will bring *total salvation* and accomplish complete *sanctification*. The entire city, from the bells on the horses to the pots in the temple and throughout Jerusalem, will be holy to the Lord (Zech. 14:19-20). This use of hyperbole by Zechariah is a way of communicating reality. For by the holy presence of the glorified Messiah, all of the people, places, and things in His city will be absolutely pure. Then, the worship of the Lord will be pure as well because Messiah Jesus will, for the third and final time, "clean house." No more will wicked people use religion for power and profit. That business of spiritual Babylon will be closed forever. But for sincere worshipers of the Lord, the gates of the city will never be shut. People from all nations will, for the ages to come, make the House of God a house of praise and prayer for all people.

In this season, as we await and anticipate the "Day of the Lord," we must remember that our bodies are the temple of the Holy Spirit. Therefore, we need to be holy as His temple, for He is holy. May we, with trust and love today, ask Him "to clean house" in our temple so that we may show forth the praises of the One who called us out of darkness into His marvelous light (1 Peter 2:9).

DECEMBER 30
Malachi 1-2

"Levi Living"

> "So shall you know that I have sent this command to you, that my covenant with Levi may stand, says the Lord of hosts. My covenant with him was one of life and peace, and I gave them to him. It was a covenant of fear, and he feared me. He stood in awe of my name. True instruction was in his mouth, and no wrong was found on his lips. He walked with me in peace and uprightness, and he turned many from iniquity."
> (Malachi 2:4-6)

Malachi shares a unique message from the Lord, for through his voice, the Lord asks some serious questions and then answers them Himself! He is like a skilled debater who anticipates His opponent's objections, verbalizes them, and then responds. The Lord knows His people and how they will profess a host of excuses. He "corners them" with their own words so He can have a straightforward conversation and a "close encounter of the divine kind" with them. Sadly, the most evasive of all the people were the priests. The ones who were supposed to teach the people the Word of God needed to hear very pointedly from the God of the Word. The Lord's charge against His priests was that they, commissioned to honor His name, have profaned God's name instead.

They did this by offering to God items unfit for an acceptable sacrifice. This disrespect despised their service's sacredness and profaned the Lord's name.

It would have been far more pleasing to God if one of them, in reverence for Him, would have closed and locked the doors to the temple and put a stop to such an irreverent show (Mal. 1:7, 10-11). They pridefully thought they alone were qualified to lead in the service of the Lord. But God assured them that "...from the rising of the sun to its setting my name will be great among the nations, and in every place incense will be offered to my name..." (Mal. 1:11) God told the priests that the ones they considered "unclean," the Gentiles, would offer pure and sincere worship to Him. The Lord warned them that continuing this kind of behavior would bring a curse upon them and their descendants, so God called them to remember their ancestor, Levi. This leader of the tribe of priests and ministers set the example by his character of how they should reform and conform their lives.

Levi's example is also the pattern for us, who, by the Lord's salvation, have become a "kingdom of priests" to our God and his representatives and his ambassadors to others (Rev. 5:10; 2 Cor. 5:20).

"Levi Living" is how we strive to live: (Mal. 2:5-7)

- *Levi viewed his life as a covenant relationship with God*
- *Levi sought to live at peace with God*
- *Levi lived in the fear of the Lord*
- *Levi lived in reverence and awe of God*
- *Levi taught God's Word truthfully to others*
- *Levi applied the Word of God to his own life*
- *Levi walked with God in peace and integrity*
- *Levi rescued many people by turning them from the wrong path*

What an example we have in Levi! He has been dead for over 3800 years, but his life still speaks for God and to us. From this last book of the Old Testament, the Lord tells us how to live in these last days. *Live like Levi!*

DECEMBER 31
Malachi 3-4

"PATHWAYS"

"For behold, the day is coming, burning like an oven, when all the arrogant and all evildoers will be stubble. The day that is coming shall set them ablaze, says the Lord of hosts, so that it will leave them neither root nor branch. But for you who fear my name, the sun of righteousness shall rise with healing in its wings. You shall go out leaping like calves from the stall."
(Malachi 4:1-2)

The journey on the *Pathways* through the Old Testament has reached the final chapters. Our time together is coming to a close. Yet, what we read in the Scriptures on this last day tells us it is *not final*. There is a day that is coming; in fact, it approaches on the road we travel, just over the horizon. And what a day it is! Malachi says this coming day will be like a burning oven that will consume like fire the evildoers and adversaries of the Lord. It is the Day of the Lord, "great and awesome" (Mal. 4:1, 4:5). How dreadful it will be for those who meet the day unrepentant, unprepared, and unsaved. The day brings them an unending, awful night of utter darkness, doom, and despair. It will be atrocious for those who follow the wide, broad, congested highway that leads to everlasting destruction (Matt. 7:13).

But, there is another *Pathway* that leads to that same great Day of the Lord, but how different is the dawning of that day for those who walk in faith and fear of the Lord! "But for you who fear my name, the sun of righteousness shall rise with healing in its wings" (Mal. 4:2). The sun of righteousness is the light of the Righteous Son. He is the Light of the world, and all who believe in Him will never walk in darkness (John 8:12). The Day of the Lord is the coming of the day of *our Lord*; and for us who trust in Him, that day is the dawn of the eternal day that will see no sunset and know no night.

What a joy it has been for me to walk a few miles on these *Pathways* of Scripture with you. Now, may the rest of your journey be bright with our Lord's living presence and warm with His living promises. Walk on, my friend.

"But the path of the righteous is like the light of dawn, which shines brighter and brighter until full day."
(Proverbs 4:18)

AUTHOR'S BIOGRAPHY

PASTOR SAM POLSON is the Lead Pastor of West Park Baptist Church in Knoxville, Tennessee. He also serves as Chairman of the Board for ABWE, the Association of Baptists for World Evangelism, and is actively involved in ministry leadership training worldwide. Sam also serves as the board chairman for CedarBrook Outreach, a ministry focusing on the physical, social, and spiritual needs of at-risk families in Knoxville, Tennessee. Previously, he served for many years on the Board of Shepherds Ministries, an educational ministry for adults with developmental disabilities. Sam was born and raised in New Castle, Indiana, where he met and married his wife, Susan. He earned his Bachelor's and Master's degrees in theology from Bob Jones University and then served seven years as an assistant pastor at Calvary Baptist Church in Findlay, Ohio. The Polsons moved to Knoxville in 1986, where Sam has served as Lead Pastor for over 36 years. Sam and Susan have three grown children and four grandchildren. Sam advises the pastoral team and staff, teaches in large and small group settings, and is most energized by witnessing people come alive to the reality of the gospel. Sam Polson's other books include: *In His Image, By Faith, SonLight* (a daily devotional), *Corona Victus: Conquering the Virus of Fear,* and *Life Changing Prayer.*

"For what we proclaim is not ourselves, but Jesus Christ as Lord, with ourselves as your servants for Jesus' sake" (2 Cor. 4:5).

Acknowledgments

The writing and publishing of a book are not commonly thought of as tasks that "take a village," but this assumption is far from the truth. The creation of *Pathways* required an ever-patient, detail-oriented, and graciously kind community, one that began with the wife of the author, Susan Polson, and ended with the husband of the publisher, Deryk Stilwell. The individuals listed below have been priceless throughout the entire process. Each and every person was required to help accomplish what you now hold in your hands, and the author and the publisher are ever-grateful. Without their diligence and belief in something that did not yet exist, it wouldn't have.

Susan Polson
Tara Hayes
LeAnn Hilemon
Debbie Trotter
Andi Walker
Stacie Weiser
Karlie Saumier
Deryk Stilwell

ABOUT CLIMBING ANGEL PUBLISHING

Climbing Angel Publishing exists for the purpose of sharing stories of hope and encouragement, aiding in the gathering together of community, and supporting the process of betterment. The following books are available at ClimbingAngel.com and major bookstores.

ADULT BOOKS: (Romans 8:28-30)

In His Image, by Sam Polson (English, Romanian, & Mandarin)
By Faith, by Sam Polson (English & Romanian)
My Birthday Gift to Jesus, by Lisa Soland
Without Ceasing, by Dr. Dennis Davidson
SonLight: Daily Light from the Pages of God's Word, by Sam Polson
Corona Victus: Conquering the Virus of Fear, by Sam Polson
Art Bushing: His Diary, Letters, & Photographs of WWII, by Art Bushing
Art & Dotty: His Diary, Their Letters & Photographs of WWII, by Art Bushing
Trimisul, by Stan Johnson (Romanian)
Life Changing Prayer, by Sam Polson
The Climbing Angel Christmas Treasury, by a variety of authors
J. Calvin Coolidge: Letters from the Korean War
Stories from Kingman, AZ: The Heart of Historic Route 66, by Loren B. Wilson
Pathways: Ancient Paths from the Pages of the Old Testament by Sam Polson

CHILDREN'S BOOKS: (Philippians 4:8)

The Christmas Tree Angel, by Lisa Soland
The Unmade Moose, by Lisa Soland
Thump, by Lisa Soland
Somebunny To Love, by Lisa Soland (English & Mandarin)
The Truth About God's Rainbow, by Lisa Soland
God's Promises, by Lisa Soland
The Boy & The Bagel Necklace, by Lisa Soland
God's Hands and Feet, by Lisa Soland
I Like To Be Quiet, by Joni Caldwell
Wheels Off!, by Karlie Saumier
Ella's Trip of a Lifetime, by Melanie Ewbank
Because You Are Mine, by Gayle Childress Greene
Jeremy Plays the Blues, by Amy Oden Simpson

CHILDREN'S BOOKS, continued...

Bad Hair Day, by Jasmyne Simpkins
I Like To Read, by Joni Caldwell
Trunks Up!, by Karlie Saumier
Perusha's Paradise, by Bette Reed Smith
Ruby and the Treasure Within, by Tonya Celeste Hobbs
Abby, the Wonder Dog & her Warrior Princess, by Melanie Ewbank

Grow into the likeness of Christ with Sam Polson's
IN HIS IMAGE!

"I challenge you to read and grow into the likeness of our Creator and Redeemer. *In His Image* will inspire, educate, and guide you in that sacred process." — Rev. Sam Phillips

"In a culture awash with self-identity talk, Pastor Sam Polson directs us to the truest identity of all...the Lord Jesus Christ Himself." — Dr. Greg Baker

"*In His Image* is a book I highly recommend to assist in family worship, private devotion, or person study."
— Dr. David Trempe

Available in:

English (ISBN: 978-0-99657-219-4)
Romanian (ISBN: 978-0-99657-218-7)
Mandarin (ISBN: 978-1-64370-036-6)
www.climbingangel.com

Learning to be a PRAYER WARRIOR is a JOURNEY

Strengthen this ability in a group at your church with Dr. Dennis Davidson's powerful book
WITHOUT CEASING!

Without Ceasing is available at a discount for small groups and church-wide initiatives.

Order direct from Climbing Angel Publishing by emailing:

ClimbingAngel Publishing@gmail.com

Learn of the
Timeless Insights for Staying on Course from Hebrews 11, **in Sam Polson's**

"BY FAITH"

"*By Faith* will be a helpful addition to the library of any serious Bible student." — Dr. Steve Euler

"Through *By Faith* you will be encouraged by the heart, the hope, and the wisdom that has encouraged my journey for almost two decades." — Pastor Rick Dunn

"Sam Polson...leads the believer down a path, living out their faith practically, in clear and logical steps. You will be blessed!" — Pastor Mark Kirk

Available in:

English (ISBN: 978-1-64370-035-9)
Romanian (ISBN: 978-1-64370-032-8)
www.climbingangel.com

www.ingramcontent.com/pod-product-compliance
Lightning Source LLC
Chambersburg PA
CBHW022026050526
44107CB00125B/1453/J